Students With Autism

Characteristics and Instructional Programming for Special Educators

JACK SCOTT, Ph.D.
CLAUDIA CLARK, M.S.

Exceptional Student Education
Florida Atlantic University
Boca Raton, Florida

MICHAEL P. BRADY, Ph.D.

Department of Educational Psychology and Special Education
Florida International University
Miami, Florida

SINGULAR PUBLISHING GROUP
SAN DIEGO, CALIFORNIA

Singular Publishing Group, Inc.
401 West "A" Street, Suite 325
San Diego, California 92101-7904

Singular Publishing Group, Inc., publishes textbooks, clinical manuals, clinical reference books, journals, videos, and multimedia materials on speech-language pathology, audiology, otorhinolaryngology, special education, early childhood, aging, occupational therapy, physical therapy, rehabilitation, counseling, mental health, and voice. For your convenience, our entire catalog can be accessed on our website at *http://www.singpub.com*. Our mission to provide you with materials to meet the daily challenges of the ever-changing health care/educational environment will remain on course if we are in touch with you. In that spirit, we welcome your feedback on our products. Please telephone (**1-800-521-8545**), fax (**1-800-774-8398**), or e-mail (*singpub@singpub.com*) your comments and requests to us.

Typeset in 10/12 Century Schoolbook by So Cal Graphics
Printed in Canada by Webcom

Library of Congress Cataloging-in-Publication Data

Scott, Jack, Ph.D.
    Students with autism : characteristics and instructional
programming for special educators / by Jack Scott, Claudia Clark,
and Michael Brady.
        p. cm.
    Includes bibliographical references and index.
    ISBN 1-56593-630-2 (softcover : alk. paper)
    1. Autistic children—Education—United States. 2. Autism—United
States. I. Clark, Claudia, 1950- . II. Brady, Michael P.
III. Title.
LC4718.S36 1999
371.94—dc21   99-27449
                                                        CIP

Contents

Preface

This book is intended to help educators who provide services to students with autism. It was created to fill the need for a comprehensive book that carefully presents the role and responsibility of educators. Other works focus on autism from the perspective of parents, or speech-language pathologists, or researchers. Some excellent books target both parents and teachers. These books all have their place. But the role of the educator differs from the roles of parents and other professionals, and the information educators require is simply not the same. Educators have an extensive background in child development and instruction, and the contexts in which they receive new information are usually structured. These contexts, whether for-credit classes or inservice workshops, rely heavily on books to present information. This book should serve these needs well, whether as a textbook in graduate and advanced undergraduate courses or for dedicated training efforts in schools and autism service agencies.

The field of autism is rapidly changing and this book will be a part of this change process. As we note many times, the field of autism has been, in many ways, *too open and too willing* to accept claims that had little or no supporting evidence. Certainly, researchers and parents who are willing and able to fund experimentation on their children have the right to explore new treatments. But the role and, we believe, the inclination of the educator must be very different. Concern should be focused on the provision of the best possible services while meeting the unique needs of all children. Educators also must work within the framework of relevant federal special education laws (primarily the Individuals with Disabilities Act) and state laws and regulations. These responsibilities include adherence to sound practices done well. Educators typically have a healthy suspicion of fads and gimmicks, a suspicion we believe to be well founded in relation to treatments for students with autism. Exploration of unproved and, in many cases, *never to be proven* approaches is the work of the researcher and not the role of the school-based teacher. But the educator is called on to conduct investigations and analyses every bit as complex and challenging in meeting the educational needs of children with disorders within the autism spectrum. Are the conceptual, pedagogical, and analytic tools available to meet these challenges? We believe they are.

The fields of special education, applied behavior analysis, and autism have a richness and depth that permit diligent educators to address virtually any instructional or management issue. Drawing on these and other fields is far more productive than seeking only approaches and techniques that have been purposely created for students with autism. For example, it is now popular to look at social skills training specifically developed for students with autism (such as Social Stories) as a panacea while failing to consider and value the knowledge and practice base of social and interpersonal skills curricula developed for persons with other disabilities. We see an expanded view as beneficial. Within this expanded view can be found an abundance of proven, practical approaches and techniques that are known to special educators in general but, sadly, are unknown to many educators who teach students with autism. Incidental teaching, discrete trial instruction, task analysis, and many prompting techniques should be first nature to any teacher of students with autism. As educators are increasingly called on to direct paraeducators and other noncertified persons, technical skill in these and many other basic teaching tools is ever more essential.

The first section of this book focuses on the general nature of autism and related disabilities. We variously use the term *autism, autism spectrum disorder,* and *pervasive developmental disabilities* and believe that all students within the autism spectrum should have access to the best programming options available to any student with autism. Chapter 1 addresses the Characteristics of the Spectrum. To give an understanding of the nature of the field, Chapter 2 provides A Brief History of Autism. Chapter 3, Medical Aspects and Etiology of Autism, focuses on the medical and science-based etiology research most important to teachers. Indeed, a full appreciation of neurological research related to etiology is beyond both the scope of this book and the interests of most educators. However, educators must be aware of some critical medical aspects, such as medication administration and seizure management, essential to quality programming for these students. Last in this section is Chapter 4, which addresses Theory and Controversy. Controversy abounds in autism and even confronting the nature of the controversy may be controversial.

Educational Programming is the focus of the second section. Here the emphasis is on teaching, instruction, behavior support and management, and the day-to-day work of the educator in planning and delivering quality programs. Chapter 5 looks at Promoting Behavioral Competence taking a stance that an understanding of any problem behavior is essential to providing the supports necessary to help students become successful. Efforts to provide behavioral supports and address problem behaviors go hand in hand with efforts to promote communication. Chapter 6, Communication: Meaning and Competence, stresses the need for creative and skilled programming to optimize the communicative opportunities for each student. Chapter 7, Social Skills and Social Competence, offers a practical and relatively simple model for facilitating social and interpersonal skills. In Chapter 8, An Educational Model for Teaching Students with Autism, we set out a model for instructing these hard to teach students. We know that these students do not learn easily and, when poorly taught, they may not learn at all. The model we provide will facilitate good instruction. Although the educators tend to focus on the school and classroom, working in partnership with parents is necessary for a quality program.

The last section deals with both present and future contexts for offering education to students with autism. Chapter 9, Parents and Families, considers these relationships from the perspective of educators. Chapter 10, Offering a True Continuum of Services, emphasizes the need to offer an array of services relevant to the needs of students. Finally, in Chapter 11, Putting It All Together, we seek to synthesize the content presented into a manageable and implementable package. We intend for this book to help influence the way educators educate.

One last word on controversy is appropriate. We recognize the degree to which controversy surrounds many issues in autism. This book reflects these controversies, but we chose not to step back from dealing with topics because some might view them as controversial. We challenge our readers to exercise high levels of discernment and judgment in considering any treatments, methodologies, or practices. Students with autism deserve the best and most empirically sound programs that we, as educators, can offer.

Acknowledgments

A book like this is a very cooperative effort and we are grateful to many people in its preparation. We are especially thankful to all of the sidebar authors. Their knowledge, skill, and breadth of experience allowed us to feature valuable and unique perspectives. Dr. Philip Drash has been instrumental in developing behavior analytic treatments for communication problems in children with autism and has been gracious in sharing his insights. Dr. O. I. Lovaas has opened the door to impressive applications of behavioral teaching specifically for young children with autism. His research has set new and high standards for effective and efficient intervention. Dr. Lovaas and his associate, Dr. Tristram Smith, offered important clarifications that greatly assisted us in valuing the benefits of program intensity in early intervention. We also are grateful to Dr. Ronald Taylor for sharing his technical expertise in the creation of this work. Dr. Cecilia Campoverde, Stephanie Wolmer, and Mapy Brown all provided valuable insights into selected aspects of the disorder and its impact on parents or educators. Dot Collins, Karen McCormack, and Cindy Carson provided ongoing assistance. We appreciate the valuable research efforts of Ajoy Kumar and Tom Brown. A special note of gratitude is due to Marie Linvill for her patience and confidence in our work and to all the staff at Singular. We would like to thank the FAU students in various sections of *Students With Autism* for their many helpful suggestions. Finally, we owe a special debt of gratitude to the many families of children and youth with autism for sharing their experiences, insights, hopes, and frustrations with us.

Dedication

This book is dedicated to my mother Albina and the memory of my father, John Scott, who shared a profound respect for all persons with disabilities, to my wonderful wife Wanda, and my dear son Peter.

JS

To my first and greatest teachers, whom I love the best—my sons, Jason and Justin.

CC

To Dick, Jim, Floyd, Luanna, and Dave Platt—my teachers who pushed, pulled, guided, and laughed—and to my students who are responsible for teaching me what's worth knowing—I thank you.

MPB

Chapter 1

CHARACTERISTICS OF THE SPECTRUM

Key Points

- Origin and evolution of the diagnosis of autism
- Incidence, IQ range, and gender ratios of autism in the general population
- Characteristics that define autism and "autistic spectrum disorders"
- Strengths of individuals with autism and how these strengths are typically expressed
- Deficits of individuals with autism and how these deficits are typically expressed
- How individuals with autism may use nontypical means to express their wants and needs

---

INTRODUCTION

The characteristics of autism overlap with those of many other disabilities, but there are distinct features of this syndrome that distinguish it from other disabilities. Even within the spectrum of autism there are extreme differences, due in part to the role played by individual biology and reinforcement histories, yet these individuals all share a consistent pattern of autism.

The characteristics of students with autism present unique challenges to professionals committed to teaching them. Indeed students with autism bring skills as well as challenges to the task of teaching. In this chapter we present the range of characteristics that comprise the syndrome of autism and delineate the core features of this unique disability.

WHAT IS AUTISM?

Kanner published a landmark paper in 1943 describing the case histories of 11 children aged 2 to 11 whose conditions "differed so remarkably and uniquely from anything reported so far" (p. 217) that he considered them a separate diagnostic entity. The children he described, although very different from each other in their abilities, family structures, and ages, exhibited a number of essential common characteristics that did not fit into any of the previously established diagnoses. The overwhelming characteristic that Kanner noted was the "inability to relate themselves . . . to people and situations." They appeared be isolated from other people, to be always alone and self-directed in their activities. Kanner wrote that these children, from the start, exhibited an "extreme autistic aloneness that, whenever possible, disregards, ignores, shuts out anything that comes to the child from the outside" (p. 242). The term "autism" was derived from the word "auto" for self. Other common characteristics of the children were excellent rote memory and an "anxiously obsessive desire for the maintenance of sameness." Kanner distinguished these children from those diagnosed with childhood schizophrenia and diagnosed these children with "inborn autistic disturbances of affective contact."

Kanner was the first person to recognize that this particular group of behaviors was different from schizophrenia and mental retardation. His observation of the specific behaviors that differentiated autism from other diagnoses has stood the test of time. Although the terminology has changed from the psychoanalytic language used during Kanner's time to more objective, descriptive definitions, the characteristics that Kanner observed and recorded are the same as those used to diagnose autism today.

The behavioral characteristics leading to a diagnosis of autistic disorder are delineated in the *Diagnostic and Statistical Manual of Mental*

Disorders, Fourth Edition (DSM-IV) of the American Psychiatric Association (APA, 1994) (Table 1–1). The essential features necessary for the diagnosis of autistic disorder include "the presence of markedly abnormal or impaired development in social interaction and communication and a markedly restricted repertoire of activity and interests" (p. 66). Although the DSM-IV definition governs much of the current thinking of professionals, the label ascribed to these individuals has varied over time, including childhood schizophrenia and borderline psychosis.

Autism is diagnosed through observation of the cluster of behaviors presented by the individual and by eliminating other disorders (such as Rett syndrome or mental retardation). The definition of autism has evolved amid speculation and research in hopes of determining physiological or psychological causes. Kanner originally noted that the parents of the children he studied tended not to be "really warmhearted fathers and mothers." He went on to note, however, that since the children's aloneness was exhibited from the beginning of life, the parents could not be exclusively responsible for their child's autism.

Bettelheim (1967), in concert with the psychotherapeutic tone of the 1960s, considered autism to be the result of "cold, unfeeling parents" and particularly targeted the mother as being the primary causative factor in the development of autism in young children. Although current research has shown that parents do not cause autism in their children, a number of professionals in the fields of psychology and medicine still look to parents as the primary causative factor when their children are diagnosed with autism.

Athough Kanner (1943) mentioned the possibility of the relevance of environmental factors to the development of autism, he also noted the possibility of a genetic or innate component in the causation of autism. Rimland (1964) was one of the first researchers to look to a physiological or neurological cause. Many other researchers since Rimland have followed the path of looking for underlying physiological causes. Although the exact causes of autism are as yet unknown, current research is beginning to find specific brain differences between children with autism and typically developing children (Bauman, 1991; Bauman & Kemper, 1994; Courchesne, 1991). Today, consensus among researchers is that (a) autism is probably caused by biological factors; (b) the exact causes remain unknown, but might be due to multiple etiologies; and (c) numerous environmental, social, and familial factors can minimize or exacerbate the symptoms of autism.

Differential Diagnosis

Autism is included in the DSM-IV as one of several pervasive developmental disorders (PDD). For a diagnosis of autism, six of the designated

Table 1-1. DSM-IV Diagnostic Criteria for Autistic Disorder

A. A total of six (or more) items from (1), (2), and (3), with at least two from (1), and one each from (2) and (3):

   (1) qualitative impairment in social interaction, as manifested by at least two of the following:
   - (a) marked impairment in the use of multiple nonverbal behaviors such as eye-to-eye gaze, facial expression, body postures, and gestures to regulate social interaction
   - (b) failure to develop peer relationships appropriate to developmental level
   - (c) a lack of spontaneous seeking to share enjoyment, interests, or achievements with other people (e.g., by a lack of showing, bringing, or pointing out objects of interest)
   - (d) lack of social or emotional reciprocity

   (2) qualitative impairments in communication as manifested by at least one of the following:
   - (a) delay in, or total lack of, the development of spoken language (not accompanied by an attempt to compensate through alternative modes of communication such as gesture or mime)
   - (b) in individuals with adequate speech, marked impairment in the ability to initiate or sustain a conversation with others
   - (c) stereotyped and repetitive use of language or idiosyncratic language
   - (d) lack of varied, spontaneous make-believe play or social imitative play appropriate to developmental level

   (3) restricted repetitive and stereotyped patterns of behavior, interests, and activities, as manifested by at least one of the following:
   - (a) encompassing preoccupation with one or more stereotyped and restricted patterns of interest that is abnormal either in intensity or focus
   - (b) apparently inflexible adherence to specific, nonfunctional routines or rituals
   - (c) stereotyped and repetitive motor mannerisms (e.g., hand or finger flapping or twisting, or complex whole-body movements)
   - (d) persistent preoccupation with parts of objects

B. Delays or abnormal functioning in at least one of the following areas, with onset prior to age 3 years: (1) social interaction, (2) language as used in social communication, or (3) symbolic or imaginative play.

C. The disturbance is not better accounted for by Rett Disorder or Childhood Disintegrative Disorder.

Source: From *Diagnostic and Statistical Manual of Mental Disorders* (4th ed.), by American Psychiatric Association, 1994, pp. 70–71. Washington, DC: American Psychiatric Association. Reprinted with permission.

What's in a Name?

Since Kanner first described autism in 1943, people have wrestled with the language used to describe the disorder. For example, autism has alternately been called childhood schizophrenia, a mental disorder, childhood psychosis, and currently, a spectrum disorder. Some critics contend that terminology is far less important than what professionals *do* with people who have the disorder. We disagree—terminology often dictates how professionals think and what they do.

Autism is a classic example of how the language used to describe a concept influences how professionals interact with the concept. Kanner's original description can best be characterized as "clinical." He provided objective and observable descriptors of characteristics and behavior. Missing from Kanner's language (and from professionals' behavior in subsequent years) were concepts regarding intervention and support.

Contrast Kanner's language and concepts with those of Bettelheim. Reflecting the state of psychology during his time, Bettelheim used language and terminology strongly based in Freudian psychology. Bettelheim described autism as a deeply rooted psychological disturbance, an understandable reaction to cold or harsh parenting methods used during infancy. Indeed, his term "refrigerator mother" summarized many psychologists' thinking about etiology and was used as the rationale for psychotherapy, counseling, and other "talking therapy" approaches to autism for many years. It was also used as a rationale for removing the child from the home and family for institutional placement. In many ways the language of this era helped establish a generation of detached "refrigerator professionals."

With the expansion of psychological services in the mid-1960s came the need to better delineate the disorders for which psychological support could be arranged and paid for. In many ways, the terminology and language used in the various DSM editions reflected the desire of professionals to describe different disorders. The DSM-IV provides a clear clinical description of a *disorder* called autism. This focus is the foundation of professionals' behavior involving assessment and differential diagnosis, but does little to inform interventions. Neither does it adequately portray the humanity of people who have the disorder.

(continued)

Finally, consider the terminology and language provided by the Autism Society of America (ASA, 1998). ASA's definition of autism includes the following:

> Autism interferes with the normal development of the brain in the areas of reasoning, social interaction and communication skills. Children and adults with autism typically have deficiencies in verbal and non-verbal communication, social interactions, and leisure or play activities. *The disorder makes it hard for them to communicate with others and relate to the outside world* [emphasis added]. *They may exhibit repeated body movements* (hand flapping, rocking), unusual responses to people or attachments to objects and resist any changes in routines. In some cases, aggressive and/or self-injurious behavior may be present.
>
> ... the majority of the public, including many professionals ... are still unaware of how autism affects people and how to effectively work with individuals with autism. (p. 3)

ASA's definition is followed by a number of statements stressing the need for interventions. ASA terminology differs from the DSM-IV in fundamental ways. While the ASA's definition includes clinical description, it also stresses the benefits of intervention. Reading the ASA material, one can picture real people who have autism; behavioral idiosyncrasies are provided within a social context.

Language *does* matter. All too often professionals retreat into clinical language and, inadvertently, clinical behavior. The clinical terminology of the DSM-IV might help some professionals *diagnose* autism. Educators and families, however, require a language of concepts based on human understanding, social supports, and effective interventions.

characteristics must be present in the individual with at least two of the indicators from the social area and one each from communication and behavior. If fewer than six total characteristics are evident, or if the required number of indicators is not present in the areas of social, behavior, and communication, a diagnosis of PDD-NOS (pervasive developmental disorder/not otherwise specified) is likely to be considered appropriate (Mesibov, 1997). Sometimes a PDD-NOS diagnosis is given when an individual does not quite meet the criteria for autism or when a child is very young. Often, neurologists, neuropsychologists, and other qualified professionals who diagnose the condition are hesitant to use a diagnosis that may, for some, be as emotionally laden as "autism."

A related diagnosis under the heading of pervasive developmental disorders is Asperger's syndrome (also known as Asperger's disorder). Asperger's syndrome has a high degree of overlap with "high functioning autism," yet there is some support for considering Asperger's syndrome a separate disorder within the PDD spectrum. Individuals with Asperger's syndrome tend to have age-appropriate communication skills, but are often slightly less developed in gross motor skills than their peers with autism. Asperger's syndrome, PPD-NOS, and the other pervasive developmental disorders are addressed in greater depth later in this chapter. The authors of this book take the position that a common core of educational services will be necessary for children with any of the pervasive developmental disorders. Although it is important for classification, diagnosis, and research purposes to accurately differentiate these disorders with the greatest degree of accuracy possible, it is not necessary to do so to provide quality education.

Incidence

Autism is among the higher incidence of the low-incidence disorders. Although there is some range in the incidence figures, a conservative estimate provided by researchers typically indicates a prevalence of 4 or 5 in 10,000 (Lotter, 1966; Rimland, 1978). The DSM-IV suggests a prevalence of 2 to 5 per 10,000. Other estimates range to 21 in 10,000 (Wing & Gould, 1979). The most recent data (during the 1994–1995 school year) show that there were 22,768 school-aged students with autism in schools in the U.S.A. (USED, 1996). Table 1–2 summarizes the differences across states in reported incidence of students with autism who received special education.

Some of the variance in the reported incidence of autism is due to difficulties in diagnosis at both ends of the spectrum. For example, individuals with severe mental retardation often duplicate the same social, communicative, and behavioral deficits that constitute autism. Individuals with both autism *and* mental retardation may be cognitively or motorically unable to perform some of the elaborate rituals that could lead to a differential diagnosis (Wing & Gould, 1979).

Difficulties exist in diagnosing autism at the milder end of the spectrum, as well. There are currently no reliable physiological or genetic markers as there are in some other disabilities (e.g., the genetic markers associated with Down syndrome). Thus, it becomes a fine distinction

Table 1–2. State Differences in Incidence of Autism

State	Number of Students Aged 6–21 with Autism	Number per 10,000 Residents
	Higher Incidence States	
Oregon	1088	16
Delaware	132	9
Michigan	1556	7
North Carolina	1056	7
New York	2224	6
Indiana	733	6
	Lower Incidence States	
Colorado	58	1
Mississippi	77	1
New Hampshire	5	<1
New Mexico	46	1
Ohio	145	1
Washington	113	1

Source: Based on 1994–1995 school year data reported in U.S. Department of Education 18th Annual Report to Congress (USED, 1996).

between the typical range of behaviors and mild levels of autism. This is particularly true with younger children, when the diagnosis is often made. For example, typically developing young children tend to be very concrete in language (a characteristic of autism) and there is a wide variance in young children's normal social development.

Some researchers believe that the incidence of autism is increasing, in part due to changes in diagnostic criteria (Sturmey & Sevin, 1994). Although more individuals are being diagnosed with autism or autistic spectrum disorder, that may be due more to increased awareness on the part of pediatricians, neurologists, and lay people than to any true increase in the incidence of the disorder (Gillberg, Steffenburg, & Schaumann, 1991). Others believe that a diagnosis of autism might depend on factors as diverse as whether high quality services are readily available, the socioeconomic status (SES) of the families of the individuals undergoing testing, and the extent to which families advocate for the diagnosis during the assessments.

Autism and IQ Scores

Approximately 80% of children with autism obtain scores in the range of mental retardation on standardized IQ tests when the tests are administered in a traditional manner (Wing & Gould, 1979); the remaining 20% show test scores ranging from normal IQs to gifted or genius IQ levels. This full range of intellectual levels can coexist with a diagnosis of autism. Rimland (1978) noted that such geniuses and eccentrics as Sir Isaac Newton and Howard Hughes shared certain characteristics of autism.

The accuracy of standardized tests must be interpreted with extreme caution, however. Since one of the key deficits of autism involves communication, any instrument that relies on expressive or receptive language may not accurately test the individual's true (or even approximate) intellectual ability. Likewise, deficits in social relatedness may influence the accuracy of standardized IQ tests when the individual being tested is minimally cooperative or is uninterested in the approval and attention of the test administrator.

As important, in many instances, the instructional *utility* of a diagnosis of autism is minimal. Standardized and developmental testing results are known to affect the educational recommendations and decisions of professionals (Linehan & Brady, 1995). The way professionals *perceive* students with disabilities influences their decisions about the services and supports they will arrange for these students (Linehan, Brady, & Hwang, 1991). When the diagnosis, rather than the student's individual differences, dictates instructional programming, the diagnosis often results in restricted rather than enhanced educational opportunities. Biklen (1990), for example, pointed out that many people with autism who were also perceived to have mental retardation did not have access to typical academic and community opportunities. Lack of *opportunity to learn* is as debilitating to students with autism as the condition itself.

There is a wide range in the level of severity and areas of deficit in autism. Individuals with autism form a highly heterogeneous population; this heterogeneity ranges from those who seem to be typical but somewhat odd to individuals who exhibit severe or life-threatening behaviors. Because of this wide range and varied expression, autism is increasingly described as a "spectrum disorder" (Siegel, 1996). The level of intellectual functioning is not directly related to the severity of autism. One student may have mild autism and severe cognitive disabilities, while another might have severe autism yet have normal intelligence.

Gender Ratios

Kanner (1943) noted that the preponderance of youngsters with autism in his sample were males. This finding has been upheld in subsequent research. Males are identified more frequently than females at an approximate 4:1 or 5:1 ratio (APA, 1994). Some studies report that females tend to have more severely affected IQ scores, as well as greater problems in language (Konstantareas, Homatidis, & Busch, 1989; Lord & Schopler, 1987) although the earlier cautions regarding standardized testing are relevant when considering these findings. Autism is not restricted to any ethnic group or socioeconomic level. The definitive characteristics of the diagnosis of autism are found in children of all cultures.

Visual Processing

A primary strength of people with autism involves visual processing (Quill, 1997). That is, people with autism often learn and interpret information from the environment through things that are *seen* rather than things that are *heard*. Visual memory may be so accurate that fluctuations in the stock market over time as reported in the newspaper or an inaccuracy in a line of computer code will be noticed immediately. It may also be so accurate that any minor deviation in the placement of desks and chairs will cause the student to become agitated until the current placement of furniture exactly matches the student's visual memory.

The relative strength of visual processing is common in students with autism. While verbal information is transitory and requires simultaneous processing and comprehension, visual information can be kept in sight until the required processing and comprehension are complete. The presentation of information in a visual format can become the primary learning modality, as will be discussed in Chapter 8.

Savant Characteristics

An unusual characteristic of a small percentage of persons with autism appears as exceptional strengths or "savant" abilities. The popular media (books, TV, movies) often present images of people with autism who also have these savant characteristics. Many of the savant skills (such as calendar calculation, map recall, musical score memory, and mathematical computation) may rely to some degree on sophisticated visual processing (Mottron & Belleville, 1993). Despite the popularity of the movies *Rainman* and *Shine*, savant skills are relatively rare. Rimland (1978) found that about 10% of individuals with autism exhibited savant skills.

Other estimates have ranged as low as 1 in 10,000. Although there is a low incidence of savant characteristics, visual strengths are common and are an important consideration for educational programming (Quill, 1997).

Teachers and parents can be faced with a dilemma as they consider responding to these exceptional abilities. A child who can recite baseball scores from memory but who cannot greet a peer has skills that are clearly out of balance. Should teachers attempt to build savant abilities further or concentrate on other less well-developed skills in the hope of encouraging a more well-rounded person? Cheatham, Rucker, Smith, and Lewis (1995) urged educators to develop savant abilities to the greatest degree possible and to provide close guidance to students to make their abilities as useful and vocationally relevant as possible. While noting that special educators, historically, have focused on a deficit model, Cheatham et al. advocated targeting savant skills as a strength.

> As educators strive to open doors to all individuals with disabilities and widen their horizons for empowerment, self determination, and independence, those with savant syndrome must not be forgotten. Educators must seek out these special abilities and encourage their development to the fullest extent possible. (p. 252)

Many students with savant skills lack basic functional skills involving social interaction, communication, and self-care. These skills are critical and educators should devote considerable time and attention to their development. In addition, educators should build on students' strengths, *including any savant abilities*, to empower these students to become more productive and independent. The student with autism and savant skills is a person with talents, talents that should be developed and on which overall success in life is very likely to rest.

COMMUNICATION ASPECTS OF AUTISM

Communication refers to the process of sharing information and ideas from one person to another. It involves encoding, transmitting, and decoding the intended message (Shames & Wiig, 1990). Speech and language comprise only a portion of the communication process. Speech refers to the verbal means of communication and consists of sound combinations, rate, intonation, and voice quality. Language refers to a socially shared code for representing concepts. Additionally, the entire range of nonsymbolic communication, including body language, gestures, eye gaze, and touch is part of the communication process.

Autism can affect any or all of these components of communication. A student may be able to make all of the known speech sounds, but not be able to *use* language to communicate. Another student may have language, that is, be able to communicate thoughts using conventional sentence structure, but may have monotonous or "robotic" speech. A third student may be able to speak and use language to communicate, but may not understand the body language, intonations, or the social nuances of the other person.

Children communicate long before they can speak (Bates, 1976; Prizant & Weatherby, 1987). For example the crying of an infant can be seen as a most basic form of (nonsymbolic) communication. As a child begins to develop more advanced forms of communication—such as gestures and vocalizations—crying usually is replaced by more conventional language.

Communication development in children with autism usually does not proceed in a typical manner. For some children with autism, the more basic, nonsymbolic forms of communication (i.e., tantrums, crying, and aggression) are so effective that they interfere with the development of more advanced symbolic forms of communication (Carr & Durand, 1985; Drash & Tudor, 1993). When students with autism develop language, the process tends not to follow a developmental progression. Instead, their language skills may be scattered across a wide range. Thus, a student might use advanced sentence structure but not use plurals or pronouns correctly.

Communication ability in individuals with autism can range from totally nonverbal to superior reading and vocabulary skills. Many individuals with autism never develop language under traditional treatments. For those who do develop language, the rate, tonal quality, pitch, or pragmatics of language may be affected. Regardless of the level of verbal language ability, Kanner (1943) found certain language deficits in common. These common deficits are still considered relevant today. Language, for a student with autism, tends to be concrete and inflexible. It is rarely used to share personal information such as thoughts and feelings. The social rewards and punishers for conventional language tend not to be effective. Even when the "amount" of language is typical, there often is a lack of conversational turn taking and appreciation of another's point of view. Generally, these students are unable to switch topics easily or to converse on topics that are not of immediate interest to them.

In addition, nonverbal communication skills such as eye contact, social distance, gestures, and body postures tend to be lacking. The understanding of what constitutes appropriate social distance differs among cultures and among different members in an individual's social group. For example, one tends to stand farther from the boss than from one's child or spouse. This is not something that is specifically taught to people without autism; instead it is learned incidentally as part of the acculturation process. Many students with autism do not use appropriate social distance without being taught the precise "code." Likewise, an individual with autism might not understand that tapping one's foot and looking at the ceiling are nonverbal signals that individuals in our culture use to communicate boredom.

The DSM-IV (APA, 1994) delineates the qualitative impairments in communication as:

1. delay or lack of spoken language;
2. significant inability to initiate or sustain conversations;
3. repetitive, stereotyped, and/or idiosyncratic language; and
4. deficit in social, spontaneous, and/or creative play.

One of the difficulties that students with autism find in conversation is the apparent lack of rules and structure. Knowing when to interrupt or interject, when to change a topic, when and how to begin and end a conversation, and how to know when the communicative partner wants to begin or end a conversation are all areas of great difficulty for students with autism. The rules of conversation, unlike the rules of mathematics or even grammar, are elusive and unstated.

In addition to these general communicative aspects of autism, people across the spectrum often face specific communicative difficulties. These include difficulties with perseveration, rate, abstract language, echolalia, and nonverbal communication.

Perseveration

Perseveration refers to the exessive repetition of a behavior, phrase, topic, or idea, the expression of which is perceived by others as "odd" in a social context. A child who perseverates on the subject of cars might speak extensively and knowledgeably about cars, but resist a communication partner's attempts to change the subject. A student who repeatedly asks, "When's lunch?" after being given the information is no longer asking for information, but is perseverating on the question. Often this perseveration serves to gain attention from the person to whom the question is directed.

Rate, Tone, and Pitch

The language of students with autism often differs from that of typical peers in rate, tone, or pitch. Rate of speech may range from faster to slower than typical range. Tonal quality may range from flat and monotonous to overly dramatic. Pitch may range from the lower to the upper ranges, sometimes being emitted as very high-pitched screams. Problems with rate, tone, and pitch exist independent of communication content. Extreme variance in these speech mechanics heightens the differences between some students with autism and their typically developing peers.

Abstract Language

Students with autism tend to be concrete in their use of language. Abstraction, idiom, and inference are complex, sometimes difficult concepts both receptively and expressively. This should not be interpreted to mean that students with autism are incapable of thinking in abstract terms, but rather that they often have difficulty expressing these thoughts and understanding them when expressed by others. Where typically developing children might relish learning an idiom such as "let the cat out of the bag," a student with autism is likely to ask why the cat had been put in the bag.

Students with autism sometimes use common words in uncommon ways. That is, although the words are the same as those used by others, the words might not have the same meaning. A teacher's request for further information may reveal differences in meaning that would not be discerned by taking a conversation at face value. For example, a student might say that she wants to "go out to eat." The teacher who arranges a trip to Wendy's would be surprised to learn that the student really wanted to eat "outside" in a park or school yard. These differences in perceived meaning sometimes cause frustration and disruption by a student with autism who is trying to communicate, uses the same words as everyone else, and still is misunderstood.

Echolalia

Echolalia is one of the inappropriate speech forms commonly seen in students with autism. Echolalia is the repetition (echoing) of words, phrases, and sometimes whole dialogs. The echolalia can be immediate or delayed and might be a repetition of the student's own words or the words of others. Researchers have established that echolalia often has a social function (Prizant, 1983; Prizant & Weatherby, 1987). For example, echolalia can serve a turn-taking function for students with autism who understand that conversation involves people taking turns speaking, but who do not have the ability to "hold up" their end of the conversation independently.

In describing her own autism, Grandin (1995) stated that her thought processes are associational. Phrases are "chunked" or memorized to stand for whole meanings based on the circumstances under which they were first learned. Echolalia or delayed echolalia may serve this function. A student may recite a Pepsi commercial to indicate that he is thirsty if he initially associated a drink with the Pepsi commercial. Teachers should look for the intended meaning of the echolalic utterance when planning to replace the echolalia with more typical speech.

Echolalia serves a host of social functions, some generalized and others highly specific. Prizant and Duchan (1981) derived multiple functional categories for immediate echolalia including conversation, turn-taking, offering a "yes" answer, and requesting. It may be that an individual with autism understands that some response is called for when a person exhibits the nonverbal behaviors of standing face-to-face and making eye contact. To keep attention focused or to keep the turn-taking process intact, the individual will make a verbal (echolalic) response.

Nonverbal Communication Problems

Much of social interaction is nonverbal. Students with autism have difficulty interpreting nonverbal cues, including facial expression, gestures, eye gaze, touch, and body language. Many of these are culture-specific behaviors; that is, people from a particular culture use similar nonverbal communications. For example, direct eye contact may be an expression of honesty or confrontation, depending on the culture. Temple Grandin and others with autism have noted their difficulties in interpreting nonverbal cues. One individual with autism wrote of needing a "handbook for aliens" (Sacks, 1993–1994) to decipher meaning from everyday nonverbal cues. Some individuals have studied books on "body language" to try to understand the meaning of nonverbal social cues.

For students who do not use words to communicate, nonverbal communication methods are their primary means of expressing themselves. Some of these students understand that vocal "noise" is used to communicate or to get others in the environment to satisfy needs. One student might use "va" to mean any circular thing that makes noise when you bang it (drum, pie plate, pan top). Another might use "gaga" with varying inflection and some gesture to mean "May I have that?" "I'm done," "yes," and "no."

Students with no recognizable language may still make their wants and needs known. A single vocalization such as "beep" or "guh" can be combined with gesture and intonation to increase the range of communication. Obviously, this is not an ideal communication system and is very limiting. Sometimes the only way to access items and activities is by communicating with other people; problem behaviors are likely to arise as a student tries and fails to make his needs understood.

Gail's Programming Dilemma

Gail is 6 years old with no clear words. She makes several noises and her parents can sometimes derive meaning from her noises and her behavior. When Gail wants something, she may begin a high-pitched noise at a low volume. This noise raises to a screech, able to be heard far away if her need is not discovered and addressed. When Gail signals a need to her parents, who are now tired of the escalation and are sensitive to her demands, they are quick to give her what she wants. Gail stops fussing, until the next time she wants something.

Gail was not able to attend a regular preschool since the staff was not willing to deal with this pattern of behavior. Now, as kindergarten placement is being considered, the parents are unsure of Gail's chances for success. They want the teacher to learn how to meet Gail's needs the way they do at home. The teacher, at the initial meeting, does not want to do this and believes that all children should request assistance in socially appropriate ways.

The programming choice here is not one way or the other, obviously. What should be done to help this child and this teacher have a successful year?

SOCIAL ASPECTS OF AUTISM

A deficit in social relatedness is essential to the diagnosis of autism. In his first descriptions of the disability Kanner (1943) wrote of "autistic aloneness." Others have described individuals with autism as being in their own worlds, aloof, and isolated. While most typical children seek out adults or peers for play, communication and social reinforcement, children with autism tend not to seek out others. Many children with autism often seem unaware of peers in their environment.

Indeed, many of these students do not seem to regard other children as people to relate to. Personal interactions might be limited to adults—and then only for caretaking functions. When this occurs, adults are used as instruments to obtain objects and activities. For example, a child might lead the teacher by the hand to a computer and push her hand toward the keyboard with no eye contact or social awareness of the teacher. In this example, the person (and the hand) is an instrument for gaining access to computers, but social contact with the adult is minimal.

Even when there seems to be a desire for social contact, the requisite interaction skills are often lacking. Clear, positive social initiations might be replaced by minor aggression or simple proximity (standing near others but not directing social interactions). Some verbal students will talk perseveratively "at" rather than "with" a peer. For others, social conversational skills may be lacking so that a student may want to ask a peer to the movies, but not know how to participate in the many turn-taking demands that such a conversation would entail.

Eye Contact

Eye contact is very difficult for many students with autism. Alternately, a student with autism might look at another person as though he were a wall, chair, or other object. A student known to one of the authors stated that he saw no necessity in looking at a person when speaking to him, since he "knew where [the other person] was."

Lack of eye-to-eye gaze is one of the common characteristics of autism in the DSM-IV criteria. Lack of eye contact should not be confused with a child's deliberate "not looking" (Volkmar, 1996). When, for example, a child's name is called or a one-step direction ("Sit with us") is given and the child turns away or closes her eyes, it is likely a learned method of expressing refusal or discomfort, not a symptom of autism. Some children will make and maintain eye contact on their own initiation, but not on the initiation of others. Not all students have this difficulty, however. Some are able to make and maintain spontaneous eye contact.

Some students with autism seem to use peripheral vision to complete tasks or to gather environmental information. It is fascinating to watch a student with autism complete a reasonably complex puzzle or sorting task while seemingly never looking directly at the task. However, eye contact and looking at people, objects, and tasks can be taught using direct instruction and methods borrowed from teachers of students with visual impairments.

Joint Attention

Typically developing children often invite others to look at an object or activity through eye gaze. They will look at the object, look at the individual, then look back at the object. If the object is at a distance, they may point, say "Look!" or otherwise draw the attention of the other person to the object. Children with autism tend not to exhibit shared attention (Mundy & Sigman, 1989). They may watch an object with complete attention without exhibiting any behaviors indicative of "sharing" the experience. Even if the object is in another person's hand, they are more likely to focus on the hand and try to take the object than to look at the person holding it.

Understanding the Core Social Deficits of Autism

Peter Mundy, Ph.D.

Imagine that you are at the circus with a child and a friend. All of a sudden, a performer does an incredible gymnastic stunt and the child looks to you, makes eye contact, and smiles. You smile back, and then you make eye contact with your friend, who nods and smiles. Each of you has just engaged in an act of joint attention. You have shared the experience of the event with the other person nonverbally. Research and theory suggest that joint attention bids are a fundamental form of human social-communication behavior. Furthermore, research and theory have begun to suggest that deficits or delays in the development of joint attention skills reflect a central or core component of the social deficits of autism.

Very early in their development, preschool children with autism display what may be a syndrome-specific deficit in the capacity to initiate joint attention bids with others. For example, children with autism will show well organized attention skills while they happily watch a mechanical toy bouncing around on a table. Other children with developmental disorders will also happily watch a mechanical toy. However, they will tend to look up at the adult who activated the toy from time to time as though to share this experience with him or her. This lack of eye contact by children with autism, however, does not appear to reflect a pervasive eye contact deficit. Children with autism display less eye contact disturbance in nonverbal requesting, social interaction, and caregiver separation and reunion attachment situations than they do in joint attention situations. Furthermore, the early joint attention deficits of autism are not limited to eye contact behaviors, but also involves deficits in gestural joint attention acts such as showing objects to others (Mundy et al., 1986; Sigman & Mundy, 1989).

Numerous observations suggest that joint attention disturbance may reflect a core component of the social deficits of children with autism. Joint attention skills develop very early in life, between 6 and 12 months of age. They are thought to provide a foundation for much of the subsequent social-cognitive and communication development displayed by preschool children (see Moore & Dunham, 1994). It is not surprising then that joint attention skill deficits have been observed in young children with autism before other important domains of disturbance, such as language or cognitive-symbolic play deficits (Mundy & Sheinkopf, 1993).

Individual differences on joint attention measures also appear to be important. Joint attention behaviors observed by a tester appear to relate to parents' ratings of the intensity of the social problems of children with autism, but not to parents' reports of the odd sensory or object use behaviors of their children. Equally important, better joint attention development among children with autism predicts better language development later in life.

Finally, it is important to note that researchers debate whether autism is caused by basic cognitive, affective, or neurological self-regulatory processes. However, joint attention development has been directly linked with each of these domains. Joint attention development is correlated with self-regulatory processes associated with the development of the frontal lobes (see Mundy, 1995 for review). Research has directly linked joint attention development to affective processes that may be central to autism as well. Finally, joint attention development may be an important precursor to social cognition and theory of mind development (Baron-Cohen, Tagger-Flusberg, & Cohen, 1993; Mundy & Sheinkopf, 1993). Theory of mind development refers to the capacity of children to understand that others have beliefs, desires, or feelings that affect their behavior. The connection between joint attention and theory of mind development may be especially important because older, verbal children may be severely handicapped by a disturbance in theory of mind skills (Baron-Cohen et al., 1993).

Thus, joint attention deficits may reflect a fundamental component of the social disturbance of autism. Indeed, one of the four core social symptoms of autism in DSM-IV (1994) is now described as "a lack of spontaneous seeking to share enjoyment, interests or achievements with other people (e.g., by a lack of showing, bringing or pointing out objects of interest)" (p. 70). Still, many important questions remain about the nature of joint attention disturbance in autism. One issue is the degree to which joint attention disturbance, or any component of the social deficits of autism are specific and central to the disorder or secondary to sensory, perceptual, cognitive, or other nonsocial fac-

(continued)

tors. The answer to this question is not at hand. However, many current theories would suggest that joint attention and the core social deficits of autism are not necessarily secondary to perceptual or sensory impairments (e.g., Baron-Cohen et al., 1993). A second important issue is the degree to which early intervention can improve the joint attention development of children with autism. This may be the single most important question before applied researchers. It is encouraging to note that several promising new methods are currently being developed and tested.

Peter Mundy, Ph.D., is Director of the Center for Autism and Related Disorders and Professor of Psychology at the University of Miami in Miami, Florida.

Body Language and Position

Children with autism may exhibit a lack of social relatedness by stiffening and arching away from adults, teachers, or caretakers when held or hugged. They may passively accept physical contact without response. They may also seek hugs and physical contact from caretakers, but it is usually on their own initiation, rather than that of the caretaker.

One of the early indicators of possible autism in babies is lack of anticipatory body movement prior to being picked up (Kanner, 1943). This lack of responsiveness is very difficult for parents and other family members to accept, especially when seen in infants or young children. An early screening indicator for autism in very young children is the lack of anticipatory posture (Gillberg et al., 1991).

As students get older, their purposeful use of body language typically falls behind that of their peers. Body language is used as nonverbal communication and the "code" is generally unknown or unavailable to these students. Without specific training in interpretation, these students tend not to understand or use body language effectively. Their movements tend to be rather stiff and minimal. This may be due in part to early correction of their natural body movements, which may have been self-stimulatory or stereotypic.

Social Play and Interaction

The difficulties students with autism find in social communication are also seen in social play and other circumstances where interaction with others is expected. Children with autism tend not to exhibit social reciprocity during play without specific instruction. The lack of structure and explicit "rules" to follow, as well as the speed with which auditory and nonverbal social signals need to be processed, make play a difficult time for these children. Indeed, some professionals note that "work is play and play is work" for these students (Mesibov, 1992). Turn taking, sharing, and joint attention during play can be taught, but are not usually developed spontaneously.

In addition to the social play skills, verbal interaction skills often need to be specifically taught. Difficulties with when to talk to another person, what to say, how long to talk, how to turn the conversation over to another person, and how to end the conversation generally need to be addressed. The cues for these skills are subtle and many teachers have little training in teaching social skills. Without instruction in these difficult skills, it is little wonder that the social interactions of students with autism can be awkward or lacking. Even when social scripts have been learned and play skills have been taught, the difficulties of having to attend to all of the cues at the same time may be overwhelming for some students. Clearly, in this circumstance, play would not be much fun.

Parallel play rather than interactive play tends to be exhibited by children with autism, particularly at the elementary level and with children with fewer skills. Given two children with autism and one pile of blocks, the children may well ignore each other completely and build separate block towers. Turn-taking skills and sharing, however, can be taught through direct instruction. In a classroom, it is sometimes easier to teach turn taking with an adult before requesting turn taking with other children. Research on social learning clearly demonstrates that teaching students to interact with other students with autism is far more difficult than teaching them to interact with peers who do not have disabilities; indeed, autism-only groupings often exacerbate students' social difficulties (Brady & McEvoy, 1989; Strain & Fox 1981). Dyadic or group games (e.g., ball throwing, parachute play, software sharing, or pushing a toy truck to a peer) can be used as the medium for teaching reciprocal interactions.

As students with autism grow older, they often want to make social contact, but lack the social skills to do so. As a result, they sometimes exhibit inappropriate behaviors directed toward others. For example, a student who wants to participate or make social contact but lacks the skill to do so appropriately might follow, watch closely, hit, or even bite a particular peer. Although the communicative intent of these behaviors is to make social contact, it is seldom *interpreted* by the peer as such.

Finding and sustaining relationships is often very difficult for students with autism. Friendship is based on shared interests and a willingness to share with another person. Students with autism often have limited interests and, as shown previously, often lack the skill needed for sharing. Interests in areas such as mathematics, computers, engineering, science, or chess can lead to inclusion in school clubs or a future career and may lead to friendships with other students who share the same interest. More obscure areas of interest may pose more difficulties in finding individuals who share them. Friendships are also hindered when nonverbal students produce inappropriate vocalizations (e.g., noises) during social interactions. Perseverating on a particular topic of conversation (e.g., fiberoptics or local bus routes) and difficulty shifting topics also challenges friendship development. Students with these characteristics have learned to form friendships when astute teachers scripted some conversations or provided a list of appropriate topics of conversation in different social settings (doctor's office, restaurant, job, parties).

Finally, students with autism usually have difficulty reading the nonverbal social cues that individuals use in social situations. While gradually moving away from another person usually means that the conversation or interaction is over, a student with autism might not recognize that the conversation is over from this cue. Direct teaching of the interpretation of nonverbal cues can help students understand the nonverbal behavior of others and thus exhibit more appropriate social behavior.

The cause of the social deficit in autism is unknown. It is possible that the core deficit of autism may be social in nature. If a student has no interest in socializing with others, communication is largely unnecessary. People generally behave in socially acceptable ways to gain social reinforcers. If social contact is not reinforcing, then there is little reason to behave in a socially acceptable manner.

Some researchers speculate that some degree of neurological abnormality exists in areas of the brain that are responsible for social relatedness (Voeller, 1986). Since there is a range of social contact exhibited by individuals, the social component of autism may be of a variable nature.

BEHAVIORAL ASPECTS OF AUTISM

The behavior of a child with autism is typically the most obvious signal to the community that the child is different. Behavioral differences can range from mild forms of stereotypic mannerisms that are seen as odd or inappropriate to prolonged episodes of self-injury and destruction of property. Regardless of the form, behavior differences are characteristic of these children. The DSM-IV lists a range of behavioral symptoms, including hyperactivity, short attention span, impulsivity, aggressiveness, self-injurious behavior, and temper tantrums.

It may be most productive to limit consideration of behavior to the portion of a person's interaction with the environment that is characterized by movement and that results in some measurable or recordable change in at least one aspect of the environment (Johnston & Pennypacker, 1980). Such a definition would exclude but not devalue other things people do (such as thinking and feeling) that are impossible to measure with available technology.

Behavioral difficulties in students with autism are most often considered as either deficits or excesses. Many of these behaviors are not unusual in themselves but are exhibited either at the *wrong times* or at a *lesser or greater frequency or intensity* than in typically developing youngsters. A look into any classroom of typically developing children will find a number of students tapping pencils, swinging feet, twirling hair, or looking out the window. These behaviors are not different in kind from a student with autism who spins, flicks his or her fingers, or gazes into the corner of the room. They may differ in degree or in the ease with which students stop and start the behavior.

It is arguably in these behavioral aspects that we see the widest range of difference among students with autism. Some have virtually no problem behaviors, others have life-threatening or highly disruptive behaviors. The behavioral component often determines the restrictiveness of educational settings arranged for students by professionals (Brady, McDougall, & Dennis, 1989). Students who rarely exhibit extreme behaviors, whatever their overall skills, are more likely to be included in typical school and community settings than students who may have more skills but who exhibit extreme behaviors.

All behavior serves a function. Generally, behavior has a history of obtaining something for the student who exhibits it. Either it has allowed the student to obtain something desired, to escape something undesired, or to provide some self-regulatory function (Cipani, 1990; O'Neill, Horner, Albin, Storey, & Sprague, 1990). In the sense that behavior allows students to interact with individuals in the environment, behavior also serves a communicative function (Carr et al., 1994; Carr & Durand, 1985; Donnellan, Mirenda, Mesaros, & Fassbender, 1984; Doss & Reichle, 1989; Reichle & Yoder, 1979).

The behavioral aspects of children with autism that concern professionals and families fall generally into three categories: stereotypic behavior, self-injurious behavior, and hyper- or hyposensitivity.

Stereotypic Behavior

Stereotypic behaviors, or "stereotypies," refer to the repetitive body movements often associated with people who have autism. Stereotypies often seen include hand flapping, finger flicking, odd hand positioning, body rocking, or spinning. For some students who engage in these stereotypies, the behaviors are produced occasionally, during stress, relaxation, or when the student is not engaged in task-related activities. For other children the behaviors are almost constant, reducing in frequency only during sleep.

Repetitive body movements traditionally were considered primarily self-stimulatory in nature. That is, they were thought to serve the purpose of self-regulation (Tinbergen & Tinbergen, 1983). An early, but continuing theory of self-stimulation (Hutt, Hutt, Lee, & Ounsted, 1964) is that the student with autism does not receive adequate stimulation from the environment. These behaviors, then, are thought to be used by children to provide increased levels of stimulation.

Not all repetitive body movements are self-stimulation. Many students with autism have restricted patterns of behavior. If a student does not have a large repertoire of behavior, then the same behavior can be used for different purposes at different times. Thus, a behavior such as hand flapping might be self-stimulatory on some occasions, but might also be used to obtain a desired item, escape a difficult task, or indicate happiness or distress (Carr & Durand, 1985; Iwata, Dorsey, Slifer, Bauman, & Richman, 1982).

Self-injurious Behavior (SIB)

When a behavior results in significant physical injury to the individual, it is labeled self-injurious behavior or SIB. Self-injurious behavior can take many forms. Biting one's own hands or arms, scratching or hitting the face, banging one's head against walls or desks, pinching one's body, and biting the tongue or lips are all forms of self-injury that have been found in some students with autism. Self-injurious behaviors, particularly when they are severe or life-threatening, can be very frightening to witness. Obviously, this form of behavior is extreme and has serious implications for educational placement. Fortunately, SIB is not common in students with autism.

One theoretical analysis (Schroeder, Rojahn, Mulick, & Schroeder, 1991) suggested that there are two types of self injurious behaviors: social and nonsocial. Their analysis suggested that a variety of conditions, situational demands, or background settings affect the rate and topography of the behavior. This is strongly supported by other research (Iwata et al., 1982), which identified environmental linkages to SIB.

Some behaviors, including self-injurious behaviors, may have a physiological component. Some self-injury may be used to reduce, relieve, or call attention to a physiological symptom or pain. For example, all of the authors of this text are familiar with students who hit their ears or heads whenever they had serious inner ear infections. Commonly, these youngsters did not have clear language or more appropriate ways of calling attention to their discomfort.

The needs of a student with autism are no different from those of any other student. The lack of an expansive behavioral repertoire, the lack of an efficient communication system, or the inability to obtain adequate stimulation and information from the environment can cause students to use atypical means of fulfilling their wants and needs. In the extreme, these means could include SIB. The need to obtain food, attention, affection, desired activities or objects, or to avoid undesired activities, objects, or punishment is the same as for a typically developing child.

Pica and Eating Disorders

One specific type of SIB, *pica*, involves ingesting nonedible materials. Pica is not specific to students with autism. Pica has been found in people with mental retardation, adolescents with psychiatric disorders, and in typically developing children. Many young nondisabled children have eaten crayons or school paste. This is pica, even though the behavior does not have lasting effects. Although many of the objects ingested are relatively harmless (paper, string, ice, insects), some may be life-threatening (metal, glass, paint, cleansing powder). Like other forms of SIB, ingesting life-threatening materials requires the intervention of professionals with expertise in behavior analysis.

Many students with autism exhibit strong food preferences. Eating one or two foods to the exclusion of all others can cause nutritional imbalances. Nutritional deficiencies have been found in individuals who exhibit pica (Danford, 1982; Feldman, 1986). Once the diet was adjusted to eliminate the deficiencies, the pica decreased. A physiological evaluation may be indicated before beginning any classroom intervention.

Most people have food preferences. Food preferences range from mild to severe. They become an eating disorder when the preferences become extreme enough to cause nutritional imbalances. For example, some students eat only one food item, such as pasta or Cheerios, and may categorically refuse any other food. Other food preferences may include eating only crunchy foods or eating only cold foods.

Finally, for some students, food preference may be due to a physiological problem called "dysphagia," or difficulty in swallowing. A medical examination, performed by a physician, speech-language pathologist, or occupational therapist, should precede any other intervention. Whenever

Communicative Intent of Self-Injury

Even if there is a physiological problem, a deficit in a student's behavioral repertoire may leave a student with few ways to communicate distress. For example, suppose that James, a young student with autism who does not speak, learned that his sinus headache could be reduced by slapping his face. When this occurred, caretakers saw the face slapping and intervened by giving loving attention, food, drinks, or medication. If the original headache was alleviated by this behavior, then face slapping when in pain has been reinforced by pain reduction. Thus the likelihood of further face slapping behavior is increased—wherever the pain is located.

The next time that James feels pain (in the stomach, for example) he might engage in face slapping. This is most likely if he does not have the language or other behaviors in his repertoire to deal with pain. Since James stopped hitting himself last time the caretakers gave food, drink, medicine, or attention, they are likely to do so again. Again, slapping his face results in attention, food, and so on.

In this example, face slapping has a very specific communicative intent: "I hurt, make it stop." Even for students who have some language, this may be an abstract concept to express. The student has learned that face slapping brings pain reduction. It also brings food, drink, and attention. Thus the student now has an all-purpose behavior that can serve to:

- bring food or drink
- bring attention
- avoid pain and, by extension,
- avoid undesired activities, tasks, and jobs.

The behavior now serves four different "functions," only one related to the original physiological problem. To show the functions that this behavior serves, an assessment of the behavior should be conducted. (This is addressed in Chapter 5.) In the example with James, slapping his face serves two obtaining functions and two avoidance functions. To reduce the behavior across all settings, then, four *replacement behaviors* must be taught. To effectively replace the behavior, each new behavior needs to be as effective and at least as easy to perform as the old behavior of face slapping.

a physiological cause could influence the exhibition of a targeted behavior, a medical examination should be performed before educational or behavioral interventions are attempted.

Hypersensitivity and Hyposensitivity

Hyposensitivity or hypersensitivity to sound or touch has been reported in some children with autism (Ornitz, 1985, 1989). *Hyposensitivity* refers to a less than typical level of response to auditory or tactile stimulation. Children with this characteristic appear not to hear many environmental sounds (i.e., a parent's voice or a train going by) or feel certain sensations (e.g., they might not cry or show distress when hurt). *Hypersensitivity* refers to more than a typical response to auditory or tactile stimulation. These students might cover their ears and scream when the air conditioner goes on, or they might show extreme distress over a minor bump or scrape. Both hyper- and hyposensitivity can be seen in the same individual.

Sound Sensitivity

Students who exhibit hyposensitivity to sound may be initially thought to be deaf. Although there is no physiological abnormality, they do not respond to environmental sounds, including a parent's voice. Some professionals believe that sound hyposensitivity is part of an auditory processing difficulty. A child who is not able to extract meaning from sound would have difficulty attending to sounds in the environment. Sounds would be meaningless, regardless of their source. Children who exhibit hypersensitivity to sound may cover their ears at certain tones, volumes, or sounds. This may be as mild as a room air conditioner turning on or the click of a light switch.

Sound sensitivity sometimes involves only certain sounds in certain contexts. A student who does not blink when two blocks are banged together might attend to the sound of candy being unwrapped across the room. Another might scream when the vacuum cleaner is turned on, but listen to music at a high volume with no discomfort. Sound sensitivity is highly dependent on context. A student may decide to play a favorite song at high volume and seem to enjoy it, but if a sibling tried to play the same song at the same volume, it might cause the student distress. For these reasons, it may be more appropriate to consider most sound sensitivity as selective.

Tactile Sensitivity

Hyposensitivity to tactile stimulation may allow a student to endure high levels of pain, even causing tissue damage, without reaction. Children may bite themselves to the point of breaking the skin or causing keloid (scar) tissue. Another child might pinch herself or hit her head with her fists hard enough to create bruises or eye damage. Because of the high frequency of these behaviors, it could be assumed that pain is not aversive or punishing for that student.

Hypersensitivity to tactile stimulation may be seen in other children. Children who are tactilely hypersensitive do not like to be touched and may react to even a light touch as though it is highly aversive. As babies, they may arch away from parents when held; some stiffen and become rigid until the unwanted touch is removed. For these children, desensitization to touch may prove helpful. Contact activities such as hugs, pats on the back, or holding hands should not be used as rewards as this contact may feel aversive to the student.

Some children who are self-injurious flinch or cry when their hands are held, exhibiting both hypersensitivity and hyposensitivity depending on the initiator of the action. For some students, a light touch may be aversive, but a firm touch (e.g., a handshake or even a restraint procedure) is highly desirable. Grandin wrote of building her own "squeeze box" to provide deep pressure to help calm herself down when upset (Grandin & Scariano, 1986). Some children have been known to crawl under a bed mattress or couch cushion to achieve firm pressure over their bodies.

CLASSIFICATION DILEMMAS

It is possible to view the varied forms of autism along a continuum. In this model, some persons have autism in a more "pure" form and with a greater degree of involvement. Others have a less typical form of the disorder with lower levels of involvement. Autism varies widely in its expression across students. It typically has pervasive deleterious effects requiring specialized educational practices, school accommodations, and teacher skill and patience. Autism is a disorder, not a disease. The complexity of autism often leads to a flawed understanding of the range, complexity, and uniqueness of students who have it.

Recently, attention has been focused on defining autism more carefully and identifying subcategories or variants of the disorder. A prime example of this is the work of Hans Asperger (1944), who identified a syndrome very similar to Kanner's autism. Asperger published his work at almost exactly the same time as Kanner. Asperger's influence was notable in many parts of Europe, but his original work had little if any impact in the United States.

Asperger's description has now been recognized in the United States and is included in DSM-IV as one of the pervasive developmental disorders. Some professionals represent Asperger's classification as the upper end of the autistic spectrum. Others maintain that it represents a separate and distinct disability. Still others advocate that Asperger described a subcategory of individuals with autism referred to by some as high functioning. These students have identifiable and classic conditions of autism that coexist with average and above average intellectual ability. The degree to which autism and Asperger's syndrome overlap remains an important question for researchers (Szatmari, 1992).

The degree to which autism overlaps related disorders is not easily answered. The technical process of dividing a disorder into subcategories, referred to as *nosology* in medicine, is heavily influenced by competing interests for grants, funding for research, and the social acceptability of the outcomes. Many parents and advocates are eager for Asperger's syndrome to be considered a fully separate and distinct clinical entity. These advocates promote separating Asperger's syndrome from autism to avoid the potential stigma associated with autism.

Other advocates for children with autism fear a dilution of services if the definition of autism is broadened by including related disorders. Mesibov (1997), for example, argued for a strict definition of autism, excluding individuals with pervasive developmental disorder/not otherwise specified (PDD/NOS). These issues are important for teachers. Although teachers generally have little direct influence on the diagnostic policies of local or state education agencies, they must be prepared to provide the best educational programs to the full range of students they are asked to teach.

Is Autism a Spectrum Disorder?

The classification of autism is aided immensely by the DSM-IV diagnostic protocol. If the DSM-IV criteria are applied and if the limiting conditions are satisfied, a diagnosis of autism is provided. Students with related disorders are eligible for special education under Public Law 101-476, the Individuals with Disabilities Education Act (IDEA) and similar legislation. However, many advocates and professionals question whether autism-specific programming should be available for students with these related disorders. To represent these students, the term autistic spectrum disorder (ASD) was developed as a more comprehensive classification.

The main advantage of obtaining a diagnosis of autism is the prospect of securing more specialized services or benefits. In many states, a child classified as autistic gets a quantitatively, if not qualitatively, "better deal" in terms of services. Florida is one state in which, until recently, autism carried one of the highest weights under the state's disability category funding formulae; and in Texas, students with autism automatically qualified for in-home family support. Although there is no guarantee that money flows directly to a given program or child, funding provides resources to schools and districts that would not otherwise be available. If a student is classified as autistic, knowledgeable parents and professionals might believe that increased funding should result in more or better services. Given confusion over diagnostic labels, and the reality that in many states differentiated services are based on labels, the preference for an autism classification is perfectly understandable.

Much of the confusion involving classification and services involves the uncertain etiologies of autism and the various related disorders. As Szatmari (1992) pointed out, "In the absence of a clear understanding of the etiology of autism, it is virtually impossible to determine whether various ASD subtypes have a similar or different etiology . . . whether ASD is the same or different cannot be answered in an absolute sense" (pp. 597–598). Given this uncertainty, a professional responsible for diagnosis must use a high degree of judgment. That judgment may be influenced by system and service delivery factors rather than the needs of the individual child.

The term autistic spectrum disorder can be used in at least two very different ways. Szatmari (1992) considered the spectrum to encompass children who meet:

> some of the characteristics of a pervasive developmental disorder (PDD), but not enough to qualify for a diagnosis of autism. The term ASD refers to the whole spectrum of *non-autistic* forms of PDD and includes previous terms such as atypical autism, autistic-like, Asperger syndrome, autistic tendencies, and so forth. (p. 583)

Szatmari maintained that ASD refers to students who have disorders similar to autism but excludes children who meet the full diagnostic criteria for autism.

A second use of the term ASD includes children with autism as well as the related disorders such as Asperger's syndrome and PDD-NOS. Siegel (1996) noted that autistic spectrum disorder can be thought "to encompass autism plus the non-autistic PDDs and is meant to correspond exactly to what DSM-IV refers to collectively as PDD—that is "pervasive developmental disorders" (p. 10).

Siegel's grouping is educationally sound because many of these children have common instructional needs. Even among students with Rett syndrome and childhood disintegrative disorder, both progressive degenerative disorders, teachers will be called on to make similar educational programming decisions. The reasonable expectation of shortened lifespan for some children may indicate the need for some curricular changes (e.g., specialized self-care skills), but does not negate the need for high quality educational programming.

For the purpose of this book we consider the autistic spectrum disorders as synonymous with the DSM-IV category of PDD. No assumption is made as to shared etiology, progression in physical well-being, or even common expression of developmental disorder. Rather, the core educational practices share sufficient similarity, generality, and utility so as to logically benefit students with any of the pervasive developmental disorders. This approach has strengths and limitations. An obvious strength is the shift of focus from medical etiology to an educational focus based on shared behavioral and learning characteristics. One possible limitation is that, by broadening the spectrum, too many children of a heterogeneous nature will be included. High value resources, required for some, could be spread too thinly. Another threat to the spectrum approach could come from those who wish to include many other diagnostic groups under ASD. If ASD becomes a popular diagnosis, undue attention will be paid to reclassification, shifting the needed focus away from programming.

PDD-NOS

Another subcategory of autistic spectrum disorder is pervasive developmental disorder/not otherwise specified. A child who presents some of the symptoms of autism but who fails to meet all of the impairment-specific criteria may be diagnosed PDD-NOS. The DSM-IV offers a clear statement as to appropriate use of this category.

> This category should be used when there is a severe and pervasive impairment in the development of reciprocal social interaction or verbal and nonverbal communication skills, or when stereotyped behavior, interests, and activities are present, but the criteria are not met for a specific Pervasive Developmental Disorder, Schizophrenia, Schizotypal Personality Disorder, or Avoidant Personality Disorder. For example, this category includes "atypical autism"—presentations that do not meet the criteria for Autistic Disorder because of late age at onset, atypical symptomatology, or subthreshold symptomatology, or all of these. (pp. 77–78)

To be classified as autistic, a child must have a total of 6 of 12 characteristics and must have at least 2 of the prescribed social impairments and at least one communication and behavior manifestation. The child must then have at least two more of the prescribed characteristics distributed across any of the three areas. For example, the child with only one social, two communication, and one behavioral characteristics would not meet the autism criteria. The child would meet the criteria for PDD-NOS. Mesibov (1997) noted that PDD-NOS was introduced so that persons with problems and disabilities related to autism, but without the number of characteristics required for a definition of autism, could obtain a classification and obtain relevant services. To Mesibov, PDD-NOS can be thought of as "subthreshold autism or a child who has atypical symptomatology that does not quite fit with the 12 characteristics one assesses under autism" (pp. 497–498). Mesibov thereby suggested that PDD-NOS, as subthreshold autism, is not actually autism. He noted that the typical child with a label of PDD-NOS will have higher language skills and greater cognitive ability. State and local education agency (LEA) policy on whether PDD-NOS qualifies as autism is mixed, as is professional consensus. However, it is our contention that a student with PDD-NOS is eligible for services under autistic spectrum disorder.

Asperger's Syndrome

Asperger's syndrome is included in the DSM-IV as one of the pervasive developmental disorders. It is called Asperger's disorder in DSM-IV, but is commonly referred to as Asperger's syndrome for educational purposes. It shares several symptoms with autism including "qualitative impairments in social interaction" and "restricted repetitive and stereotyped patterns of behavior, interests, and activities." To meet the diagnostic criteria, a student must show at least two areas of social impairment such as failure to develop peer skills or inability to show emotional or social reciprocity. The student must also show at least one deficit in the behavioral realm. These deficits include stereotypies or rigid adherence to rituals. The social impairment must occur at a degree that significantly affects overall life functioning. The full DSM-IV criteria are shown in Table 1–3. The main difference between Asperger's syndrome and autism involves communication. Communication is presumed to be within normal limits in children with this disorder although, as might be expected of a person with severe limitations in recognizing social messages, pragmatic deficits are common. Because pragmatic deficits constitute an essential area of communication functioning, this reduces the true differences between children diagnosed with Asperger's syndrome and autism. Certainly, important issues remain to be resolved as this new diagnostic category becomes established.

Hans Asperger received minimal recognition in the United States and many other English-speaking countries until 1981 when his original work was first translated into English (Frith, 1991). By this time autism was the most prominent of the pervasive developmental disorders. Asperger's original reports are significant as they help recognize a milder form of autism than that identified by Kanner.

The children identified by Asperger differed from those identified by Kanner in one substantial way. Asperger's population did not show the significant communication deficits that Kanner observed. Today people recognize Asperger's population as having a milder form of autism, featuring a less severe expression of characteristics.

Table 1–3. DSM-IV Diagnostic Criteria for Asperger's Disorder

A. Qualitative impairment in social interaction, as manifested by at least two of the following:

   (1) marked impairment in the use of multiple nonverbal behaviors such as eye-to-eye gaze, facial expression, body postures, and gestures to regulate social interaction

   (2) failure to develop peer relationships appropriate to developmental level

   (3) a lack of spontaneous seeking to share enjoyment, interests, or achievements with other people (e.g., by a lack of showing, bringing, or pointing out objects of interest to other people)

   (4) lack of social or emotional reciprocity

B. Restricted repetitive and stereotyped patterns of behavior, interests, and activities, as manifested by at least one of the following:

   (1) encompassing preoccupation with one or more stereotyped and restricted patterns of interest that is abnormal either in intensity or focus.

   (2) apparently inflexible adherence to specific, nonfunctional routines or rituals

   (3) stereotyped and repetitive motor mannerisms (e.g., hand or finger flapping or twisting, or complex whole-body movements)

   (4) persistent preoccupation with parts of objects.

C. The disturbance causes clinically significant impairment in social, occupational, or other important areas of functioning.

D. There is no clinically significant general delay in language (e.g., single words used by age 2 years, communicative phrases used by age 3 years).

E. There is no clinically significant delay in cognitive development or in the development of age-appropriate self-help skills, adaptive behavior (other than in social interaction), and curiosity about the environment in childhood.

F. Criteria are not met for another specific Pervasive Developmental Disorder or Schizophrenia.

Source: From *Diagnostic and Statistical Manual of Mental Disorders* (4th ed.), by American Psychiatric Association, 1994, p. 77. Washington, DC: American Psychiatric Association. Reprinted with permission.

Unlike Kanner who implicated a parental role in the development or cause of autism, Asperger saw *symptoms of the disorder in many of the parents.* In all 200 families in the original Asperger study, one or more parent showed some symptoms of the disorder (Frith, 1991). This observation made a strong case for genetic transmission. Piven, Palmer, Jacobi,

Childress, and Arndt (1997) put forward similar suggestions. They used structured family history interviews to identify the increased likelihood of symptoms in relatives of children with autism. These authors suggested that further investigation is needed to examine what may be a familial autism pattern, albeit expressed in milder forms. This recent work aligns with Asperger's observations made more more than 50 years ago.

It is important to remember that Aperger's disorder is a *pervasive* developmental disorder. It is not a mild disorder nor a medicalization of extreme social awkwardness. With these serious social and interactional problems come many other problems. Social problems are not confined to interaction but can extend to the child's reflection on his or her own social awkwardness. This can cause deleteriously low self-regard. Increased risk for suicide, an important characteristic noted in the literature, can be seen as an end product of extreme social ineptness. Both parents and professionals continue to search for effective education interventions (Myles & Simpson, 1998). The student with Asperger's syndrome requires extensive support in school.

Rett Disorder

Rett disorder is rare and no reliable estimates of prevalence are available. Nearly all cases of Rett disorder have been reported in females (APA, 1994). Unlike autism, the disorder is progressive and degenerative. As children with Rett reach preschool age, they experience a decline in intellectual capacity and purposeful movement. Hand movement is commonly affected, yielding a characteristic hand-washing pattern. Other stereotyped behaviors and major socialization problems are common (Olsson & Rett, 1985). The etiology is unknown but the disorder becomes obvious after a period of normal development. At about 5 months of age, head growth decelerates. Across the next several years students lose many of their motor and communication skills. These patterns clearly delineate Rett disorder from autism and the other pervasive developmental disorders. It is important for a teacher to have some awareness of the characteristic pattern of Rett to help screen for the disorder. Many girls in past years had been misdiagnosed as autistic when they had Rett disorder (Witt-Engertrom, & Gillberg, 1987). This misdiagnosis should decline with more widespread knowledge of the key indicators (Table 1–4) of Rett disorder. Although the incidence of this disorder is quite low, there is some limited literature on effective instructional programming (Feigen & Brady, 1988). In general, students with Rett disorder will benefit from the range of services made available to children with autism.

Table 1–4. DSM-IV Diagnostic Criteria for Rett Disorder

A. All of the following:

    (1) apparently normal prenatal and perinatal development

    (2) apparently normal psychomotor development through the first 5 months after birth

    (3) normal head circumference at birth.

B. Onset of all of the following after the period of normal development:

    (1) deceleration of head growth between ages 5 and 48 months

    (2) loss of previously acquired purposeful hand skills between ages 5 and 30 months with the subsequent development of stereotyped hand movements (e.g., hand-wringing or hand washing)

    (3) loss of social engagement early in the course (although often social interaction develops later)

    (4) appearance of poorly coordinated gait or trunk movements

    (5) severely impaired expressive and receptive language development with severe psychomotor retardation.

Source: From *Diagnostic and Statistical Manual of Mental Disorders* (4th ed.), by American Psychiatric Association, 1994, pp. 72–73. Washington, DC: American Psychiatric Association. Reprinted with permission.

SUMMARY

Autism is a spectrum disorder that affects children in all socioeconomic levels and cultures. It is one of the highest of the low incidence disorders and affects between 2 and 21 per 10,000 people. It affects males more often than females. The characteristics of autism include relative strengths in visual processing and relative deficits in auditory processing. Students with autism typically have difficulties with communication and social relatedness. In addition, the lack of efficient communication skills combined with an inadequate behavioral repertoire can cause problem behaviors.

There is substantial variation in the levels of severity of autism. Although the diagnostic criteria are specific and based on observable behaviors, the range of differences in the exhibition of these behaviors (from mild to severe and from rare to frequent) constitutes a wide spectrum of variability. When combined with an equally wide range of academic skills (from very delayed levels to highly advanced), the spectrum of variability is even more pronounced.

The range of expression of autism now poses a complicated set of questions for diagnosticians and teachers. Although IDEA specifically mentions only autism, most advocates consider that students with closely related disorders are included under the term autistic spectrum disorders. This would include all of the PDD diagnoses. For educational purposes the authors of this book take the position that students with autism and any of the pervasive developmental disorders, and even some other children with closely related disorders, will benefit from the array of educational opportunities provided to a student with classic autism.

REVIEW QUESTIONS

1. What are the three key areas in which students with autism differ from their peers?

2. Describe four demographic characteristics of students with autism.

3. Based on DSM-IV criteria, how would a student with autism be differentiated from other students with pervasive developmental disorders?

4. Based on the recommendations of the authors, which disorders are included within Autistic Spectrum Disorder?

REFERENCES

American Psychiatric Association. (1994). *Diagnostic and statistical manual of mental disorders* (4th ed.). Washington, DC: Author.

Asperger, H. (1944). Die Autistischen Psychopathen; im Kindesalter. *Archiv für Psychiatrie und Nervenkrankheiten, 117,* 76–136.

Autism Society of America. (1998). What is autism? *Advocate: The Newsletter of the Autism Society of America, 30,* 3.

Baron-Cohen, S. Tagger-Flusberg, H., & Cohen, D. (Eds.). (1993). *Understanding other minds: Perspectives from autism.* Oxford, UK: Oxford University Press.

Bates, E. (1976). *Language and context: The acquisition of pragmatics.* New York: Academic Press.

Bauman, M. (1991). Microscopic neuroanatomic abnormalities in autism. *Pediatrics, 87*(5), 791–795.

Bauman, M. & Kemper, T. (1994). Neuroanatomic observations of the brain in autism. In M. Bauman & T. Kemper (Eds.), *The neurobiology of autism* (pp. 119–145). Baltimore: Johns Hopkins Press.

Bettelheim, B. (1967). *The empty fortress.* New York: Free Press.

Biklen, D. (1990). Communication unbound: Autism and praxis. *Harvard Educational Review, 60,* 291–314.

Brady, M. P., McDougall, D., & Dennis, H. F. (1989). The schools, the courts, and the integration of students with severe handicaps. *Journal of Special Education, 23,* 43–58.

Brady, M. P., & McEvoy, M. (1989). Social skills training as an integration strategy. In R. Gaylord-Ross (Ed.), *Integration strategies for students with handicaps* (pp. 213–231). Baltimore, MD: Paul H. Brookes.

Carr, E. G., & Durand, V. M. (1985). Reducing behavior problems through functional communication training. *Journal of Applied Behavior Analysis, 18,* 111–126.

Carr, E. G., Levin, L., McConnachie, G., Carlson, J. I., Kemp, D. C., & Smith, C. E. (1994). *Communication-based intervention for problem behavior.* Baltimore, MD: Paul H. Brookes.

Cheatham, S. K., Rucker, H. N., Smith D. J., & Lewis, W. G. (1995). Savant syndrome: Case studies, hypotheses, and implications for special education. *Education and Training in Mental Retardation and Development Disabilities, 30,* 243–253.

Cipani, E. (1990). The communicative function hypothesis: An operant behavior perspective. *Journal of Behavior Therapy and Experimental Psychiatry, 21,* 239–247.

Courchesne, E. (1991). Neuroanatomic imaging in autism. *Pediatrics, 87,* 781–790.

Danford, D. E. (1982). Pica and nutrition. *Annual Review of Nutrition, 2,* 667–680.

Donnellan, A. M., Mirenda, P. L., Mesaros, R. A., & Fassbender, L. L. (1984). Analyzing the communicative functions of aberrant behavior. *Journal of the Association for Persons with Severe Handicaps, 9,* 201–212.

Doss, S., & Reichle, J. (1989). Establishing communicative alternatives to the emission of socially motivated excess behavior: A review. *Journal of the Association for Persons with Severe Handicaps, 14,* 101–112.

Drash, P., & Tudor, R. (1993). A functional analysis of verbal delay in preschool children: Implications for prevention and total recovery. *Analysis of Verbal Behavior, 11,* 19–29.

Feigen, J., & Brady, M. P. (1988). What to ask of a school setting: Procuring local school services for children with Rett syndrome. In *Educational and therapeutic intervention in Rett syndrome.* Fort Washington, MD: International Rett Syndrome Association.

Feldman, M. D. (1986) Pica: Current perspectives. *Psychosomatics, 7*(27), 519–523.

Frith, U. (1991). *Autism and Asperger syndrome.* Oxford, UK: Cambridge University Press.

Gillberg, C., Steffenburg, S., & Schaumann, H. (1991). Is autism more common now than ten years ago? *British Journal of Psychiatry, 158,* 403–409.

Grandin, T. (1995). *Thinking in pictures and other reports from my life with autism.* New York: Vintage.

Grandin, T., & Scariano, M. M. (1986). *Emergence: Labeled autistic.* Novato, CA: Arena.

Hutt, C., Hutt, S., Lee, D., & Ounsted, C. (1964). Arousal and childhood autism. *Nature, 204,* 908–909.

Iwata, B. A., Dorsey, M. F., Slifer, K. J., Bauman, K. E., & Richman, G. S. (1982). Toward a functional analysis of self-injury. *Analysis and Intervention in Developmental Disabilities, 2,* 3–20.

Johnston, J. M., & Pennypacker, H. S. (1980). *Strategies and tactics of human behavioral research.* Hillsdale, NJ: Lawrence Erlbaum.

Kanner, L. (1943). Autistic disturbances of affective contact. *Nervous Child, 2,* 217–250.

Konstantareas, M. M., Homatidis, S., & Busch, J. (1989). Cognitive, communication and social differences between autistic boys and girls. *Journal of Applied Developmental Psychology, 10,* 411–424.

Linehan, S., & Brady, M. P. (1995). Functional versus developmental assessment: Influences on instructional planning decisions. *Journal of Special Education, 29,* 295–309.

Linehan, S., Brady, M. P., & Hwang, C. (1991). Ecological versus developmental assessment: Influences on instructional expectations. *Journal of the Association for Persons with Severe Handicaps, 16,* 146–153.

Lord, C., & Schopler, E. (1987). Neurobiological implications of sex differences in autism. In E. Schopler & G. B. Mesibov (Eds.), *Neurobiological issues of autism* (pp. 191–211). New York: Plenum.

Lotter, V. (1966). Epidemiology of autistic conditions in young children. *Social Psychiatry, 1,* 124–137.

Mesibov, G. (1992). Lecture given at Division TEACCH, Chapel Hill, NC.

Mesibov, G. B. (1997). What is PDD-NOS and how is it diagnosed? *Journal of Autism and Developmental Disorders, 27,* 497–498.

Mottron, L., & Belleville, S. (1993). A study of perceptual analysis in a high-level autistic subject with exceptional graphic abilities. *Brain and Cognition, 23,* 279–309.

Mundy, P., & Sigman, M. (1989). Specifying the social impairment in autism. In G. Dawson (Ed.), *Autism: Nature, diagnosis and treatment* (pp. 3–21). New York: Guilford Press.

Mundy, P., Sigman, M., Ungerer, J., & Sherman, T. (1986). Defining the social deficits of autism: The contribution of nonverbal communication measures. *Journal of Child Psychology and Psychiatry, 27,* 657–659.

Myles, B. S., & Simpson, R. L. (1998). *Asperger syndrome.* Austin, TX: Pro-Ed.

Olsson, B., & Rett, A. (1985). Behavioral observations concerning differential diagnosis between the Rett syndrome and autism. *Brain Development, 7,* 281–290.

O'Neill, R. E., Horner, R. H., Albin, R. W., Storey, K., & Sprague, J. R. (1990). *Functional analysis of problem behavior: A practical assessment guide.* Sycamore, IL: Sycamore Press.

Ornitz, E. M. (1985). Neurophysiology of infantile autism. *Journal of the American Academy of Child Psychiatry, 24,* 251–262.

Ornitz, E. M. (1989). Autism at the interface between sensory and information processing. In G. Dawson, (Ed.), *Autism: Nature, diagnosis and treatment* (pp. 174–209). New York: Guilford Press.

Piven, J., Palmer, P., Jacobi, D., Childress, D., & Arndt, S. (1997). Broader autism phenotype: Evidence from a family history study of multiple-incidence autism families. *American Journal of Psychiatry, 154,* 185–190.

Prizant, B. M. (1983). Echolalia in autism: Assessment and intervention. *Seminars in Speech and Language, 4,* 63–77.

Prizant, B., & Duchan, J. (1981). The functions of immediate echolalia in autistic children. *Journal of Speech and Hearing Disorders, 46*, 241–249.

Prizant, B., & Weatherby, A. (1987). Communicative intent: A framework for understanding social and communicative behavior in autism. *Journal of the American Academy of Child Psychiatry, 26*, 472–479.

Quill, K. A. (1997). Instructional considerations for young children with autism: The rationale for visually cued instruction. *Journal of Autism and Developmental Disorders, 27*(6), 697–714.

Reichle, J. E., & Yoder, D. E. (1979). Assessment and early stimulation of communication in the severely and profoundly mentally retarded. In R. L. York & E. Edgar (Eds.), *Teaching the severely handicapped* (Vol. 4, pp. 180–218). Seattle: American Association for the Education for the Severely/Profoundly Handicapped.

Rimland, B. (1964). *Infantile autism: The syndrome and its implications for a neural theory of behavior.* New York: Appleton-Century-Crofts.

Rimland, B. (1978, August). Inside the mind of the autistic savant. *Psychology Today*, pp. 69–80.

Sacks, O. (1993–1994, December/January). An anthropologist on Mars. *The New Yorker*, pp. 106–120.

Schroeder, S. R., Rojahn, J., Mulick, J. A., & Schroeder, C. S. (1991). Self-injurious behavior. In J. L. Matson & J. R. McCartney (Eds.), *Handbook of behavior modification with the mentally retarded* (pp. 141–180). New York: Plenum.

Shames, G. H., & Wiig, E. H. (1990). *Human communication disorders: An introduction.* Columbus, OH: Merrill.

Siegel, B. (1996) *The world of the autistic child: Understanding and treating autistic spectrum disorders.* New York: Oxford University Press.

Sigman, H., & Mundy, P. (1989). Social attachments in autistic children. *Journal of the Academy of Child and Adolescent Psychiatry, 28*, 74–81.

Strain, P., & Fox, J. (1981). Peer social initiations and the modification of social withdrawal: A review and future perspective. *Journal of Pediatric Psychology, 6*, 417–433.

Sturmey, P., & Sevin, J. (1994). Defining and assessing autism. In J. Matson (Ed.), *Autism in children and adults* (pp. 13–36). Pacific Grove, CA: Brooks/Cole.

Szatmari, P. (1992). The validity of autistic spectrum disorders: A literature review. *Journal of Autism and Developmental Disabilities, 22*, 583–600.

Tinbergen, N., & Tinbergen, M. (1983). *"Autistic" children: New hope for a cure.* London: George Allen & Unwin.

U.S. Department of Education. (1996). *U.S. Department of Education Annual Report to Congress.* Washington, DC: Author.

Voeller, K. (1986). Right-hemisphere deficit syndrome in children. *American Journal of Psychiatry, 143*, 1004–1009.

Volkmar, F. R. (1996). Diagnostic issues in autism: Results of the DSM-IV field trial. *Journal of Autism and Developmental Disorders, 26*, 155–157.

Wing, L., & Gould, J. (1979). Severe impairments of social interaction and associated abnormalities in children: Epidemiology and classification. *Journal of Autism and Developmental Disorders, 9*, 11–12.

Witt-Engerstrom, I., & Gillberg, C. (1987). Rett syndrome in Sweden. *Journal of Autism and Developmental Disorders, 17*, 149–150.

Chapter 2

A BRIEF HISTORY OF AUTISM

Key Points

- Itard's contribution to autism and special education
- The influence of Kanner and Asperger
- Parental blame and the influence of psychogenic etiologies
- Modern developments involving biological conditions, behavioral advances, and unproven treatments

INTRODUCTION

Although autism was first identified as a distinct clinical syndrome in 1943 (Kanner, 1943), the unique educational needs of children with autism and the specialized support and training needs of classroom teachers and parents only recently were recognized. Early school programs were often organized around psychodynamic conceptualizations of the disorder. As the etiology of autism was better understood, the orientation of school programs for these students changed. When it became clear that autism had an organic-biological basis rather than a psychological or psychogenic etiology, programs shifted from treating "underlying psychopathology" to focus on teaching skills and developing active partnerships with parents and families.

This chapter traces the history of autism by emphasizing the role of key persons. Several individuals had a tremendous influence on our understanding of the disorder. They set the stage for new developments and defined practice. This chapter is organized around three person-defined eras. The first era is represented as the early years prior to Kanner's 1943 clinical description. Second, the Kanner era is presented. Finally the modern era, which began with Rimland and flows into the current understanding of the educational and treatment needs of students with autism, is presented. Table 2–1 provides a summary of important contributions to the field of autism.

ITARD AND THE EARLY HISTORY OF AUTISM

It is impossible to know when the first child with autism was recognized as being distinct from other children with disabilities. Persons with autism were a part of the undifferentiated and often abused group of "idiots" and "insane" persons for countless centuries. As social forces moved to a greater recognition of rights for all people and concern for the well-being of those with disabilities, the first detailed clinical description of a child who may have been autistic appeared.

In 1799, a young boy, later named Victor, was found in the rugged country of southeastern France (Itard, 1932). He had been spotted and even briefly apprehended prior to this time but survived on his own in the wild. The boy was brought to Paris, and a young physician, Jean Marc Itard, became fascinated with the prospect of "civilizing" the child. Fortunately, records of the child's medical examinations and Itard's diligent work survived. Itard firmly believed that Victor was primarily impaired due to environmental deprivation and that, with vigorous and skillful mental and moral education, Victor could acquire normal patterns of behavior and development. Itard had a massive under-

Table 2-1. Important Figures in Autism

Key Person	Historical Context	Highlights and Impact
Itard (1800–1805)	Education only for a restricted and privileged minority	Pioneered special education with a "feral child," Victor, a child with autism.
Bleuler (1905)	Rise of psychiatric involvement in the lives of persons with severe mental illness and other disabilities	First to use the term "autism" to describe the departure from reality associated with schizophrenia.
Kanner (1943)	Autism not differentiated from other severe disorders	Provided the first detailed description of children with autism. Suggested biological etiology of "affective contact." Hints at parent role in cause.
Asperger (1944)	Autism not differentiated from other severe disorders; more verbal persons with autism did not receive separate consideration	Brought attention to social and communication deficits in autism.
Bettelheim (1950–1960s)	Psychiatric theorists seek to explain autism with psychoanalytic models	Popularized the notion that parents cause autism by rejecting the child. Blameful parents should be treated; are not fit to assist with treatment of their child.
Schopler (from 1960)	Progressive professionals see benefits of working with parents. Parent-blaming model is crumbling.	Established parent-friendly autism services and state-wide network of diagnostic, technical assistance, school program support and advocacy. Developed systematic teaching procedures.
Lovaas (from 1960)	Most persons with autism still shunted into public residential facilities; autism seen as diagnosable but incurable.	Developed behavioral programs for institutionalized children. Developed intensive, home-based early intervention program in which 47% of children achieve normal outcomes.

(continued)

Table 2–1. *(continued)*

Key Person	Historical Context	Highlights and Impact
Rimland (from 1963)	Psychiatric theories and parent causation are challenged as "normal" parents voice opposition toward psychiatric and parent causation theories.	Established alternative to psychoanalytic and parent causation theories. Formed national parent autism organization, now Autism Society of America.
Biklen (from 1984)	Rejection of scientific, research-based approaches to autism; enthusiasm with new age treatments.	Popularizes facilitated communication (FC), a method of physically supporting the person with autism to communicate using literacy skills. FC gains countless devotees yet fails rudimentary tests of authorship.
Grandin (from 1988)	Society considers autism as a life of isolation, rejection, and dependency.	Earned Ph.D. from the University of Illinois at Urbana in 1988. Leading expert on the design and construction of livestock facilities. Shared intriguing insights into her disorder.
Maurice (from 1993)	Parents distressed with low/no impact interventions. Demand for best available, not merely "appropriate" services.	Writes *Let Me Hear Your Voice*, detailing search for effective treatments for children with autism. Encourages thousands of parents to establish home-based, intensive behavioral treatment programs. Works to establish a parent organization which selectively supports only scientifically validated treatments.

taking as Victor had no speech and was completely devoid of typical social perceptions or skills. He did have the skills that had proven successful in the wilderness. Detailed treatments of Itard's work can be found in Itard's original (1932) translation and in Lane (1976).

Itard, considered by many as the father of special education, identified five main "aims" or goals for Victor and in so doing provided insight into the boy's deficit areas.

1. To interest him in social life . . .
2. To awaken his nervous sensibility . . .
3. To extend the range of his ideas . . .
4. To lead him to the use of speech . . .
5. To make him exercise the simplest mental operations. (Itard, 1932, pp. 10–11)

Itard did not believe that Victor was retarded or that retardation was the primary cause of his problems. The boy's ability to elude captors, escape, and survive in a harsh and rugged territory all pointed, for Itard, to high degree of native intelligence.

In 1806, Itard (1932) reported his 5 years of progress to the Minister of the Interior. He had hoped that with intensive and skilled intervention Victor would approach a normal level of functioning. In spite of valiant effort, progress was far more limited than Itard had expected as excerpts from his report illustrate:

> The education of this young man is still incomplete and must always remain so . . . The intellectual faculties are developing slowly and painfully . . . The emotional faculties . . . are subordinated to an utter selfishness. (p. 63)

Although candid about the limited progress, Itard also cited important successes:

1. Improvement of his sight and touch . . . contributed powerfully to the development of his intellectual faculties;
2. Therefore he [has] both a knowledge of the conventional value of the symbols of thought and the power of applying it by knowing objects, their qualities and their actions.
3. That in spite of his immediate taste for the freedom of open country and his indifference to . . . social life, Victor shows himself sensible of the care taken of him. (Itard, p. 64)

To the teacher of students with autism, Itard's report will sound, apart from its archaic language, applicable to a classic student with autism. Victor lived to be about 40 and required care throughout his life. Itard went on to achieve great success in the education of people with hearing impairments and in the field of otology (the science of the ear). In spite of his technical accomplishments, Itard's defining contribution to the field of education was philosophical rather than scientific, as illustrated by the concluding passage from the previous report. This statement may well mark the beginning of special education as a discipline. Victor, the "wild" (and probably autistic) boy, was both Itard's student and his teacher.

> To be judged fairly, this young man must only be compared to himself. Put beside another adolescent of the same age, he is only an ill-formed creature, an outcast of nature as he was of society. But if one limits oneself to the two terms of comparison offered by the past and present states of young Victor, . . . one can question whether Victor is not more unlike the Wild Boy of Aveyron arriving in Paris, than he is unlike other individuals of his same age and species. (Itard, p. 67)

Here we clearly see Itard discarding the view that education and treatment should result in full recovery or cure to be valuable. Instead, Itard embraced the idea that individual progress provides the true measure of intervention success. Special educators will recall Itard's legacy and his impact on Seguin and, through his notes and reports, on Maria Montessori. Educators owe much to Itard and his work with Victor, a child with autism who was quite likely the first special education student (Graham, 1991; Hunter, 1993).

Uta Frith (1989) also asserted that Victor had autism. She cited as ' key indicators of Victor's autism: "(a) evidence of a serious impairment in reciprocal social interactions, (b) evidence of specific intellectual impairment, (c) evidence of characteristic impairment of sensory attention, (d) evidence of stereotypies, and (e) evidence of extreme autistic aloneness." Frith did not believe Victor's condition in the wild was entirely shaped by nature. As a child with autism his preference for being left alone—autistic aloneness—was a natural element of his feral existence. If a child without autism was left alone, that child might have sought human contact and more quickly found his way back to civilization. Instead, Victor sought to remain alone and was especially successful at it for many years.

Whether Victor had autism or not may be of little practical consequence. He had many of the defining features and his long-term progress was similar to that of many students with autism, especially those who are not the beneficiaries of skilled early intervention. Educators teaching students with autism may take some degree of pride in the notion that the first student in special education was a child with autism. Although autism, in a modern sense, is relatively new, the provision of skilled special education to students with autism can be traced directly to Victor and his teacher, Itard.

THE KANNER ERA

Leo Kanner

It is very difficult for modern educators to fully appreciate the historical prominence of psychodynamic conceptualizations in viewing disabilities and differences in children. From the time autism was first clinically documented in 1943 until the mid-1960s, psychological causation, or what may be termed "psychogenic" etiologies for autism, held sway just as they did for an array of other child emotional, mental, or behavioral problems. Consider also that teachers, principals, psychologists, and society in general historically have been more deferential to the authority of experts than is common today. In the case of autism, these experts would have been psychiatrists.

Leo Kanner, a key figure in autism, provides an almost perfect illustration of these forces within the professional community. Kanner was a central figure in child psychiatry (Sanua, 1990). His textbook, *Child Psychiatry* (Kanner, 1935), was revised three times and was widely used in the early to the middle 20th century. From his post as Director of the Child Psychiatry Clinic at Johns Hopkins University, Kanner was regarded as the leading authority in child mental disorders. He wrote 8 major books and over 300 articles. In 1971 he founded the *Journal of Autism and Childhood Schizophrenia*. Kanner maintained an active consulting practice until a few years before his death in 1981. Although revered by many for his keen clinical insights and humanity, he was maligned by others who believed he unfairly blamed parents for contributing to the development of autism in their children.

Kanner became interested in a cluster of behaviors that set some children, then labeled as psychotic or schizophrenic, apart from the other children with moderate to severe disabilities. His classic 1943 paper, *Autistic Disturbances of Affective Contact,* provided detailed descriptions of 11 children and an analysis of what he labeled, "inborn autistic disturbances of affective contact" (Kanner, 1943, p. 50). Kanner's descriptions of the children and identification of the defining syndrome features established the foundation for the modern understanding of autism.

Kanner's clinical descriptions and his summary of the defining features of this new syndrome are now a half century old but they are instantly recognizable as descriptions of autism. The consistent diagnostic features across the children in Kanner's study were:

- an inability to relate to others
- extreme autistic aloneness
- failure to assume an anticipatory posture

- excellent rote memory
- delayed echolalia
- literalness
- an all-powerful need for being left undisturbed
- [noises and motions that are] monotonously repetitious
- limitation in the variety of spontaneous activity

On the positive side, Kanner noted that these children tended to have good, "cognitive potentialities, . . . all have strikingly intelligent physiognomies, . . . [which give the] impression of serious-mindedness, [and] physically, the children were essentially normal" (p. 47).

Kanner was an astute observer and he had the good fortune to study children with many shared characteristics. His observations were later to bring him severe criticism as some professionals emphasized the association Kanner noted between parent emotionality and the condition of their children. When placed in the full context, one can have little doubt that Kanner believed autism was of organic origin, possibly mediated by family-influenced environmental factors. It is important to consider that Kanner's selection of cases was not random but probably favored persons of higher educational levels. The last two paragraphs from his 1943 article are worthy of careful attention:

> One other fact stands out prominently. In the whole group, there are very few really warmhearted fathers and mothers. For the most part, the parents, grandparents, and collaterals are persons strongly preoccupied with abstractions of a scientific, literary, or artistic nature, and limited in genuine interest in people. Even some of the happiest marriages were dismal failures. The question arises whether or to what extent this fact has contributed to the condition of the children. The children's aloneness from the beginning of life makes it difficult to attribute the whole picture exclusively to the type of the early parental relations with our patients.
>
> We must, then, assume that these children have come into the world with innate inability to form the usual, biologically provided affective contact with people, just as other children come into the world with innate physical or intellectual handicaps. If this assumption is correct, a further study of our children may help to furnish concrete criteria regarding the still diffuse notions about the constitutional components of emotional reactivity. For here we seem to have pure-culture example of inborn autistic disturbances of affective contact. (p. 50)

These statements make a strong case for a biological etiology. However, in years to come, Kanner was drawn to speculating about the role of parents in causing autism. He was the source of many contradictions and was, oddly enough, one of the leading voices for *not* blaming parents for causing mental problems in their children. Kanner died in 1981. Many of his colleagues and co-workers are still active in the field of autism. His legacy may still be too fresh to receive the balanced appraisal it deserves.

Kanner continued his work with children with autism in several informative longitudinal studies of persons evaluated at his clinic. In a 1971 study appearing in the *Journal of Autism and Childhood Schizophrenia,* Kanner focused on what might now be considered "best outcome" cases. Eleven of 96 children, by now young adults, had made reasonably good adjustments and were:

> mingling, working, and maintaining themselves in society. They have not completely shed the fundamental personality structure of early infantile autism but . . . they expended considerable effort to fit themselves—dutifully, as it were—to what they came to perceive as commonly expected obligations. (p. 31)

Bleuler and the Term "Autism"

Kanner (1943) used the term "infantile autism" but he was not the first to use the term autism in relation to disabilities. This distinction belongs to Bleuler, a Swiss psychiatrist who coined the term in 1919 (Wing, 1976). Bleuler examined the onset of schizophrenia in adults. He gave special attention to the loss of reality perception and the transition into an isolating, divergent perception of reality experienced by people with schizophrenia (Wing, 1976). Bleuler applied the term "autism" to this transition. He made no reference to what we would now recognize as autism. The later use of this term by Kanner may have been unfortunate. Psychiatrists had previous familiarity with this term but only as it related to adults with schizophrenia. Needless confusion led many to believe that autism in children was a form of early onset schizophrenia. Some of the confusion may continue to this day. In any case, Bleuler coined the term and its prime meaning has evolved to focus on the child's self-contained social world.

Kanner's Autism and Asperger's Syndrome

In an interesting coincidence, Hans Asperger, an Austrian like Kanner, was also trained in medicine and child development in Vienna. Both produced groundbreaking reports on children with autism within a year of one another. There is no evidence that these two men collaborated or even had an early awareness of each other's work (Frith, 1989). Asperger, working in Austria and writing in German, portrayed children very similar to those described by Kanner with only a few important differences. Asperger's children tended to have more highly developed language skills and generally higher intelligence and may be seen as representing the "upper range" of the autistic population. Asperger's work was largely unknown to the English-speaking world until fairly recently. In 1989, Uta Frith provided a translation of Asperger's 1944 article and a critical analysis, which led to a long overdue appreciation of this work. Both Kanner and Asperger understood aspects of autism, and their combined work yields a fuller range or spectrum of this disabling condition. The fact that Asperger's writings could have gone unappreciated in the English-speaking world for almost 50 years and then be linked with Kanner's in such an important manner will be more fully explored in the chapters that follow.

How do children with Asperger's syndrome differ from those with Kanner's autism? Sachs (1994), a clinician-researcher with a gift for summing up complicated matters, provided this brief appraisal:

> The ultimate difference, perhaps, is this: people with Asperger's syndrome can tell us of their experiences, their inner feelings and states, whereas those with classical autism cannot. With classical autism, there is no "window," and we can only infer. With Asperger's syndrome there is self-consciousness and at least some power to introspect and report. (p. 107)

Historical Context

The statements made about parents' roles in the development of autism in their children have in the past, and continue today, to cause great controversy. Kanner was one of the central persons in this controversy. It is possible to assert that Kanner was merely a person of his time and that his views reflected the prevailing wisdom of psychiatric practice. This is countered by the pivotal role Kanner had in shaping psychiatric practitioners' views toward autism and the family. It is also possible to see Kanner's statements relating the "association between autism and certain family variables" as relatively benign and innocuous. He does not specifically blame the parents but merely points to apparent associations. Indeed, Kanner's 1943 writings are mild in comparison to later writings and lectures on the subject of autism.

The degree to which Kanner blamed parents remains unclear. What is clear is that the psychiatric community of his time controlled both the treatment and popular understanding of autism and they believed that parents caused the disorder.

Bruno Bettleheim helped take these views to an absurd extreme, setting himself up in later years as a target for criticism. Selections from his widely read *Truants from Life* (1955) and *The Empty Fortress:*

Infantile Autism and the Birth of the Self (1967) are replete with parent-blame. Consider just one example:

> The infant, because of pain or discomfort and the anxiety they cause, or because he misreads the mother's actions or feelings, or correctly assesses her negative feelings, may retreat from her and the world. The mother, for her part, either frustrated in her motherly feelings, or out of her own anxiety, may respond not with gentle pursuit, but in anger or injured indifference. This is apt to create new anxiety in the child, to which may now be added the feeling that the world (as represented by the mother) not only causes anxiety but is also angry or indifferent as the case may be. (Bettelheim, 1967, p. 72)

In a fascinating historical twist, the Bettelheim legacy has come in for serious reconsideration since his death in 1990. A least two major biographies have been written (Pollack, 1997; Sutton, 1996), both highly critical of his theories, his methods, and his essential truthfulness. Early work he claimed to have done with a girl with autism in Vienna, work that served as the basis for many of his theories, never took place (Pollack, 1997). Bettelheim's first wife provided treatment for the child and he was not involved. He distorted the nature and extent of his training. He was not trained in medicine, psychology, nor in psychoanalysis. After his death, former staff and students from the Sonia Shankman Orthogenic School, the site for his most significant "work" in autism, revealed the extent of his psychological and physical abuse. Pollak's biography exposes Bettelheim as a highly manipulative, egocentric, and abusive person who was harsh to students and staff.

Bettelheim was not a compassionate, insightful sage but a troubled individual. He lied extensively about his background and training. His maligning of parents of children with autism caused irreparable harm and unnecessary guilt to generations of parents. His poorly grounded theories unjustly fostered distrust of parents and blamed them for causing autism in their children. Bettelheim lacked data to back up his theories and claims of successful treatment. He relied on unsystematic anecdotal notes and the validity of much of this content must now be questioned.

There is one important message educators should take from the Bettelheim legacy. As they frame their own practices and consider the advice they give to parents, educators must give special recognition to researchers who have gathered data, systematically analyzed the data, and then made their findings available to the professional community for scrutiny. Some theories and hypotheses stand up to this scrutiny; others do not. The research process drives scholarship and continues to advance shared knowledge about what works and what does not. Teachers should demand that the theories they value and support and the approaches they recommend to others have a scientific and educationally sound basis in fact. Only in this way will parents, teachers, and persons with autism be spared from the harm of the next Bettelheim and the next array of useless treatments.

Rimland (1994) summed up the nature of the assault from the parent-blamers. Not only had parents, primarily mothers, been blamed for causing autism in the child, but parental denial of responsibility was a further indication of their emotional poverty and additional evidence of their guilt. As parents had caused the problem and were now invested in denying their responsibility, they could not be trusted, if we were to believe Bettelheim and his followers, to assist in the treatment process. Anna Freud (1946) noted the role of parents in sabotaging treatment as another reason for keeping them out of the child's therapy program. The proper parent role was to accept psychotherapeutic assistance and prepare to welcome the child back after he or she had received treatment in a residential psychiatric facility.

Bettelheim's views held sway for many years, but by the early 1960s, these specious views were challenged. Fortunately, a parent with the right professional credentials and strong leadership skills stepped forward.

THE MODERN ERA

Bernard Rimland

Bernard Rimland, a U.S. Navy psychologist, became concerned that his infant son, Mark, was not developing normally. Rimland, who has told the story to many audiences, relates how Mark had a unique and troubling cry that resonated throughout the newborn nursery. Rimland and his wife searched for answers to their son's strange behavior. Ultimately, they spotted a description of autism in a college text and instantly knew they had the name for Mark's condition (Rimland, 1994). As they considered the parental causation theories, one can only guess as to their incredulity. As a psychologist employed to screen and evaluate Navy personnel, Rimland knew normal from abnormal in individuals and knew that Mark's parents (his wife and himself) did not cause this disorder. Rimland was determined to become familiar with all of the available literature and information on autism, a major undertaking even at that early stage of knowledge about autism. He became convinced that a biological condition, likely of neurological origin, was responsible for this disorder, not bad parenting or "refrigerator mothers."

Rimland was determined to destroy the parent causation argument, which had become the key element in the psychogenic etiology theory. In 1964 he published *Infantile Autism: The Syndrome and Its Implications for a Neural Theory of Behavior* in which he argued against a psychological etiology and in favor of a neurological etiology. Rimland gave three reasons why it was important to examine closely the evidence for a psychogenic versus a biological causation:

1. *If* the cause was psychogenic, the specific causes needed to be identified to stop the disease process.
2. *If* the professional community was led to believe the cause is psychogenic, then biologically oriented researchers would avoid autism as a field of study.
3. The cause or causes of autism were of importance to basic research in psychology and psychiatry, especially as it related to the impact of heredity on behavior.

Rimland then presented his summary. The case for a psychological basis for autism rests on the assumptions that:

- no abnormalities in either physical or neurological dimensions have been found consistently;
- many parents of children with autism have atypical emotional responses;
- children raised in emotionally barren environments such as hospitals and orphanages often have emotional difficulties;
- behavioral deficits and excesses are seen as the child's "punishment" of the parents;
- certain psychological stressors in the child's early life can be seen as "trigger points" to the onset of autism;
- providing a highly reinforcing environment has beneficial effects on children;
- first-born children and only children tend to have a higher incidence of autism, again pointing to parental emotional response as a causative factor.

With this groundwork laid, Rimland offered his case for a biological causation of autism.

1. Some clearly autistic children were born of parents who did not fit the autistic parent personality pattern.
2. Parents who did fit the description of the supposedly pathogenic parent almost invariably had children who developed normally, without autism.
3. With very few exceptions, the siblings of children with autism did not have the disorder.

4. Children with autism were behaviorally unusual "from the moment of birth."
5. There was a consistent ratio of three or four boys to one girl.
6. Virtually all cases of twins reported in the literature were identical: both twins had the disorder.
7. Autism could occur or be closely simulated in children with known or organic brain damage.
8. The symptomatology was highly unique and specific.
9. There was an absence of gradations of infantile autism which would create "blends" from normal to severely afflicted. (pp. 51–52)

Although not all of Rimland's assertions are consistent with the information now available, the strength of his case in 1964 was apparently overwhelming. Kanner, who wrote the foreword to Rimland's book, was resigned to this criticism of his work. He was clearly distressed that, prior to 1963, autism had become a "pseudo diagnostic wastebasket" (p. v) and an especially useful diagnosis for those seeking to promote *psychodynamic* treatments. As an accurate observer and careful scientist, Kanner had to be concerned with the damage being done by clinicians who labeled everything as autism and who disregarded his original reports and assumptions of inborn, biological (innate) "autistic disturbances of affective contact."

Rimland's work can be seen as a watershed. He achieved at least five main goals. In brief, Rimland:

1. established biological causation as the most likely etiology;
2. ended the demonization of parents—parents who had *caused* their children to become autistic;
3. put hard line psychodynamic proponents, such as Bettelheim, on the defensive;
4. opened the door for parents to join professionals in partnerships to help address the complex problems confronting children with autism; and
5. laid the groundwork for the creation of a sustained movement to create a national organization. This was to become the National Society for Autistic Children in 1965.

The National Society for Autistic Children was the clearest expression of this new parent-professional partnership. This organization, now the Autism Society of America (ASA), has over 225 chapters in 46 states (ASA, 1998) with a total membership of over 22,000.

O. Ivar Lovaas

Ivar Lovaas began working with people with autism in California in the late 1950s. As a behavior analyst, he focused on observed behavior and managing environmental consequences to teach new and more productive behaviors. He addressed severe problem behaviors and language development. In spite of intensive efforts, Lovaas achieved limited long-term results with older children treated in hospital settings. To overcome the pervasive impact of autism he redirected his programs in three major ways:

1. He focused on younger children, who were 2–5 years of age, believing that the younger children might possess greater adaptability and be more capable of overcoming the biologically induced impact of autism than older children.
2. Treatment was transferred away from institutional sites and placed, when possible, in the homes of the children with the parents in an important support role.
3. Program intensity was dramatically increased, with children receiving 40 hours of training per week.

This effort was named the Young Autism Project, and Lovaas claimed dramatic results. Lovaas (1987, p. 7) reported that, "47% of the experimental group achieved normal intellectual and educational functioning in contrast to only 2% of the control group subjects." Results such as these renewed both a sea of controversy about the benefit of behavioral treatment and a ground swell of enthusiasm from parents seeking the most efficacious treatments for their young children with autism.

Catherine Maurice

Catherine Maurice, a mother of two children with autism, explored an array of options and became distressed with the lack of both success and empirical validation for the treatments proposed for her children. She learned of the success Lovaas had achieved and arranged for Bridget Taylor and others to assist her in implementing the program in her home (Maurice, 1993). Her account of the treatments for her children, Anne-Marie and Michel, became the basis of a best-selling book, *Let Me Hear Your Voice*. In addition to promoting the benefits of intensive behavioral intervention, Maurice also detailed several problem practices of clinicians. This included providing widespread misinformation and guesswork regarding effective treatments. She was especially critical of professionals who issued blanket condemnation of behavioral treatments when they knew little or nothing about them.

Her children have continued to progress and, as reported by Perry, Cohen, and DeCarlo (1995), "Follow up . . . of the siblings demonstrated that recovery was enduring" (p. 232). Maurice has become a champion for empirically validated and scientifically sound treatments for children with autism. She was perhaps the first to openly confront the prevailing and accepted view that all treatments should be afforded the same status. Scientific validation was either unnecessary or unwarranted according to this perspective. Maurice challenged this view vigorously, asserting that treatments based on applied behavior analysis (ABA) had, by far, the strongest empirical support. She linked with other professionals and parents who shared her views to produce a manual for effective home intervention (Maurice, Green, & Luce, 1996). She also has helped create the Association for Science in Autism Treatments, a national movement designed to promote intensive behavioral interventions, and an organization devoted to this purpose.

As Maurice discovered, the nature of behavioral treatment is often grossly misunderstood. Many still believe it is grounded in harsh punishments and entails an essential dehumanization of the child. These charges are easily refuted by the facts and by a growing convergence between progressive behavior analysts and others who are concerned about effective treatments for children with autism. Carr (1994) argues that behavior analysis is essentially about the purpose or functions of behavior and as such may well represent the most useful form of treatment available for a wide range of disabling conditions. In any case, the notion that behavioral treatment is characterized by harsh punishments and the robotic application of aversives may be most effectively refuted by the thousands of parents who have sought, and in most cases have privately paid for, intensive behavioral treatment for their young children with autism.

Behavioral technology has evolved in large part to deal with problems relating to the generalization of newly learned skills (Stokes & Baer, 1977) and an over-reliance on contingency management. The emerging technology of positive behavioral support (PBS) (Horner et al., 1990) emphasizes analyzing the communicative functions of problem behaviors, teaching functional communicative alternatives, systematic analysis and modification of antecedent conditions, and regulation or elimination of aversive or punishing consequences. The PBS approach is especially well suited to community-based programs and schools, which have a responsibility to foster positive behavior and enhance communication. Horner and his colleagues provided a strong and reasoned statement that is very important to persons concerned with the education and care of students with autism when they wrote:

> A consistent message for families, teachers, and community service providers is that positive programming is the expected technology. The routine use of procedures that deliver pain (shock, pinching, slaps), procedures that result in harm (bruises, cuts, broken bones), and procedures that are disrespectful or dehumanizing (facial sprays, shaving

cream in the mouth, foul smells) are no longer acceptable. Families, teachers, and community service personnel should turn toward (a) developing competence in the technology of positive programming and (b) addressing internal policies and procedures to prevent the abuse of severe, intrusive procedures. (p. 130)

Temple Grandin

In recent years, professionals involved in special education and the care and treatment of students with disabilities have become more familiar with the nature of autism. Research discoveries have reached classrooms and had an impact on the lives of students. The public has developed a familiarity with the term autism, but in many cases they has received inaccurate or sensationalized views of the disorder. Often, the odd aspects of the behavior of students with autism were emphasized and the humanization of these individuals was compromised. Temple Grandin, a person with autism, has had a profound impact on these perceptions.

Grandin retains the memory of her early development (Grandin & Scariano, 1986). She was the beneficiary of an especially strong and supportive family and some excellent teaching. Grandin was able to follow her interests, and they led to her professional success in the livestock handling equipment field. She earned a master's degree from Arizona State University in Animal Science and a doctorate from the University of Illinois in 1988. She currently teaches in the Department of Animal Science at Colorado State University. Dr. Grandin credits much of her success to her ability to deal with a problem on a purely visual-spatial basis. Most people address problems in a language-based mode. Grandin's visualization ability allows her to focus on the factors relevant to cattle or other animals and to problem solve directly from these sources of information. Her success is apparent. Her equipment designs are widely used in the livestock industry, and she publishes widely in two fields: animal sciences and autism (Sachs, 1994).

Grandin has achieved what mainstream society can easily consider as success. She holds an important position at a state university, is a popular speaker, and the devices and processes she creates are widely used. Yet it is the nature of her success (and perhaps her willingness to share information about it) that sets her apart from other successful persons with autism. She exploits and fully utilizes the special abilities that are a part of her autism. For Grandin, autism is not a bad thing and may even have benefits. In an article in *The New Yorker,* entitled "An Anthropologist on Mars," Sachs cites Grandin as ending a lecture with this comment: "If I could snap my fingers and be non-autistic, I would not—because then I wouldn't be me. Autism is part of who I am."

(Sachs, 1994, p. 124). Her life is different, but she is secure in who she is. She reported to Sachs:

> I do not fit in with the social life of my town or university. Almost all of my social contacts are with livestock people or people interested in autism. Most of my Friday and Saturday nights are spent writing papers and drawing. My interests are factual and my recreational reading consists mostly of science and livestock publications. I have little interest in novels with complicated interpersonal relationships, because I am unable to remember the sequence of events. Detailed descriptions of new technologies in science fiction or descriptions of exotic places are much more interesting. My life would be horrible if I did not have my challenging career. (p. 125)

A summary statement she gave to Sachs provided the title for the article. "Much of the time," she said, "I feel like an anthropologist on Mars."

Grandin has changed society's perception of what it means to have autism. She speaks frequently on the topic of autism and has been influential in increasing the knowledge of teachers and parents regarding the perceptions of those with autism. She has provided a list of teaching and interaction suggestions for this book, which appear on the next page.

Unproven Treatments

Although great strides have been made in understanding the nature of autism and in providing appropriate teaching practices and intervention strategies, there has also been an increase in unproven or controversial treatments. According to Silver (1995), a treatment can be considered controversial if any of the following conditions are met:

1. the treatment is made public in the absence of replicated research,
2. the treatment is not supported by data, or
3. the treatment is used in isolation when it should be used in combination with other treatments or assessments.

Facilitated Communication

One of the most controversial of the unproven treatments has been facilitated communication (FC). Brought to the United States by Biklen in the early 1990s, FC was initially used by Crossley (Crossley & McDonald, 1980) to assist people with cerebral palsy to communicate. She used the method with children with autism in 1985 (Biklen, 1990).

Approaching a Child with Autism

Temple Grandin

I am a person with autism and today I am on the faculty of a major university. One of the reasons I am successful is because I had very good teachers. At age 2½, I was placed in a special education class with an experienced teacher. Based on my own experiences, I have listed some tips for teachers who work with students with autism.

1. Many people with autism are visual thinkers. I think in pictures. I do not think in language. All my thoughts are like videotapes running in my imagination. Pictures are my first language and words are my second language. Nouns were the easiest words to learn because I could make a picture in my mind of the word. To learn words like "up" or "down" the teacher should demonstrate them to the child. For example, take a toy airplane and say "up" as you make the airplane take off from a desk.

2. Avoid long strings of verbal instructions. People with autism have problems remembering sequences. If the child can read, write the instructions down on a piece of paper. I am unable to remember sequences. If I ask for directions at a gas station I can only remember three steps. Directions with more than three steps have to be written down. I also have difficulty remembering phone numbers because I cannot make a picture in my mind.

3. Many children with autism are good at drawing, art, and computer programming. These talent areas should be encouraged. I think there needs to be much more emphasis on building up the child's talents.

4. Many autistic children get fixated on one subject such as trains or maps. The best way to deal with fixations is to use them to motivate school work. If the child likes trains, then use trains to teach reading and math. Read a book about a train and do math problems with trains. For example, calculate how long it takes for a train to go between New York and Washington.

(continued)

5. Use concrete visual methods to teach number concepts. My parents gave me a math toy that helped me to learn numbers. It consisted of a set of blocks, which had a different length and a different color for the numbers 1 through 10. With this I learned how to add and subtract. To learn fractions my teacher had a wood apple that was cut up into four pieces and a wood pear that was cut in half. From this I learned the concept of quarters and halves.

6. I had the worst handwriting in my class. Many autistic children have problems with motor control in their hands. Neat handwriting is sometimes very hard. This can totally frustrate the child. To reduce frustration and help children enjoy writing, let them do it on the computer. Typing is often much easier.

7. Some autistic children will learn reading more easily with phonics and others will learn best by memorizing whole words. I learned with phonics. My mother taught me the phonics rules and then had me sound out my words.

8. When I was a child, loud sounds like the school bell hurt my ears like a dentist's drill hitting a nerve. Children with autism need to be protected from sounds that hurt their ears. The sounds that will cause the most problems are school bells, PA systems, buzzers on the scoreboard in the gym, and the sound of chairs scraping on the floor. In many cases, the child will be able to tolerate the bell or buzzer if it is muffled slightly by stuffing it with tissues or duct tape. Scraping chairs can be silenced by putting slit tennis balls on the ends of the legs or installing carpet. A child may fear a certain room because he is afraid he may be suddenly subjected to squealing microphone feedback from the PA system. The fear of a dreaded sound can cause bad behavior.

9. Some autistic children are bothered by visual distractions and fluorescent lights. They can see the flicker of the 60-cycle electricity. To avoid this problem, place the child's desk near the window or try to avoid using fluorescent lights. If the lights cannot be avoided use the newest bulbs you can get. New bulbs flicker less.

10. Some hyperactive autistic children who fidget all the time will often be calmer if they are given a padded weighted vest to wear. Pressure from the garment helps to calm the nervous system. I was greatly calmed by pressure. For best results, the vest should be worn for 20 minutes and then taken off for a few minutes. This prevents the nervous system from habituating to it.

Temple Grandin is a faculty member in the Department of Animal Science at Colorado State University in Fort Collins, Colorado.

Facilitated communication is defined as, "an alternative means of communication in which students are given physical and emotional support to type on an electronic keyboard or point at letters on an alphabet board" (Biklen, 1990; Biklen & Schubert, 1991).

Using this means of communication, a child's hand or forearm was supported by the "facilitator" and the child was assisted in initiating a pointing response to letters on a keyboard or alphabet board. Unexpected literacy skills were revealed which, combined with the positive philosophy that FC proponents hold regarding the competence and value of the individual, were embraced by parents (Mundy & Adreon, 1994).

However, Green (1994), Braman, Brady, and Williams (1991) and many others found no evidence of unexpected literacy or independent (student-generated) communication. Investigations using standard research protocols found that students with autism failed to produce messages when the facilitator was unaware of what the message should be. This raised great doubts about the initiator or author of the messages. When authorship cannot be clearly ascribed to the child with a disability, such as when a child is typing on a keyboard independently, teachers must be extremely skeptical of the validity of the resulting communication.

One of the most telling studies was performed by Montee, Miltenberger, and Wittrock (1995). They evaluated the authorship of messages presented under three conditions: (1) the facilitator and subject had access to the same information, (2) the facilitator did not have access to the information, and (3) the facilitator had been given false information. The results showed overwhelmingly that correct answers occurred only when the facilitator had access to the correct information. In the false information condition, the answers given were the same as those given to the facilitator. Although this study and others like it have shown strong evidence of facilitator influence, *there is no evidence that the facilitator deliberately manipulated the information presented.*

Proponents of FC, as well as independent researchers (Braman et al., 1991), have asked that more research be done. Unfortunately, to date, only researchers who have a vested interest in proving the efficacy of this treatment have found positive results and then only with a small number of children. Instead of providing a new direction for the field, there is a growing consensus that FC has been a misdirection for many students with autism, while providing a serious distraction for the field.

Educators cannot afford to waste time, money, and the positive energy of families and professionals on unproven techniques, particularly when more effective (and proven) treatments are available. Taking a cue from Carl Sagan, "extraordinary claims demand extraordinary evidence." Facilitated communication has failed to meet this standard.

Dolphin Therapy

Another unproven treatment that has been used with children with developmental delay, brain damage, Down syndrome, and pervasive developmental disorder is Dolphin/Child Therapy (Jerome & Grant, 1993). After making a correct response to a target question or exhibiting a specific skill, the children are taken into the water by an adult who stays in close proximity. The children are allowed to swim with or take a ride holding the dorsal fin of a dolphin.

Nathanson and de Faria (1993) researched the effects of access to dolphins in water and of access to favorite toys in water on verbal and nonverbal responses of children with mental disabilities. Upon giving a correct response to a specific question, the child was allowed to interact with the dolphin in one condition and was allowed to play with a favorite toy in the water for 15 seconds in the second condition. A higher number of correct responses was found when the child was allowed to interact with the dolphin than when the child was allowed to play with a favorite toy. Although supporters of the technique attribute these gains to an inherent, "special bond" between the dolphin and the child with disabilities, it is likely the reinforcement value of the activity (rather than any inherent factor in the dolphin) contributes to skill acquisition in dolphin therapy.

Again, the novelty of a treatment, uncritically analyzed, promotes unwarranted enthusiasm. FC, dolphin therapy and a long list of other poorly or unsupported exercises characterize the field of autism, for many persons, as one lacking in discernment and good sense.

CURRENT ISSUES AND TRENDS

Key Legislation

When President Bush signed Public Law 101-476, The Education of the Handicapped Act Amendments of 1990, he ushered in a new era for the education of children with autism. This legislation, which changed the name of the federal law to the Individuals with Disabilities Education Act (IDEA), brought several important changes in the law, including a global replacement of the term "handicapped" with the term "disabilities" and expanded transition services, and provided for an extension of services to younger children. Transition services can be defined as a coordinated set of activities based on a student's unique and individual needs that promote a smooth movement from school to postschool activities. Most significantly, in the context of autism, the law added two new disabilities to the federal definition of disabilities. One group was students with traumatic brain injury (TBI); the other was students with autism.

As with the other disability categories, states interpret the federal definition in a variety of ways. Florida, for example, uses the following definition:

> *Autistic.* One who has a disability reflected in severe disorders of communication, behavior, socialization, and academic skills, and whose disability was evident in the early developmental stages of childhood. The autistic child appears to suffer primarily from a pervasive impairment of cognitive and perceptual functioning, the consequences of which are manifested by limited ability to understand, communicate, learn, and participate in social relationships. (Florida Department of Education, 1992, p. 7)

With these federal changes, autism achieved recognition as a unique and distinct disability. Consider that, in the earliest version of the federal law, autism was included as one of the named disabilities under the category of serious emotional disturbance (SED). By 1975, the presumed neurological basis of autism was well accepted and only a small minority of professionals still supported the concept of a psychogenic or emotional rather than a biological etiology. This unfortunate classification decision engendered a host of concerns that ultimately resulted in the removal of autism from the SED category and its placement under the other health impaired (OHI) category in 1981. This was not fully satisfactory, but it separated autism from the SED classification. What was needed was a clearer statement of the unique nature of autism and clarification that it was not a disorder with an emotional etiology. The 1990 reauthorization provided this clarification.

In 1997, IDEA was reauthorized by President Clinton. The law was scheduled for reauthorization in 1995, but advocates, fearing a legislative climate less appreciative of disability issues and eager to reduce the perceived burdens placed on the states by the federal government, sought a continuation of the existing legislation. When ultimately passed, the reauthorization mandated that districts provide functional behavioral assessments for students with significant challenging behavior, including students with autism. Today, IDEA and related and supporting legislation continues to set a national agenda for the provision of special education services to children with autism.

Inclusive Schools

Special education services are being questioned as never before. Placement of students with disabilities remains one of the primary issues facing the field of special education. The federal mandate that students be served in the least restrictive environment has been taken by many parents and advocates to mean that students with disabilities should always be educated with their nondisabled peers. The issue of placement is of grave concern to parents and teachers of children with autism (Myles, Simpson, Ormsbee, & Erickson, 1993). A strong tradition within the autism community is that "one size does *not* fit all" and that choices are key components of any true continuum of services offered by local schools.

Efforts to place all children with autism in regular classes have met with criticism. Reflecting on many years of educational practice, Rimland (1995) offered this perspective:

> I have no quarrel with inclusionists if they are content to insist upon inclusion for their children, or for children of other parents who feel that it is optimum for their children. But when they try to force me and other unwilling parents to dance to their tune, I find it highly objectionable and quite intolerable. Parents need *options*. (p. 291)

Parents' and teachers' reservations about "including" students with autism are not surprising and reflect reactions of other educators and disability professionals (Brady, Hunter, & Campbell, 1997). Some advocates have embraced inclusion in the hope that, once included, a child with disabilities will be guaranteed a better education and a more effective service delivery system. However, many parents and teachers of these children fear that a focus on *placement* draws attention away from effective programming. Mesibov (1990) has been particularly critical of inclusive schools, arguing that opponents of separate, autism-only services base their objections on philosophy at the expense of existing program options. Mesibov (1990) noted that, "What we need today are more, not fewer, options for individuals with handicaps" (p. 383). Unfortunately, in many districts, an inclusive education has not yet become one of the options available for students with autism (Brady et al., 1997).

History and the Future

What are the key issues facing the future of autism research and service delivery? Pfeiffer and Nelson (1992) surveyed 99 experts in the field of autism by asking them to rate progress in areas including research, treatment, and future directions for the improvement of service delivery. They reached the following conclusions:

1. Substantial progress has been made in basic and applied research in autism. Most experts recommend comprehensive treatment featuring behavioral and psychological components.
2. A sense of optimism exists that progress will continue in identifying the biological, genetic, and neurological factors that may contribute to autism.
3. Research on treatment responsiveness is needed to understand which types of interventions are likely to work best with which subgroups of persons with autism under an array of environmental and contextual variables.
4. The field of autism is increasingly community-based and family-focused. Better family supports, alternative community-based programs, and creative training opportunities are needed as are continued access to quality residential services for persons with autism who have more severe disabilities.

SUMMARY

Considerable progress has been made in recent years, especially in treatment and the delivery of effective services. The history of the field points clearly to a strong tradition of individualization of services. Options are essential for families and persons with autism. With categorical recognition and enthusiasm for intensive early intervention, attention has been focused on the provision of specialized educational services to students with autism.

Enthusiasm for innovative approaches that have yet to establish a solid research base indicates the desire of parents or teachers to find treatments that match the uniqueness of the disorder. However, uncritical acceptance of testimonials and poorly examined practices have the potential to undermine support for proven approaches especially in a social-political context that demands accountability and cost-effectiveness for the expenditure of public funds. Research and common sense applied to successful practices has brought about a dramatic increase in the understanding of the disorder. Educators can now, if appropriately supported, provide quality programs in a variety of settings for students with autism. Yet a full understanding of autism eludes even the most knowledgeable persons in the field. Sachs (1994) captured the essence of the problem faced by those seeking to fully understand this complex disability when he wrote:

> Autism as a subject touches on the deepest questions of ontology, for it involves a radical deviation in the development of the brain and mind. Our insight is advancing, but tantalizingly slowly. The ultimate understanding of autism may demand both technical advances and conceptual ones beyond anything we can now even dream of. (p. 126)

We believe Sachs is correct. The history of autism is replete with controversy and change; the future of autism rests on our hard work and dreams.

REVIEW QUESTIONS

1. Why is Itard referred to as the "father" of special education?

2. What were the differences between the children and youth described by Kanner and Asperger?

3. Why were parents removed from the treatments designed for children with autism prior to the 1960s?

4. What contributions did Rimland make to our understanding of autism?

5. What dangers lie in promoting unproven treatments?

REFERENCES

Asperger, H. (1944). Die "autistichen Psychopathen." im Kindesalter, *Archives für Psychiatrie und Nervenkrankheiten, 117,* 76–136.

Autism Society of America. (1998). Autism Society of America services and benefits. *Advocate, 30*(1), 2.

Bettleheim, B. (1955). *Truants from life.* Glencoe, IL: The Free Press.

Bettleheim, B. (1967). *The empty fortress: Infantile autism and the birth of the self.* New York: Free Press.

Biklen, D. (1990). Communication unbound: Autism and praxis. *Harvard Educational Review, 60,* 291–314.

Biklen, D., & Schubert, A. (1991). New words: The communication of students with autism. *Remedial and Special Education, 12*(6), 46–57.

Brady, M. P., Hunter, D., & Campbell, P. (1997). Why so much confusion? Debating and creating inclusive schools. *Educational Forum, 61,* 240–246.

Braman, B., Brady, M. P., Lynch Linehan, S., & Williams, R. E. (1995). Facilitated communication for children with autism: An examination of face validity. *Behavioral Disorders, 21,* 110–118.

Carr, E. (1994). Emerging themes in the functional analysis of problem behavior. *Journal of Applied Behavior Analysis, 27,* 393–399.

Crossley, R., & McDonald, A. (1980). *Annie's coming out.* New York: Penguin.

Florida Department of Education. (1992). *A resource manual for the development and evaluation of special programs for exceptional students, Volume II-K: Autism.* Tallahassee: Bureau of Education of Exceptional Students Division of Public Schools.

Freud, A. (1946). *The psychoanalytic treatment of children.* London: Imago.

Frith, U. (1989). *Autism: Explaining the enigma.* Cambridge, UK: Blackwell.

Graham, L. (1991). Wild boys and idiots: The beginnings of special education. *B.C. Journal of Special Education, 15*(1).

Grandin, T., & Scariano, M. M. (1986). *Emergence: Labeled autistic.* Novato, CA: Arena.

Green, G. (1994). The quality of the evidence. In H. C. Shane (Ed.), *Facilitated communication: The clincal and social phenomenon* (pp. 157–226). San Diego: Singular Publishing Group.

Horner, R. H., Dunlap, G., Koegel, R. L., Carr, E. G., Sailor, W., Anderson, J., Albin, R. W., & O'Neill, R. E. (1990). Toward a technology of "nonaversive" behavioral support. *Journal of The Association for Persons with Severe Handicaps, 15,* 125–132.

Hunter, I. M. L. (1993). Heritage from the wild boy of Aveyron. *Early Child Development and Care, 95,* 143–152.

Itard, J. M. G. (1932). *The wild boy of Aveyron* (G. Humphrey & M. Humphrey, Trans.). New York: Appleton-Century-Crofts.

Jerome, R., & Grant, M. (1993, October 25). The dolphin treatment. *People Weekly, 40,* 175–176.

Kanner, L. (1935). *Child psychiatry.* Springfield, IL: Charles C Thomas.

Kanner, L. (1943). Inborn disturbances of affective contact. *Nervous Child, 2,* 217–250.

Lane, H. (1976). *The wild boy of Aveyron.* Cambridge, MA: Harvard University Press.

Lovaas, O. I. (1987). Behavioral treatment and normal educational and intellectual functioning in young autistic children. *Journal of Consulting and Clinical Psychiatry, 55,* 3–9.

Maurice, C. (1993). *Let me hear your voice.* New York: Knopf.

Maurice, C., Green, G., & Luce, S. C. (1996). *Behavioral intervention for young children with autism.* Austin, TX: Pro-Ed.

Mesibov, G. (1990). Normalization and its relevance today. *Journal of Autism and Developmental Disorders, 20,* 379–390.

Montee, B. B., Miltenberger, R. G., & Wittrock, D. (1995). An experimental analysis of facilitated communication. *Journal of Applied Behavior Analysis, 28,* 189–200.

Mundy, P., & Adreon, D. (1993). Commentary: Facilitated communication: Attitude, effect, and theory. *Journal of Pediatric Psychology, 19,* 677–680.

Myles, B. S., Simpson, R. L., Ormsbee, K., & Erickson, C. (1993). Integrating preschool children with autism with their normally developing peers: Research findings and best practices recommendations. *Focus on Autistic Behavior, 8,* 1–18.

Nathanson, D. E., & de Faria, S. (1993). Cognitive improvement of children in water with and without dolphins. *Anthrozoos, 6*(1), 17–29.

Perry, R., Cohen, I., & DeCarlo, R. (1995). Case study: Deterioration, autism, and recovery in two siblings. *Journal of the American Academy of Child and Adolescent Psychiatry, 34,* 232–237.

Pfeiffer, S. I., & Nelson, D. D. (1992). The cutting edge in services for people with autism. *Journal of Autism and Developmental Disorders, 22,* 95–105.

Pollak, R. (1997). *The creation of Dr. B: A biography of Bruno Bettelheim.* New York: Simon & Schuster.

Rimland, B. (1964). *Infantile autism: The syndrome and its implications for a neural theory of behavior.* Englewood Cliffs, NJ: Prentice-Hall.

Rimland, B. (1994). Recovery from autism is possible. *Autism Research Review International, 8,* 3.

Rimland, B. (1995). Inclusive education: Right for *some.* In J. M. Kauffman & D. P. Hallahan (Eds.), *The illusion of full inclusion* (pp. 289–292). Austin, TX: Pro-Ed.

Sachs, O. (1994, December 27/January 3). An anthropologist on Mars. *New Yorker,* pp. 106–125.

Sanua, V. D. (1990). Leo Kanner (1894–1981): The man and the scientist. *Child Psychiatry and Human Development, 21*(1), 3–23.

Silver, L. B. (1995). Controversial therapies. *Journal of Child Neurology, 10,* 96.

Stokes, T. F., & Baer, D. M. (1977). An implicit technology of generalization. *Journal of Applied Behavior Analysis, 10*(2), 28–46.

Sutton, N. (1996). *Bettelheim: A life and a legacy.* Boulder, CO: Westview Press.

Wing, L. (1976). *Early childhood autism* (2nd ed.). London: Pergamon.

Chapter 3

MEDICAL ASPECTS AND ETIOLOGY OF AUTISM

Key Points

- Some medical conditions coexist with autism
- Many professionals provide information for assessment
- Medical conditions have likely educational implications
- Advances in understanding the etiology of autism
- Common medications prescribed for students with autism
- School procedures involving administration of medications

INTRODUCTION

Teachers who teach students with autism will be faced with medical issues that are frequently associated with the syndrome. In this chapter we examine these medical issues and their educational implications for teachers, including the management of medications and seizures.

Rationale for Knowing About Medical Conditions

It is common for parents to believe that their children have numerous complications, some requiring extensive specialized treatment or accommodation. Although a few students with autism do indeed have very complicated health concerns, most tend to have fairly good health. Because of the communication limitations found in students with autism, small and easily manageable health problems often become much more complex. Fortunately, as Kanner (1943) noted in his initial delineation of the disorder, most students with autism are quite healthy.

Several medical issues must be considered by educators including medication, seizures, food and related allergies, and health compromising safety concerns. In addition, this chapter reviews the medical research relating to etiology or the cause of autism. Speculation on the etiology of autism is abundant; fortunately, serious scientific research is moving closer to identifying the most likely causes of this disorder. Still, no clear biological markers currently exist to identify autism in children and to rule out other disorders.

The Need for Medical Involvement

The first clinical report on children with autism contained a detailed description of their medical status. In Kanner's (1943) report of autism in 11 children, he offered this summary of their medical status:

> Physically, the children were essentially normal. Five had relatively large heads. Seven of the children were somewhat clumsy in gait and gross motor performance, but all were very skillful in terms of finer muscle coordination. Electroencephalograms were normal in the case of all but John, whose anterior fontanelle did not close until he was 2½ years old, and who at 5¼ had two series of predominately right sided convulsions. (pp. 47–48)

The pattern Kanner described was that of relatively healthy and medically normal children. Although their behavior (especially their social relatedness) was beyond normal limits, their health profiles were not extraordinary. Today, it is clear that some students with autism have serious health and medical problems, but most are healthy. Maintaining good health can present a challenge for parents and educators. This is due, in part, to deficiencies in the natural feedback mechanisms that adults use to assess a child's well-being. For example, a student may not be able to communicate the fact that she has a severe toothache or suffers from stomach pain. If distress is communicated by displaying a problem behavior, adults may not interpret the situation correctly. This may delay or postpone needed treatment and result in a health crisis that could have been easily managed at an early stage.

Parents and teachers of students with autism are brought into contact with a host of medical professionals. Some of these contacts are brief and only for diagnostic purposes. Other contacts are ongoing and frequent. It is not unusual for a large number of health professionals and others to be simultaneously involved with a child. Educators should be aware of the roles of the professionals likely to be involved with a student with autism.

PEDIATRICIAN.   A pediatrician is an MD or OD who specializes in children from birth to 18 years old. A pediatrician is usually the first source of medical information for a family and may be the first person, apart from a family member, to identify signs of autism and to make recommendations for diagnosis and treatment.

NEUROLOGIST.   A neurologist is a medical doctor who has completed specialized training in the treatment and study of the nervous system. Neurologists increasingly rely on advanced imaging techniques for diagnostic purposes. These doctors may also specialize in prescribing and monitoring one or more medications to manage symptoms associated with autism.

CLINICAL SOCIAL WORKER.   A clinical social worker seeks to understand the family context and then assists the family in identifying resources to deal with a medical condition or disability. They usually consider the "big picture" and are the professionals most likely to help the family plan for long-term outcomes.

SPEECH-LANGUAGE PATHOLOGIST.   A speech-language pathologist (SLP) is trained to assess and treat problems in language development and speech production. SLPs are also skilled in treatment of problems relating to swallowing. In addition, SLPs assist in assessing a student's need for augmentative or assistive communication and in developing and monitoring the use of these systems.

AUDIOLOGIST.   Most diagnostic work-ups will call for a complete audiological evaluation conducted by a qualified audiologist. An audiologist is a specialist in hearing and sound processing. Some audiologists further specialize in an age range of patients; it is advisable for parents to select an audiologist with training and experience with children.

PSYCHIATRIST.   A psychiatrist is a physician who has completed a residency in Psychiatry. Psychiatrists view problems primarily as the result of a disorder of the mind, which is then expressed in the body. As the etiology of autism is now understood to be biological, the role of the psychiatrist has diminished in recent years, although many psychiatrists have developed specialized skills in diagnosing children with autism and evaluating their need for medication.

OCCUPATIONAL THERAPIST (OT).   This therapist often helps students with tasks of daily living and vocational fitness. The OT focuses on the skill limitations that may be due to biological impairment. They often assess fine motor skills and the ability to integrate intentions with motor expression. Many OTs are proponents of "sensory integration," one of the many controversial therapies advanced for students with autism in recent years. Examples of the types of problems that an OT can help with include holding a pen or pencil, turning the pages in a book, or holding a spoon or fork.

PHYSICAL THERAPIST (PT).   Physical therapists traditionally focused on the large muscle groups where mobility, gait, and posture are key concerns. A PT might teach a student to climb stairs or move from one class to another. In emerging practice, OTs and PTs assess and help treat many of the same problems.

BEHAVIOR ANALYST.   Professionals with training and experience in applied behavior analysis are increasingly involved in the diagnosis and treatment of autism. Behavior analysts assess patterns of behavior to determine the functions or purposes of problem behaviors. This is the newest of the professions described in this section, and parents and teachers should be aware that only a relatively small number of states (Florida, Texas, California, Oklahoma, New York) have established a credentialling process for behavior analysts. In light of the important changes made to IDEA in 1997 relating to functonal behavioral assessment, many states are developing appropriate credentials for these professionals.

FAMILY SERVICES COORDINATOR.   The family services coordinator (FSC) serves as a specialized social worker helping the family cope with a diagnosis of disability, explore needs for resources, create a family services plan (FSP), and monitoring family satisfaction with services provided. The FSC is a role described under IDEA for the Part C (formerly Part H) program for children birth to 3 years of age. As screening and assessment systems are refined under the Part C programs, students with autism are more likely to be identified under the age of 3 years and will be eligible for specialized services from the FSC.

DEVELOPMENTAL PSYCHOLOGIST. This professional conducts assessments in a variety of skill areas and organizes comprehensive evaluations of the cognitive status and learning ability of students. They may or may not have specialized training and experience in diagnosing autism and related disabilities. However, in most districts, a licensed psychologist will have a critical role in applying the diagnostic criteria for autism adopted by the state education agency.

Transdisciplinary Assessment and Diagnosis

In the past professionals from different disciplines conducted separate assessments and typically wrote separate reports. This method of assessment reflects a traditional medical model in which independent experts provided their insights and recommendations. This process was relatively inefficient and, for a student with autism, was often highly intrusive. Increasingly, early developmental evaluations that include medical, health care, and educational professionals are conducted in an "arena assessment" format. The professionals form a circle around the child while one member of the team, often assisted by a parent, conducts direct assessment activities with the child. Other team members observe and score items that are pertinent to their areas. An OT, for example may conduct an assessment, then present other items from the assessment protocols of other team members. In this way the student is subjected to less "handling" and a team consensus is likely to emerge as each team member directly observes all assessment tasks. This also provides an opportunity to examine the implications of a student's problems across the areas of expertise held by the many professionals. For example, a health care professional might show the practical implications of a student's seizure disorder on community mobility, language development, and self-care skills. Arena assessment is most common for very young children and is an example of best practices in transdisciplinary cooperation. These assessments help to determine eligibility for services under Part C of IDEA.

THE FAMILY SERVICES PLAN. With the widespread availability of services for families of young children with disabilities (Part C of IDEA), families are receiving specialized support several years prior to the time a child begins kindergarten. Part C services are typically provided by different agencies according to a state plan. In many states, these services are delivered under a medical services umbrella organization. The family services plan (FSP), referred to as the individualized family support plan (IFSP) in some states, becomes the agreement for services between the Part C agency and the family. This document is the plan of services for the child *and* family. Services under Part C differ from those for students age 3 to 21 in that they are family-centered and not solely child-centered. The rationale is that the child is entirely dependent on the family and the family is the paramount provider of supports and services for the child. This promotes efforts to enhance parents' skills and to empower them as active advocates and planners for their child.

EARLY PARENT CONTACT WITH THE MEDICAL COMMUNITY.   Parents of young children with autism will have had a great deal of contact with the medical community. Certainly Part C services, in most states, will bring them into contact with many clinicians in the "healing arts" as they obtain a developmental evaluation and a diagnosis of autism or other pervasive developmental disorder. In some cases, this diagnostic process is clearcut. For other children, it may take many visits to clinicians over many months to establish a diagnosis. Educators will frequently hear of cases in which clinicians hesitated to provide a diagnosis of autism. Some parents either *shop* for such a diagnosis or, alternatively, they *object* to a diagnosis of autism. In these situations, they may terminate involvement with one clinician and seek other services. Some clinicians, especially those less skilled in diagnosing autism, may suggest that a child has a less severe condition such as a language delay, or they may elect to ascribe a more general diagnosis such as "developmental delay." Such labeling may be fully appropriate in some cases, but in others failure to recognize autism early may result in a failure to marshal resources needed for an effective early intervention effort. This could result in a critical loss of opportunity.

Another reason for clinician caution in diagnosing autism is the tremendous importance of the diagnosis process. Autism is a behaviorally defined syndrome. It is not a disorder that can be definitively diagnosed by means of any biological marker or test. The diagnostic process calls for ruling out other disorders that could produce symptoms similar to autism. Rett syndrome is one of the disorders that could be mistaken at an early stage for autism. In some cases, brain tumors have produced symptoms that mimic autism. Failing to differentially diagnose a brain tumor and instead providing a diagnosis of autism could be a mistake with the most serious, if not fatal, consequences. Fortunately, clinician skill and training, advanced imaging techniques, and comprehensive diagnostic procedures can help avert this kind of misdiagnosis. The key point is that many parents gain important and close contact with medical professionals. In the vast majority of cases, parents get their introduction to autism from these professionals as well.

THE DSM-IV. As noted in Chapter 1, the *Diagnostic and Statistical Manual of Mental Disorders*, Fourth Edition (DSM-IV) provides the diagnostic framework for autism and other developmental disabilities. The DSM-IV is clear that autism can occur in association with other medical conditions. This association (referred to as comorbidity) can complicate diagnosis and treatment and is important to recognize.

The DSM-IV classifies autism as one of the pervasive developmental disorders, which includes Asperger syndrome, Rett syndrome, childhood disintegrative disorder, and pervasive developmental disorder/not otherwise specified. In each of the disorders, a diverse group of other general medical conditions (e.g., chromosomal abnormalities, congenital infections, structural abnormalities of the central nervous system) are sometimes observed. In addition, many of the pervasive developmental disorders are also typically associated with some degree of mental retardation. Rett syndrome is one of the PDDs that requires lifelong medical management to preserve quality of life; it is therefore absolutely essential that the diagnostic process be thorough.

RETT SYNDROME. In the past, students with Rett syndrome often were misdiagnosed as having autism. A student with Rett syndrome typically continues to regress and experiences a progressive loss of key motor capabilities. Until recently, Rett syndrome was thought to occur only in females. Recent reports indicate that, in rare instances, males may have the disorder as well. The cause of Rett's disorder remains unknown but several factors have been suggested, including various structural defects within the mitochondria in cells (Coker & Melnyk, 1991) and certain enzyme deficiencies. Unlike autism, Rett's disorder is progressive. A student with the disorder becomes more impaired over time and by the age of 12 or 14, many students with Rett syndrome are incapacitated. Life expectancy data for students with Rett syndrome are not conclusive. Haas (1988) noted that:

> Several middle-aged Rett patients have been identified but they are relatively few considering the size of the Rett population. Is the life expectancy normal with adequate attention to seizure control, nutrition, and orthopedic complications? We do not yet know. (p. S4)

In the past, many children lived only into late childhood or early teenage years. Careful medical management is critical to extending the life span and maximizing quality of life for students with this disorder.

Of special concern here is the fact that autism constitutes the most frequent misdiagnosis of Rett syndrome. Indeed, autism was the likely diagnosis for a child with Rett syndrome prior to the work of Dr. Andreas Rett in Vienna in the late 1960s (Percy, Zoghbi, Lewis, & Jankovic, 1988). Percy et al. (1988) provided guidelines for differential diagnosis of this disorder relying primarily on the motor-behavioral features of these children in contrast to children with autism. Prominent features included abnormal respiratory pattern, "ataxia/apraxia, slowness of movement, hand stereotypies, and the absence of hand function" (p. 66). Failure to differentiate Rett syndrome from autism has a profound negative impact on the course of medical treatment for a child with Rett syndrome.

THE ROLE OF A FAMILY PRACTICE PHYSICIAN. What kind of information do family practice physicians receive about autism? Edwards and Bristol (1991) reviewed information provided to physicians. Physicians learn that autism "is not rare among the severe developmental disabilities" (p. 1755) and that "No single underlying biomedical etiology for autism has been identified; studies suggest that neuralgic and genetic components are involved" (p. 1757). Edwards and Bristol also noted that, if physicians hold incorrect assumptions, they will fail to recognize autism and neglect to suggest effective treatments. They addressed four myths:

1. parents cause autism;
2. all children with autism have potentially normal intelligence;
3. [that] these children cannot be reliably tested with standard instruments; and
4. that autism represents a juvenile form of schizophrenia.

Their advice to physicians is valuable for teachers who should understand what information pediatricians receive. They noted that laboratory tests for fragile X and other genetic anomalies, blood analysis, and advanced imagining and an electroencephalogram may be indicated for some children.

Physicians should know that an effective diagnosis includes comprehensive psychoeducational assessment, which in turn leads to effective early intervention. Edwards and Bristol (1991) write:

> At present no cure for autism exists. Psychotherapy for either the child or the parent has not shown to be effective. However, psychoeducational and behavioral therapies are effective in improving both the autistic symptoms and the overall outcome for patients and their families. (p. 1760)

COMMON HEALTH AND MEDICAL PROBLEMS

Students with autism require skilled medical attention from competent and sensitive health care providers (Gualtieri, Evans, & Patterson, 1987).

But it is easy for teachers to believe that most students with autism are likely to have complicated medical issues, when this is not actually the case. Confusion is understandable. Rutter, Baily, Bolton, and Le Couteur (1994, p. 311) noted that, "There is a general agreement that autism has an organic basis but there is less agreement on the frequency with which it is associated with known medical conditions." Wing and Gould (1979) reported that 17% of students with autism with IQs over 50 had an identifiable medical condition. Students with autism who had lower IQs were even more likely to have medical complications. Ritvo and colleagues (1990) sampled students covering the full range of IQ levels and found that 12% had conditions known to cause central nervous system pathology. As in the Wing and Gould study, students with lower IQs had a greater likelihood of medical conditions with CNS impact. Tuchman, Rapin, and Shinnar (1991) studied 314 students with autism and 237 students with dysphasia but not autism. They determined a low rate of medical conditions that could account for the presence of each diagnosis. Only 5% of the students with autism and 4.4% of the students with dysphasia had identified medical conditions. Rutter et al. (1994, p. 315) summarized the situation this way, "Known medical conditions are much more common when autism is accompanied by severe retardation and especially if there is profound retardation."

Barton and Volkmar (1998) suggested that reliance on the relatively nonstringent earlier versions of the DSM criteria led to an overdiagnosis of children with low IQs and a correspondingly high rate of medical conditions. Noting the "consistent finding of increase in medical conditions with decreasing IQ," they noted "that the more fundamental relationship may be between severe mental handicap and medical conditions rather than with autism as such" (p. 277). In most cases, the etiology of autism remains unknown. When autism is found in association with a known medical condition that affects CNS development, the IQ of the student will tend to be lower. This, however, need not impair the ability of educators and medical team members to craft an effective program of intervention.

Seizures and Seizure Management

Seizures are episodes of abnormal electrical activity in the brain that disturb normal functioning of the central nervous system. They can vary in severity and type, ranging from minor changes in alertness or staring into space to loss of consciousness accompanied by violent and uncontrollable shaking. Electroencephalograms (EEGs) are usually administered to locate the source of the seizure. However, EEG results may not be definitive as some students with abnormal EEGs never have seizures and others with normal EEGs have them frequently. In most cases, carefully monitored anticonvulsant medication will help control the intensity and frequency of seizures. Side effects of the medications (e.g., drowsiness or increased activity) are common and likely to be of concern to teachers. All personnel involved in a child's care must have detailed knowledge of the child's medication regimen. Additionally, teachers should be aware that, after a seizure, many students will be tired, distractible or have difficulty "getting back to work" for a period of time.

Kanner (1943) noted that one of his 11 original children with autism had epilepsy. In the follow-up report on the original group of 11, an additional person had developed a seizure disorder as an adult (Kanner, 1971). The association between autism and epilepsy is clear and has been reported by many researchers (Deykin & MacMahon, 1979; Fish & Ritvo, 1979; Rutter, 1970), but the actual link has not been precisely identified.

Until recently, it was assumed that the onset of epilepsy typically occurred during puberty and was brought on by increases in hormonal levels. This view has been replaced by an understanding that onset is most common during early childhood. Studies by Olsson, Steffenburg, and Gilburg (1988) and Volkmar and Nelson (1990) suggested that most students with autism who develop epilepsy do so in early childhood. The assumption that epilepsy developed during puberty may have been fostered by the greater severity of some forms of seizures then and by the physical size of the student.

Epilepsy is commonly associated with autism. Gillberg (1991b) estimated that approximately one third of people with autism develop seizures by adulthood. Gillberg further noted that, in spite of the rather large population of persons with autism and epilepsy, relatively little information is available. Most treatment recommendations are based on clinical experience. Antiepileptic drugs are not intended to treat the symptoms of autism, but rather to manage or eliminate seizures for individuals with autism who also have epilepsy.

Teachers may find it hard to appreciate the complications involved in determining the right program of medication for a student with autism and epilepsy. Successful treatment involves high levels of clinical judgment. A passage from Gillberg's (1991b) study illustrates this complexity.

> Antiepileptic pharmacological treatment should always be weighted against the frequency (or rather infrequency) with which most children with autism and epilepsy actually suffer from major seizures. It is arguable whether a mildly mentally retarded child with autism who has seizures of a few minutes duration or twice a year or less should receive any kind of pharmacological treatment. Of the 66 patients referred to above, 5 did not receive any kind of treatment. In 4 of these cases the reason was that the rate of seizures was low (<3 each year) and when antiepileptic drugs had been tried, they had led to severe behavioral

side effects. However, there is no good rationale to suggest a minimum frequency of fits at which pharmacological treatment is always indicated. Before a decision is made, type of epilepsy, etiology, and consideration of potential hazards with drug treatment must always be made. (pp. 70–71)

Seizure control even with the best medication management is not assured. According to the Epilepsy Foundation of America (1996), approximately 85% of persons with epilepsy are able to achieve a reasonable degree of symptom suppression by means of medication. This leaves a significant number with more complex and hard to manage seizures.

Types of Seizures

Seizures usually fall into one of four general categories: generalized tonic-clonic seizures, petit mal seizures, simple partial seizures, and complex partial seizures (Tsai, 1998).

With **tonic-clonic seizures**, students experience the sudden onset of a major seizure. Students typically lose consciousness and fall unless assisted. The tonic phase of the seizure involves extreme tightening of muscles and very rapid respiration and heart rate, which can last several minutes. This is followed by the clonic phase, which is characterized by jerky movements, usually cycling to a higher and then lower degree several times, with erratic arm and leg movements lasting several minutes. Last is the restoration of full consciousness. This is gradual and may take place within several minutes or may last several hours. Students are usually unaware of the seizures, but postseizure headaches and muscle aches are common. Extreme sleepiness is also common and students should be allowed to slowly regain control afterwards.

Petit mal seizures, by contrast, are less obvious. They usually last only a few seconds and involve brief loss of awareness and control. During a petit mal seizure, a student is likely to stare vacantly ahead or her eyes may roll upward. Ongoing physical activity may cease. A student may drop a drink or pencil and then just as suddenly regain awareness without realizing that she has had a seizure. After a petit mal seizure, the student will usually experience no physical side-effects.

With a **simple partial seizure**, students will be aware during the seizure yet experience specific motor, sensory, or autonomic symptoms (Tsai, 1998). Students with simple partial seizures may be able to manage their own care during the time of the seizure, but may require assistance to avoid further distress.

The **complex partial seizure** is similar to the simple partial seizure but differs in that it involves a loss of consciousness. This loss of consciousness may come after some initial symptoms that parallel the simple partial seizure. As the seizure moves to the complex partial seizure, it may take on a number of strange forms, including highly disorganized behavior, repetitive, purposeless movements, visual distortions, and in some cases hallucinations. With complex partial seizures the student should be moved to a safe setting in which constant supervision and support are provided.

The Epilepsy Foundation America issues and updates a set of recommendations for assisting persons who have seizures (EFA, 1996). This information is summarized in Table 3–1.

Educational Implications of Seizures

Teachers of students with autism will almost certainly have one or more students who have seizures. While a teacher will have no role in prescribing medication or in diagnosis, a teacher's observations are essential to the management of seizures. Seizures in students with autism are not always immediately obvious. Caregivers and teachers often fail to recognize seizures and sometimes misinterpret seizures as signs of uncooperative or disruptive behavioral episodes. Knowledgeable teachers who are familiar with their students are better prepared to spot a seizure. They will see the student experience a loss of focus. This may be especially obvious in a preferred or well-tolerated activity. They may notice the student begin to shake or cease movement while at the same time becoming oblivious to his or her surroundings.

Comprehensive planning is essential. The IEP should contain suggestions for managing seizures and these suggestions should be an important topic at the IEP meeting. For example, if the side effect of a medication for seizure control includes irritability, a teacher should expect this behavior in the initial hours following administration of the medicine. This could influence whether a teacher reacts to a student's irritability as a compliance problem or as a medication effect.

Some states require that medical reports be made available as part of the initial eligibility determination for students with more severe disorders. If the student is taking prescription medication for seizures, or if seizures have been reported but the student's pediatrician does not believe medication is appropriate, then a plan for dealing with in-school seizures is needed. Management suggestions may differ depending on the nature, frequency, and severity of the seizures. For students with autism, the following general guidelines should be considered:

1. Look for signs of seizure activity and prepare to respond quickly at the first indications of a seizure.
2. When possible, help the student with major seizures move to a comfortable and private location. Seizures can involve some

Table 3–1. Treatment Suggestions for Epileptic Seizure

Seizure Type	What To Do	What Not To Do
Generalized Tonic-clonic	• Obtain medical information • Protect from nearby hazards • Loosen shirt collars • Protect from head injury • Turn on side to keep airway clear; reassure when consciousness returns • Call parents • If multiple seizures, or if one seizure lasts longer than 5 minutes, call an ambulance	• Don't put any hard implements in the student's mouth • Don't try to hold tongue; it can't be swallowed • Don't give liquids during or just after seizure • Don't use artificial respiration unless breathing is absent after muscle jerking subsides • Don't restrain
Petit mal	• No first aid necessary, but report to parents for the purposes of medical evaluation	• Don't draw unnecessary attention
Simple partial	• No first aid necessary; if seizure becomes convulsive, administer first aid • No immediate action needed other than reassurance and emotional support • If first episode, recommend medical evaluation to parents	• Don't draw unnecessary attention
Complex partial	• Speak calmly and reassuringly • Guide gently away from obvious hazards • Stay with student until completely aware • Consider the need for special assistance in returning home	• Don't grab hold unless sudden danger • Don't restrain • Don't shout • Don't expect instructions to be followed

Source: Adapted from *Seizure Recognition and First Aid*, by the Epilepsy Foundation of America, 1996. Landover, MD: Author.

degree of embarrassment, which is easily minimized if the student has a degree of privacy. At the conclusion of the seizure, the student should be returned to the classroom as naturally as possible.

3. Never attempt to put anything in the student's mouth during a seizure.

4. Move the student to a comfortable position on the ground, in a chair, or on a couch. A responsible adult should provide direct supervision and be in immediate contact with the student when a seizure involves involuntary motor movement.

5. Anticipate potential danger during activities if the student is known to have seizures. This is a high-judgment task for teachers yet an important one. The greatest degree of care and support should be provided in any activity in which the student could be placed in danger if a seizure were to occur. Barring a student with seizures from certain activities (e.g., using a playground slide) is unduly restrictive and unwise. In some cases, however, parents and physicians may request restriction of certain activities.

6. Document all seizure and precursor activity and share these observations and data with parents. This relates back to IEP planning and completes the information cycle. Parents can then communicate this information to the child's pediatrician as part of the ongoing medical management of the seizures.

7. Tell classmates how to assist the student with seizures. Peers may be the first to spot signs of a seizure and may be in the best position to offer assistance. Peers can learn to help the student with a seizure to a comfortable place while calmly calling for help; they can "spot" the student to prevent a possible fall while serving in a buddy role. Even if peers are not in a "first response" role, their knowledge can increase their comfort level and provide real support for the student with a seizure.

8. Any seizure management plan must be designed to meet the individual needs of the student. The teacher must ensure that every adult who has regular contact with the student knows how to respond to a seizure.

Food Preferences and Food Refusal

Food preferences and food refusal patterns are common in students with autism. Although young children exhibit periods during which they "fuss" about food, most soon outgrow this. Other children's selectivity or other preferences can be easily accommodated and, when they do not impose a dietary problem, are not cause for alarm. For some students with autism, however, food becomes the context for major behavioral challenges. In addition to bothersome confrontations, parents may become concerned that their child does not have an adequate diet or that the child might have possible allergies or other biologically based reasons for the refusal.

Although some food problems may be related to biology, the interplay of environment can make problems greater or might alleviate the problem altogether. Parents can easily become anxious and torn between advice to ignore the problem on one hand and to take a get-tough policy on the other. Children's nutrition is closely linked to their physical health, as well as their mental and emotional development (Martin, 1973). For many children, critical or sensitive periods can be isolated for some forms of feeding disorders (Illingworth & Lister, 1964). Extreme measures were routinely used in the past when a child would not eat. One treatment still in use in certain extreme circumstances consists of inserting a feeding tube through the child's mouth directly into the stomach. Children typically resist this treatment and parents may be uncomfortable with its obvious intrusiveness.

A second and less intrusive approach is forced oral feeding. In this approach, the child is assisted in putting food in his or her mouth. The food must be swallowed before more food or drink is given. What differentiates this approach from "assisted feeding" is the contingency aspect. In forced feeding, the morsel of food placed in the child's mouth must be swallowed before any other food is given. It is essentially compliance training. Assisted feeding allows the student to taste a targeted food with whatever level of assistance is required. The first step in assisted feeding may simply be to touch the food item to the lips. The rest of the student's food is then given to him.

Although forced feeding has some clinical support (Ives, Harris & Wolchik, 1978), parents and teachers recognize that it has limited social acceptability. Teachers should never *initiate* any forced feeding of any student. Some students have physiological abnormalities that make swallowing difficult. A swallowing assessment, conducted by an experienced professional is a minimal prerequisite before embarking on any behavioral approach to feeding issues. A teacher should not be asked to participate in a program of forced feeding until all treatment issues have been addressed and procedural and ethical safeguards have been satisfied. Parents must provide full informed consent to a comprehensive plan that is developed and agreed to by medical professionals, district level specialists, and administrators.

The best current practices for helping children with serious feeding problems are largely derived from work by Riordan and her colleagues (1984) at Johns Hopkins University. In an important initial study, four children at risk due to food refusal and who had no had clear medical barriers to normal oral food consumption were treated with behavioral interventions. The treatment differed slightly for each child but the common elements consisted of:

1. Preintervention assessment in which an array of foods were presented to the child with careful observation and measurement of degree of acceptance or refusal.
2. Delivery of some form of reinforcement when, and only when, the child ate the targeted foods. Preferred foods functioned as reinforcers for most children with brief access to toys used with one child.
3. Challenging and disruptive behaviors and food refusals were ignored during treatment and in follow-up conditions.
4. During a maintenance phase, reinforcement was delivered intermittently and other changes were made, such as increasing the time between food intake and reinforcement.
5. To assure long-term benefit, the parents were extensively trained and closely supervised during practice feedings of their child. They were also given detailed instructions for maintaining the program.

Critical to the success of this approach was the assessment of preferred versus nonpreferred foods and whether the child accepted the food, refused the food, or accepted it but then expelled it. In treatment, preferred food served as reinforcers for nonpreferred foods. Children were given small amounts of the nonpreferred food and very quickly presented with the preferred food. Expulsion of the nonpreferred food resulted in expulsion of the preferred food as well. Certainly, as parents seek humane and effective treatments for children with severe feeding problems and seek to avoid unnecessary and potentially dangerous tube feeding, behavioral treatments like those described by Riordian et al. (1984) continue to be a treatment of choice.

Safety as a Health Issue

Students can and should be taught how to be safe. Typically developing children learn safety from observing the safety behaviors of parents and siblings as well as from direct teaching. Parents may tell childen why they are riding in car seats or state and then restate rules for play near bodies of water. It is harder for students with autism to learn these skills and for families to teach them effectively; however, these skills must be taught actively and directly and be reinforced in all relevant environments. Accidents are the second leading cause of death in children over the age of 5 years; and the accident rate for children with disabilities far exceeds that of children without disabilities.

Safety education must be emphasized in educational programs for students with autism (Berkell, 1992). Powers (1989) noted that students with autism exhibit a "combination of poor judgement and good motor skills," which can be dangerous. Good programming requires active exposure to real world environments in which to practice and maintain newly learned safety skills. This involves an element of risk, but these risks must be balanced with the even greater risks of not teaching safety skills. Key elements of a safety program for students with autism should include:

1. street crossing;
2. kitchen and home safety;
3. edible/nonedible discriminations;
4. community living;
5. dealing with the unknown; and
6. interacting with known versus unknown persons

The range of safety concerns will vary broadly as the spectrum of autism embraces a very wide range of students. Some students will require close and skilled supervision for extended portions of their lives. Fortunately, the preference for sameness and routine can allow for good safety behaviors, once well taught and effectively generalized, to become lifelong habits.

ETIOLOGY OF AUTISM: WHAT IS THE ORIGIN?

The etiology of autism remains unknown. While it is possible to determine etiology in a few cases, the vast majority of cases have no clear cause. Multiple causes are almost certainly likely. Complicating matters is the fact that students with identical symptoms may have different etiologies.

Although the various causes of autism are not known, a fair amount is known about what does not cause autism. Parents do *not* cause autism. This is especially important in light of the history of autism, with its tradition of parental blame and the dominance of psychogenic explanations. Today, research suggests possible multiple etiologies including brain, neurological, or genetic differences, birth trauma, and other miscellaneous reasons.

The Brains of Children With Autism

What, if anything, is different in the appearance and function of the brains of children with autism? As a disorder with a presumed neurological etiology, it is reasonable to assume that the brains of individuals with autism would provide clear evidence of difference. Further, these differences should be of such magnitude as to be seen as responsible for or strongly contributing to the disorder we recognize as autism.

Although no consistent gross anatomical differences have been found in the brains of individuals with and without autism, some interesting research has been emerging. Hashimoto, Tayama, Miyazaki, Murakawa, and Kuroda (1993) conducted magnetic resonance imaging of children and adults with autism. Their research found that the cerebella and brainstems of persons with autism were smaller than those of individuals in a control group. They noted that the size of the cerebellum and the brainstem increased as the child developed in both the children with autism and controls. The pattern of development led Hashimoto et al. to suggest that these brain differences are not the result of a progressive degenerative process, but rather of some insult occurring fairly early in pregnancy. Hashimoto and colleagues stated, "The brain abnormalities responsible for this disorder have their origin during the first 6 months of gestation" (p. 14).

Courchesne et al. (1988) suggested that the damage occurs even earlier—possibly as early as the third or fifth month of gestation. The work of a growing number of researchers (Akefeldt & Gillberg, 1991; Bauman, 1991; Bauman & Kemper, 1994; Courchesne et al., 1988) provided evidence that the morphology, or structure, of the brain of persons with autism exhibits differences from those of persons who do not have autism.

Other studies failed to find evidence of smaller cerebellar regions. In the accompanying sidebar, Dr. Roberto Tuchman, a neurologist specializing in children with autism, provides a summary of recent research about the cause or causes of autism.

In many ways, current brain research represents a continuation of a search begun many years age. Most special educators are familiar with the early work of Werner, Strauss, Kephart, and later Cruickshank and colleagues. These researchers sought to discover the neuroanatomical differences directly accountable for the disability. Cruickshank (1966), for example, maintained that specific and hard-to-detect abnormalities in brain structure accounted for a wide array of serious learning and behavioral problems. Although this thesis was appealing intuitively, it often had disappointing effects. One of the authors recalls participating in a school consultation with the eminent scholar and jointly observing a preschool child with autism. After observing the child for about an hour, Dr. Cruickshank met with the parents and teacher. He complimented the teacher for being a wonderful teacher, but went on to state that she was exactly the *wrong* teacher for this particular child. It was clear to Dr. Cruickshank (but not to the child's physician) that this child had brain damage. This damage might not appear in X rays or imaging techniques but Dr. Cruickshank was sure that, if the parents made contact with the right researcher in Holland, he would surely isolate the cause of all this child's

Neurological Aspects of Autism

Roberto Tuchman, M.D.

In the absence of a biological marker, diagnosing autism and delineating its boundaries remain somewhat arbitrary clinical decisions. Great strides have been made in the past decade in categorizing subgroups of children with autistic spectrum disorder. Present research endeavors are focusing on the neurobiological underpinnings of these clinical subgroups.

An important goal of any proposed criterion to diagnose autism and related disorders should be to reduce inconsistencies among researchers and clinicians regarding the behavioral versus biological delineation of autistic disorders. The diagnoses of an associated medical or neurological condition in an individual with autism defines the clinical symptoms at the neurobiological level, but does not exclude a behaviorally defined diagnosis of autism. For example, an individual with behavioral symptoms meeting the diagnostic criteria for autism who has a chromosomal analysis diagnostic of fragile X syndrome has both autism and fragile X. In this example, the behavioral symptoms are consistent with a diagnosis of autism (with all of the implications this may have in terms of management and prognosis), and the biological cause for the autism is fragile X (with all of the implications this may have in terms of genetics and prognosis).

The diverse biological disorders associated with autistic spectrum disorders support the hypothesis that the behavioral manifestations of autism may be secondary to a wide variety of insults to the brain. The heterogeneity of autistic disorders may be due to different etiologies or to a combination of factors such as an interplay between etiology, genetic predisposition, and environmental factors. The diagnosis of autism is similar to that of mental retardation; careful clinical evaluation (i.e., speech and language evaluation, neuropsychological assessment) and medical workup (i.e., chromosomal studies, DNA for fragile X, neuroimaging, or neurophysiologic studies) need to be carried out to allow for subtyping according to both behavioral phenotype and etiology. It is only through careful subgrouping of individuals with autistic spectrum disorders that we will achieve an understanding of the pathophysiology of this disorder and be able to provide for specific medical intervention and prognosis.

(continued)

Autistic spectrum disorders may have multiple etiologies. These etiologies include:

Some of the Disorders Associated with Autism

Congenital/Acquired	Genetic/Metabolic
Rubella	Chromosome anomalies*
Toxoplasmosis	Tuberous sclerosis
Cytomegalovirus	Neurofibromatosis
Moebius syndrome	Leber's congenital amaurosis
Hypomelanosis of Ito	Phenylketonuria
Dandy-Walker syndrome	Histidinemia
Cornelia-deLange syndrome	Ceroid lipofuscinosis
Soto syndrome	Hyperlactatemia
Goldenhar syndrome	Celiac disease
Williams syndrome	Purine metabolism disorders
Microcephaly	Adrenoleukodystrophy
Hydrocephalus	Duchenne musculardystrophy
Joubert syndrome	Angelman syndrome
Herpes encephalitis	
Infantile spasms	
Lead ingestion	
Meningitis	
Temporal lobe tumors	

*Chromosomal anomalies include fragile X, autosomal and sex chromosome anomalies

It is important to realize that these disorders are not always associated with autism. In the majority of individuals with autism, no specific etiology is found using presently available diagnostic tools.

Our present understanding of the neuropathology of autism is based on the work of Bauman, who found consistent neuropathological changes in the limbic system and in cerebellar circuits. A developmental maturational curtailment involving the circuitry of the limbic system has been postulated. These investigators have suggested that whatever happened to the brains of individuals with autism occurred around 30 weeks of gestation (Bauman, 1991; Bauman & Kemper, 1994; Kemper & Bauman, 1993).

Neuroradiological studies in autism continue to provide diverse results. Cortical abnormalities include enlargement of the left lateral ventricle, bilateral ventricular enlargement, and cortical malformations such as polymicrogyria, schizencephaly, and macrogyria (Berthier, Bayes, & Tolosa, 1993; Berthier, Starkstein, & Leiguarda, 1990; Courchesne, 1991; Nowell, Hackney, Muraki, & Coleman, 1990; Piven et al., 1990). None of these findings is consistent with or specific to autism. Abnormalities of the posterior fossa structures reported in autism include hypoplasia of cerebellar vermal lobules VI and VII and diminished size of the brainstem (Courchesne et al., 1988; Hashimoto, Tayama, Miyazaki, Murakawa, & Kuroda, 1993; Kleiman, Neff, & Rosman, 1992). Findings of cerebellar abnormalities have not been consistently reproduced and some investigators have stated that previous reports of posterior fossa abnormalities may be related to technical and methodological factors (Holttum, Minshew, Sanders, & Phillips, 1992; Piven et al., 1990).

The most consistent neurochemical finding in autism has been an elevation in platelet serotonin levels. Despite extensive research, neither the relationship of this finding to concomitant mental retardation nor the mechanism of the hyperserotoninemia has been elucidated. Cook has suggested that hyperserotoninemia in autism may be heterogeneous with one subgroup of subjects with increased 5-HT uptake and another subgroup with decreased 5-HT2 binding (Cook et al., 1993). A role for other monoamine neurotransmitters has been suggested; however, aside from serotonin, the only other consistently replicated neurochemical finding in autism has been elevated norepinephrine plasma levels (Cook, 1990). Research on the role of brain opioid systems in the development of social behavior and on the role of the immune system in autism may provide new insight into pharmacotherapeutic interventions (Buitelaar et al., 1992, 1989; Sahley & Panksepp, 1987; Zimmerman, Frye, & Potter, 1993).

Electrophysiological studies of autistic children have included clinical EEG studies and evoked potential studies. Clinical EEG studies performed on autistic children have revealed abnormal EEGs in 13% to 83% of the cases studied (Ornitz, 1987; Tuchman, Rapin, & Shinnar, 1991). The clinical diagnostic criteria used for autism, the associated medical disorders that coexist, and the methods of recording and interpreting clinical EEGs likely account for the variability in rates among different studies. Evoked potential studies have shown no consistent abnormality in either the brainstem auditory evoked potential (BAEP) or the middle latency responses (MLRs) of nonretarded autistic disor-

(continued)

der patients (Grillon, Courchesne, & Akshoomoff, 1989). Abnormalities in endogenous or event related potentials have been consistently reported and suggest cortical processing abnormalities (Ciesielski, Courchesne, & Elmasian, 1990; Courchesne, Courchesne, Hicks, & Lincoln, 1985; Lincoln, Courchesne, Harms, & Allen, 1993; Lotspeich & Ciaranello, 1993; Minshew, 1991).

Genetic studies have demonstrated an increased recurrence risk for autism of approximately 4% to 8% in families with one autistic child (Folstein & Piven, 1991; Ritvo et al., 1989a). The relationship of genetic factors to the expression of a pervasive developmental disorder and the role of nongenetic events in determining the severity of the disorder need further investigation (Vukicevic & Siegel, 1990).

Summary

Research over the past 20 years has provided conclusive evidence to support the concept of autism as a neurobiological complex developmental disorder that is behaviorally defined. The search for pathophysiologic mechanisms for autism has accelerated dramatically over the past decade through contributions from the fields of neuropathology, neuroimaging, neurophysiology, neurochemistry, and genetics.

Dr. Roberto Tuchman is a child neurologist who specializes in autism and other developmental disabilities. He is affiliated with several prominent institutes in South Florida.

problems. Isolating the cause and fully understanding the psychological-physiological implications of any damage, for Cruickshank, was essential.

This approach is taken by many experts even today. For educators, whether or not there is some level of brain damage makes little difference in selecting important goals and effective teaching methods. Obviously, careful examination for tumors and malignancy is essential for *health* reasons, but the implications for educators are minimal.

Fortunately, a dedicated group of scientists continues to pursue these questions and they publish their work in peer-reviewed journals allowing international appreciation and critiques of their work. These scientific endeavors may, over the course of the next decade, yield conclusive evidence of different causes of autism and the development of ways to prevent the disorder. Yet, even if a structural or clearly biological difference is found, it is unlikely that an effective *medical intervention* will result in dramatic improvements for students who already have autism.

Neurological Etiologies

What are the linkages between an atypical CNS and the multiple sets of behaviors displayed by a student with autism? This question is especially relevant for the core social behaviors and cognitive processes supporting social interaction. Mundy and Sheinkopf (1993) pointed out the problems in bridging the research on the neurology of autism with the research on the social behavior of children with autism. After reviewing the major neurological models, they stated:

> Whereas some models argue for a direct link between the neurological process and its behavioral manifestations, others argue that such a relationship is mediated by dysfunctions in attention, arousal, sensory processing, or cognition. Nevertheless, all of these may be interpreted to predict specific relationships between neurological function and behavior in child with autism. (p. 208)

If neurological factors do indeed predispose a child to autism, it should be possible to link specific types of neurological difference or damage to specific types of abnormal behavior. It will be especially important for future research to demonstrate these linkages, particularly in students' social behavior as these skills may well constitute the central deficit in students with autism. This has not yet been done but, as Mundy and Sheinkopf (1993) indicate, linking these areas of research is an important goal for future research into the causes of autism.

Genetic Differences

Many autism researchers hope to find clear evidence of a genetic marker in autism. At this time, no clear genetic marker for autism has been found. However, some studies suggest that some combinations of autism and mental retardation accompanied by mild physical disabilities can be detected by means of chromosomal analysis. Gillberg and his colleagues (Gillberg, Steffenburg, Wahlstrom, Sjostedt, & Eeg-Olofson, 1991) in Sweden reported a chromosomal defect in six boys who had a partial trisomy of chromosome 15. It is important to note, however, that these boys had mental retardation and other physical problems in addition to autism. No clear chromosomal link for autism in individuals without other problems has been conclusively demonstrated.

Piven, Palmer, Jacobi, Childress, and Arndt (1997) examined the genetic liability for autism in relatives of children with autism. Their work suggested that milder forms of autism are more likely when close relatives also have autism. Piven et al. (1997) wrote:

> In this study we have replicated and extended the finding of others that the relatives of autistic probands show familial aggregation of behaviors that are milder than but qualitatively similar to the defining features of autism. Within this study, the findings for the parents in the autism families were replicated in the grandparents and in the aunts and uncles in the autism families. These findings suggest that the social and communication deficits and stereotyped behaviors examined in this study may be expressions of the genetic liability for autism. (p. 189)

Great care must be taken in any interpretation of these findings. However, as continued research in the area of genetic factors relating to autism comes closer to finding the pattern(s) most closely linked with autism, it would not be surprising to find that some of these patterns do yield a familial association. Some parents of students with autism are likely to have some aspects of the disorder.

What if some parents are co-afflicted? This is the case in some forms of deafness and it is not recognized as either good or bad, but simply a co-affliction. The pattern noted by Kanner (1943) was not due to parental *transmission* of feelings of rejection or hostility, but may have represented some degree of co-affliction. Asperger was not subtle in his conclusions. Of the 200 cases evaluated in his research, one or the other parent had signs of the disorder in every case. Asperger's assessment, however, was free of parent blaming and so it may have been (and may now be) easier for parents to consider the implications.

The implications are important for the overall program for the student in the present and in the future. At a very basic level, the presence of some attributes of autism in one or both parents bodes well for the ultimate life success of the child. If the parent has found ways to deal with the disorder without sophisticated therapeutic and educational interventions, the child may also be successful. As parents consider their own strengths in helping their children, a co-afflicted parent has unique insights into dealing with the world. These insights may seem odd to a mainstream clinician, but they are of immense value to the students struggling with their place in the world.

Birth Trauma or Anesthesia

Complications at or near the time of birth have been considered for their contribution to increased risk for autism. Lord, Mulloy, Wendelboe, and

Schopler (1991) examined pre- and perinatal factors and used sibling birth circumstances as control conditions. They reported, "Overall, results support the minor contribution of nonspecific (or not-yet-identi-fied) prenatal factors in the etiology of autism, even when the disorder is not associated with severe mental retardation. However, these differences are relatively small and may be related to birth order" (p. 207).

Nevertheless, parents may become very concerned when their child is diagnosed with autism and search for perinatal incidents as the cause. Any drugs used near the time of birth, including prescribed barbiturates like Seconal (Jensen, 1991), may increase the likelihood of the child having autism. Gualtieri (1991), responding to a question as to whether barbiturate drugs taken during gestation may be a cause of autism, wrote:

> To this question, the answer is perhaps, or probably yes. The problem comes, though, when one considers the list of potential neurotoxins: the potential hazards of natural events like viruses, autoimmunity, or maternal immunoreacticity; of environmental pollutants; of a host of drugs (including alcohol); and even electromagnetic fields. One has to consider the effects not only of single teratogens but also of several potential toxins, at sub-threshold doses, working in concert. It is a question with staggering dimensions. (p. 256)

Some parents have suspected immunizations as a cause of autism. Parents often describe a close temporal relationship between their child receiving a vaccine and the onset of autistic symptoms. Any decision not to immunize a child can cause a major problem as these immunizations prevent dangerous illnesses, and possibly death for some children. Several experts have tried to explain the association of immunization to autism. A child is most likely to receive immunizations at about the time that child would begin to show clear signs of the disorder. The two are most likely linked only by time, not in a cause-and-effect manner. The best advice for parents is to have their children immunized.

Other Possible Causes of Autism

Martin (1995) suggested that a novel class of viruses called "stealth" viruses could be responsible for some cases of autism. He suggested that these viruses are derived from the herpes virus and in laboratory trials can be shown to produce chronic noninflammatory neurological disease in animals. Martin was able to isolate this virus in a 10-year-old child with autism who had symptoms consistent with impaired neurosensory functions due to persistent viral infection. This work is by no means conclusive but is mentioned to point to the possibility of a poorly understood disease process that may cause autism in some people.

PHARMACOLOGICAL INTERVENTIONS

Medical interventions are considered more intrusive than behavioral interventions. Medical interventions include the use of various drugs to assist the student in reducing the frequency or severity of behaviors that interfere with learning. Teachers should be aware of the medications that students take, their potential for changing behavior in students, and their possible side effects. Teachers can be valuable sources of information for parents by sharing behavior changes in their students during classroom hours.

No unique drugs are used to treat children with autism. That is, no drugs are prescribed only to children with autism. Medications used to treat students with autism are commonly used to address problems found in other students with developmental disabilites, seizures, or mental illness.

Categories of Medications

Generally, medications fall in to eight broad categories:

1. Antianxiety medications;
2. Anticonvulsants;
3. Antidepressants;
4. Antipsychotics;
5. Beta-blockers;
6. Opiate blockers;
7. Sedatives; and
8. Stimulants

These categories are delineated by their effects on the individual. As with any medication, side effects may occur.

Antianxiety medications are sometimes prescribed to reduce anxiety, anxiousness, or "nerves." Side effects may include increased behavior problems. Trade names include Valium and Librium.

Anticonvulsants are given to control seizures. Side effects may include drowsiness, gum swelling and tenderness, negative behavioral and cognitive performance. Trade names include Depakote, Dilantin and Tegretol.

Antidepression medications are sometimes prescribed to reduce anxiety, compulsive behaviors, depression, mania, or panic. Side effects may include agitation, insomnia, decreased appetite, and hyperactivity. Trade names include Tofranil and Elavil (to reduce anxiety), Lithium and Depakote (to treat bipolar disorder), and Anafranil and Prozac (to reduce compulsive behavior).

Antipsychotics are in the tranquilizer family of drugs. They are sometimes prescribed to treat severe behavior problems such as aggression, self-injury, agitation, or insomnia. Side effects may include involuntary twitching, tremors, stiffness and sleepiness. Trade names include Haldol, Mellaril, and Thorazine.

Beta-blockers are sometimes prescribed to decrease aggression and hyperactivity by preventing the rush of adrenalin that accompanies these behavior patterns. Side effects may include drowsiness, irritability, and lowered blood pressure. Trade names include Clonidine, Catapres, and Inderal.

Opiate blockers are sometimes prescribed to reduce self-injury. They sometimes improve socialization and general well-being. These drugs block the production of endorphins. Side effects may include drowsiness. Trade names include Naltrexone and Trexan.

Sedatives are sometimes prescribed for insomnia. Side effects may include excitation. Trade names include chloral hydrate, Noctec, and Benadryl.

Stimulants are sometimes prescribed for hyperactivity, attention, or concentration problems. Side effects may include decreased appetite, sadness, tantrums, and hyperactivity after medication wears off. Trade names include Ritalin and Dexedrine.

Teachers who are alert to the effects and possible side effects of the medications children take can assist parents in evaluating the effectiveness of a given medication. Communicating with parents regarding behavior change (both positive and negative) is important. Some medications take several weeks to reach peak effectiveness. Many need to be monitored by the physician on a regular basis. Behavior changes can alert the physician to alter the level of medication, if necessary. Because the teacher typically sees the student for a large part of the day, teacher and parent collaboration is necessary for a full accounting of the effects of medication.

Medication Administration

Teachers of students with autism must be prepared to share responsibility for the administration of medication. Mulligan-Ault, Guess, Struth, and Thompson (1988) found that, in over 85% of the classrooms for students with severe disabilities, at least one student required the administration of medication during school hours. In 47% of these classrooms, the teacher was responsible for administering the medication. Many different systems of medication administration management and responsibility are used in schools. Teachers should carefully review the district procedures for medication administration. Typically, parental request forms, a physician's authorization (prescription), secure storage procedures, and delineation of responsibility are elements of a district policy. A teacher given responsibility for the administration of medication should insist on thorough training by a qualified medical professional. In no other area of teacher responsibility, perhaps with the exception of physical safety, are mistakes so harmful.

Special provisions must be made to deal with medication. Procedures should be carefully crafted to anticipate the characteristics of these children. For example, students with autism are not likely to remind a teacher of their need for medication. Some students will have unusual reactions to medication even when administered correctly. Obviously, medication mistakes can result in fatalities and needless suffering. Regardless of an educator's preferences or biases in relation to medication, many students with autism will require assistance with medication on a daily basis. Sound practices in this regard are an essential responsibility of educators in close cooperation with the family and other team members.

Dickey (1987) offers "Five Rights" relating to medication administration. These five rights call for the person responsible for administering medication to ensure that the **right dose** of the **right medication** is provided to the **right person** at the **right time** by means of the **right route**. These five rights guide each and every administration of medication. In addition, no first dose of any new medication should be administered at school, since potentially severe reactions could result. Documentation of all medication administrations and even failure to administer must be accurate and complete.

Students with autism may resist taking medication. For the student known to be resistant, the parents, teacher, and a medical professional should explore the array of options that can be used if the student becomes resistant. These include breaking the medication into smaller pieces, mixing it with pleasant tasting foods or drinks, or modifying the manner of administration (e.g., liquid rather than capsules). Parent participation in such preincident planning is essential. In no case should an actively resistant child be forced to take a medication. This can result in the child choking or aspirating on the medication especially if the child is lying down (Graff, Mulligan-Ault, Guess, Taylor, & Thompson, 1990). If medication refusal is chronic, a functional assessment should be conducted to establish what function the refusal serves. Any intervention designed for medication refusal should be instructional and/or preventive. Wong and Whalley (1986) recommend the simplest approach: wait 20–30 minutes, then try again.

School Drug Policy

Every school should have a policy dealing with medication or operate under a sound district policy. Schools serving the needs of children with autism must give special attention to this issue. Teachers and staff can face career-destroying consequences for errors of commission or omission if a child should suffer ill effects or die. Any comprehensive policy must, at minimum, address the following points:

1. Procedures for receiving medications and maintaining information about their correct use.
2. Procedures for secure storage of medications.
3. Controlled administration and documentation of administration.
4. Procedures for noting and acting on adverse or unusual reactions including immediate parent notification.
5. Procedures for over-the-counter medications with regulation prohibiting their use except as directly authorized by parents with the concurrence of appropriate medical professionals at the school or within the district.
6. For medication intended to influence behavior, direct observation, recording, charting, and analyzing of key indicator behaviors both before and during treatment. This information to be shared with the family and, with the parents' consent, the prescribing physician.
7. Policy statement on how the IEP will reflect the medication administration plan and, when needed, educator responses to the effects of medication on the child.

These guidelines can help provide reliable administration of medication and protect educators, students, and families from the potentially dire consequences of errors.

Endorphins, Medications, and Behavior

An interesting hypothesis for the common failure of children with autism to develop early bonding was advanced by Panksepp and colleagues (Panksepp & Lessing, 1991). Panksepp suggested that, as mothers hold and comfort their newborns, endorphins are released into the bloodstream. This rush of endorphins is pleasurable to the infant and has the effect of increasing the desire of the child for more social interaction. The child becomes, in effect, "addicted" to the social bonding due to the very positive neurochemical consequences. For many children with autism, this process does not work. These children tend to have very high levels of endorphins and therefore get little or no neurochemical pleasure from being held and cuddled. As these levels tend to remain high during early childhood, the child has little motivation to seek physical comfort from parents. This hypothesis is strengthened when drugs designed to reduce the abnormally high levels of endorphins are given, thereby permitting the child to be more receptive neurochemically to the rewarding affects of physical contact. Drugs such as Naltrexone act in such a manner.

Studies on the effect of Naltrexone have been mixed. The neurochemical impacts may be complex and are further complicated when personality factors of the child and parents are considered. It is certainly possible that a window of opportunity exists during which the neurochemical pleasures of infant-parent bonding are most pronounced. Research continues on these and related social-biochemical associations.

SUMMARY

In addition to the educational and behavioral challenges that students with autism face, many of these students also have a host of difficulties of a medical nature. This results in a "forced partnership" among families, educators, and medical professionals. Families typically are introduced to autism through medical professionals involved in the initial diagnosis and evaluation of their children. Although many families spend considerable effort and energy searching for possible causes, determining etiology is not critical for successful educational programming.

Although most students with autism are healthy, a significant proportion have seizure disorders and require medications to control these seizures. These drugs often have side effects that have a serious impact on students' ability to learn. School districts must have policies in place to safeguard their students and their teachers regarding medical issues and possible complications. The IEP is the logical vehicle for educators' involvement in medical issues faced by students with autism.

REVIEW QUESTIONS

1. What medical problems commonly found in students with autism do educators need to be familiar with?

2. What are the educational implications of the medical problems of students with autism?

3. If we knew what caused autism, how would educators alter their instructional programs?

4. Are there benefits for educators knowing the causes of autism?

5. What procedures and safeguards should be in place regarding the administration of medication in your classroom?

REFERENCES

Akefeldt, A., & Gillberg, C. (1991). Hypomelanosis of Ito in three cases with autism and autistic-like conditions. *Developmental Medicine and Child Neurology, 33*, 737–743.

American Psychiatric Association. (1994). Diagnostic and statistical manual of mental disorders (4th ed.). Washington, DC: Author.

Barton, M., & Volkmar, F. (1998). How commonly are known medical conditions associated with autism? *Journal of Autism and Developmental Disorders, 28*, 273–278.

Bauman, M. (1991). Microscopic neuroanatomic abnormalities in autism. *Pediatrics, 87*(Suppl.), 791–795.

Bauman, M., & Kemper, T. (1994). Neuroanatomic observations of the brain in autism. In M. Bauman & T. Kemper (Eds.), *The neurobiology of autism* (pp. 119–145). Baltimore, MD: Johns Hopkins University Press.

Berkell, D. E. (1992). *Autism: Identification, education, and treatment.* Hillsdale, NJ: Lawrence Erlbaum.

Berthier, M. L., Bayes, A., & Tolosa, E. S. (1983). Magnetic resonance imaging in patients with concurrent Tourette's disorder and Asperger's syndrome. *Journal of the American Academy of Child and Adolescent Psychiatry, 32*, 633–639.

Berthier, M. L., Starkenstein, S. E., & Leiguarda, R. (1990). Developmental cortical anomalies in Asperger's syndrome: Neuroradiological findings in two patients. *Journal of Neuropsychiatry and Clinical Neuroscience, 2*, 197–201.

Buitelaar, J. K., van Engeland, H., de Kogel, C. H., de Vries, H., van Hooff, J. A., & van Ree, J. M. (1992). Deficits in social behavior in autism and their modification by a synthetic adrenocorticotrophic hormone (4–9) analog. *Experientia, 48*, 391–394.

Ciesielski, K., Courchesne, E., & Elmasian, R. (1990). Effects of focused selective attention tasks on event-related potentials in autistic and normal individuals. *Electroencephalography and Clinical Neurophysiology, 75*, 207–220.

Coker, S., & Melnyk, A. (1991). Rett syndrome and mitochondrial enzyme deficiencies. *Journal of Child Neurology, 6*, 164–166.

Courchesne, E. (1991). Neuroanatomic imaging in autism. *Pediatrics, 87*, S781–S790.

Courchesne, E., Courchesne, R., Hicks, G., & Lincoln, A. (1985). Functioning of the brain-stem auditory pathway in non-retarded autistic individuals. *Electroencephalography and Clinical Neurophysiology, 61*, 491–501.

Cruickshank, W. M. (1966). *The teacher of brain-injured children: A discussion of the bases for competency.* Syracuse, NY: Syracuse University Press.

Deykin, E. Y., & MacMahon, G. (1979). The incidence of seizures among children with autism. *American Journal of Psychiatry, 136*, 1310–1312.

Dickey, S. (1987). *A guide to the nursing of children.* Baltimore, MD: Williams and Wilkins.

Edwards, D. R., & Bristol, M. M. (1991). Autism: Early identification and management in family practice. *American Family Physician, 44*, 1755–1764.

Epilepsy Foundation of America. (1996). *Seizure recognition and first aid.* Landover, MD: Author.

Fish, B., & Ritvo, E. (1979). Psychoses of childhood. In V. Noshpitz (Ed.), *Basic handbook of child psychiatry* (pp. 249–303). New York: Basic Books.

Folstein, S., & Piven, J. (1991). Etiology of autism: Genetic influences. *Pediatrics, 87*, S767–S773.

Gillberg, I. C. (1991a). Autistic syndrome with onset at age 31 years: Herpes encephalitis as a possible model for childhood autism. *Developmental Medicine and Child Neurology, 33*, 920–924.

Gillberg, I. C. (1991b). The treatment of epilepsy in autism. *Journal of Autism and Developmental Disorders, 21*, 61–77.

Graff, J. C., Mulligan-Ault, M., Guess, D., Taylor, M., & Thompson, B. (1990). *Health care for students with disabilites: An illustrated medical guide for the classroom.* Baltimore, MD: Paul H. Brookes.

Grillon, C., Courchesne, E., & Akshoomoff, N. (1989). Brainstem and middle latency auditory evoked potentials in autism and developmental language disorder. *Journal of Autism and Developmental Disorders, 19*, 255–269.

Gualtieri, T. (1991). Response to Mr. Jensen's letter. *Journal of Autism and Developmental Disorders, 21*, 255–257.

Gualtieri, T., Evans, R. W., & Patterson, D. R. (1987). The medical treatment of autistic people: Problems and side effects. In E. Schopler & G. Mesibov (Eds.), *Neurolobiological issues in autism* (pp. 374–388). New York: Plenum.

Haas, R. H. (1988). Rett syndrome. *Journal of Child Neurology, 3*(Suppl.), S1–S4.

Hashimoto, T., Tayama, M., Miyazaki, M., Murakawa, K., & Kuroda, Y. (1993). Brainstem and cerebellar vermis involvement in autistic children. *Journal of Child Neurology, 8*, 149–153.

Holttum, J. R., Minshew, N. J., Sanders, R. S., & Phillips, N. E. (1992). Magnetic resonance imaging of the posterior fossa in autism. *Biologica Psychiatry, 32*, 1091–1100.

Illingworth, R. S., & Lister, J. (1964). The critical or sensitive period with special reference to certain feeding problems in infants and children. *Journal of Pediatrics, 65*, 839–848.

Ives, C. C., Harris, S. L., & Wolchik, S. A. (1978). Food refusal in an autistic type child treated by a multi-component forced feeding procedure. *Journal of Behavior Therapy and Experimental Psychiatry, 9*, 61–64.

Jensen, R. A. (1991). Autism and the use of hypnotic barbiturates in obsterics and pediatrics. *Journal of Autism and Developmental Disorders, 21*, 254–255.

Kanner, L. (1943). Autistic disorders of affective content. *Nervous Child, 2*, 217–250.

Kanner, L. (1971). Follow-up study of eleven children originally reported in 1943. *Journal of Autism and Childhood Schizophrenia, 1*, 119–145.

Kemper, T. L., & Bauman, M. L. (1993). The contribution of neuropathologic studies to the understanding of autism. *Neurology Clinics, 11*, 175–187.

Kleiman, M., Neff, S., & Rosman, N. (1992). The brain in infantile autism: Are posterior fossa structures abnormal? *Neurology, 42*, 753–760.

Lincoln, A. J., Courchesne, E., Harms, L., & Allen, M. (1993). Contextual probability evaluation in autistic, receptive developmental language disorder, and control children: Event-related brain potential evidence. *Journal of Autism and Developmental Disorders, 23*, 37–58.

Lord, C., Mulloy, C., Wendelboe, M. & Schopler, E. (1991). Pre- and perinatal factors in high-functioning females and males with autism. *Journal of Autism and Developmental Disorders, 21,* 197–209.

Lotspeich, L. J., & Ciaranello, R. D. (1993). The neurobiology and genetics of infantile autism. *International Review of Neurobiology, 35,* 87–129.

Martin, H. P. (1973). Nutrition: Its relationship to children's physical, mental, and emotional development. *American Journal of Clinical Nutrition, 16,* 766–775.

Martin, W. J. (1995). Stealth viruses isolated from an autistic child. *Journal of Autism and Developmental Disorders, 25,* 223–224.

Minshew, N. (1991). Indices of neural function in autism: Clinical and biologic implications. *Pediatrics, 87*(Suppl.), S774–S780.

Mulligan-Ault, M., Guess, D., Struth, L., & Thompson, B. (1988). The implementation of health related procedures in classrooms for students with severe multiple impairments. *The Journal of the Association for Persons with Severe Handicaps, 13,* 100–109.

Mundy, P., & Sheinkopf, S. (1993). Social behavior and the neurology of autism. *International Pediatrics, 8,* 205–210.

Nowell, M., Hackney, D., Muraki, A., & Coleman, M. (1990). Varied MR appearance of autism: Fifty-three pediatric patients having the full autistic syndrome. *Magnetic Resonance Imaging, 8,* 811–816.

Olsson, I., Steffenburg, S., & Gillberg, C. (1988). Epilepsy in autism and autistic-like conditions: A population-based study. *Archives of Neurology, 45,* 666–668.

Ornitz, E. M. (1987). Neurophysiologic studies of infantile autism. In D. J. Cohen & A. Donellan (Eds.), *Handbook of autism and pervasive developmental disorders* (pp. 148–165). New York: John Wiley.

Panksepp, J., & Lessing, P. (1991). A synopsis of an open-trial of Naltrexone treatment of autism with four children. *Journal of Autism and Developmental Disabilities, 21,* 243–249.

Percy, A. K., Zoghbi, H. Y., Lewis, K. R., & Jankovic, J. (1988). Rett syndrome: Qualitative and quantitative differentiation from autism. *Journal of Child Neurology, 3*(Suppl.), S65–S67.

Piven, J., Berhier, M., Starkstein, S., Nehme, E., Pearlson, G., & Folstein, S. (1990). Magnetic resonance imaging evidence for a defect of cerebral cortical development in autism. *American Journal of Psychiatry, 147,* 734–739.

Piven, J., & Palmer, P. (1997). Cognitive deficits in parents from multiple-incidence autism families. *Journal of Child Psychology and Psychiatry, 38,* 1011–1021.

Piven, J., Palmer, P., Jacobi, D., Childress, D., & Arndt, S. (1997). Autism phenotype: Evidence from a family history study of multiple-incidence autism families. *American Journal of Psychiatry, 154,* 185–190.

Powers, M. D. (1989). *Children with autism: A parent's guide.* Rockville, MD: Woodbine House.

Riordan, M. M., Iwata, B. A., Finney, J. W., Wohl, M. K., & Stanley, A. E. (1984). Behavioral assessment and treatment of chronic food refusal in handicapped children. *Journal of Applied Behavior Analysis, 17,* 327–341.

Ritvo, E. R., Jorde, L. B., Mason-Brothers, A., Freeman, B. J., Pingree, C., Jones, M. B., McMahon, W. M., Petersen, P. B., Jenson, W. R., & Mo, A. (1989). The UCLA-University of Utah epidemiologic survey of autism: Prevalence. *American Journal of Psychiatry, 146,* 194–199.

Ritvo, E. R., Mason-Brothers, A., Freeman, B. J., Pingree, C., Jenson, W. R., McMahon, W. M., Peterson, P. B., Jorde, L. B., Mo, A., & Ritvo, A. (1990). The UCLA-University of Utah epidemiologic survey of autism: The etiologic role of rare diseases. *American Journal of Psychiatry, 147,* 1614–1621.

Rutter, M. (1970). Autistic children: Infancy to adulthood. *Seminars in Psychiatry, 2,* 435–450.

Rutter, M., Baily, A., Bolton, P., & Le Couteur, A. (1994). Autism and known medical conditions: Myth and substance. *Journal of Child Psychology and Psychiatry, 35,* 311–322.

Sahley, T., & Panksepp, J. (1987). Brain opioids and autism: An updated analysis of possible linkages. *Journal of Autism and Developmental Disorders, 17,* 201–216.

Tsai, L. (1998) Medical interventions for students with autism. In R. L. Simpson & B. S. Myles (Eds.), *Educating children and youth with autism* (pp. 277–314). Austin, TX: Pro-Ed.

Tuchman, R., Rapin, I., & Shinnar, S. (1991). Autistic and dysphasic children: II. Epilepsy. *Pediatrics, 6,* 1219–1225.

Volkmar, F. R., & Nelson, D. S. (1990). Seizure disorders in autism. *Journal of the American Academy of Child and Adolescent Psychiatry, 29,* 127–129.

Vukicevic, J., & Siegel, B. (1990). Pervasive developmental disorder in monozygotic twins. *Journal of the American Academy of Child and Adolescent Psychiatry, 29,* 897–900.

Whaley, L. F., & Wong, D. L. (1987). *Nursing care of infants and children.* St. Louis, MO: C. V. Mosby.

Wing, L. & Gould, J. (1979). Severe impairments of social interaction and associated abnormalities in children: Epidemiology and classification. *Journal of Autism and Developmental Disorders, 9,* 11–30.

Wong, D. L., & Whaley, L. F. (1986). *Clinical handbook of pediatric nursing.* St. Louis, MO: C. V. Mosby.

Zimmerman, A., Frye, V., & Potter, N. (1993). Immunological aspects of autism. *International Pediatrics, 8,* 199–204.

Chapter 4

THEORY AND CONTROVERSY

Key Points

- The history of autism has helped create an unusual and complicated set of beliefs, traditions, and theories of autism
- The field is heavily influenced by tolerance of nonscientific theoretical orientations
- Behavioral theories have made tremendous contributions, while challenging unvalidated and counterproductive practices, yet this orientation serves as a lighting rod for criticism
- Research on autism has a mixed impact on current educational practices

---

INTRODUCTION

Perhaps more than any other field in education, psychology, and the human services, controversies have surrounded autism, the nature of autism, and the interventions used to help people with autism. Many of these controversies challenge the very nature of our understanding of autism, but many controversies have pitted parents against professionals. This chapter explores some of these controversies and presents strategies for evaluating new treatments.

WHAT IS A THEORY?
WHY IS THEORY IMPORTANT?

What guides the search for understanding in autism? People have many different ways of knowing about this disorder. Some of these ways are guided by science and research, with an emphasis on controlled experimentation, data gathering, and replication. Other approaches are guided by personal experience. In yet another way, philosophy drives the search for understanding. In autism, our understanding often appears to be driven by what people *wish to see* happen.

Controversy in the field of autism is closely tied to theory. Controversy over theory is common in academic disciplines and often helps fuel a healthy competition among adherents of different viewpoints. But autism is quite unlike the academic discussions of geologists (on plate tectonics, for example) or biologists (on the pace of evolution) in that the challenges are immediate and theoretical discourse actively shapes what families and professionals do with children. Controversy is neither good nor bad if it leads to solving the problems faced by students with autism and their families. Controversy regarding theories, even the most poorly supported and implausible, can yield important insights that may allow professionals to select more effective treatments and practices.

What is a theory? In psychology, a *theory* is "a general principle formulated to explain a group of related phenomena" (Chaplin, 1975, p. 538). The same source defines a *principle* as a "working hypothesis or a maxim for conduct or for scientific investigation" (p. 407). Again taking a definition from Chaplin, an *hypothesis* is "an assumption which serves as a tentative explanation." From another point of view, an hypothesis is a "question put to nature to be answered by an experiment or series of observations" (Chaplin, 1975, p. 24). A theory of autism, then, can be seen as a statement of how autism is caused or expressed in a person, coupled with a series of statements or assumptions that can be *tested* or *directly observed*, either by experiment or observation. A theory that is not testable is not worthy of being called a theory. Some theories may challenge existing knowledge but the challenge must contain testable elements. Through testing, experimenting, and observing, theories are strengthened or dismantled.

Are theories even necessary? Many behavioral researchers would say no. Skinner (1956), for example, proposed that direct observation of a behavioral phenomenon and investigation of controlling variables was sufficient to understand that phenomenon. Instead of relying on theory, Skinner argued for active hypothesis testing. A body of knowledge would grow and evolve that need not be tied to theory but to established empirical evidence. Of course, even this argument against the need for theories can be seen as a theory of sorts but it illustrates the difference in value placed on theory among different autism researchers.

Schlinger (1995) applied a behavioral view to a comparison of theories of child development. He considered that the work of researchers is guided by their theoretical orientation. To understand in part why such disparity exists between behavioral and developmentally oriented researchers one must gain facility with the language used to understand the phenomenon under study. He made an important point in the following selection.

> How we talk about our subject matter determines, to varying degrees, what we do about it. For instance, if developmental psychologists talk about hypothetical cognitive events as explanations of behavior, that may determine the kinds of research methods they use to study the behavior, or the kinds of strategies they might employ in applied settings. A behavior analysis of the traditional language of developmental psychology may help to elucidate more objective controlling variables and to suggest more scientific ways of studying the behavior. (Schlinger, 1995, p. x)

Behavioral researchers seek observable events, record them, and then analyze them, whereas cognitive developmentalists typically work with hypothetical constructs. These differences result in differences in what is sought or studied and what, ultimately, is found.

It is quite appropriate for educators to ask what role theory plays in delivering programs for students with autism. Theories involving neurology and learning are excellent examples. Unlike some areas of disability, there is no clear linkage between possible neurological damage in autism and specific educational interventions. Smith (1991) noted that it is not yet known how to directly link neural findings to effective educational activities for a specific child. This is particularly true for students with autism. Without firm linkages, a high degree of teacher judgment is needed when selecting interventions. These teacher judgments will be based primarily on teachers' theoretical understanding of autism. Educators might be perplexed, and with good reason, as to why researchers and other leaders in autism seem to be so fond of some treatments, views, or approaches and so negative toward others. But without an understanding of their own theoretical orientations, educators are left without the judgment tools and the discernment needed to negotiate the minefield of controversy. Without these tools, a biological explanation is just as valid as a psychogenic one and a program based on sensory interventions is just as logical as one based on behavioral concepts.

Theory and Research in Autism

Research in many fields of study is relatively unified. Theories are generated, experiments conducted, evidence gathered, and, based on the evidence, some theories and claims gain credibility while others are seen as less plausible. To some degree, the study of the nature of autism and treatments works this way. But, unlike that of other disability areas, a strange set of factors converge to make research in autism unusual. Just as the characteristics of students with autism have been promoted as unique, so too are the factors surrounding the *culture of autism*. This culture has had a complicated impact on theory and research. It has, at its worst, allowed very wasteful (and even harmful) treatments to become established. It has also contributed to a lack of discernment on the part of many educators and parents. This is clearly changing.

Catherine Maurice, in the publication of *Let Me Hear Your Voice*, confronted these problems head on (Maurice, 1993). Maurice argued that supporters of remarkable discoveries should provide *evidence* before their claims are taken seriously. She further called for a general agreement on the scientific formats used to investigate these discoveries. Maurice's cautions are not merely of academic interest; evidence regarding the validity of a discovery *prior to its popular acceptance* will result in good and useful applications while minimizing wasteful applications. The authors of this text firmly believe that reasonable criteria for testing theoretical assertions can and must be put forward. Evidence can and must be presented to peers for their appraisal. Perhaps most importantly, testable hypotheses must be presented, which in turn can be investigated by researchers. Results can then be either replicated or not replicated and the field given the chance to make important decisions about the value of treatments.

The way an individual perceives a person with autism or any disability is largely influenced by his or her experiences, knowledge and view of what autism is. Professionals in education, psychology, medicine, and other fields often have very different perspectives on autism. These variations in perspective shape the way new information is presented and received. For researchers, their perspective shapes the questions they pose and influences their interpretations of the data obtained. Our understanding of autism is also influenced by our situation and the consequences of viewing the disorder in this way. An obvious example is the heart-felt thanks and enthusiastic reception Rimland received for advocating a biologically based model of autism, decisively countering the parent blaming, psychogenic tradition.

The alliance between the parent-led advocacy community and the professional community is especially close in the field of autism. This is both a strength and a potential source of weakness. The combined assault on the problems posed by autism has effectively gathered attention and resources. Close cooperation has allowed the professional community to know the needs of those touched by autism. However, it is a weakness when *fashionable thinking* replaces adherence to the canons of rigorous scientific investigation and systematic research of critical topics. To some extent, the family-professional alliance in autism has hindered the effort to reduce fallacious claims by promoters who prey on the hopes (and resources) of others. Educators and parents are faced with a bewildering array of often wildly contradictory claims about the effectiveness of some treatments. Families' beliefs in untested treatments often cause professionals to stop asking the hard questions and providing clear, scientifically sound (but sometimes unpopular) advice. When alliances result in professionals who are unwilling or unable to say that certain treatments are of little or no value (and are possibly even harmful), a real problem exists. Consider that the Autism Society of America (ASA) maintains a policy of neither endorsing nor condemning any treatment for autism and the scope of the problem may be obvious.

Notes On Terminology in Special Education

It would be wonderful if our selection of terms could be limited to everyday English. Unfortunately, special educators have unique ways of using some fairly common terms. Consider the following:

> *Therapy* generally means the treatment of disease or a pathological condition (Bolander, 1992). While this may seem consistent with the goals of special education, a related term, *treatment*, often used as a synonym for therapy, shows otherwise. Treatment means "the care and management of a patient; the application of medicinal remedies or surgery in combating disease or pathological conditions; therapy" (Bolander, 1992, p. 267). By these definitions, the person being helped is a *patient* and the nature of services are *medically* oriented. Many educators of students with autism recognize the tendency toward "medicalization" of school programs for these students.

Next, consider the term *education*: "The process of training and developing the knowledge, skill, mind, character, etc., especially by formal schooling; teaching; training" (McKenchie, 1983, p. 576). This is what teachers do and the focus of their attention is on individuals referred to as *students*. The teachers' mission is broad, encompassing academics, daily living, character and social ability, and vocational preparation. While the teachers' mission is extensive, it does not include medical treatment nor therapy in the sense that members of the healing arts understand it.

Schools are required by IDEA and other legislation to provide *related services* to help students take advantage of educational opportunities and benefit from special education. Related services refer to the array of developmental, corrective, and other supportive services required for a student with disabilities to benefit from special education. Related services include special transportation services, speech and language therapy, audiology, psychological services, physical and occupational therapy, school health services, counseling and medical services for diagnostic and evaluation purposes, rehabilitation counseling, social work services, and parent counseling and training.

The provision of these services (therapy, treatment, education, and related services) is among the most controversial aspects of special education today. The extent to which a related service is required is rarely easy to determine. The costs of services, as well as concerns about providing services that may interfere with other learning (such as socialization) tend to make school districts conservative in approving such services. It is interesting that the first case based on PL 94-142 involved the provision of related services (*Board of Education v. Rowley*, 1982). The Supreme Court ruled that Amy Rowley, a child with a hearing impairment who received some related services was not entitled to a full-time interpreter. The court held that since Amy was making satisfactory progress without the interpreter, the appropriateness of her education and special education was being demonstrated. The Rowley case set an important precedent. If a student is making satisfactory progress, a school's program for the student can be seen as "appropriate." Of course this raises a host of questions about the ambitiousness of the goals and objectives, the nature of progress for students with disabilities, and the systems of measurement and evaluation used.

Since "appropriate" (not *best* or *maximum feasible*) benefit remains the federal standard for students with disabilities, a fairly modest set of expectations is fostered in special education. This frequently comes into conflict with the culture of autism. Many parents of children with autism are well aware of and believe they should expect the best education and related services shown to be effective. Perhaps it is the pervasiveness of autism, coupled with the startling progress some students make under optimized programs, that drives families to seek *best* practices rather than settling for less. In response to the advocacy efforts of families and professionals, several states have gone beyond the federal minimum and have raised their standards and commitments to all students with disabilities in their state constitutions.

CONTROVERSY INVOLVING THEORY AND TREATMENT

The history of autism is replete with high levels of speculation and extreme positions. Itard was influenced by theories of "wolf children," where a naive child with a disability like Victor merely awaited the benefits of civilization (Wing, 1976). (Unlike more modern controversies, Itard was apologetic when his success with young Victor failed to support his theoretical ambitions.) Kanner clarified that autism differed from other conditions, but hinted that parents might be responsible for the disorder. Bettelheim (1967) was more outrageous in his speculations and his absurd parent-blame theories of causation. But Bettelheim's controversy today is not in the extent of his theoretical "weirdness," but the degree to which it targeted parents. Several current theories and treatments rival Bettelheim's in their outlandishness. It is one thing to propose a theory as a brainstorming exercise, but when the theory leads to elaborate and expensive treatments with little attention to their effectiveness, major problems are to be expected.

Autism is not the only disability that has inspired controversy. The field of learning disabilities (LD), the largest of the special education categories, also had an early history of controversy (O'Shea, O'Shea, & Algozzine, 1998; Silver, 1987). O'Shea et al. (1998) listed 10 major controversies (including "brain retraining" and interventions based on scotopic sensitivity syndrome). They concluded that, "Despite the reported absence of supportive data, followers continue to support unorthodox assessment and treatment practices" (O'Shea, et al., 1998, p. 127). Silver (1987) provided these summary comments about controversial LD therapies:

> Parents of children or adolescents with disabilities want the best treatment. They are vulnerable to any person who reports having a quick solution and possibly a cure. It is important that professionals be informed of these controversial therapies so that they can educate parents on what is known about these treatments. . . . Professionals must educate parents on proposed new treatments. **Parents need to ask**

themselves why this amazing approach is not used by everyone [emphasis added]. If the person proposing the treatment tells them that "most professionals are biased and do not believe the finding because they are different from the traditional treatments," they should feel free to ask to see the data supporting the concept and the treatment. They should not accept without question popular books published by the person proposing the treatment or information provided in a flyer or on a television show by the person proposing the treatment. They should not put their son or daughter through something unproved and unlikely to help. (pp. 599–100)

These comments could just as well be applied to the field of autism. Unfortunately, the level of self-awareness of the controversies found in the LD field typically has been missing in autism. Relatively few objective analyses of controversial theories and interventions have appeared in the autism field. As we have stated frequently in this book, the field has been hesitant to engage in serious self-policing of unwise therapies and bogus claims. Rather, the field has developed a tendency to accept, and sometimes embrace, concepts and interventions, no matter how odd, and regardless of how little evidence exists to support them. Other theories and treatments, on the other hand, remain controversial *in spite of* the objective evidence that supports them. Finally, many ideas are controversial because they challenge existing concepts, but with familiarity and collected evidence of support, such controversy subsides. Some of the theories, interventions, and controversies include (a) theory of mind, (b) facilitated communication, (c) sensory theories, including sensory integration and auditory integration, (d) personal history as a source of knowledge (e) psychogenic theories, and (f) controversy surrounding research by Lovaas.

Theory of Mind

One of the theories to gain prominence recently is referred to as Theory of Mind (TOM) (Baron-Cohen, 1995; Frith, 1989). This is an extension of cognitive theory with special application to autism. Students with autism present a unique opportunity for research for social-cognitive theorists. These students may have the intelligence and general perception of their environment, which suggests that they should develop reasonable social skills with skillful teaching and treatment. Students' difficulties with social awareness and skills, combined with their apparent capacity, has led some researchers to redefine autism as a condition characterized by a deficit in "perspective-taking." Said another way, students with autism fail to develop the skill to share experiences and events with others (or to share "joint attention"). This failure to develop joint attention is a prerequisite to understanding the perspectives of others and was described by Mundy in Chapter 1.

Among the main deficits in autism is an appreciation that other people work from an intentional stance, or maintain their own points of view. This is critical in the development of communication, especially for conversation. Hadwin, Baron-Cohen, Howlin, and Hill (1997) suggested that, "effective conversation relies on an understanding that people know different things and that these states of knowledge can be shared" (p. 520–521). This inability to appreciate that others are thinking is the basis for a theory of mind. According to this theory, a student with autism fails to generate swiftly evolving hypotheses about why people do what they do and fails to recognize that others may have information that he or she does not have. This student may not conceive of other people as thinking, sensing beings who construct their own frames of reference. As a result the student with autism may see others as "objects." Students might know of their own needs and rely on whatever strategies are successful to meet their needs. The key strategy these students lack, however, is the ability to infer or comprehend the intentions of others.

Baron-Cohen (1995) refers to this characteristic in students with autism as "mindblindness" and likens it to blindness or hearing impairment. Baron-Cohen's theory relies on four concepts including:

1. Typically developing students interpret social behavior by assigning motives, beliefs, etc. to others;
2. Students with autism lack at least some of this "mind reading" skill;
3. These skills are part of the cognitive structure of the brain; and
4. Four developmental mechanisms in an individual promote perspective sharing. These mechanisms include:
   - *Intentionality Detector*: interprets motion as goal and desire;
   - *Eye-Direction Detector*: detects presence of another's eyes, computes whether eyes are directed toward self or elsewhere, and infers what is being seen by another;
   - *Shared-Attention Mechanism*: builds triadic representations (Agent, Self, Object);
   - *Theory-of-Mind Mechanism*: infers the full range of mental states (volitional, perceptual and epistemic) into social behavior.

Baron-Cohen and others take this further by suggesting a deficit in a sub-anatomical theory of mind "module." This promotes the idea that a module component could be identified and perhaps repaired, or the deficits otherwise mitigated, as might be the case in a computer system repair. Indeed, this theory draws many parallels to information processing and computer networking. However, serious research involving the existence of a "mind module" is years away. How TOM differs from simply saying the child with autism is less capable of learning complex social information is not clear. Several examples are found in the TOM description on the following page.

Theory of mind has given rise to some interesting instructional efforts. Hadwin et al. (1997) looked at the cognitive and communication problems of students with autism and sought to teach conversational enhancement skills and use of "mental state terms" for conversation. The students were taught to identify obvious facial and body language signs for emotions, and later to appreciate that emotions have cognitive "causes." Play was used as one instructional tool. Some limited improvement was noted in understanding emotions and belief statements, but broader changes in social communication skills were not seen. Conversational skills did not improve nor did the use of descriptive terms about mental states.

It is difficult to explain these results. The authors noted that progress may have been made but was poorly generalized to the test situation. The authors noted that improvement might have been detected with longer term instruction. Our own interpretation includes the possibility that relying on primarily cognitive teaching strategies resulted in relatively weak learning. In any case, this study points to the challenge of using teaching strategies based on theory of mind in classroom applications.

If successful interventions or teaching strategies can be found to substantially improve the TOM capacities of students with autism, then the theory itself is weakened. If, on the other hand, a number of studies convincingly demonstrate that TOM deficits are essentially intractable and a fixed attribute of autism, then the theory may be strengthened. Ironically, this theory incorporates a subtle disincentive to find and validate effective strategies for teaching students with autism how to better perceive the intentions of others.

Researchers from various schools of thought explore these questions in a variety of ways; some recent studies have yielded provocative findings as to the nature, and even the actual existence, of "mindreading" capability. Charman and Lynggaard (1998) used photographs to improve student performance on the classic Smarties Test. The Smarties Test is a test of false belief (Perner, Leekam, & Wimmer, 1987) in which students are shown a container of Smarties, a candy known to them, and asked what they believe is inside. Students typically say "Smarties." They are then shown that pencils, not Smarties are inside the container. These students are then asked, "What will other students think is inside the container when they see it?" Students without autism report that naive students will say that Smarties are inside. Students with autism typically report that naive students will say that pencils are inside. The failure of

Theory of Mind

Jessica Marcus

Picture yourself enjoying a scoop of ice cream at the local Baskin and Robbins, watching the events unfold around you. A small child walks repeatedly up and down the rows of ice cream, pausing briefly to gaze at certain of the flavors. Pointing to first one, then another, she eventually leaves the parlor with a smile on her face and a scoop of Rocky Road on a sugar cone. Her behavior needs no explanation. We simply take the perspective of a young child having a difficult time deciding which flavor to choose (they all look so good) and finally (considering the three samples she tasted) making a well-informed decision. Observing other people and understanding their behavior often depends on this ability to ascribe mental states to others.

By the time typically developing children reach school-age, they are able to infer what other people might know, think, or believe in a given situation. Perspective taking is one source of social cognition and key to the development of theory of mind (TOM). Someone without the ability to imagine or represent states of mind that another person might incorporate would have great difficulty providing possible motives or reasons for the behavior of others. It could even be unclear why a child would pace, in such an unusual manner, back and forth in front of the ice cream counter.

Theory of mind includes not only the ability to take the beliefs of others into account, but also the ability to appreciate the difference between one's own belief and the belief of someone else. Without an appreciation of this difference, it would be impossible for you to understand why anyone would choose Rocky Road ice cream when your personal favorite is vanilla. Without an awareness of this difference, the behavior of others would appear mysterious and confusing at best. Individuals with autism may suffer from deficits in theory of mind, which limit their ability to secure meaning from the social world. The inability to recognize that other people have their own thoughts and feelings, that these thoughts and feelings may be different from their own, and that there can even be different beliefs concerning a single event can provide for an unpredictable and often threatening social environment.

(continued)

Research suggests that the development of joint attention skills may be directly related to the evolving theory of mind and emerging social cognition. Beginning in the early stages of infancy, social interactions routinely involve blinking and gaze direction as clues to focus the attention of others to given events. By the end of the first year of life, infants have the ability to conclude that they and someone else are attending to the same event and can interpret the actions of others as goal-directed and driven by desires. Toddlers can develop elaborate pretend scenarios and understand the charades of others. By the age of 5, children think and talk about states of mind, regularly explaining behavior in terms of underlying motives and intentions. From early games of peek-a-boo, pouring juice for teddy bear, sharing toys, and playing house to making moral judgments, understanding a comedy, or appreciating a compliment, social skills depend on such familiar concepts as knowing, thinking, feeling, believing, wishing, imagining, and perceiving. An inability to conceive of these mental states is analogous to a blindness, leaving persons with autism without the ability to predict the reactions and behaviors of others.

Research indicates that children with autism have difficulty connecting the mental states of others with actual states of affairs. In the classic Sally-Anne experiment, Sally put her marble in a basket and left to go for a walk. While Sally was away, Anne took the marble from the basket and hid it under a box. Typical 3- and 4-year-old children not only know the marble actually is under the box, they also know that Sally, having been tricked, will look for the marble where she originally left it—in the basket. Children with autism, to the contrary, suspected Sally would return to the room and immediately retrieve the marble from under the box. In fact, across a variety of experimental paradigms, we find that individuals with autism show an inability to recognize not only differences between people's mental states and actual states of affairs, but also the existence of mental states entirely. Far from operating on the premise that their own mental states are shared, they function without the propensity to even consider that mental states occur.

Our relationships with others depend on communication. This includes sharing information on many different levels, all of which are mediated by a working theory of mind. We are able to pull together a coherent interpretation of events, using information from a variety of sources, and share it in a very specific way that hinges on understanding mental states. Social relationships require coordination between the mental states of each participant, ensuring that intentions are understood and the information shared is relevant. Social language is saturated with phrases and expressions that compel each participant to continuously decipher obscure meanings and hidden intentions. It makes sense, then, that the level of social skill demonstrated by individuals with autism appears clearly linked to perspective-taking ability.

Social skills training for persons with autism has been a target of intervention in recent years. A variety of techniques, including modeling, coaching, role-play, chaining behaviors, communication books, conversation menus, and turn-taking, have proved helpful in promoting more positive social encounters. Many of these approaches, however, assume basic social-cognitive skills that students with autism may not have. Targeting theory of mind abilities and mental state concepts with problem-solving principles and cognitive strategies, on the other hand, appears to ease some aspects of this impairment. Understanding the range of impairments in theory of mind, common to individuals with autism, may help us to facilitate their own endeavors to understand.

Jessica Marcus is a doctoral candidate in Psychology at the University of Miami in Miami, Florida.

the student with autism to anticipate a natural answer (Smarties in a Smarties can) is seen as a deficit in inference of the other students' perspective—a deficit in theory of mind. Students with autism believe that other students will know what they know. This is one of the classic elements of TOM.

Charm and Lynggaard (1998) made a few changes in the Smarties Test to determine whether students with autism truly showed a deficit in TOM or rather were confused by the verbal demands of the request. In their modification, students were shown the Smarties tube and photographs of four items that conceivably could have been in the Smarties tube. When asked what they believed to be inside the container, students selected the Smarties photo. Next, the students were shown the contents of the container in which pencils instead of Smarties had been placed. Students were asked to identify the photo of what they believed to be in the container. The students selected the photo of the pencils. Then a False Belief Question was asked, (paraphrase) "Before we opened the tube, what did you think was inside (indicating the Smarties tube)?" The results of the modified Smarties Test differed dramatically from the original test. When students with autism were given photographic cues to support their communication, more than twice as many accurately identified the predictions of naive students. The authors suggested that, "prosthetic, or alternative routes to understanding simple social interactions can be taught . . . to circumvent the developmental impairment in theory of mind" (Charman & Lynggaard, 1998, p. 40).

A major challenge to TOM is evident in the results of Charman and Lynggaard and is found in the behavioral literature dating as far back as 1964 when Lindsley advocated the use of behavioral prostheses. In short, Charman and Lynggaard provided students taking the Smarties Test with a prosthetic means of organizing their knowledge and communicating their ideas. Such is the lesson of many educators when they discover that students with autism can perform in ways similar to people without autism when they are provided supports, permanent prompts, guides, or skilled training. Essential TOM capacities, if they do exist, appear as mutable and amenable to change as other developmental characteristics and patterns of behavior.

Another major challenge to TOM is presented by the apparent recovery of some children with autism. Lovaas (1987), for example, reported recovery for 47% of intensively treated children with no special attention given to any defective social cognition module. If Lovaas is correct, intensive treatment resolves intensive problems, and the difficult characteristics of autism are not immutable. From a behavioral perspective, a simpler alternative exists for why these students typically show such poor skill in social cognition and in reading the intentions of others. The tasks embraced by TOM proponents challenge students with autism because of their social basis and requirements for heightened response energy. In the absence of natural reinforcers and success for trying, these students reduce their efforts to try to figure out what others are doing or what others may want them to do and resort to other, less socially sensitive approaches.

Facilitated Communication

Facilitated communication or FC is a means of promoting communication by having a nondisabled person physically support the arm or hand of a student with autism while the student types or writes a message. FC was initially brought to the United States by Biklen (1990) after watching similar demonstrations by Crossley and her colleagues (Crossley & MacDonald, 1984) in Australia. FC has appealed to professionals and families alike, in part because it *assumes* competence in students with autism and proposes that students can express their thoughts, feelings, and desires when given emotional and physical support. This support is provided by a trusted person who maintains hand-to-hand (or sometimes hand to arm or shoulder) contact with the student who, in turn, types his or her message. Initial claims described students with autism writing poetry, prose, and sometimes just the mundane expressions of everyday life.

FC became controversial almost immediately on its introduction to the autism community in the United States. Although the technique appeared similar to augmentative communication procedures used by some students with physical disabilities, it differed in several ways. Most notably, initial proponents underplayed the role of *teaching* needed to help students learn to use the system, and instead stressed that people with autism primarily needed a method of help to *produce* their messages. Several aspects of FC also were challenged by professionals with expertise in learning and communication disorders (Green, 1994a; Prior & Cummins, 1992; Shane, 1994). First, the claims of remarkable vocabulary and literacy skills in children (sometimes under 3 years of age) often stretched credibility, particularly in the absence of any education or training in language arts, reading, spelling, or written expression. Although it certainly is possible that people with no previous reading or writing abilities might demonstrate literacy, the number of children using FC to describe the "prison of autism" and other metaphors caused many in the field to wonder whose ideas were really being expressed (Shane, 1994).

Second, adherents of FC quickly developed an almost cultlike following, while skeptics attacked their claims with increasing vehemence. These positions rapidly devolved into an *us vs. them* debate that lingers to this day. Proponents wrote that "belief in" FC took precedence over refinement of instructional methods to promote it, and that failure to promote communication competence was often a problem of the nondisabled community's commitment to supporting people with autism. Among the more bizarre claims was that FC worked in part due to the ability of students to read the minds of adult facilitators (Haskew & Donnellan, 1992). Some adults were said to be capable facilitators because they easily developed extra-sensory bonds with students; FC difficulties, according to this view, could be caused by "crossed signals" during an ESP transmission. One student with autism, for example, was said to have difficulty typing an accurate message because he was channeling for a second student with autism rather than conveying his own thoughts!

Skeptics point out that the *assumption* of independent communication *while one person was producing the message of another* contains an inherent problem: authorship (Rimland, 1991). Although potential coercion by an adult was seen as an obvious, if rare, possibility, a more subtle concern involved the possibility of *unintended* influence of a facilitator over the student. For example, adults who wanted to "hear" a particular message from a student might inadvertently help the student produce the message by unintentionally applying directional pressure to the student's hand while typing. These concerns exploded during the late 1980s and through the 1990s when graphic claims of sexual abuse via FC resulted in children being removed from their families (Calculator & Hatch, 1995; Hostler, Allaire, & Christoph, 1993). In an environment rife with argument over the veracity of FC, judges were now being called on to evaluate the believability of claims using this means of communication.

In most political, social, and scientific environments, decisions are made based on the accumulation of evidence. With FC, even the proposition that evidence should be gathered has been controversial. Early calls to study FC were met by harsh criticism and concern that the act of *studying* FC would undermine the confidence of people with autism who relied on it and thereby cause irreparable harm to those being studied (Biklen, 1990). Obviously, objective evaluation is extremely difficult when professionals claim that the very act of studying a phenomenon will damage the people in the study. Instead, proponents suggested that the efficacy of FC should be established by collecting nonobtrusive case studies of FC success. In such an atmosphere, few claims have been valued or trusted by people within the autism community.

In spite of these difficulties, research on FC was conducted and evidence was gathered. Several experimental studies were conducted using traditional double blind methods (Wheeler, Jacobson, Paglieri, & Swartz, 1993; Intellectual Disability Review Panel, 1989; see Green, 1994b for a summary). These studies typically posed questions to students with autism and their adult facilitators. The facilitators were grouped into one of two conditions: (a) those who *knew* the "correct" answers to the questions asked of the students and (b) those who *did not know* the answers. The results across these studies have been unequivocal. Unless the adult facilitators knew the correct answers in advance, students with autism rarely responded correctly. The reaction to these initial experiments by FC proponents was critical and acrimonious. The studies were criticized for their "clinical" or sterile treatment of participants, and the methodologies were said to undermine the trust needed for valued communication. Using criteria supplied by Biklen and his colleagues (Biklen, 1993; Biklen & Schubert, 1991), more naturalistic evaluations were conducted to establish authorship under nonclinical, more "respectful" conditions (Braman, Brady, & Williams, 1995). Unfortunately, even more naturalistic evaluations of FC have failed to show evidence of independent communication.

Where then does FC stand in light of the controversy it spawned? FC remains a popular intervention with many families and professionals, and at least one national institute generates considerable financial support from this treatment. To date, however, the majority of the independent studies of this phenomenon have failed to demonstrate its efficacy.

Indeed, the few empirical demonstrations of support for FC exist in its supporters' own publications rather than in independent, refereed literature (see Biklen & Cardinal, 1997). Although the research to date does not paint FC in a good light, it should be noted that only a few variations of the technique have been studied (primarily the hand-to-hand procedure). There remain personal reports of people with autism who have learned to use variations of the technique. For example, several adolescents and adults with autism have reported (verbally) that they prefer to communicate in writing and that this occurs best with hand-to-shoulder "facilitation." If promoters expect their advocacy of FC to be taken seriously, they must pursue their claims in a manner respectful to the individuals with autism who use it, as well as the public at large who expect honest investigation when establishing the veracity of a treatment. Until then, the FC claims remain beyond rational proportion, and the phenomenon continues to be a prototype of "pathological science" (Wolfensberger, 1994).

Sensory Theory

The DSM-IV (1994) notes that "abnormal responses to sensory stimuli" is one of the many criteria for autism. That is, students with these "abnormal responses" may have either a heightened (hypersensitive) or lessened (hyposensitive) perception of kinesthetic, auditory, or visual sensory input than students without autism. Because autism is likely affected by some yet unknown neurological circumstance, the set of behaviors we see and identify as autism may be *actually* a function of an array of sensory mechanisms. An autistic response to sensory input could involve functioning at the point where sensory stimuli are routed to the brain or it could involve the point where the brain processes the sensory information that is received. According to those supporting a sensory theory of autism, the problem is primarily at the input or processing level.

Much of the early sensory development theory was proposed by Ayres (1972) in her work with students with learning disabilities. Ornitz and Ritvo (1968) first suggested that a perceptual inconstancy resulted from core neurological deficits in autism. This inconsistency was usually expressed by either excessive or inadequate modulation or damping of sensory input. In some cases, too much sensory input was allowed, while in other cases too little input entered the processing system. An example of this physical damping seen in many students with autism involves holding their hands over their ears in noisy environments. This example often is used as anecdotal evidence for a sensory hypothesis. Other, apparently self-stimulatory behaviors in students with autism are also described as evidence of an attempt to provide sensory input which may not be provided by the environment. For sensory information to be useful, it must be quickly processed by the brain in a relatively consistent fashion. A lag in processing can distort the input and render it meaningless. Those who advocate a sensory theory use the metaphor of a poor cellular phone connection (with static, echo, and voice delay) as a way of appreciating the sensory deficits in autism and the ensuing difficulties that result from this experience.

The sensory theories make sense intuitively. It is sometimes easy to spot situations that place sensory demands on students with autism. For example, some sensory-rich conditions trigger episodes of problem behavior for students (e.g., a noisy cafeteria). Ameliorating these sensory demands can bring immediate relief to the student and caregivers. Parent and teacher sensitivity to a student's sensory status can lessen the occurrences of problem behaviors associated with sensory demands. But the sensory theory has weaknesses as well. The reaction we may see as a student struggles with a "sensory" demand situation may have begun as a fairly normal response to unwelcome sensation. Awareness of the student's distress by parents or teachers, coupled with termination of normal environmental demands, can result in *sheltering* the student from the real world. In addition, allowing the student to escape sensory demands by showing distress teaches the student an effective (but stigmatizing) communication skill.

One of the authors saw a very positive example of parents dealing with what could have developed into a problematic sensory issue. The child and family (and 200 or so other people) attended a benefit dinner in a large church hall. The sound system was very poor and sounds were loud and garbled. The ambient noise from the crowd was also high. The parents sensed that their child was struggling with the situation. They comforted her and let her know that they recognized that the noise was a challenge for her. But they stayed and they helped their daughter to stay in the event. The mother's parting words were "She has to learn to deal with loud situations sometime and this is as good a time as any." Certainly, not every situation affords a "good time" to deal with a challenging environment, but it is normal and developmentally appropriate to expose students to a range of sensory environments and to provide them with suitable support to enable them to be successful.

The traditional approach to treating students with autism from a sensory perspective has been controversial, in part due to the absence of research supporting the efficacy of sensory treatments. Interventions typically involve sensory "process training" and might involve exposing students to various gradations of sensory input. In addition, careful attention is given to the sensory aspects of a learning environment. Distracting or irritating sensory input is reduced or eliminated. Two types of treatments based on a sensory theory of autism have received substantial attention among families and some professionals in the last decade, and both have been surrounded by controversy. These interventions include (a) sensory integration therapy and (b) auditory integration training.

Sensory Integration Therapy

Sensory integration treatments use a controlled increase or reduction of input into the tactile, vestibular (movement) and proprioceptive (body position) senses to assist in the "organization" of these sensory stimuli. These treatments are considered successful if the senses are "integrated" so that students can effectively act on the environment. Proponents of sensory integration claim that, when the human senses do not integrate as they should, learning, development, and behavior are adversely affected. A summary of the underlying theory behind sensory integration is provided on the next page.

Sensory integration therapy does not usually involve specific skill development, so progress can be difficult to measure. Therapists trained in sensory integration provide stimulation activities to help students develop "underlying abilities" that presumably facilitate skill acquisition. Sensory integration therapy is typically pleasurable for students and often includes many gross motor activities. The goal of treatment is for students to process complex sensory information more effectively. The ability to process complex sensory information is thought to lead to improvements in school achievement, emotional adjustment, behavioral control, and increased language development (Sensory Integration International, 1991). The recommendations of therapists who practice sensory integration therapy do hold some appeal for classroom teachers. Such recommendations typically include motor and sensory based adaptations, such as providing a quiet study area or carrel for a student who becomes easily stimulated or minimal use of language, visual schedules, and written transcripts of lessons for students who have difficulty processing auditory information.

Controversy about sensory integration stems from a number of sources. The degree of sensory difference can be difficult to determine accurately, and the interaction of the difference with past learning is very complicated. Consider a student who has a strong preference for a very quiet environment. Each time a noise is introduced the student might react with behaviors that communicate distress. If these "distress behaviors" are responded to quickly, and strengthened by allowing them to result in the removal or reduction of the noise, the student would be far more likely to engage in the distress behaviors in the future. Are the student's current preferences for a quiet environment a true product of the student's sensory system or merely the result of learning? The controversy surrounding SI is not simply one of its effectiveness. Some evi-

Sensory Integration and Autism: Viewing Behavior from a Different Perspective

Sonia Kay

The flapping hands, the shifting eyes, the repetitive play, and the limited food repertoire: What do these behaviors have in common? These unusual behaviors are frequently observed in students with autism and they all can be interpreted as responses to sensory stimuli. The theory of sensory integration developed by Ayres in 1972 analyzes behavior in terms of sensory components.

Sensory integration is defined as the receipt, organization, and processing of sensory stimuli for use in responding to the environment. As infants, sensory stimuli are received as early as 9 weeks into gestation and continue to affect the function of an individual throughout life. The first and most primitive stimuli received are those that allow the individual to develop postural control in response to gravity (vestibular), protective and discriminative abilities based on touch (tactile), and body awareness based on input from the joints and muscles (proprioceptive). All of these sensory systems have direct neuronal connections to the limbic system, which governs affective and emotional responses. In addition, these stimuli have neurological connections to each other, to the visual and auditory systems, and to the cortex. Thus, these basic sensory systems are the foundation for the development of higher level skills such as gross and fine motor responses, attention to task, play skills, self-care skills, and social interaction. If there is a dysfunction in the processing of these basic sensory stimuli, the development of adaptive responses to the environment will likewise be impaired. Sensory integration treatment is based on these concepts.

Ayres and subsequent proponents of the theory of sensory integration view elements of the abnormal behaviors of the student with autism as a disorder in the sensory modulation system and/or a disorder in sensory registration; both are dysfunctions in processing sensory stimuli. However, recent research has also discovered that autism may be caused by underlying neurological abnormalities. Because sensory integration treatment is most effective with sensory processing dysfunctions, it can only be a part of an integrated treatment approach.

Sensory stimuli are frequently uncomfortable to students with autism. This seems to be a problem in sensory modulation, the ability of the individual to modify his or her response to the intensity of the stimuli. The behaviors of the student with autism can be viewed on a continuum from hyporesponsivity to hyperresponsivity to sensory stimuli. Overreaction, or hyperresponsiveness, can result in defensive or protective behaviors. Examples of hyperresponsive reactions include screaming, covering one's ears, and running from the room when a vacuum cleaner is turned on. Once the student with a hyperresponsive reaction becomes upset, calming and reorienting to the environment is prolonged and difficult. A study by Ayres and Tickle (1980) indicated that students with hyperresponsive reactions may benefit from sensory integrative treatments.

Underreaction, or hyporesponsiveness, can result in a failure to respond to environmental stimuli. Examples of hyporesponsiveness include not crying after a fall or not responding to noises. Some students with autism may not demonstrate sensory registration (i.e., recognize and focus on relevant environmental stimuli). A sensory registration disorder can result in inability to understand an activity or situation and decreased or absent inner drive to meet environmental challenges. This would explain the purposeless wandering and poor visual attention of some students with autism. The repetitive play schemas may be due to this lack of inner drive. If it does not occur to a child that there is another way to interact with a toy, the child might continue the same pattern over and over.

The treatment of students with autism with sensory integrative methods is usually performed by an occupational therapist trained in sensory integrative techniques. The treatment includes sensory experiences that help the brain to organize sensory information and allow learning to occur. Treatment methods include the use of suspended equipment for vestibular stimulation, weight-bearing and deep pressure for proprioception, and a variety of brushing and tactile experiences. Sequential presentation of stimuli in amount, intensity, and speed generates adaptive responses. The sequence of therapy within the therapist-designed environment is based on the goals for specific students. The overall goal of therapy is to create an environment in which students can successfully respond to sensory stimuli and become ready to learn from the environment. As students' sensory needs are met,

(*continued*)

students can access and organize information to elicit functional behavior such as play, self-care, and initiation of social interaction.

Sensory integrative concepts may also be applied in an educational setting. By understanding the effect of various types of stimuli on the nervous system, educators can include the needed activities in the structure of the day to prepare students for learning. For example, heavy work activities, such as moving heavy objects or pulling on a rope, are calming. Sitting on an unstable surface like a ball or swing would cause arousal and alertness.

In addition, sensory integrative concepts allow educators another perspective from which to understand students' behavior. Behaviors can be analyzed in terms of causative sensory events. For example, if a student begins jumping and flapping his or her hands after a 15-minute table top activity, it could be interpreted as a need for vestibular and proprioceptive input for arousal or organization. If a student is known to be tactiley defensive (hyperresponsive to touch), it would be better to decrease tactile input by putting the student at the end of a line or in a front seat to prevent inadvertent tactile stimuli, which might induce a tantrum or aggressive behavior. Thus, educators can design the environment for maximum performance and prevention of maladaptive behavior.

It is important for parents and all caregivers to look at a child's behavior in terms of sensory responses. The parent may understand why daily activities at home might be uncomfortable for the child by analyzing the sensory components of these activities. Then, it would be possible to grade the stimuli and build the child's tolerance. This could result in more appropriate behavior and a more peaceful household.

Additional research on the effectiveness of sensory integration for students with autism is needed. However, experience demonstrates that, in combination with the use of behavioral techniques, good educational strategies, and communication facilitation, sensory integration treatment can positively affect the lives of students with autism and their families.

Sonia Kay is an occupational therapist with the Child Development Center at St. Mary's Hospital in West Palm Beach, Florida.

dence suggests that it may be counterproductive. Mason and Iwata (1990) assessed the effects of SI on self-injurious behavior. They reported that exposure to sensory integration therapy was as likely to increase self-injury as to decrease it, whereas interventions based on differential reinforcement of other behavior (DRO), access to toys, and simple response interruption effectively reduced self injury.

The measurement tradition of sensory integration therapists can be difficult for educators to appreciate. Typically, the measures fail to operationalize behaviors and relate to highly subjective hypothetical processes. For example, specific skills such as holding a pencil, eating with a fork, and washing one's hands (skills that are easy for educators and parents to evaluate) are seldom selected as student target behaviors for sensory integration. Without clearly assessable outcomes, teachers may not be able to evaluate whether the therapy has indeed had any positive impact on the student.

Finally, educators must consider that the debate over the relative value of *process versus skills-oriented instruction* in special education was effectively settled long ago. Hammill and colleagues (Hammill & Larson, 1974, 1978; Hammill, Goodman, & Wiederholt, 1974; Hammill & Wiederholt, 1973) summarized the relative effectiveness of psycholinguistic process training, visual motor training, and perception training and brought the field of special education to an inescapable conclusion: Intervention aimed at underlying processes is far less efficient and effective than intervention aimed at direct teaching of important skills. This conclusion is in stark contrast to the thrust of the sensory integration therapies. Unlike the field of autism, the use of sensory- and process-based approaches, once dominant in the learning disabilities field, are now of little importance. Referring to the LD field, Mercer (1997, p. 56) stated: "To date, neither approach [Ayres' theory of sensory integration or modality preference based instruction] has presented data to counter the criticisms leveled at earlier ability-oriented treatments. Overall, the perceptual-motor approaches have had little effect."

Another element of the controversy surrounding SI is that an array of behaviorally based treatments founded on sound empirical research is available to deal with some types of sensory challenges. Reliance on sensory integration and other process treatments is not the result of a lack of effective and validated approaches. Herein lies a major source of controversy. In contrast to treatments that are based on sensory theory, behavioral treatments seek to address the outward and observable manifestations of problematic sensory differences. Behavioral approaches are also highly sensitive to the interaction of sensory differences and the possible functions served by protests or gestures that alert parents and teachers to the distress of the child. Several behavioral approaches are noteworthy.

Rincover, Cook, Peoples, and Packard (1979), for example, examined the sensory basis for some problem behaviors and the sensory feedback obtained by engaging in these problem behaviors. They referred to interventions based on "masking" this feedback as *sensory extinction*. One child, for example, flapped her hands in front of her eyes, yielding both kinesthetic and visual sensation. Masking the sensory feedback reduced the sensory reinforcement and consequently the problem behavior itself. An alternative behavioral approach involves *sensory replacement*. Favell, McGimsey, and Schell (1982) replaced the stimulation that a student received through eye-poking by providing access to visually stimulating toys. In a similar vein, Gunter et al. (1984) replaced students' loud vocalizations by providing an alternate source of auditory input in the form of popular music through headphones. Each of these interventions differs from the emphasis on sensory integration therapy by: (a) directly targeting important behaviors that have a sensory basis, (b) allowing direct measurement of the impact of the intervention, and (c) avoiding placement of the student in a separate therapeutic environment to benefit from the intervention.

Auditory Integration Training

Auditory integration training (AIT) represents a special case of sensory-based treatments and was first championed by Stehli (1992), who reported the success (actually a "miracle") with her daughter using one method of auditory training. Berard (1993) helped expand the case for auditory integration. His work, *Hearing Equals Behavior*, made bold claims for the centrality of auditory processing deficits in the behavior and overall skill deficits of students with autism and similar disorders. Berard suggested that the underlying deficit for many students with autism was a failure to integrate auditory information.

Proponents of auditory integration claim that some students with autism have unusually acute hearing and others appear especially sensitive to certain kind of sounds. These students try to block sounds by covering their ears or flee from an environment they find too noisy. When students do this repeatedly, they develop many defensive reactions and, over time, these reactions strengthen into patterns of problem behavior. Additionally, by blocking out sounds, students miss much important information essential to learning. Proponents of AIT suggest that this unusual hearing capacity can be changed. They maintain that, by subjecting students to several hours of specially processed music, students' auditory processing systems will in effect, *recalibrate* in a more normal manner. Two theoretical summaries of AIT are provided on the following pages.

Although at least six different forms of auditory integration training are identifiable, they all share essential features and a common theoretical basis. In general, AIT exposes students to a series of specially pro-

Auditory Integration Training for Children with Autism: An Audiologist's Perspective

Richard S. Saul, Ph.D.

The central nervous system, functioning as the body's network for communication, has the enormous task of analyzing, structuring, and integrating incoming sensory stimuli. Additionally, it must simultaneously inhibit these stimuli thereby resisting system overload (Smaldino, Saul, & Carlson, 1983). Breakdowns in this complex sequence of neural events may result in notable behavioral consequences. Recently attention in the field of autism has focused on the unusual sensitivity to sound observed in some children. These children exhibit behavior consistent with perceiving certain sounds as too loud or overwhelming (Berard, 1993).

Auditory integration training (AIT) is a technique in which the child listens to music presented through earphones. The music output is filtered electronically to randomly select various frequencies from the music source. A typical treatment is completed over a 10-day period, with the child receiving therapy twice per day in 30 minute sessions. A hearing test (audiogram) is obtained prior to treatment to ascertain areas of hypersensitivity or peaks of unusually acute hearing. This sensitivity to sound is determined by behavioral audiometry. If areas or peaks of hypersensitivity are found, these frequencies are filtered out of the auditory stimuli to avoid presenting uncomfortable or aversive sounds to the child (Rimland & Edelson, 1991).

Based on claims made about the success of this treatment in reducing adverse reactions to certain sounds, a climate of hopeful anticipation exists. Theoretical constructs underlying the use of this technique include strengthening the muscles of the middle ear to prevent sensory overload, providing stimulation to the coordinating mechanisms of the cerebellar and vestibular systems, and modulation to the reticular activating system (Berard, 1993).

There is evidence from the auditory processing literature that various aural habilitation procedures can be applied to the treatment of children with auditory processing disorders (Sloan,

(continued)

1986). Treatment approaches, including desensitization to background noise, for example, have been successfully used to treat individuals with difficulty focusing and attending in a noisy environment. However, children with autism do not represent a homogeneous group. Some may have auditory involvement of this nature; others may not. Therefore, essential auditory as well as behavioral information must be obtained by trained personnel— those with a concomitant understanding of auditory phenomena, acceptable test-retest variability, and appropriate modifications of test procedures used with special populations. Some pointed questions include:

> What specific decibel levels, if any, represent hyperacute sensitivity to sound?
>
> What characterizes an appropriate auditory screening procedure for candidacy? (Gravel, 1994).
>
> What represents a significant change in auditory function, post-treatment?

Reports of significant changes in hearing tests after AIT have not been well documented. Additionally, because the acoustic stimuli used in AIT training are presented at relatively intense levels, the effects of these levels on hearing also need to be more fully addressed. Considering the divergent group of practitioners administering the technique, the various procedures and modifications, including the equipment's sound output levels, must be carefully monitored.

In a recent report by Zollweg, Vance, and Palm (1995), no significant differences in hearing thresholds before and after AIT training was found. Does this indicate that AIT is not viable? Certainly not. It does, however, indicate that anecdotal evidence of auditory benefits must be further translated into carefully controlled research. Further investigation can determine the validity of these procedures by defining, in operational terms, the specific changes in the involved behaviors.

Richard S. Saul, Ph.D., is a faculty member in the Department of Communication Disorders at Florida Atlantic University in Boca Raton, Florida.

THE ABC'S OF AIT

Renai Jonas, CCC, Ed.D.

Auditory integration training (AIT) is a relatively new technique in the United States. It made its debut in 1990 when an article entitled "Fighting for Georgie" appeared as a condensed version of "The Sound of a Miracle," a mother's eloquent account of her 11-year-old autistic child's experience with AIT.

There are six forms of AIT: The Tomatis, the Berard, the Clark, the Stehli, the Walkman, and the Disc methods. The Tomatis method was developed by Alfred Tomatis, a French otolaryngologist and psychologist. This treatment is based on neurophysiological and psychosocial theory. Training requires 45 to 200 hours spread over 4 to 12 months. Advocates of this technique claim that it is useful for children or adults with language, behavior, and learning problems, as well for persons with other problems. The Tomatis Listening Training device is used by these practitioners.

The Berard AIT technique is an offshoot of the Tomatis method. Guy Berard, a French otolaryngologist, worked with Tomatis and claimed that this method eliminated the annoying and chronic ringing (tinnitus) in his own ears. However, Berard believed only in the mechanical and physical, not the psychological aspects of the technique and developed his own device now known as the Audiokinetron. Berard posited that individuals do not hear efficiently due to hearing loss, distortions, or hypersensitivity to select frequencies. He described his technique as "physical therapy to the ear," whereby an intense program of sound stimulation varying in pitch and intensity was said to activate the middle and inner ear. Berard stated that this procedure reduced hypersensitivity and improved listening, attention, cognitive abilities, behavior, and/or social skills. The Berard method is used for individuals diagnosed with dyslexia, learning disabilities, pervasive developmental delays, attention deficit disorder, bipolar disorders, and autism.

The third AIT technique, the Clark method, was developed by an engineer after his child with autism underwent AIT in France with Berard. The Clark technique is an adaptation of the Berard method and uses a device called the BGC Audio Enhancer. The fourth method is known as the Stehli method.

(continued)

This uses the Audioscion, which was developed by the parents of a child with autism who also received Berard AIT. The child's experience is cited in *Sound of a Miracle.*

The fifth and sixth methods are home treatments with specific music recorded on an audiotape or compact disc, played through a Walkman or compact disc player via headphones. In some cases, the Berard procedures are utilized or adapted.

Areas of Reported Change

The following changes in children's behavior have been reported by various clinicians and parents as a result of exposure to one of the AIT methods.

Behavioral: Changes in stereotypy, aggression, sleep patterns, activity level, self-control, organizational skills, anxiety, and self-injury.

Speech and language: Improvements in attention and focusing, auditory directions, and language and communication proficiency.

Auditory: Changes in sound sensitivity and hearing ability.

Educational: Improvement in learning ability and overall school performance.

Sensory: Improved sensory perceptual skills.

Psychological: Improvements in test performance, auditory memory span, auditory closure, and visual motor skills.

Medical Outcomes: Increased glucose utilization.

Treatment Procedures

Treatment procedures for the Berard, Clark, and Stehli methods include a hearing test to determine sound sensitivities, sound distortions, and hearing levels. Test results may alter procedure protocols. Next, the individual listens to 10, 1-hour sessions of specifically selected music fed through an AIT device via headphones. This is done for 5 consecutive days, twice a day, with a minimum of 3 hours between sessions. A second hearing test is then administered to determine if the settings on the AIT device require modification for the remainder of the training. Ten more sessions are conducted in the same manner, ending with a final audiogram.

FDA Regulations

AIT devices are not currently approved by the Food and Drug Administration (FDA) and therefore cannot be sold in the United States. These devices are classified as Class III medical devices because proponents claim they are used to treat medical conditions. (All new medical devices that enter the U.S. marketplace are considered Class III medical devices.)

In September 1993, the FDA banned importation of the Audiokinetron. In 1995, the Florida Health and Rehabilitative Services seized both the equipment and records of one AIT practitioner because the device was not FDA approved. Since then, AIT has been discontinued in the State of Florida. Efforts are being made to downgrade classification of the equipment to a Class II medical device (similar to an audiometer), which would make it easier to attain FDA approval. Research will be necessary to demonstrate that AIT is not harmful and, in fact, is effective. AIT continues to be available in many states in the United States (except Florida) and abroad.

Theoretical Basis

To date there are approximately 21 explanations for how AIT might work. These fall into four categories involving (a) auditory sensitivity, (b) auditory awareness, (c) biochemical changes, and (d) neurological changes. More than 20 studies with varying research designs, sample demographics and sizes, and test measures were reported between 1980 and 1995.

The Do's and Don'ts of AIT: What a Teacher Should Know

It is important for families to be informed of the following information and facts about AIT:

1. AIT does not help all individuals with autism and is not a cure.
2. This technique should not be performed if a child is under the age of 3-1/2 years, has ear wax build-up, ear infections, or pressure-equalizing tubes (PE tubes).

(continued)

3. AIT equipment is not FDA approved and is not currently used in the State of Florida.

4. Individual using AIT may exhibit negative behaviors after or during the procedure; the family must be informed of this possibility in advance and prepared to deal with these behaviors.

5. Longitudinal studies are necessary to determine the duration of treatment outcomes.

6. After AIT, it is contraindicated to listen to music via headphones, although an individual is able to receive verbal instructions and speech via headphones. Instructional computer programs may be used as long as music is not a part of the program.

7. Medical problems that occur during or after AIT should be discussed with a physician. These may not be related to AIT.

8. AIT has not met scientific standards that would justify its use for treatment and it is considered experimental by the American Speech-Language-Hearing Association (1994). Furthermore there is no certifying board to regulate and standardize this procedure and equipment.

9. To date, the risks and safety factors of AIT use have not been completely addressed.

Renai Jonas, Ed.D., is a speech-language pathologist in private practice in Boca Raton, Florida.

cessed sounds, songs, and other input designed to integrate students' auditory processing. The actual mechanism by which this auditory integration occurs remains unclear. The claims made for AIT are fairly dramatic. One claim is that students' abnormal auditory processing ability can be altered by AIT. Although this claim should be fairly easy to validate, research support has been mixed. If AIT does in fact produce a change in auditory ability, these changes should be measurable with standard audiological techniques. An expectation for demonstrable and clinically significant improvement, and the absence of it among the AIT supporters, has contributed to the relatively short shelf-life of AIT.

Gillberg, Johansson, Stefenburg, and Berlin (1997) investigated the Berard method with nine students with autism between the ages of 3 and

16 years. Students were rated on the CARS and ABC, and then rated 9 months later by an evaluator blind to the purpose of the investigation. No significant differences for any of the total or subscores were detected on either the CARS or the ABC, although the ABC sensory score did decline slightly. The moderate reduction in sensory problems could be a chance finding, particularly given the lack of similar results on the CARS' scores. Gillberg et al. concluded that this study of AIT "did not provide any support for a positive effect on autistic symptoms" (p. 98). Rimland and Edelson (1995) also examined AIT, with equally unimpressive findings. They examined the Berard method applied to eight children, with another nine serving as controls. Assessment was conducted by means of a daily journal, Aberrant Behavior Checklist (ABC), Fisher's Auditory Problems Checklist (FAPC), and the Hearing Sensitivity Questionnaire (HSQ). One important finding of the study was that AIT did not appear to decrease sound sensitivity for children in the experimental group, although modest differences in scores on several subtests were noted.

The research on AIT can be criticized on at least five points:

1. Research on AIT has been limited. There simply is not enough objective evaluation to establish the utility of AIT.
2. The effect of AIT reported to date has been quite small, lacks practical meaning, and pales when compared to other treatments.
3. The modest effects reported for AIT may not reflect any real change in behavior, but rather the views of the rater at the time of assessment. Direct observation is essential in future studies to determine change more objectively.
4. The lack of real change in hearing ability is one of the important findings. To the degree that *any* effects have been found, these might be a function of *systematic desensitization* of children to certain sounds, as Siegel (1996) suggested, and this should be the focus of future studies.
5. The gains reported for AIT may be more easily accounted for by means of a placebo effect. Given the difficulties with objective rater measurement, families involved in the AIT studies may be especially disposed to believing that their children have improved in behavior and learning ability.

In 1993, the Food and Drug Administration (FDA) issued a ban on the importation of the SAPP Audiokinetron, one of the devices used for AIT (ASHA, 1994). The FDA ban and subsequent regulatory actions have had a dual impact on AIT. On one hand, it has fostered the sale of unregulated (and far less expensive) AIT *products and media* in place of more sophisticated equipment. For example, compact discs containing the processed sounds are now available. These are sold not as regulated medical devices, but as training materials. Second, the FDA ban on AIT equipment, and the resulting absence of a market for these devices, has eroded the demand for effectiveness data. Without a requirement that AIT proponents demonstrate the effectiveness of the equipment they use, there has been no compelling reason to conduct this research, especially if the marketing of AIT can proceed in its absence. The newsletter of the American Speech-Language-Hearing Association (ASHA, 1994) featured a report on three AIT methods and offered this recommendation:

> We have reviewed three methods [Tomatis, Berard, & Clark] of AIT that have been offered as treatments for a variety of communication, behavioral, emotional, and learning disorders. These methods have not yet met scientific standards for efficacy that would justify their inclusion as mainstream treatments for these disorders. Nonetheless, parents, consumers, and professionals should continue to see new information as it becomes available . . . it is recommended that consumers be informed that AIT is experimental in nature before they participate in treatment. (p. 58)

What does this mean? AIT remains unvalidated and experimental. If the potential value of the technique attracts the attention of serious researchers, they will conduct studies yielding firm conclusions on the effectiveness of the technique. Alternatively, researchers may elect to bypass this field of study, and only persons with a vested interest in AIT will evaluate this phenomenon, relying on anecdotal evidence and testimony. The message to educators, however, is clear: As an experimental set of treatments, school districts should not be obligated to consider AIT for a student's individualized education plan (IEP). Any consideration by an IEP team to add AIT would have to address the experimental nature of the treatment and proceed with the utmost caution.

Personal History as a Source of Knowledge

It has become popular to learn about a disability by listening to what persons with the disability can tell us. In the field of autism, people with greater levels of involvement do not tell their stories very often (or very well) because of their limited communication skills. Instead, the public has learned about personal perspectives of autism from those with more communication prowess who, while providing useful and interesting insights, are less representative of the broader population of persons with autism. Indeed, Sachs noted that the essential distinction between autism and Asperger's syndrome is the inability of the former to be introspective and to share insights into their own condition (Sachs, 1994). If

Sachs is correct, we may never have direct literary reports offering insight into autism, but instead obtain insights only from people with skills and capabilities not representative of the whole spectrum of autism. Several individuals have stepped forward to offer their stories, and in so doing have provided either insight or controversy.

Temple Grandin

Temple Grandin, by all accounts, is an extraordinary person who has overcome major obstacles resulting from her autism to achieve academic success. She provides an excellent example of how a person with autism can productively share insights into the disorder. Her success has also provided a valuable case history for considering family intervention and therapeutic interactions.

Grandin was diagnosed with autism as a young child. Her parents took an active interest in her education and treatment, seeking what they believed to be practical approaches, consistent with their lifestyle and work. As a child, they expected Grandin to behave and to fulfill basic responsibilities. They recognized her disorder but did not allow it to become an excuse for misbehavior. They apparently had a functional understanding of the communicative purposes of problem behavior and knew how to both promote and demand good behavior. Grandin has credited much of her success to the quality of her care and education, although her education was not what would be now be considered "autism-sensitive." She received a great deal of attention at home from her family and a governess and later at a small private school for typically developing children.

Grandin has also credited her mother and family for much of her success. She wrote, "Mother helped me each day after school. Thanks to her, my reading ability was above grade level. . . . She improved my reading skills by having me read aloud and sound out words and she made me feel grown-up by serving me tea [actually hot tea-flavored lemon water]" (Grandin & Scarino, 1986, p. 37). Frequent help and practice, coupled with many positive interactions, caused Grandin to later write, "She helped me educationally and raised my self-esteem" (p. 37). Her development was strong in some areas, but she faced many obstacles. She wrote, "But in spite of my creative talents, I lacked the ability of getting along with people. As a rule they didn't warm to my erratic way of behavior, my stressed way of talking, my bizarre ideas, my jokes and tricks. And my grades overall were deplorable" (p. 63). Fortunately, a gifted teacher helped Grandin direct her abilities in constructive ways. She says of this teacher, "Mr. Carlock didn't see any of the labels, just the underlying talents. Even the principal had doubts about my getting through tech schools. Mr. Carlock believed in building what was within the student. He channeled my fixations into constructive projects. He didn't try to draw me into his world but came instead into my world" (p. 87).

School for Grandin was challenging and she struggled with content in many courses. Yet she persevered and, with the help of good teachers and her family, graduated and prepared for college. During college, Grandin channeled her interests in animal care into the study of the behavior and management of livestock. This work continued through graduate school, and she ultimately earned a Ph.D. in animal science. Today, Grandin is as well known for her inventions and contributions to the livestock industry, as for her insights into autism. Her success has become an important milestone for both the autism community and indeed, the entire disability community.

Donna Williams: A Reconsideration

Donna Williams gained notoriety in 1993 with the publication of her book, *Nobody, Nowhere*. She recounted her struggle with autism offering vivid, poetic descriptions of her fascination with lights and patterns, and sharing her memories as a socially isolated, uncomprehending little girl. Her descriptions of the speech of others as "gabble" still are wonderful. In conjunction with her books, Williams has given many speaking engagements. Many who heard her on National Public Radio will remember her insistence on questions being posed in a prescribed order. Ever so carefully, the interviewer asked if she would consider a question out of sequence. Donna was cautiously willing to oblige. Here was a person with autism who had broken the bonds of isolation through literature, and while still autistic, made an important contribution to the world.

The only problem was that Williams, if we believe the reports of people who knew her during college, was almost certainly not autistic. A report by the Australian Broadcasting Corporation Radio National investigated the claims made by and in support of Williams (Gollan, 1996). The report raised, "disturbing questions about whether Donna can be seen as in any way typical of an autistic person, and whether she should be seen as autistic at all" (p. 11). Interviews with college classmates suggested that she was not autistic. It was during her senior year in college that an autistic persona emerged. Apparently, after researching a term paper on autism, Williams began an exploration of the nature of autism in a very personal way. Classmates noticed that she began to act increasingly autistic and even to think in a way a person with autism might think. But adult-onset autism as the result of a philosophical-academic adventure is not recognized as a valid form of the disorder. Dr. Kathleen Dillion, a professor of psychology at West New England College and an expert on autism, was reported to be, "one of the few specialists who is willing to speak on the record about her doubts about Donna's diagnosis. She thinks that Donna's symptoms owe more to the abuse she suffered as a child than to autism" (Gollan, 1996, p. 8). The Australian reporter, Kathy Gollan, interviewed classmates and inquired about signs of obsessive behavior, rigid thinking, lack of social skills, and degree of intuitive thinking. She did not find support for a diagnosis of autism. She did find that Donna apparently regressed into an autistic persona at times. Marcia Devlin, a fellow student said, "It seemed so acted. She seemed like she was making a point all the time of everyone knowing at every moment that she was autistic. And it appeared to me, and to other people I spoke to, that when she needed to understand something for her benefit, like when she had to understand what was needed for an assignment, she switched out of the 'autism,' understood what she needed to know, and then went back into it again" (Gollan, 1996, p. 7). Volkmar also was questioned in the report about Williams' diagnosis and the fact that it was not confirmed by any reports from her early years. According to Volkmar, "It's hard for me to know what to make of Donna Williams. Donna Williams' books in my view, while very interesting, are not typical of the experience of at least the 20, 30 or 40 higher functioning autistic people that I have come to know fairly well" (Gollan, 1996, p. 10).

Volkmar's comments may be the most charitable conclusion that can be reached. Donna Williams' situation is at least highly uncharacteristic of persons with autism. The other conclusion to be reached is that she is not now, and never was, a person with autism.

How could Williams' self-diagnosis and proclamation of autism have occurred and how could it have gone uncontested? A simple or parsimonious explanation is that she attracted attention (in a form highly reinforcing to her) and/or avoided some other demands contingent on the demonstration of autistic behaviors. Certainly, the notoriety accompanying the publication of a break-through book must have provided rich social and monetary reinforcement, even prestige. Many in the autism community may have wanted to believe that a person with autism had the literary talents Williams demonstrated and were disinclined to question her status.

What does this mean? Certainly more conclusive evidence is needed to support Donna's claim that she is or ever was autistic. A convincing case either can be assembled or it cannot. Given the solid evidence available to discount her claim, she or her supporters have an obligation to offer proof. If proof is not forthcoming, her claim is likely to be discounted and the search for the meaning of this adventure takes a different turn. Why in this era would someone who is not autistic claim to be so? Do we, as a culture, place some special value on persons with autism? Do we assign them a distinctive role? Perhaps the English-speaking, book-buying public was altogether too gullible and too ready to believe someone who claimed to be at the same time severely impaired and a gifted, even brilliant writer.

It may well turn out that Donna Williams did not write a work of non-fiction. She may have rather, created a skillful profile of a person with autism. Ironically, this person may not have been Donna Williams, but simply a literary creation. If so, her chosen title, *Nobody, Nowhere*, takes on a very special meaning. Such escapades can be seen as amusing, but for the fact that hundreds of thousands of persons legitimately have autism. They and those who care about them are in no way helped by such creative writing. It is difficult enough for the public to appreciate the reality of autism without having such confusing information featured in the news. Neither does it help the autism community to be used in this way. Greater skepticism is called for, obviously, as well as a full accounting of the story of Donna Williams. Gullibility is not a good thing. Perhaps Donna Williams teaches us, once again, to be suspicious and slow to embrace the unsupported claim.

Psychogenic Theory

The notion that autism is caused by a psychological process—psychogenesis—was handed an almost fatal blow by Rimland (1964), as was described in Chapter 2. Yet proponents of a psychological causation can still be found. Tustin (1975) argued that autism may be best understood as the young child's response to the trauma of developing into a separate person. A few children, according to Tustin, cope with this trauma by forming a protective shell that we diagnose as autism. Within a theoretical framework rich in speculation about mother-infant symbiosis and the significance of play objects, it is not surprising that some psychodynamic theorists will regard this as a logical extension of their beliefs. Empirical and clinical validation of Tustin's views remains to be provided, and none of the post-Bettelheim psychogenic theories have ever gained a wide following. As noted previously, Bettelheim (1967) was the most vocal proponent of psychogenesis. In his view, parental rejection and emotional coldness caused autism. Contradictory evidence has been abundant and persuasive (Rimland, 1964).

The history of parent blame associated with psychodynamic clinicians lingers. Today, no reputable researcher suggests that parents cause autism; rather, psychodynamic clinicians advance their position that autism is a function of the trauma caused by parent and child separation and by the difficulty in establishing independent identities. Although parents are not blamed directly, the disorder is still framed by the dynamic interplay and psychological connections between adults and their children. Many of the actions of professionals today continue to have their roots in the psychogenic tradition. Maurice (1993), for example, pointed out that many of the adjunct therapies (music therapy, art therapy, play therapy) are designed toward psychological healing and are guided by specialized therapists. Such services pay little attention to the development of useful skills, the hallmark of an instructional model. No doubt music, art, and play have contributions to make for students with (and without) autism, but such contributions are *instructional* in nature, not curative and therapeutic.

In an effort to put psychotherapy in a proper context in relation to autism, Riddle (1987) wrote:

> It is understandable that the very idea of "psychotherapy", burdened by this history, should be distasteful for families and other professionals. (pp. 539–540)

Riddle is correct. The burden of blame remains and constitutes a barrier. And like so many other controversies in autism, psychogenic theorists have benefited from a public that is far too willing to suspend its skepticism.

Controversy Surrounding Research by Lovaas

One of the most contentious and acrimonious issues in autism involves the research of Lovaas. Lovaas and his colleagues refined a set of early and intensive behavioral interventions for young children with autism. In a study published in 1987, Lovaas reported that 47% of the children in an intensive treatment group reached essentially normal levels of functioning; these children were described as having recovered from autism. These findings helped ignite interest in home-based, intensive behavioral intervention nationwide. The ensuing demand for services from parents fueled a controversy that shows little sign of diminishing.

Earlier in his career, Lovaas conducted behavioral intervention with older persons with autism, but recognized the challenges to achieving long-term and durable gains. By the early 1980s, he believed that interventions would become more effective if three conditions were in place:

1. Intervention should be started very early in the child's life (the children in his study all began treatment before 46 months of age);
2. Interventions should be intensive and behaviorally based (his intensive group received 40 hours of one-on-one intervention each week in carefully supervised programs); and
3. Interventions should be delivered in the child's home.

To Lovaas, these conditions maximized the likelihood of learning, and, for some children, recovery from autism. These interventions provided opportunities for parents and other caregivers to maximize the intervention across all of the child's waking hours and to promote generalization of newly learned skills. Parents became a central part of the intervention, and as they learned behavioral techniques, they were able to identify therapeutic and counter-therapeutic interaction patterns with their children.

The nature of intensive behavioral intervention called for skilled one-on-one instruction. After assessment and program development, the child was placed within a Lovaas-prescribed sequence of skills. During the early stages, discrete trial (DT) teaching was the norm. In DT, a behavior therapist or teaching assistant presented a simplified teaching task to a child. For example, a child might be asked to, "Point to the yellow ball" when presented with two colored picture cards. A correct response would be followed with active praise and, as necessary, food reinforcers; an incorrect response would result in an informative "No" response and re-presentation of the item. Massed trials, typically 10 presentations, would be presented on each skill. Work periods would be interspersed with brief play periods throughout 40 hours of intervention each week. As the child progressed, more natural teaching formats, still maintaining the intensive mode, were incorporated. Programming for generalization was a feature throughout, but became a more important element as the child mastered more skills. As children made substantial progress, they were transitioned into local schools, often into general education classes. The preference during the study was to select orderly non-special education settings in the hope of permitting a continuation of progress.

Lovaas' results were startling. Following the treatment, mean IQs for the experimental group were 83.3; in contrast, mean IQs for children in control group 1 were 52.2. (These values were significant at the $p<.001$ level.) Nine children in the experimental group were judged to be recovered on the basis of class placement, intellectual testing, and measures of adaptive behavior. None of the children in Control Group 1 achieved recovery status. In a subsequent study by McEachin, Smith, and Lovaas (1993) treatment gains were reassessed. They noted that "The 9 experimental subjects who had achieved the best outcomes at age 7 received particularly extensive evaluations indicating that 8 of them were indistinguishable from average children on tests of intelligence and adaptive behavior" (p. 359).

Soon after publication of this work, parents began to clamor for intensive, behavioral, home-based intervention, which soon became personified as "Lovaas treatment." Chance (1991) helped to popularize the intervention by publishing a review of the study in *Psychology Today*. Maurice (1993) detailed her success using very similar techniques with her own children in a best selling book, *Let Me Hear Your Voice*. Both of these authors helped to build a momentum among parents eager to optimize their children's potential. As of 1998, well over 6,000 families in the

United States had established home-based behavioral intervention programs for their children with autism (L. Parles, personal communication, February 1998).

The Lovaas (1987) study has been criticized on many counts (Mundy, 1993; Schopler, Short, & Mesibov, 1989). The criticism, both in print and in other forums, has at times exceeded the bounds of civility found in academic discourse. Lovaas, in his 1996 presentation at the Association for Behavior Analysis, labeled some of the criticism as "vicious and unproductive." For many observers of this phenomenon, it seems strange that a study would receive such harsh criticism after using family-friendly interventions based mostly on positive reinforcement. Lovaas' results are not outside of the scope of gains reported in peer-reviewed journals by other, comprehensive, intensive behavioral interventions. Rogers (1996) reported on the results of six independent intensive early intervention projects, each of which produced impressive gains for children with autism. The Lovaas study, one of those reviewed by Rogers, is only incrementally more effective than the others. All six studies pointed to the critical role of early, structured, behavioral intervention.

The most comprehensive critique of the Lovaas work was provided by Gresham and MacMillan (1997). Their evaluation focused on weaknesses in internal, external, and construct validity and treatment integrity. The most serious of these challenges involved Lovaas' selection of measurement instruments, his use of different measures for pre- and post-testing, and his use of a non-standard pro-rated mental age (PMA). In addition, Gresham and MacMillan criticized Lovaas for using reinforcement techniques to optimize compliant responding during post-testing. This suggested that increased test-taking performance rather than fundamental knowledge gains were being measured.

Schopler et al. (1989), one of the first critics, focused on the selection and assignment of children to experimental and control conditions. Random assignment was not used; rather assignments were based on availability of personnel and parent wishes. Schopler et al. (1989) also noted that the relatively high functioning levels of children in the study were not characteristic of most children with autism; Mundy (1993) agreed that assignment and selection problems weakened the study. Because the children in the experimental group had more sophisticated skills than those in the other groups, they had a better prognosis even without intervention (Gresham & MacMillan, 1997; Mundy, 1993).

Threats relating to external validity deal with the degree to which the findings of a study can be applied to other settings and children. A key aspect of the critique of the study's external validity also involves whether the children in all parts of the Lovaas study were representative of students across the autism spectrum. If the Lovaas findings are based on children who are unlike the general population of children with autism, then many children are not likely to achieve the substantial benefit found by Lovaas.

Gresham and MacMillan (1997) concluded, "We have argued here that [the Lovaas project] is at best experimental, is far from providing a cure for autism and awaits replication before school districts are required to provide it on a wholesale basis" (p. 196). They also noted the wide array of interventions that might be productively used by school districts and suggested that school districts consider other interventions.

Obviously, such criticisms have resulted in careful replies by Lovaas and his colleagues. Smith and Lovaas (1997) provided a point-by-point reply to these criticisms and argued that an important objective of the Gresham and MacMillan critique,

> Is to help school personnel deal with requests from parents for the UCLA program and that they proceeded to try to meet this objective by focusing exclusively and relentlessly on the alleged shortcomings in the UCLA program. While attempting to help school personnel is laudable, Gresham and MacMillan's strategy is, we think, misguided and unhelpful. School personnel have a legal mandate to work collaboratively with parents to provide appropriate services for children with autism. To fulfill this mandate, they need balanced discussions, not polemics. (p. 214)

Smith and Lovaas raised another objection to Gresham and MacMillan's article, noting that it:

> incites antagonism where none need exist. When parents request support for the UCLA program from schools, they are doing so because they have concluded that their children will not benefit from other services offered to them, not because they want to provoke a lawsuit. Their goal is to reduce their children's need for services over the course of the children's lives, not to obtain more than their fair share of help. (p. 214)

Competent researchers, both independent and associated with Lovaas and his colleagues, will continue to investigate the impact of intensive early intervention for young children with autism. One message is clear: intensive and early behavioral intervention offers many young children with autism dramatic improvement potential, appears to harm none, and can be provided within a realistic cost-benefit mode to a large number of children. Yet, the intensity of the critique leveled at Lovaas should cause advocates for children with autism to consider the functions of such critiques, particularly when scant criticism is directed at many widely embraced approaches for which no *empirical support* is provided. Multiple, intense criticisms of research that *willingly undergoes empirical validation and peer review* results in the creation of a climate of "clinical indeterminacy" (Feinberg & Beyer, 1997) in which *no treatment* is ever completely validated, yet all treatments are acceptable if they find favor with some families, advocates, and professionals. Perhaps these arguments are best viewed within the context of academic and scholarly differences, and functionally as conflicts in self and programmatic interests. The strength and often personal nature of the criticism leveled at Lovaas shows the significance of his project. At a more global level, that criticism is not merely about the methodology or results of one study, but rather the critical issue of what society will do in response to any research that shows impressive and unequivocal results involving youngsters with autism.

Is There No End? Additional Controversies

The examples presented in this chapter are among the most visible controversies facing the field today. Unfortunately, they are not the *only* examples of controversy. Families and educators face a deluge of other treatments, poorly tested and overly-popularized, each with its own adherents. Few show evidence that their "miracles" have any positive impact on the students who so need their support. Such treatments are characterized by five features:

1. Dissemination of information about the treatments comes primarily through the popular or commercial media rather than through peer-reviewed, objective sources.
2. The validity for their use is based primarily on *emotional* testimonials. The testimonials typically involve a small number of professionals who promote the treatments and develop close personal links with families. These alliances are then used to challenge the prevailing belief systems and power structures in the field.
3. The treatments tend to be expensive and often require highly specialized (and expensive) personnel. Quasi-business entities are created to foster wide dissemination, training, and marketing. These entities seldom engage in serious research or support independent validation of their treatments.
4. Treatment procedures generally are described in only the vaguest of terms and are alleged to work for people with a broad array of disabilities. Use of the treatments by professionals other than the central proponents is resisted.
5. The benefits of the treatments typically are described only in subjective terms. Adherents typically support the idea that subjective benefits (often seen only by the therapists or families involved) are superior to objectively measurable (publicly demonstrated) benefits. Proponents typically criticize calls for empirical or scientific validation of the treatment.

Ironically, many of these controversial treatments are supported or presented as viable options by organizations best positioned to guard against exploitation of people with autism and their families (American Society of Autism, 1997). The more obvious of these include cranial-sacral therapy, the Doman/Delacato Method, and dolphin therapy. Space limitations preclude a detailed presentation of all the unproven interventions available in autism; however, a few of these treatments are summarized in Table 4–1.

Cranial-sacral therapy

Cranial-sacral therapy is based on a study by Upledger (1983) who suggested that children with a number of disorders may have two related physical problems. First, he suggested that the bones of the cranium were not functioning properly because they failed to move in a free and easy manner. Second, he suggested that pressure exerted by cerebrospinal fluid moving through the cranium and spinal column created a dynamic system of fluid and air pressure which, when not operating correctly, would yield an array of physical problems. Treatments based on these ideas involve direct physical manipulation of a child's head and spine; movement activities, often on large balls, are used to correct problems with "fluid distribution."

Although these treatments are promoted as being of benefit to students with autism, no studies that meet any of the standard criteria for reviewing research (see Gresham & Macmillan, 1998, for an example) provide any support for these treatments. These treatments should be approached with the greatest degree of caution.

Table 4–1. Controversial Treatments Supported by Autism Advocates

Pet Therapy	Facilitated Communication
Art Therapy	Music Therapy
Auditory Intergration Training	Perceptual Therapy
Dietary Interventions	Sensory Integration Therapy
Dolphin Therapy	Vision Therapies
Cranial-Sacral Therapy	Mega-vitamin Therapy
Holding Therapy	Shamanism
Play Therapy	Psychoanalysis

Data, Dolphins, and Autism:
Real Progress is Being Made in Autism
but Baloney Treatments Help No One

Jack Scott, Ph.D.

Autism is a serious developmental disorder. It is fairly common for a rare disorder, occurring once or twice within a population of 2,000 children. Until fairly recently, a diagnosis of autism might have been the worst thing a family could hear, as it meant having a child who would be physically present yet socially and emotionally isolated, alone in a world that might come close to the *real world* but rarely into direct contact with it. Dustin Hoffman gave a powerful portrayal of an adult with autism in the movie *Rainman*. Even a determined and creative sibling (Tom Cruise) learned enough at the end of the movie to send his brother back to the institution. But the Rainman grew up in a time when there were few or no effective treatments for autism. Well into the 1960s parents were blamed for causing autism by "rejecting" their child. Mothers came in for special vilification. Remember the term, "Refrigerator Mother?" It was the brutal label stuck like some refrigerator magnet of shame on these blameless and victimized moms. Now, anyone who knows anything about autism, knows one thing: nothing parents do can *cause* autism.

Although the cause (and probably a variety of causes exist) is still elusive, treatments are plentiful and the claims for some of them will make you wonder why anyone still has autism. The array of so-called treatments is daunting with auditory integration training, sensory integration training, facilitated communication, vitamin therapy, special diets, holding therapy, even swimming with dolphins—all touted as offering impressive gains; some even offer the potential for *cure*. Yes, these treatments can be expensive and involve lots of hocus-pocus, but proponents will offer emotional testimonials. What the proponents will not offer, and cannot provide, is solid data or research attesting to the effectiveness of the treatment. If these treatments are so great, why on Earth are the data either *not available* or *not gathered* in a way to convince reasonable citizens and taxpayers.

(continued)

The most absurd recent fad, facilitated communication (FC), shows how vulnerable parents and some overly optimistic educators can be about unvalidated, new age, and sensational treatments. Children with autism and profound communication handicaps were alleged to have "unexpected literacy," and if a skilled "facilitator" guided their arms, children could type out cogent messages. Surprisingly, these messages were often enriched in a philosophy of empowerment for persons with disabilities strikingly similar to the philosophy of the supporters of the FC technique. The research in support of FC is laughably weak; controlled studies show that the technique generally is a farce. Gina Green, director of research at the New England Center for Children, has labeled this entire episode the "scandal of facilitated communication." Yet while proponents of FC and other odd techniques magnify scraps of support, other interventions *do* exist that have undergone close scrutiny. These interventions make up a growing body of supports backed by solid evidence pointing to dramatic but hard-won gains for young children with autism.

Ivar Lovaas, professor of psychology at UCLA, pioneered the use of intensive behavioral treatments for young children with autism. These treatments are based on B. F. Skinner's work in behavior analysis (a science) with the emphasis on positive reinforcement, clear task structure, repeated opportunities to practice the behavior (called trials), and careful observation and data gathering (data has always been important to behavior analysts). This includes lots of practice! Forty hours per week of one-to-one instruction is common in parent-directed home programs. Parents get professional support (when it is available and they can afford it) and recruit and train teaching assistants—college students, talented high school students, relatives, church volunteers and others—to do the training. The child progresses through structured activities and learns to apply new skills in a variety of situations. Some, not many, school districts fund all or part of these home programs. Fewer still make this treatment available in schools. Some states, recognizing the immense long-term savings and societal benefit, routinely fund these programs. Alaska, thanks to Todd Risley, may be the most progressive in this regard. But Alaska is the exception. In most places, parents labor to recruit and train helpers and struggle with the costs. Reasonable as they may be on an hourly basis, 40 hours per week of anything is expensive.

I teach in Boca Raton in Palm Beach County, Florida, an area with many affluent families who can afford the full intervention. I have seen tremendous results as children who were clearly autistic with severe impairments are now seen by their peers as more or less normal. Some no longer qualify for special education. For every affluent family who can arrange for the program, I know many more who can only dream about the opportunity passing their children by. I and many of our students and faculty help in these programs, but the task is much bigger than we can manage. It is certainly a much bigger undertaking for families in rural areas, far from professional resources and groups of talented and eager college students. Children who *could* live more normal lives are being cheated. The school systems in most states believe this is not their responsibility. If they provide 40 hours of intensive treatment for one kid they might be asked to do it for *all* kids. Anyway, they will argue, they don't have to provide the most effective treatment—only some "appropriate" level of educational service. Most social or developmental service agencies also will not touch this. They tend to fund expensive residential placements or delay needed treatments for children living at home until they are older, more difficult to manage, and (so absurdly) active threats. So much for a stitch in time.

Thousands of families across the U.S., and now world-wide, have established home-based behavioral programs based on Dr. Lovaas' work. Many more would like to do so but cannot due to lack of either financial or technical resources. The treatment works to help children with autism learn to learn. Not every child learns this, but enough of them do so that the manager of your local large grocery store would, if he or she saw the data, tell you it was a good deal and that it would probably save our society money in the long run. The research is piling up. Replication projects, most with university affiliations, are operating in over 10 sites. Confirmation of the gains for all and the "recovery" for approximately one-half of the children is on the way. But even with stacks of data, I fear that our society will not acknowledge the value of these treatments. Of course, the policy makers will fritter away 5–10 years, and schools may work hard to "stonewall" family requests for support and funding. Affluent families will seek out the treatment and manage to have it implemented. They have this right, and they deserve to do everything

(continued)

they can to help their children. Are we, as a society and a country, so short-sighted and so heartless as to deny access to these treatments for young children who could, in many cases, no longer be disabled? It is no miracle cure and, as the Beach Boys say, "it's not a fad cause it's been going on so long." It is hard work for the family, child, teacher, and teaching assistants. In academic circles we love to talk about partnerships, especially with families. I can tell you, for a fact, that this is ground zero for creative parent-professional partnerships. The challenge is great and the results are smiling back at you.

Some privileged children are having their turn with intensive behavioral treatment, but all kids who can benefit need access to these treatments. Young children with autism need access to the best we, as a society, have to offer. Right now, the best is an intensive, home-based behavioral program. I hope that in this great country we can find a way to allow these children without a voice to get their turn!

Jack Scott, Ph.D., is a professor of special education and teaches courses in autism at Florida Atlantic University in Boca Raton, Florida.

Doman/Delacato Method

The Doman/Delacato method, a popular but discredited procedure in special education in the 1960s and 1970s, resurfaced during the 1990s as a means of helping children with autism. The research base for these treatments is sparse, with support chiefly in the form of "how-to" manuals (Doman, 1975). The Doman/Delacato method rests on the suggestion that children with brain damage pass through stages of neurological development. If children do not master the components of one stage, they are thought to have unrepairable problems that preclude moving on to "higher" stages. Treatments characteristic of the Doman/Delacato method are designed to help children master lower stages, often by going back to crawling. The original training is now streamlined and in most cases no longer takes extensive blocks of time.

Although the treatments have undergone modest change and the targeted populations have shifted over the years, one core feature of the Doman/Delacato method remains consistent: No scientific studies have provided any support for these treatments. Many parents are aware of this deficiency, but others still seek out these treatments in the hope of affecting a cure for their children. Certainly, the absence of independent effectiveness research should serve as a "red flag" for families and educators.

Dolphin therapy

Dolphins have been used in the treatment of students with autism (Livermore, 1991). Bottlenose dolphins and students with autism are brought together in the water for interaction and play for sessions of up to 20 minutes. Many guesses as to how the dolphins might assist students are available. In general, they rely on the idea that dolphins are "sensitive" to the needs of students with autism and seek to reach out and help via play and other expressions of concern. Smith (cited in Livermore, 1991) noted that dolphins communicate acoustically and with variety of body movements. She suggested that dolphins attend to the subtle body cues of students with autism and understand their thoughts and actions. St. John (1991) referred to a "secret language" that is shared when dolphins and students communicate. The suggestion of mystical sharing resonates with a public likely to have a distorted view of autism and little accurate knowledge of dolphin behavior.

Nathenson (also cited in Livermore, 1991) studied the impact of dolphin therapy on the retention and attention skills on students with mental retardation. He used the dolphins as both a stimulus and reinforcer and reported gains in learning rates. Nathenson noted, "I can't say I know exactly why it happens" (cited in Livermore, 1991). Our parsimonious explanation is that the opportunity to play with these animals is likely very reinforcing. In addition, the novelty, attention, and general quality of life enhancement accompanying repeated trips to the Florida Keys are factors likely to increase students' motivation and desire to learn. The problem with dolphin therapy, of course, is that the mechanism for change, if any change in fact occurred, is wholly unknown and relies on mystical explanation.

Playing with dolphins is expensive and poses inherent problems involving generalization in students' gains and in the dolphins' own way of life. Concerns over the possible exploitation of the dolphins, as well as the safety of both the dolphins and people, have led to regulatory efforts to limit these activities. Are dolphins able to offer a unique connection to students with autism? The limited research fails to make the case, and the modest results are far better explained by established principles of reinforcement. Will families spend thousands of dollars on these treatments, and bypass validated treatments? We hope not.

Summary

Each of the treatments discussed here has important weaknesses; several of these approaches rest their "successes" on the fact that their unsupported claims have gone without challenge for many years. What is needed in the field of autism is a means for navigating through these claims. The following section presents such a means by advocating a *scientific attitude* when considering treatments in autism.

THE ROLE OF SCIENCE IN AUTISM TREATMENT

If educators and others are to benefit from research and practice efforts, what systems will they use to guide their judgments? Given that unsupported and unsupportable claims have been able to earn a place in the field, we propose that the traditions of sound empirical research and scientific investigation provide the best framework for decision making. Science has earned a special place in our culture and has facilitated much of the technological progress we now take for granted. Applying scientific thinking will not be satisfactory to all. Many, most notably the proponents of some unvalidated treatments, will oppose a framework based on rational thinking. Their claims will certainly be deflated when scientific methods of evaluation are applied to their treatments. A greater emphasis on the scientific method, however, will raise the discernment level in the field; this can only raise the quality of education, treatment, and care of students with autism and do so with the resources likely to be available.

The field of autism should seek a more scientific orientation. Recent debacles, such as the unfettered claims involving facilitated communication, have a negative effect on the general public. The public can see the autism community as lacking in good sense and less worthy of financial and other support. As a national agenda for autism research is strengthening, funding agencies must be convinced that the proposals they fund are sound and a wise use of limited funding. The notable success of the National Association for Autism Research (NAAR) in quickly securing millions of dollars for research owes much to the clear and unequivocal scientific foundation of this organization. An important point brought to light by NAAR was the relatively weak federal support for autism research in contrast to other disability areas. This may have been due, in part, to the perceived lack of discernment in the field.

Funding for research on autism does not take place in a vacuum but in the context of multiple, often competing demands for social services. The gross deficiencies found in many schools, especially inner-city schools, contrast dramatically to schools in more affluent suburbs. Kozol (1991) has described this imbalance as one of "savage inequalities" and spotlights this competition for resources. Educators of students with autism can see the dramatic progress that can be achieved with good programming and know that efforts to increase research and dissemination dollars will prove very cost-effective. Funding agencies must be assured that the projects they back (and the field of autism in general) can tell a good result from a bad one and maintain the judgment to act on new information.

What are the hallmarks of a scientific approach to looking at human problems? Poling, Methot, and LeSage (1995) noted that:

> Science is a search for regularities in the natural world, a search that employs many strategies. Science is what scientists do, and scientists do many different things that affect the behavior of other people. (pp. 1–2)

They offered five characteristics that describe the behavior of scientists.

1. Scientists are concerned with empirical phenomena. This requires detailed, controlled, and objective observation of events which are recorded and analyzed. Others must also appraise the events.
2. Scientists disclose orderly relations between classes of events. These relations are used to explain natural relations, such as the relation between a behavior and variables within the environment which may affect it. Scientists seek to understand these relations and test their understanding by altering different conditions. When scientists can control the behavior reliably, they can be relatively confident that they understand the nature of the relationship of the variables. Active manipulation of variables is used in some experiments, but in human applications, we often observe naturally occurring variations.
3. Scientists attempt to predict and control their subject matter. The use of the term "control" is problematic for those who approach this discussion non-scientifically. Control does not mean that the scientist seeks to exert control over others. Rather, the word confirms the nature of a relation between factors that may be at work within a person's life. The current emphasis on functional assessment is clearly person-centered and empowering, while being at the same time an effort to understand the nature of variables that *control* a person's behavior.
4. Scientists assume that the phenomena they study are orderly and predictable. Scientists work on the assumption that things happen in response to laws of the universe. The roles of fate, psychic ability, and demons fail to meet the standards set by scientists for considering why things happen. This may be the characteristic of science most widely misunderstood. It has become popular in academic circles to assert that "old ways" of viewing the world are outmoded, and that new paradigms of investigation are required. Kuhn (1962) was among first to suggest that revolutions in scientific thinking would result when shared rules, research traditions, or other ways of knowing changed. When these shared rules are changed, a "paradigm shift" is said to have occurred. Many educators are infatuated with the notion of a scientific paradigm shift, yet have little sense of the shared rules and accumulated knowledge in the field. When paradigm shifts result in acceptance of knowledge previously shown (under the "old" para-

digm) to be harmful or wasteful to students, we suggest that a *regression* rather than a revolution in thinking has occurred.
5. Scientists make assertions that are tentative and testable. Science is self-checking and open to new information. This may be the most elegant and powerful characteristic of science. Assertions of scientists can be checked and the accuracy of their findings shown through replication. If independent scientists replicate a set of procedures, then confidence in this knowledge is increased. If no one can replicate the findings, confidence is decreased. (pp. 2–4)

In the practice of education, professionals must make countless decisions; obviously, they cannot set up formal, scientific experiments to analyze every situation. But educators can and must hold a set of principles to discern and appraise situations, and render sound judgments. They must have the skills to appreciate the research literature and to determine the value of the information offered to them. They must make judgments based on evidence. Such is the nature of science in everyday life. Sidman (1960) suggested that those who adopt the ideals of science will look for criteria, rules, and experimentation to find sound ways to evaluate information.

Skinner's (1953) statements on science presaged much of the problem faced by the autism community 40 years later. He wrote:

Science is first of all a set of attitudes. It is a disposition to deal with the facts rather than with what someone has said about them. Rejection of authority was the theme of the revival of learning, when men dedicated themselves to the study of "nature, not books." Science rejects even its own authorities when they interfere with the observation of nature. (p. xx)

Scientific thinking has brought tremendous benefit to civilization, but in many ways, the American public is scientifically naive, and falls victim to the most dazzling array of nonsense. Consider the popularity of psychic telephone advice, the X-Files, UFOs, and magic of all sorts. Sagan (1995) noted that the issues in medicine, technology, and other areas can seem so far beyond the grasp of average people that they are inclined to withdraw from engagement of these issues. He asked:

So how do Americans decide these matters? How do they instruct their representatives? Who in fact makes these decisions, and on what basis? (Sagan, 1995, p. 7)

The same questions face educators of students with autism, and one thing is clear: Turning away from logical and rational decision making will not improve the picture. Sagan offered advice on how to spot the more blatant offenses. Such tactics become essential with the proliferation of outrageous claims. Sagan labeled this the "fine art of baloney detection" and offered nine essential tools that should be in a *baloney detection kit*, including:

Whenever possible there must be independent confirmation of the "facts."

Facilitate real debate on the evidence by proponents representing all point's of view.

Do not give "authorities" special status as they have been wrong in the past. In science there are no authorities.

Spin more than one hypothesis and think of all the possible ways in which it could be explained. What survives will be better working hypotheses.

Avoid getting overly attached to your own personal hypothesis or theory because it is yours.

Quantify by attaching some numerical value to the measures. This is especially important when considering competing hypotheses.

If there's a chain of argument, every link in the chain must work—not just most of them.

Apply Occam's Razor—which urges us when faced with two hypotheses that explain the data equally well to select the simpler.

Ask whether the hypothesis can be . . . falsified. Propositions that are untestable, unfalsifiable are not worth much. You must be able to check assertions out. (Sagan, 1995, pp. 210–211)

These guidelines were not written with autism in mind, but their potential value to the field is obvious. Many of these elements are in place but others emerge a glaring weaknesses.

Pseudoscience and Antiscience and Autism

Psuedoscience and antiscience must be addressed in any thoughtful examination of treatments for student with autism. Green (1996) wrote that, "pseudoscience treats phenomena that do not have the hallmarks of scientific methods or evidence as if they were scientific" (p. 16). Television infomercials featuring lab-coated persons with scientific instruments are common examples of pseudoscience. Antiscience challenges or flatly rejects science, may assert that factual information is unobtainable, and that any fact is only in the mind of the beholder. (For further discussions of these issues see Jacobsen, Mulick, and Schwartz, 1995;

Randi, 1982; Stanovich, 1992; and Wolfensberger, 1994.) These issues are directly relevant to autism. Green (1996) summarized the situation accurately when she wrote:

> Many therapies that are currently being promoted for autism are pseudoscientific or anti-scientific. They are said to produce high success rates very rapidly with a wide range of disorders. Little training or expertise is required to administer them; belief and faith, on the other hand, are essential . . . little or no objective evidence is offered in support of claims about the therapies—only testimonials, anecdotes and personal stories. (p. 16)

Green recommended that parents and professionals carefully consider the evidence. Her suggestions are incorporated into the guidelines for treatment selection provided at the end of this chapter. Increased sophistication on the part of parents and professionals is necessary to cope with the perils of unsupported claims in autism.

Beyond both pseudoscience and antiscience are examples of "pathological science" (Wolfensberger, 1994), "the science of things that aren't so." Wolfensberger described the trend toward fads and crazes in human services as wasteful and harmful to persons with disabilities. He noted:

> This craziness for crazes consists of a mindless surrender by much of science and the lay public to any number of fads or crazes that flash across the scene in bewildering variety, boosted by much hoopla and hype, often cloaked in scientific language and accompanied by claims to a scientific, research, and intellectual base. (p. 58)

As an example of pathological science, Wolfensberger suggested that excessive dogmatism led the promoters of facilitated communication to actively ignore the role of critical external examination. The absence of rigorous inquiry resulted in intense confrontation between proponents and detractors. The Wolfensberger critique has become one of the more provocative pieces of scholarship in special education.

The lack of accepted criteria for evaluating autism treatments is clearly evident in the Autism Society of America's option policy (Autism Society of America, 1997). This policy promotes the right of access to all available treatments. It states, in part:

> Each family and individual with autism should have the right to learn about and then select, the options that they feel are most appropriate for the individual with autism. . . . The ASA believes that all individuals with autism have the right to access appropriate services and supports based on their needs and desires (p. 4).

The ASA newsletter clearly indicates that the organization does not, as policy, endorse treatments. In this context, parents and professionals are left alone to determine effective interventions. This failure to provide direction is criticized openly, even within the *Advocate*. Woodward (1997) wrote:

> I have been concerned about the lack of direction from ASA on autism treatments. . . . It is unfortunate that ASA, in its efforts to represent the broad diversity within the autism community, has been on the lagging edge of science (p. 7).

The climate of uncritical acceptance was challenged directly by a group of behavioral scientists (Green, 1996; Maurice, 1996; Smith, 1996). Smith, for example, offered assessments for a full range of treatments. He summarized:

> Investigations have indicated that . . . [facilitated communication and psychoanalysis] . . . are based on erroneous theories and harm children with autism and their families. The remaining treatments (speech and language therapies, Sensory Integration Therapy and Auditory Integration Training) may offer some benefits, although this has yet to be demonstrated, and the available evidence on one treatment (Sensory Integration Therapy) is not promising. If the treatments are beneficial, they probably do not improve all areas of functioning; rather, improvements are likely to be continued to the few specific behaviors targeted for treatment. (p. 52)

This assessment is consistent with the published research and should have been welcomed by the autism community. Although many did value this appraisal, it engendered bitter criticism from key leaders in the field. The nature of the criticism by the supporters of the poorly performing therapies prompted Maurice (1996, p. 3) to comment:

> Autism will not be cured through personal attacks . . . it will not be overcome through enthusiastic and precipitous endorsement of every fad and miracle cure; it will not respond to personality cults, media celebrities, and religiously-held beliefs; it will not be alleviated through mountains of impassioned testimonials and correspondingly weak data. It will be cured in the end through science: good science, peer-reviewed, replicated, objectively validated.

This is the logical path for educators. The supporters of unvalidated treatments must be willing to conduct the needed studies, write up their findings, and share these data in reputable journals and other peer-reviewed forums. The era of uncritical acceptance of autism treatments has passed. A scientific way of thinking should become primary in the appraisal of all claims, both new and old.

What Criteria Should Then Be Applied?

In fields outside of education, a change in the climate of tolerance for unvalidated treatments is apparent. For example, the recent editorial on alternative treatments in the *New England Journal of Medicine* pointed to less tolerance toward controversial and unsubstantiated treatments in medicine.

> It is time for scientific community to stop giving alternative medicine a free ride. There cannot be two kinds of medicine—conventional and alternative. There is only medicine that has been adequately tested and medicine that has not, medicine that may or may not work. Once a treatment has been tested rigorously, it no longer matters whether it was considered alternative at the outset. If it is found to be reasonably safe and effective, it will be accepted. But assertions, speculation, and testimonials do not substitute for evidence. Alternative treatments should be subjected to scientific testing no less rigorous than that required for conventional treatments (Angell & Kassirer, 1999, p. 60).

This strong statement appearing in one of the leading medical journals is indeed noteworthy. A similar standard is needed in education in general, special education in particular, and with the greatest urgency in autism. Although the autism community as a whole may not yet be prepared to embrace this standard, we believe that educators should and will be in the forefront of such an effort. Toward this end, we propose the following criteria when educators consider interventions for students with autism and related disabilities.

1. What is the nature of the claims?
   - What are the qualifications of the individuals doing the studies?
   - Are the claims based on empirical research or testimonials?
   - Are the claims being made substantiated by the research findings?
   - Can the claims be explained by different, simpler factors?
2. Are there professionals in the field who challenge the efficacy of the intervention?
   - Are these challenges adequately addressed?
   - Are the challenges dismissed as "old thinking" or ignored?
3. Are there financial and/or professional incentives associated with the intervention?
   - Are the proponents of the intervention positioned to gain financially from its acceptance?

- Are there professionals who are not financially involved in the intervention who recognize its effectiveness?
- What are the positions of the relevant professional and consumer organizations?

4. For whom has this intervention been effective?
   - What features do the students share?
   - What happened to the individuals for whom it was not effective?
   - How would a teacher know whether this intervention was working?
   - How would a teacher know whether the intervention was not working?

5. Are there any risks associated with the intervention?
   - Do the potential risks associated with the intervention outweigh the likely positive effects?
   - Will the intervention interfere with the student's routines or quality of life?
   - Will the student have to give up other successful interventions to access this intervention?
   - Are there financial, emotional, or other risks to the family of the student?

6. Are there decision rules involving the intervention?
   - Is guidance provided about the amount of time per day needed for the intervention?
   - How many days, weeks, or months will be needed of the intervention?
   - How are decisions made involving whether to continue, strengthen, or decrease the intervention?
   - Is guidance provided so that the intervention will promote functional skills?

SUMMARY

In the final analysis, a fundamental test of any theory is its utility. Do explanations derived from a given theory allow educators and parents to more successfully help students with autism? How do educators select interventions for students who need substantial support? Certainly, educators need to learn to hone their "baloney detection" skills. These skills are needed to cull through the controversies summarized in this chapter; unfortunately, additional controversies abound.

For far too long, professionals and families have been unwilling to discriminate proven from unproven interventions. It is time for educators to establish *effectiveness* as a primary standard in selecting interventions. *This should not be controversial!* Keeping students and families from harm is just as (or even more) important as treatment effectiveness. Not all treatments currently available are helpful, and some even pose significant risks. These risks may go beyond abusing a family's good faith and emotional well-being.

Unscrupulous practices have been identified in several areas of special education (Silver, 1987). Bogus remedies and fraudulent medical treatments abound and are estimated to cost millions of dollars each year. The costs and unneeded pain and suffering are incalculable. Developing a *scientific attitude* as a way of thinking about autism interventions holds promise for educators, families, and students. We must never allow the proposition that practices validated as effective are controversial.

REVIEW QUESTIONS

1. What are some of the defining features of a theory?

2. How has the unique history of the field of autism helped to shape support for a broad array of poorly researched treatments.

3. What are some of the most noteworthy controversies in the field of autism?

4. How does the lack of a scientific attitude on the part of promoters of unvalidated interventions contribute to controversy?

5. How do science, pseudoscience, and antiscience relate to consideration of interventions for students with autism?

6. What scientific attitudes should an educator apply when evaluating claims for autism interventions?

REFERENCES

American Society of Autism. (1997). Resources for therapies and treatments. *Advocate, 29*(1), 20–23.

American Speech-Language-Hearing Association (1994). Auditory integration training. *Asha, 36,* 55–58.

Angell, M., & Kassirer, J. P. (1999, January/February). Alternative Medicine: The risks of untested and unregulated remedies. *Skeptical Inquirer*, pp. 58–60.

Ayres, A. J. (1972). *Sensory integration and learning disorders*. Los Angeles: Western Psychological Services.

Ayres, A. J. (1975). *Sensory integration and the child*. Los Angeles: Western Psychological Services.

Ayres, A. J. (1979). Sensorimotor foundations of academic ability. In W. M. Cruickshank & D. P. Hallahan (Eds.), *Perception and learning disabilities in children* (Vol. 2, pp. 301–358). Syracuse: Syracuse University Press.

Ayres, A. J., & Tickle, L. S., (1980). Hyperresponsivity to touch and vestibular stimuli as a predictor of positive response to sensory integration procedures by autistic children. *American Journal of Occupational Therapy, 31*, 444–453.

Baron-Cohen, S. (1995). *Mindblindness*. London: MIT Press.

Berard, G. (1993). *Hearing equals behavior*. New Canaan, CT: Keats.

Bettelheim, B. (1967). *The empty fortress*. New York: Free Press.

Biklen, D. (1990). Communication unbound: Autism and praxis. *Harvard Educational Review, 60*, 291–314.

Biklen, D. (1993). Re: Wheeler et al. "OD Heck study." In *Facilitated Communication Advanced Workshop* (pp. 43–49). Syracuse, NY: Syracuse University.

Biklen, D. & Cardinal, D. (Eds.) (1997). *Contested words, contested science: Unraveling the facilitated communication controversy*. New York: Teachers College Press.

Biklen, D., & Schubert, A. (1991). New words: The communication of students with autism. *Remedial and Special Education, 12*(6), 46–57.

Board of Education of the Hendrick Hudson School District v. Rowley (1982). 458 US 176.

Bolander, A. (1992). *The new Webster's medical dictionary*. Hartford, CT: Lewton.

Braman, B., Brady, M. P., & Williams, R. E. (1995). Facilitated communication for children with autism: An examination of face validity. *Behavioral Disorders, 21*(1), 110–118.

Brocket, S., Edelson, S., & Woodward, D. (Eds.). (1995). *The sound connection, 3*(2), 1.

Calculator, S., & Hatch, E. (1995). Validation of facilitated communication: A case study and beyond. *American Journal of Speech-Language Pathology, 4*, 49–58.

Casti, J. L. (1989). *Paradigms Lost: Images of man in the mirror of science*. New York: William Morrow.

Chance, P. (1987, December). Saving grace. *Psychology Today*, pp. 42–44.

Chaplin, J. P. (1975). *Dictionary of psychology*. New York: Dell.

Charman, T., & Lynggaard, H. (1998). Does a photographic cue facilitate false belief performance in subjects with autism? *Journal of Autism and Developmental Disorders, 25*, 33–42.

Chu, S. (1991, September). Sensory integration and autism: A review of the literature. *Sensory Integration Quarterly*, pp. 3–6.

Crossley, R., & MacDonald, A. (1984). *Annie's coming out*. New York: Viking Penguin.

Doman, G. (1974). *What to do about your brain-injured child*. New York: Doubleday.

Favell, J. E., McGimsey, J. F., & Schell, R. M. (1982). Treatment of self-injury by providing alternative sensory activities. *Analysis and Intervention in Developmental Disabiltes, 2*, 83–104.

Feinberg, E., & Beyer, J. (1997). Creating public policy in a climate of clinical indeterminacy: Lovaas as the case example du jour. *Infants and Young Children, 10*(3), 1–10.

Fisher, A. G., Murray, E. A., Bundy, A. C. (Eds.). (1991). *Sensory integration: Theory and practice*. Philadelphia: F. A. Davis.

Fox, S. (1992). The emergence of auditory training in the treatment of autism. *Advance for Speech-Language Pathologists and Audiologists, 11, 1*.

Frith, U. (1989). *Autism*. Oxford: Basil Blackwell.

Gardner, R., Sainato, D. M., Cooper, J. O., Heron, T. E., Heward, W. L., Eshelman, J. W., & Grossi, T. A. (1994). *Behavior analysis in education: Focus on measurably superior instruction*. Pacific Grove, CA: Brooks/Cole.

Gerlach, E. K. (1993). *Autism treatment guide*. Eugene, OR: Four Leaf Press.

Gillberg, C., Johansson, M., Stefenburg, S., & Berlin, O. (1997). Auditory integration training in children with autism: Brief report of an open pilot study. *Autism, 1*, 97–100.

Gollan, K. (1996, July 29). Autism: A special report. *Australian Broadcasting Corporation, National Radio Transcripts*, 1–11. http://www.ABC.net.au/rn/talks

Grandin, T. (1995). *Thinking in pictures*. New York: Doubleday.

Grandin, T., & Scariano, M. M. (1986). *Emergence: Labeled autistic*. Novato, CA: Arena Press.

Gravel, J. S. (1994) Auditory Integration Training: Placing the burden of proof. *American Journal of Speech Language Pathology, 3*, 25–29.

Green, G. (1994a). Facilitated communication. *Skeptic, 2*, 68–76.

Green, G. (1994b). The quality of the evidence. In H. Shane (Ed.), *Facilitated communication: The clinical and social phenomenon* (pp 157–225). San Diego: Singular Publishing Group.

Green, G. (1996). Evaluating claims about treatments for autism. In C. Maurice, G. Green, & S. Luce (Eds.), *Behavioral interventions for young children with autism* (pp. 15–28). Austin, TX: Pro-Ed.

Gresham, F., & MacMillan, D. (1998a). Autism recovery? An analysis and critique of the empirical evidence on the Early Intervention Project. *Behavioral Disorders, 22*, 185–201.

Gresham, F., & MacMillan, D. (1998). Early Intervention Project: Can its claims be substantiated and its effects replicated? *Journal of Autism and Developmental Disorders, 28*(1), 5–13.

Gunter, P., Brady, M. P., Shores, R. E., Fox, J., Owen, S., & Goldzweig, I. (1984). The reduction of aberrant vocalizations with auditory feedback and resulting collateral behavior change of two autistic boys. *Behavioral Disorders, 9*, 254–263.

Hadwin, J., Baron-Cohen, S., Howlin, P., & Hill, K. (1997). Does teaching theory of mind have an effect on the ability to develop conversation in children with autism? *Journal of Autism and Developmental Disorders, 5*, 519–537.

Hammill, D. D., Goodman, L., & Wiederholt, J. L. (1974). Visual-motor processes: Can we train them? *Reading Teacher, 27*, 469–478.

Hammill, D. D., & Larson, S. C. (1974). The effectiveness of psycholinguistic training. *Exceptional Children, 41*, 5–14.

Hammill, D. D., & Larsen, S. C. (1978). The effectiveness of psycholinguistic training: A reaffirmation of position. *Exceptional Children, 44*, 402–414.

Hammill, D. D., & Wiederholt, J. L. (1973). Review of the Frostig Visual Perception Test and the related training program. In L. Mann & D. Sabatino (Eds.), *The first review of special education* (Vol. 1, pp. 33–48). Philadelphia: Journal of Special Education Press.

Haskew, P., & Donnellan, A. (1992). *Emotional maturity and well being: Psychological lessons of facilitated communication* (Movin' on: Beyond facilitated communication). Danbury, CT: DRI Press.

Hostler, S., Allaire, J., & Christoph, R. (1993). Childhood sexual abuse reported by facilitated communication. *Pediatrics, 91,* 1190–1192.

Intellectual Disability Review Panel. (1989). *Investigation into the reliability and validity of the assisted communication technique.* Community Services Victoria, Australia: Author.

Itard, J. M. (1962). *The wild boy of Aveyron.* (Translated by George & Muriel Humphrey.) New York: Appleton Century Crofts.

Iwata, B. A., Zarcone, J. B., Vollmer, T. R., & Smith, R. G. (1994). Assessment and treatment of self-injurious behavior. In E. Schopler & G. Mesibov (Eds.), *Behavioral issues in autism.* New York: Plenum.

Jacobson, J.W., Mulick, J., Schwartz, A. (1995). A history of facilitated communication: Science, pseudoscience, and antiscience. *American Psychologist, 50,* 750–765.

Kozol, J. (1991). *Savage inequalities: Children in America's schools.* New York: Crown Publishers.

Kuhn, T.S. (1962). *The structure of scientific revolutions.* Chicago: University of Chicago Press.

Lindsley, O. (1964). Direct measurement and prothesis of retarded behavior. *Journal of Education, 147,* 62–81.

Livermore, B. (1991). Water wings: Swimming with dolphins may be the boost special kids need. *Sea Frontiers, 37*(2), 44–52.

Lovaas, O. I. (1977). *The autistic child: Language development through behavior modification.* New York: Irvington Publishers.

Lovaas, O. I. (1987). Behavioral treatment and normal educational and intellectual functioning in young autistic children. *Journal of Consulting and Clinical Psychology, 55,* 3–9.

Lovaas, O. I. (1997). The UCLA Young Autism Project: A reply to Gresham and MacMillan. *Behavioral Disorders, 22,* 202–217.

Lovaas, I., Calouri, K., & Jada, J. (1989). The nature of behavioral treatment and research with young autistic persons. In C. Gillberg (Ed.), *Diagnosis and treatment in autism* (pp. 285–305) New York: Plenum Press.

Madell, J. (1995). *AIT treatment outcomes.* Presented at ASHA teleseminar.

Mason, S. A., & Iwata, B. A. (1990). Artifactual effects of sensory-integrative therapy on self-injurious behavior. *Journal of Applied Behavior Analysis, 23,* 362–370.

Maurice, C. (1993). *Let me hear your voice.* New York: Knopf.

McEachin, J., Smith, T., & Lovaas, O. I. (1993). Long term outcomes for children with autism who received early intensive behavioral treatment. *American Journal on Mental Retardation, 97,* 359–372.

McKenchie, J. L. (1983). *Webster's new twentieth century dictionary.* New York: Simon & Schuster.

Mercer, C. (1997). *Students with learning disabilities.* Upper Saddle River, NJ: Merrill.

Mundy, P. (1993). Normal versus high-functioning state in children with autism. *American Journal on Mental Retardation, 97,* 381–384.

Ornitz, E., & Ritvo,E. (1968). Perceptual inconstancy in early infantile autism. *Archives of General Psychiatry, 18,* 76–98.

O'Shea, L. J., O'Shea, D. J., & Algozzine, R. (1998). *Learning disabilites: From theory toward practice.* Columbus, OH: Merrill.

Parham, L. D., & Mailloux, Z. (1996). Sensory integration. In Smith, Allen, & Pratt (Eds.), *Occupational therapy for children.* St. Louis: Mosby.

Perner, J., Leekam, R., & Wimmer, H. (1987). Three-year olds' difficulty with false belief: The case for a conceptual deficit. *British Journal of Developmental Psychology, 5,* 125–137.

Poling, A., Methot, L. L., & LeSage, M. G. (1995). *Fundamentals of behavior analytic research.* New York: Plenum Press.

Prior, M., & Cummins, R. (1992). Questions about facilitated communication and autism. *Journal of Autism and Developmental Disorders, 22,* 331–337.

Randi, J. (1982). *Flim-flam!* Buffalo, NY: Prometheus Books.

Riddle, M. A. (1987). Individual and parental psychotherapy in autism. In D. J. Cohen & A.M. Donellan (Eds.), *Handbook of autism and pervasive developmental disabilities* (pp. 528–541). Silver Spring, MD: Winston and Sons.

Rimland, B. (1964). *Infantile autism: The syndrome and its implications for a neural theory of behavior.* New York: Prentice-Hall.

Rimland, B. (1991). Facilitated communication: Problems, puzzles, and paradoxes. *Autism Research Review International, 5,* 3.

Rimland, B., & Edelson, S. (1991). *Improving the auditory functioning of autistic persons: A comparison of the Berard Auditory Training Approach with the Tomatis audio-psycho-phonology approach* (Tech. rep. No. 111). San Diego: Autism Research Institute.

Rimland, B., & Edelson, S. M. (1992). *Auditory integration training in autism: A pilot study* (Tech. rep. No. 111). San Diego: Autism Research Institute.

Rimland, B., & Edelson, S. (1995). Brief report: A pilot study of auditory integration training in autism. *Journal of Autism and Developmental Disorders, 25,* 61–70.

Rincover, A. (1981). *How to use sensory extinction.* Austin, TX: Pro-Ed.

Rincover, A. Cook, R. Peoples, A., & Packard, D. (1979). Sensory extinction and sensory reinforcement principles for programming multiple adaptive behavior change. *Journal of Applied Behavior Analysis, 12,* 221–233.

Rogers, S. (1996). Brief report: Early intervention in autism. *Journal of Autism and Developmental Disorders, 26,* 243–246.

Sagan, C. (1995). *The demon haunted world.* New York: Random House.

Sachs, O. (1994, December 27/January 3). An anthropologist on Mars. *New Yorker,* 106–125.

Schlinger, H. D. (1995). *A behavior analytic view of child development.* New York: Plenum Press.

Schopler, E., Short, A., & Mesibov, G. (1989) Relation of behavioral treatment to "normal functioning:" Comment on Lovaas. *Journal of Consulting and Clinical Psychology, 57,* 162–164.

Sensory Integration International. (1991). *A parent's guide to sensory integration.* Torrance, CA: Author.

Shane, H. (Ed.). (1994). *Facilitated communication: The clinical and social phenomenon.* San Diego: Singular Publishing Group.

Sidman, M. (1960). *Tactics of scientific research: Evaluating experimental data in Psychology.* New York: Basic Books.

Silver, L. B. (1987). The "magic cure:" A review of the current controversial approaches for treating learning disabilites. *Journal of Learning Disabilites, 20,* 498–504.

Simpson, R. L., & Myles, B. S. (1998). *Educating children and youth with autism.* Austin, TX: Pro-Ed.

Singer, M. T., & Lalich, J. (1996). *"Crazy" therapies: What are they? Do they work?* San-Fransisco: Jossey Bass.

Skinner, B. F. (1953). *Science and human behavior.* New York: Free Press.

Skinner, B. F. (1956). A case study in scientific methods. *American Psychologist, 11,* 221–233.

Sloan, C. (1986). *Treating auditory processing difficulties in children: Clinical updates in speech-language pathology.* San Diego: College-Hill Press.

Smaldino, J., Saul, R., & Carlson, D., (1983). Toward an understanding of auditory processing in autism. *Seminars in Speech and Language, 4,* 43–51.

Smith, C. R. (1991). *Learning disabilites: The interaction of learner, tasks and setting.* Boston: Allyn & Bacon.

Smith, T. (1996). Are other treatments effective? In C. Maurice, G. Green, & S. Luce (Eds.), *Behavioral interventions for young children with autism* (pp. 45–59). Austin, TX: Pro-Ed.

Smith, T., & Lovaas, O.I. (1997). The UCLA Young Autism Project: A reply to Gresham and MacMillan. *Behavioral Disorders, 22,* 202–218.

Snow, C. E., Burns, M. S., & Griffin, P. (1998). *Preventing reading difficulties in young children.* Washington, DC: National Academy Press.

St. John, P. (1991). *The secret language of dolphins.* New York: Summit Books.

Stanovich, K. (1992). *How to think straight about psychology.* New York: HarperCollins.

Stehli, A. (1991). *The sound of a miracle: A child's triumph over autism.* New York: Doubleday.

Stehli, A. (1995). *Dancing in the rain.* Westport, CT: Georgiana Organization.

Tustin, C. (1995). *Autism and childhood psychosis.* London: Karnac.

Upledger, J. E. (1983). Cranialsacral function in brain dysfunction. *Osteopathic Annals, 11,* 318–324.

Veale, T. K. (1995). *Auditory integration training: A review of current research.* Paper presented at the 1995 National Conference on Autism, Raleigh, NC.

Watkins, C. L. (1997). *Project Follow Through: A case study of contingencies influencing instructional practices of the educational establishment.* Concord, MA: Cambridge Center for Behavioral Studies.

Wheeler, D., Jacobson, J., Paglieri, R. & Swartz, A. (1993). An experimental assessment of facilitated communication. *Mental Retardation, 31,* 49–60.

Wing, L. (1976). *Early childhood autism.* New York: Pergamon Press.

Williams, D. (1993). *Nobody, nowhere.* New York: Times Books.

Wolfensberger, W. (1994). The "facilitated communication" craze as an instance of pathological science: The Cold Fusion of human services. In H. Shane (Ed.),

Facilitated communication: The clinical and social phenomenon (pp. 57–122). San Diego: Singular Publishing Group.

Woodward, K. G. (1997). Research and the options policy. *Advocate, 29*(2), 7.

Zollweg, W., Vance, V., & Palm, D., (1995, November). *A double-blind, placebo controlled study of the efficacy of Auditory Integration Training.* Paper presented to the annual convention of the American Speech-Language-Hearing Association, Orlando, FL.

Chapter 5

PROMOTING BEHAVIORAL COMPETENCE

Key Points

- The nature of behavioral challenges in students with autism
- The necessity for behavioral interventions
- Determining the function of problem or challenging behavior
- Increasing a student's behavioral repertoire
- Continuum of educative behavioral interventions
- Improvement of quality of life as an intervention

INTRODUCTION

Students with autism often display serious disorders in their personal and social behavior. The methods used to alter problem behavior have changed substantially in the past two decades. This chapter reviews current methods of altering problem behavior. This includes an analysis of the function that problem behavior serves, the design of educative interventions to replace the problem behavior with more socially acceptable behavior, and the role that an improved quality of life plays in reducing challenging behavior.

THE NATURE OF PROBLEM BEHAVIOR

One of the primary difficulties exhibited by students with autism is a "markedly restricted repertoire of activities and interests" (APA, 1994). These difficulties are often observed as tantrums or distress behaviors during transitions or with deviations from established routines. Problem behavior can make it very difficult to include students with autism in typical classroom, community, or home environments. Whereas some aspects of the disability of autism may be private (such as unusual responses to sensory stimuli or atypical perceptions of the motivations of others), the behavior of a person with autism is immediately observable to others. Problem behaviors may differ for a wide variety of reasons. Some behaviors are influenced by biological factors; others are due to past learning. When problem behaviors are obvious or interfere with learning, educators are likely to devalue the student.

Some students with autism exhibit a *preoccupation* with one or two narrow interests and are unwilling to move on to other subjects or activities. Some exhibit stereotyped body movements such as hand flapping, hand biting, or spinning. These behaviors can isolate the student from peers, reduce the opportunities for social interactions, and interfere with normalization.

Some behaviors can be viewed as *excesses*; these behaviors occur over longer durations or at a higher frequency or rate than would be considered normal in students without autism. Perseveration on particular topics or with specific parts of objects is considered a behavioral excess. Teachers uninitiated to autism often have the greatest difficulty with excess behavior.

Other behaviors can be viewed as *deficits*; these behaviors may be missing or occur with lower duration, frequency, or rate. Deficits often include behaviors used as substitutes for more appropriate behaviors. (For example, a student's deficit in communicating frustration might result in frequent tantrums.) Difficulty initiating social contact is a common example of a behavioral deficit in students with autism.

A fourth category of problem behaviors are those that are exhibited *out of context*. These are behaviors that are appropriate to specific settings or circumstances, but become problematic when displayed outside those circumstances. Taking off clothes is an appropriate activity in one's own room, but is obviously not appropriate at the supermarket. Clapping hands may be appropriate at the end of a play, but not at a funeral.

When an intervention is needed, the choice of intervention is influenced by whether the behavior is a preoccupation, an excess, a deficit, or displayed out of context. Formal intervention may be needed to reduce or increase a particular behavior's duration, frequency, or rate or to target a more appropriate replacement behavior for acquisition. It may be necessary to teach students to recognize the contextual cues that make a particular behavior appropriate to a specific setting. Teachers should not assume that the student can perform an appropriate behavior unless it has been observed repeatedly or directly taught as a replacement behavior.

Traditionally, educators provide strong negative consequences for challenging behavior. Schloss and Smith (1998) noted that the traditional discipline model for public schools has been to respond to "behavior that violates the expectations of the educator [with] unpleasant conditions expected to deter the future occurrence of the behavior" (p. 25). Even when teachers use only punishers considered acceptable in regular classes or schools, this orientation is reactive and is counterproductive to learning. Punishment is generally regarded as an outdated, unnecessary intervention (Repp & Singh, 1990). Unfortunately, some teachers and many parents still view punishment as an acceptable intervention, often the intervention of choice, for students with autism. In past years, the target of punishment-based interventions was simply to make the student stop performing a problem behavior. If the student did not stop performing the targeted behavior, unpleasant consequences (punishers) were applied. If the application of punishers was not effective, the teacher's focus shifted to removing the student from the classroom.

In contrast, good educational programming for students with autism requires proactive and creative responses by adults to the challenges presented by these students. While punishers might suppress a specific behavior, students *do not learn to engage in useful and productive behavior with punishers.*

The Development of Behavioral Interventions

The field of applied behavior analysis (ABA) has given rise to most of the effective and efficient interventions for students with autism. ABA is relatively young; the first issue of the *Journal of Applied Behavior Analysis* in 1968 serves as a convenient starting point. In spite of the recency of the development of ABA, the field has evolved rapidly. Today it is possible to identify six overlapping phases in this short history that are relevant for educators of students with autism.

1. *Definition of the field and demonstrations of the power of interventions based on positive reinforcement in applied settings.* Authors such as Baer, Wolf, and Risley (1968) and Repp and Deitz (1974) exemplify this stage of the field.

2. *Recognition of the need for more effective generalization of newly learned skills, with an emphasis on the selection of relevant targets for intervention and systematic generalization programming.* Stokes and Baer's (1977) now classic work on generalization best illustrates this phase in the development of ABA. In an innovative application of photographic activity schedules, MacDuff, Krantz, and McClannahan (1993) provided an example of an autism-specific study in which generalization of gains was the essence of the intervention.

3. *Discovery of the functions served by problem behavior and appreciation of the need for functional assessment prior to an intervention.* The findings of Iwata, Dorsey, Slier, Bauman, and Richman (1982) and Carr, Newsom, and Binkoff (1980) illustrate this stage in the development of the field. These studies demonstrated the relationship between severe problem behavior and the environment.

4. *Refinement of functional assessment procedures; attention to the social acceptability of interventions and the need to develop a positive orientation to behavior change in increasingly normalized settings.* Horner et al. (1990) helped define this phase in general, and Koegel, Koegel, Hurley, and Frea (1992) provided specific application to children with autism.

5. *Appreciation of the communicative functions of most, if not all, problem or challenging behaviors.* These problem communications are often best addressed by means of skill training, including Functional Communication Training in which the person is taught to use alternative, more socially acceptable forms of communication. Durand and Carr (1991) exemplify this emphasis.

6. *Movement toward teaching parents and primary caregivers to use proactive strategies to forestall the development of problem behaviors and to teach productive behavior.* This research links early intervention to functional assessment. Mullen and Frea (1994) provide an example of this trend. A separate but related trend is the movement for parents to *establish intensive, home-based early intervention programs.* Although

many of these programs follow a model similar to that described by Lovaas (1987), a significant number feature a compilation of intensive behavioral teaching strategies (Maurice, 1996).

Interventions that evolved from applied behavior analysis research have done much to improve the lives of persons with autism. Much of the early work in ABA focused on arranging consequences—positive and negative—for various target behaviors. The focus on consequences, however, led to problems in generalizing newly acquired behaviors and in maintaining these behaviors over time. Consider, for example, how it would be possible to reinforce a child for engaging in a behavior during an intervention, but at the end of the formal intervention, to no longer have a system in place for delivering reinforcers. In the early development of ABA, this situation was often present. In addition, the experimental nature of ABA often resulted in more emphasis on research designs that would establish behavioral relationships and less emphasis on improving the quality of life of individuals involved in the studies.

In response to these limitations, ABA as a field, and many active researchers in autism and special education in particular, initiated a search for more natural ways to intervene. A philosophy of benign, effective intervention is a prominent feature of the new face of ABA. Providing access to quality behavioral services has always been important for the behavioral community (Van Houten et al., 1988) but, increasingly, issues of human dignity and the right of a person with disabilities to be free from some classes of intrusive intervention are being considered (Horner et al., 1990).

An important element of the new understanding of problem behavior is the notion that *problem behavior often serves a communicative function* and that treatment will be effective when the person learns new and more efficient means of communicating (Carr et al., 1994; Carr & Durand, 1985). Finally, those asked to intervene are asked to consider the overall quality of life of the person displaying problem behaviors. This has emerged along with recognition that it is unfair and unethical simply to promote compliance; educators must also help people to learn the skills needed to succeed in real world settings.

Evolution to Positive Behavioral Support

The shift in the type, nature, and philosophy of interventions that target problem behavior has generally become known as *positive behavioral support* or PBS. To date, much of the PBS research has involved students and adults with autism. Nevertheless, PBS has been slow to impact the practice and training of special educators, school psychologists, and others likely to have direct contact with students with autism. Hobbs, Westling, and Hatoum (1996) examined the ABA textbooks used in large special education teacher training programs. None of the books fully presented the PBS approach in a comprehensive manner; the coverage that was provided was highly variable and often not cohesive. Hobbs et al. noted that each presented its own strengths but none of the texts that were used had an explicit PBS focus.

A central tenet of PBS is that interventions for students with problem behavior should be based on the realization that many of these students have limited opportunities to learn or to make choices. Interventions that target problem behavior are most effective when they fulfill an educative purpose, thereby enabling a student to engage in behavior that is equally as productive and efficient as the problem behavior. Changing behavior through PBS can result in broad changes in a person's lifestyle.

Some in the behavioral community regard PBS as a radical departure from ABA; others advocate using PBS "versus" ABA (Turnbull, 1997). We believe these characterizations are wrong. PBS represents a natural and logical progression in ABA and an increased sophistication in intervention effectiveness. In many ways the evolution of PBS mirrors the changes in education itself. As students with moderate to severe disabilities were increasingly included in typical schools and communities, a different emphasis in teaching and support was inevitable. An emphasis on values, with calls for the restriction or elimination of certain classes of punishers, has revitalized the *emphasis on teaching* students with the most difficult challenges and has led many parents to regain their enthusiasm for behavioral interventions. PBS represents the evolution of behavior technology and a development of those approaches most suitable for addressing challenging, problem behaviors in home, school, and community. Certainly as parents' homes and neighborhood schools have become the natural places for children with more serious disabilities, interventions suitable for these very normal settings must be developed. The evolution toward positive behavioral support represents the most vivid example of this process.

What is positive behavioral support? Anderson, Albin, Mesaros, Dunlap, and Morelli-Robbins (1993) provided four defining elements, which can be summarized as:

1. A focus on educative approaches, proactive strategies, and hypothesis-driven interventions;
2. A shift from decelerative behavior change procedures to multicomponent interventions and comprehensive supports;
3. Broadened criteria of success for an intervention that emphasize behavior change in the context of quality of life;
4. Development of long-term support and intervention plans rather than "quick-fix" strategies.

In addition to these defining elements it is important to recognize the philosophical underpinnings of PBS. In an article titled, "Toward a Technology of Nonaversive Behavioral Support," Horner et al. (1990) made a clear statement of the values supporting this direction in behavioral services. Three key points are emphasized: (a) the expectation of positive technology, (b) emphasis on social validation and human dignity in determining the appropriateness of behavioral programs, and (c) recommendations for prohibition or severe restriction on the use of intrusive punishers. This article has been an important bridge between technology and human values. The authors base their thesis on clear statements that offer "a commitment to the value that people with severe disabilities who exhibit challenging behaviors should be treated with the same respect and dignity as all other members of our communities." To further these ends, they are opposed to "an emphasis on behavioral suppression by means of aversives" and strongly in favor of "a focus on positive procedures that educate and promote the development of adaptive sets of behaviors" (p. 125).

Horner et al. (1990) went on to operationalize positive behavioral support. They offered nine competencies that we believe teachers of students with autism should have. These competencies include:

1. *An emphasis on lifestyle change.* No matter how technically sophisticated, narrowly focused interventions will not help a person overcome a poor quality of life. Support efforts must increasingly focus on upgrading the lifestyles of students with autism and seek never to degrade their lifestyles simply to improve their behavior.

2. *Functional analysis: Assessing antecedents and consequences.* Intervention must be based on systematic behavioral assessment of the functions served by the problem behaviors.

3. *Multicomponent interventions: Durable change efforts demand multiple changes.* The student with autism will typically be expected to change, but adults in the environment must be willing to arrange multiple interventions to support this change. This includes engineering the environment to make it more responsive to the needs of the student.

4. *Manipulating ecological and setting events.* This suggests a shift from "contingency management" to more active changes of the settings to enable the student to function most successfully.

5. *Emphasis on antecedent manipulations.* Managing consequences traditionally has been the main strategy in applied behavior analysis, but PBS emphasizes events that come *before* challenging behaviors. Antecedent manipulations are usually conducted by persons responsible for teaching and/or caring for students with autism.

6. *Teaching adaptive behavior.* If students with autism display challenging behaviors, then they need to be taught new and more adaptive behaviors. These new behaviors will allow them to communicate and act more effectively without resorting to problem behaviors.

7. *Building environments with effective consequences.* Daily environments must be analyzed and modified so that effective consequences are "natural" (albeit sometimes arranged) by-products of students' behaviors in those environments.

8. *Minimizing the use of punishers.* Although limited use of some traditional punishers (such as verbal reprimands) may be needed, punishment in general should be used as little as possible. Punishers that are not likely to be used on other members of society need not be considered. If a more intrusive intervention is contemplated, then it should be carefully reviewed by human rights and dignity committees.

9. *Distinguishing emergency procedures from proactive programming.* Students, on occasion, tantrum or become violent. Safe and nonaggressive procedures are needed to ensure the safety of everyone in the environment. This is necessary whether the student has autism or no disability at all. These limited-use, emergency procedures must not be confused with behavioral supports. Emergency procedures that are used on a regular basis become routine. This should not happen.

Where Horner et al. (1990) identified these competencies for PBS, several states have identified more generic behavior competencies that teachers should possess. An example is presented on the following page.

PBS and Other Intensive Programs

As PBS becomes more prominent, questions of growing relevance involve the interplay between PBS and other behavioral interventions that fall under the rubric of discrete trial interventions. Many parents and others who seek the most intensive behavioral interventions for their children have advocated for home-based interventions based on systematic, discrete trial teaching formats (Scott, 1996). These formats typically require intense family effort and result in impressive gains for children.

With thousands of families of children with autism managing such programs in the United States, this issue is critical. Many parents begin intensive home interventions with weak professional support, yet their children are able to make rapid progress. As parents seek support from PBS-oriented professionals, they may be discouraged from participating in these more intensive interventions. Common objections to the more intensive, discrete trial programming include concerns about the gener-

Behavioral Qualifications for Teachers of Students with Autism

Michael Hemingway

Teachers of students with autism must be especially enthusiastic, caring, and competent; the students who depend on these teachers for learning and support require them to be so. Teachers' personal, moment-to-moment interactions with students are indicators of their enthusiasm and caring. Students' expanding knowledge, skills, and abilities will confirm a teacher's competence.

A delineation of competencies expected among teachers would help promote learning of these competencies by teachers. The following list of competencies comes from what is known about functional and efficient learning. The list is short but demanding! It is important to note that this list *does not represent all educational competencies*, but rather those necessary for behavioral interventions for students with autism.

Knowledge, Skills, and Abilities in Applied Behavior Analysis

A recent occupational analysis of the practice of ABA identified the following content in which teachers and entry-level practitioners should be competent:

- Ethical issues in applied behavior analysis;
- Characteristics of applied behavior analysis;
- Principles of behavior;
- Individualized behavioral assessment, including generating hypotheses regarding behavior-environment relationships;
- Identification of functional behavior change targets for students, including intermediate and ultimate outcomes. This includes teacher identification of what the student should do outside of instructional settings, as well as changes needed in life-style indicators such as choice, employment opportunities, making and having friends);
- Selecting and using behavior change procedures including contextual/ecological factors, antecedents, es-

(continued)

tablishing operations, consequences, complex molar systems, and such procedures as shaping and chaining;
- Procedures that promote generalization and maintenance of behavior change.

Specialized Teaching Strategies

These competencies reflect specific skills needed by teachers to plan, deliver, and evaluate instructional programs for students with autism. Teachers should be able to:

- Teach students to make requests, as well as to respond to different types of teacher mands:
- Identify and use alternative methods of communication. This includes the use of signing, picture-language exchange systems, and a variety of augmentative communication devices;
- Use direct instruction, precision teaching, and discrete trials training formats;
- Design and/or use functional curricula.

The strength of these competencies will vary from teacher to teacher, as will the diversity of the needs, interests, and competencies of their students. If a student does not progress or learn as expected, teachers and other professionals (including behavior analysts, speech-language therapists, and curriculum designers) need to improve their own skills and abilities to serve these students. Regardless of these factors, teachers must ultimately look to their students for confirmation that what is being taught, and the methods being used, are the kindest and most effective that we, as a society, have to offer.

Michael Hemingway is a Senior Behavior Analyst for the Florida Department of Children and Families in Tallahassee, Florida.

alization of new skills, the artificial nature of interventions, and the removal of the child from contact with other children during these interventions. In spite of these limitations, significant gains are made by children in these intensive behavioral programs (Rogers, 1996).

Unfortunately, few parents and professionals have learned to bridge the perceived barriers between PBS and discrete trial interventions. Both PBS and discrete trial interventions have value; both are effective and both have a place in teaching students with autism. Among the few authors to bridge the perceived barriers are Bambara and Warren (1993). They note the efficacy of discrete trial teaching formats, but offer a range of delivery systems from high intensity to naturalistic approaches.

No discussion of PBS and autism would be complete without addressing the "communication hypothesis" for problem behavior. This hypothesis is based on the growing understanding that problem behavior serves important functions for many students. This is especially likely when a student has limited or no verbal communication. The communication hypothesis and functional communication training, one of the primary techniques for strengthening the communicative competence of persons with challenging behaviors, are discussed in detail in Chapter 6. It is essential to consider the high degree of overlap between behavioral and communication interventions for students with autism and to understand that neither realm functions satisfactorily in isolation as the "answer" to the challenges presented by these students.

PBS and a Focus on Environment

Current approaches to behavioral support involve examining problem behaviors as a pattern of excesses and deficits exhibited in an environmental framework. The environmental context has become an important focus of attention in the PBS tradition. Active management of reinforcers has become secondary to a broader consideration of the many, often complex variables affecting students' behavior.

Central to this approach is the attempt to *determine the function* that a behavior serves for a student, to *target aspects in the environment* that act as antecedents to the problem behavior, and to *assess the consequences of the particular behavior*. Once this information is known, interventions can be designed that involve actively changing features of the environment. These environmental changes make desirable behaviors more likely. Improved behavior sets the stage for successful, nonproblematic interactions.

Although a clear environmental structure can assist in the reduction of many behavior problems, some challenging behavior will persist in individual students. Behavioral interventions can assist the teacher in reducing maladaptive behavior while teaching and/or increasing more adaptive behavior.

Functional Assessment of Behavior

Functional assessment of behavior, sometimes referred to as a functional analysis (Carr et al., 1994), is a procedure designed to assist teachers and other professionals in understanding the function or functions served by a particular behavior. Functional assessment assumes that behavior serves a logical purpose or function and that behavior, even problem behavior, has meaning for the student. Understanding the purpose of the behavior is necessary before designing an intervention or teaching an appropriate alternative behavior. Failing to assess the purpose of problem behavior leads to poor intervention success (Iwata et al., 1982) and, perhaps most importantly, ignores the communicative intent of these behaviors. Since much problem behavior serves a communicative function (Carr et al., 1994), failing to appreciate what the student is communicating deprives the teacher of many opportunities to understand the child more fully.

Challenging behavior needs to be addressed in terms of its function or purpose for the individual student *in a particular setting*. A challenging behavior can be considered a response to something that occurs in the environment. For some students with autism, events such as transitions, fire drills, and assemblies may cause a behavior problem. For others, being given a nonpreferred task (or any task) may "trigger" the problem behavior. A lack of attention becomes the trigger for others. Whatever the cause, historically, the problem behavior generally has been effective in obtaining a desired consequence for the student. The behavior thereby serves a purposeful, communicative function (Carr et al., 1994) for the student. It is not a random act nor a fixed characteristic of the student's autism.

When a student with autism lacks a rich behavioral repertoire, the same behavior may be used for different purposes. For example, a student who slaps his face when presented with a difficult task may also slap his face when a fire drill occurs or when the teacher has not praised him recently. Slapping could be used as an escape behavior (getting the student out of an undesired activity), an attention-seeking behavior (causing adults to come and pay attention), or even self-stimulation. Because the same behavior might serve many purposes, an analysis of antecedent events is crucial if teachers are to help turn this behavior around. Face slapping for attention requires a different approach than face slapping used to escape difficult tasks.

A classroom teacher might begin a functional assessment by addressing the following questions:

- What is the student doing?
- Where is the student doing it?
- Who is the student doing it to or with?
- When is the student doing it?
- What happens when the student does it?

Functions of Problem Behavior

Glen Dunlap, Ph.D.

For some time, two vital assumptions have guided work in behavior management: problem behaviors are assumed to be *lawful*, meaning that they occur in an understandable context and are susceptible to scientific analysis, and they are somehow *governed by the environment*. These assumptions are basic precepts of a behavioral orientation and have driven the development of great advances in behavioral interventions over the last half of this century.

Unfortunately, these two assumptions offer only a limited understanding and a restricted array of intervention options. Recently, these assumptions have been broadened and elaborated, and our perspective has fundamentally transformed the way we view and intervene with problem behavior. We now consider problem behaviors to be not merely lawful and related to the environment, but also **meaningful** and **purposeful** *from the perspective of the person displaying the behavior*. Problem behaviors, no matter how bizarre or destructive, are viewed as serving a comprehensible purpose, or specific **function**. Furthermore, because the vast majority of problem behaviors have purposes that involve the social environment, we also interpret problem behaviors as having a *communicative* function. Typically, the underlying purpose of the problem behavior is to "ask" or "demand" that another person either provide something (such as attention or a preferred activity) or remove an unpleasant stimulus or circumstance (such as a task demand or an irritating noise).

Since the mid-1980s, an expanding body of research has focused on the functions of problem behaviors. The basic notions of functionality have been demonstrated repeatedly, and the perspectives have been validated as extremely useful for reducing unwanted behaviors and promoting desirable alternatives. Research has refined our understanding. We now know that functions are idiosyncratic, functions do not rely on verbal or conscious *deliberation*, and they are independent of a behavior's topography. For example, we might call a student's behavior "aggression" or a "tantrum" but our terms do not mean that the student's problem behavior supported those functions. *Form*

(continued)

and function are often unrelated. Aggression might be exhibited to attract the attention of one person, for example, but at other times it might serve the function of repelling an undesirable companion. To identify the function of a particular problem behavior, it is crucial to focus on the specific individual, the individual's preferences, and the specific circumstances in which the problem behavior occurs. This process of identification, called functional assessment, has been the subject of many authors' recommendations. Typically, the procedures are easily accomplished.

The implications of this *functional view* of problem behaviors are substantial, especially for intervention. The functional perspective implies that problem behaviors have some kind of legitimacy and value that need to be appreciated if optimal interventions are to be created. Intervention must be based on a functional understanding, not on a general cookbook-style formula. Simple suppression of problem behaviors through punishers or procedures such as "time out" is difficult to justify. Displaying a problem behavior may be a person's most effective means of communication; punishment of a communicative attempt can be as destructive as the problem behavior itself.

The presence of a problem behavior is evidence of a specific skill deficiency. The person displaying the behavior lacks a sufficiently effective communicative alternative. Research has shown that, when such an alternative is taught, it will displace the problem behavior, as long as it is at least as productive in achieving the same outcome. Thus, a functional perspective on problem behavior has urgent implications for what to teach.

The occurrence of problem behavior should be understood as a message, or signal, that something is wrong in the person's environment, *at least from that person's perspective.* Either an offensive circumstance is present or a condition of deprivation exists. A functional understanding should permit a support provider (e.g., a teacher) to ameliorate the situation, remove the offending stimulus or provide some measure of environmental enrichment. If these steps are based on an accurate understanding of the function of the behavior, they can serve to prevent the problem behavior from occurring by removing the source of the problem behavior's motivation.Considerable research has demonstrated the power and feasibility of this approach, but its efficacy is entirely dependent on an understanding of the behavior's function.

The growing recognition that problem behaviors are functional, that they are idiosyncratic, and that we can come to understand them has transformed our approach and our regard for the human condition. As we learn to base our interventions on this understanding, we gain sensitivity and an appreciation that people with disabilities are as individualistic in their preferences and challenges as everybody else and that a respect for these characteristics can be extremely valuable in our efforts to provide support in an effective, humane, and constructive way.

Glen Dunlap, Ph.D., is director of Community Development Programs, and Professor at the Department of Child and Family Studies, Florida Mental Health Institute, at the University of South Florida in Tampa, Florida.

Finding the answers to these questions helps determine the purpose of the behavior. To intervene effectively, understanding the purpose of a given behavior is necessary. In the above example, a functional assessment can show the purpose (or different purposes) that the face slapping serves. Each purpose can then be addressed differently, even though the behavior is the same *topographically* (i.e., it looks the same).

Several reference guides are available to help teachers conduct functional assessments (Cipani, 1990; O'Neill et al., 1997). Although each has its own particular set of procedures, in general, teachers who use a functional assessment can follow six steps:

1. Provide an operational description,
2. Observe the student,
3. Determine the purpose of the behavior,
4. Analyze the information,
5. Manipulate the environment to test the function of the behavior, and
6. Plan and implement the intervention.

Providing an Operational Description

A functional analysis begins with an operational description of the behavior that will be targeted and evaluated. An operational description needs to be precise enough so that other observers see the same behavior in the same way. "Being disruptive" is not an operational description. "Hitting peers" and "spinning toys" are operational definitions.

Observing the Student

The next step is to record the times and situations when the targeted behavior does and does not occur across the full range of daily routines. To do this, teachers (or other adults) should observe the student over an extended period of time and note the times and situations in which the behavior occurs. This can be done quickly by making periodic observations of the student during the course of the teaching day. Teachers can use published materials or make their own charts. Figure 5–1 illustrates the use of a simple format for recording observations.

Determining the Purpose of the Behavior

The third step in conducting a functional assessment is to observe and record what the targeted behavior produced for the student. Teachers should observe what happens when the behavior is exhibited, then note what occurs after the behavior. The teacher should be alert to the actual consequences. Among the most likely consequences are that the student gets attention or access to some activity or object, is removed from the situation, or is ignored.

Analyzing the Information to Establish a Hypothesis

After several days of observations, the teacher or support team should examine the data to see if any discernible patterns emerge. An increase in behaviors during specific activities or at a specific time of day should alert the teacher to attend closely to the antecedents during these times; the function of the behavior might be more obvious in one situation than in others.

Careful analysis of the information gathered may show patterns in antecedents or consequences that, unknown to the teacher, may be maintaining the behavior. This analysis is used to *generate potential hypotheses* regarding conditions that maintain the behavior. Iwata et al. (1982) identified three major hypotheses that account for the vast majority of challenging behavior. These are:

1. Positive reinforcement (i.e., attention, objects, or activities),
2. Negative reinforcement (i.e., escape or avoidance of people or tasks), and
3. Sensory or automatic reinforcement (e.g., self-stimulation or sleeping).

A functional analysis will show if adults are inconsistent in responding to the student's behavior or whether the behavior consistently receives reinforcers (e.g., attention). The analysis might also show that a

Challenging Behavior Observation Sheet

Student:

Date:

Directions: Each time the student produces a challenging behavior write down the behavior and time in the left column. Then, respond to the questions by moving from left to right.

Behavior and time	What's the task?	Is the student successful with the task?	Where is the teacher?	Who is near the student?	What did the teacher do after?	What did peers do after?	What else went on in the environment?	What purpose do you think this behavior served?
1								
2								
3								
4								
5								
6								
7								
8								
9								
10								

Figure 5-1. Challenging Behavior Observation Sheet.

particular activity generally precedes the behavior (e.g., the sound of a specific teacher's voice that always occurs before a student screams). Other information might show that the behavior occurs when the student is hungry or thirsty.

Some typical classroom routines inadvertently maintain an unwanted behavior. Typically in a classroom, a teacher will use a verbal reprimand or a model to decrease a behavior. For example, if a student is not on task, the teacher may request that he "get to work." For a student who was exhibiting off-task behavior to get teacher attention, being off task was successful in obtaining the teacher's attention. Teachers should remember that attention need not be *positive* to be reinforcing. Even negative attention can be a positive reinforcer.

Analysis of the information can help confirm or deny the tentative hypotheses regarding the function of the behavior. Sometimes the available information may be enough to craft a hypothesis and begin intervention. In other circumstances, it may be necessary to manipulate the environment to further test the hypothesis prior to beginning the intervention.

Manipulating the Environment to Test the Functions

If after the first four steps an intervention based on the function of the behavior is not obvious, systematic manipulations of the environment should begin. Teachers should make these manipulations and then examine whether any changes occur in the problem behavior. These manipulations, whether natural to the environment or arranged by the teacher, are tests to check whether the teacher clearly understands the function of the behavior.

For example, consider an antecedent-behavior-consequence (ABC) analysis that indicates that Mario hits Bobby most frequently on the playground when Bobby is on the swings. The usual consequence is that the teacher scolds Mario and makes him sit down beside her for the rest of recess. Having learned the typical sequence of events, the teacher should make several changes to test her understanding of the function served by hitting. For example, the teacher's working hypothesis is that Mario's hitting is maintained by proximity to the teacher (a positive reinforcement hypothesis). One test of this hypothesis would be to have Mario sit somewhere other than by the teacher. A decrease in hitting then would suggest that the hitting was unintentionally reinforced by the teacher's attention, thus confirming the hypothesis. A second manipulation might involve pairing Mario and Bobby during other activities and in other settings. A decrease in hitting in these circumstances would suggest that the hitting served as a means of helping Mario escape from the playground (a loud, undefined area with numerous social demands). This would deny the positive reinforcement hypothesis and, instead, lend support to a negative reinforcement hypothesis (escape).

If a behavior is aggressive or self-injurious, ethical considerations preclude systematic manipulations that are likely to increase the behavior. In such cases, care should be taken to provide interventions under the auspices of a qualified professional in behavior analysis or a related field. Any manipulation must have the full and informed consent of the family and, where possible, the student and adhere to the policies and procedures of the school system or agency.

Planning and Implementing the Intervention

The last step of a functional assessment is actually the first step in teaching. When a teacher is confident that the function served by challenging behavior has been identified, an intervention should be designed. Because problem behavior typically has a communicative function, one of the core interventions is to *teach an acceptable communication alternative* to the problem behavior. Any alternative behavior that is taught should be as effective in obtaining the desired consequence, and should be at least as easily performed *and efficient* as the maladaptive behavior (Durand & Carr, 1991).

Once a teaching plan has been developed, it can be implemented. Initially, there may be a temporary undesirable change in the intensity, duration, or frequency of the problem behavior. For example, a program to replace screaming with requesting might result in a temporary (typically 2 to 3 days) increase (an extinction burst) in screaming if extinction was used as part of the intervention. It is sometimes difficult to pick the right intervention initially. Occasionally several different interventions will be attempted before an effective program is found.

If it is necessary to target a behavior for reduction, teachers must also teach a different, more appropriate behavior (a "fair pair") that can serve the same purpose. Ideally, the behavior targeted for increase should already be in the student's repertoire and should be one that the student can use efficiently. That is, the student should be able to perform the behavior, although not at the desired frequency or strength or in response to the appropriate antecedents. For example, a student who cries when frustrated with a difficult task and who has some language could be taught to say, "I need help." A nonverbal student in the same circumstance might be taught to place a "help" sign on his desk or tap the teacher on the arm. In each case, the behavior selected for decrease is the inappropriate behavior (crying) and the behavior selected for increase is talking, placing a sign, or tapping the teacher. Trying to reduce a problem behavior without increasing a replacement often results in the student finding another problem behavior to serve the initial purpose.

Instructional Model for Behavioral Interventions

If the initial 25 years of ABA can be characterized by the validation of effective behavioral interventions, the last decade has seen an effort to establish decision models to guide educators' efforts to use these interventions. A precursor to modern decision models is the Gaylord-Ross (1980) heuristic that included medical, ecological, and instructional procedures. Prior to selecting any particular intervention, Gaylord-Ross prescribed thorough behavioral assessment to establish the conditions under which the challenging behaviors were most likely to occur (similar to the functional assessment now regularly a part of PBS).

An instructional model to guide behavioral interventions also was described by Colvin and Sugai (1988). They pointed out that teachers seldom resort to punishment procedures for students' *academic errors*, but often use punishers as the first intervention when students' errors involve social or personal behavior. Colvin and Sugai suggested that teachers learn to apply the instructional model used to remediate academic deficiencies to problem behavior as well. For teachers of students with autism, this means that challenging behavior would elicit *instructional interactions* from teachers rather than *management procedures*. This is particularly relevant given the skill deficits that typically accompany autism.

Behavioral excesses and deficits can be addressed instructionally using the same process used to teach new social, academic, motor, or life skills. Behavioral programming, like all other instruction, should be developed and implemented in a manner that is consistent with a student's IFSP or IEP. Teaching appropriate behavior is particularly important when teaching students with autism. Many of these students do not know what an appropriate behavior is in a particular setting or circumstance. If they have successfully used challenging behavior to access reinforcement, then they may have no substitute behavior in their repertoire. Students who cry and tantrum when not allowed access to preferred toys, for example, may have a history of receiving preferred toys when they tantrum. In lieu of attempts to manage these tantrums, teachers applying an instructional model would select a replacement behavior (e.g., pointing or asking), then begin teaching that new skill.

Selecting a Replacement Behavior

When selecting a replacement behavior, an improvement in a person's quality of life should be a primary outcome (Winett & Winkler, 1972). If a student exhibits a specific problem behavior (e.g., hyperventilating) and has no other means of expressing protest, a useful intervention would be to teach a more appropriate, but equally effective, means of expressing protest (e.g., saying or signing "stop"). Behaviors that are likely to increase the student's ability to participate in family and community activities or to increase access to less restricted environments are good choices to improve students' quality of life. Any replacement behavior targeted for instruction must be socially valued, simple, and efficient for the student to perform (Durand, 1990). If the replacement behavior is more difficult than the challenging behavior, the challenging behavior will continue to be used. A behavior that is already in the child's repertoire, although perhaps at a low rate, is often a good choice for a replacement behavior. The replacement behavior also should be one that is likely to be reinforced in typical home and community settings. Communication is a behavior that readily crosses settings and is highly likely to be reinforced. Ideally, the adults at home and in the classroom should agree on a replacement behavior and promote it in both settings.

A second common replacement behavior that is likely to be responded to positively by others is compliance. Compliance is a generalized set of behaviors of responding positively to the requests of others. Some modern theories of education shun the language and concept of children's compliance. For many advocates of "child-centered education," for example, compliance has become synonymous with a loss of self-direction, creativity, and equality. To these educators, compliance has become heavily laden with negative emotional connotations. *We do not support this deconceptualization.* Compliance is not a concept or skill that reduces students' choices. All students face situations where they would fare better or learn more easily if they comply with social expectations. (This holds for all people, whether young or old, with or without disabilities.) The important factors in deciding whether to comply with social norms involves *having the skill to comply* and *having the skill to predict consequences* of compliance and noncompliance. Many students with autism do not have the skills to comply and predict consequences of their choices unless they are taught to do so. Failing to teach students to comply with basic requests sets them up for future problems. Students without the ability to comply with requests and predict the consequences of their choices ultimately will lose the opportunity to make their own choices regarding social relationships and living arrangements. This typically involves placement in more restrictive settings. Compliance is an empowering cluster of skills.

Any replacement behavior that a teacher selects must be one that is likely to be reinforced by others in the student's life (Heward, Dardig, & Rossett, 1979). This has been referred to as the *relevance of behavior rule* by Ayllon and Azrin (1968). It makes little sense for teachers to orchestrate a special intervention, and for a student to be the subject of an intervention, that simply will not increase the level of positive reinforcement in the future. Using the relevance of behavior rule as a selection criterion prevents teachers from selecting inefficient or even wasteful target behaviors.

Continuum of Educative Behavioral Interventions

An instructional model for replacing challenging behavior with new skills will be successful only if the interventions that make up the model are effective. There is no shortage of effective behavioral strategies (Lovaas, 1981; Repp & Deitz, 1979; Skinner, 1968; White, 1986). What many teachers lack, however, is a systematic means for selecting one intervention over another.

One means of selecting potential interventions involves arranging the array of behavioral interventions on a continuum that integrates their effectiveness with their corresponding acceptability in community settings (Brady, 1984). In such a continuum, all potential effective interventions are listed in order of their "restrictiveness." As the perceived restrictiveness of an intervention increases, the likelihood of the technique being acceptable in typical school or community settings decreases. Indeed, some effective interventions are only minimally acceptable to large segments of society.

In his critique of traditional placement continua, Taylor (1988) pointed out that placing restrictive options on any service continuum legitimizes those options for service providers. Thus a continuum of effective interventions risks legitimizing the more restrictive procedures. A continuum of effective interventions sensitive to this danger, then, would eliminate options that are restrictive, *even though they might be effective in some circumstances*. Figure 5–2, a Continuum of Educative Behavioral Interventions, presents one such model. This continuum does not present all effective behavioral interventions, but clusters those consistent with the instructional approach to challenging behavior presented in this chapter.

The Continuum of Educative Behavioral Interventions shown in Figure 5–2 culls interventions from the larger set of traditional and modern practices that have been validated as effective. These interventions promote teaching of new skills and are clustered into four classes of procedures, consistent with educators' perceptions of the social acceptability of the interventions (Witt & Elliot, 1985). Educative behavioral procedures most acceptable include *restructuring of setting factors that empower students*. The second cluster includes *antecedent procedures involving changes in cues, prompts, and delivery strategies*. The third cluster includes *reinforcement procedures involving changes in content and schedules, noncontingent reinforcement, and differential reinforcement*. The fourth cluster includes *consequence and correction procedures that combine reinforcer removal with delivery of instruction*.

LEVEL 1 (SETTING FACTOR) PROCEDURES.   Level 1 (setting factor) procedures include three recent behavioral innovations that empower students by altering the perceived value of, and increasing the students'

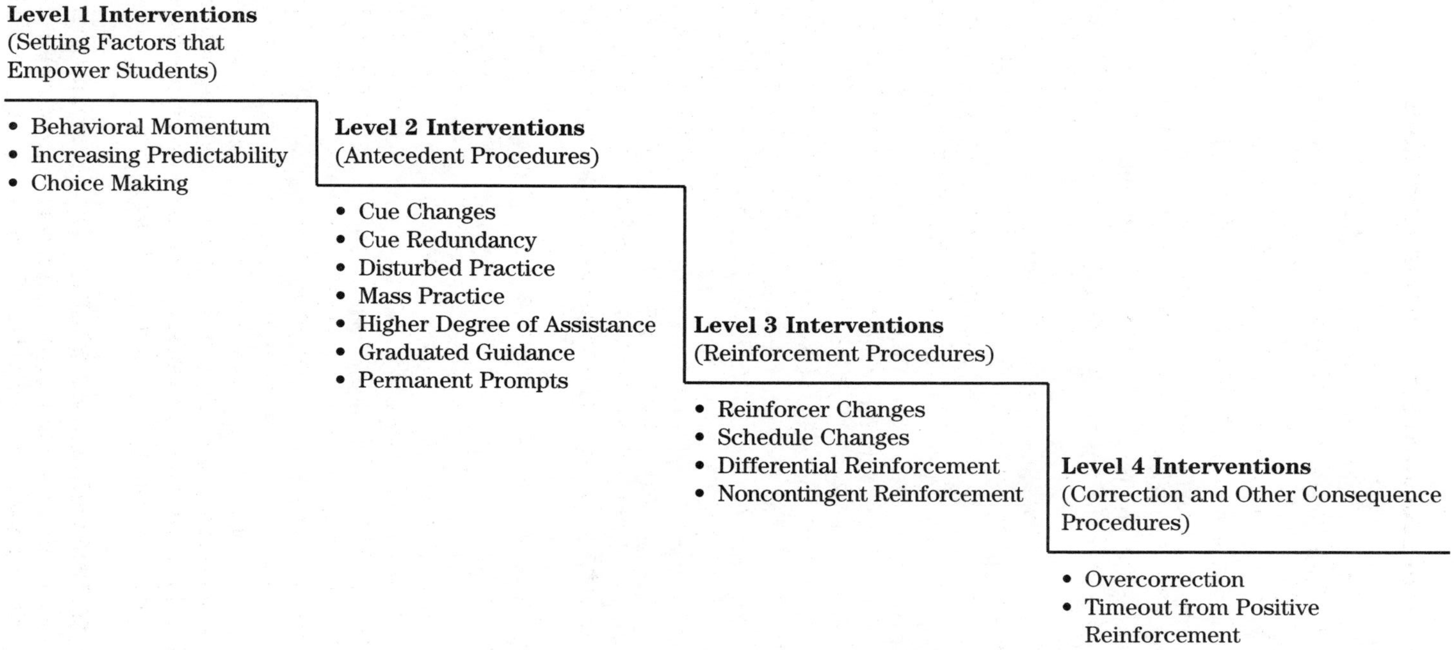

Level 1 Interventions
(Setting Factors that
Empower Students)

- Behavioral Momentum
- Increasing Predictability
- Choice Making

Level 2 Interventions
(Antecedent Procedures)

- Cue Changes
- Cue Redundancy
- Disturbed Practice
- Mass Practice
- Higher Degree of Assistance
- Graduated Guidance
- Permanent Prompts

Level 3 Interventions
(Reinforcement Procedures)

- Reinforcer Changes
- Schedule Changes
- Differential Reinforcement
- Noncontingent Reinforcement

Level 4 Interventions
(Correction and Other Consequence
Procedures)

- Overcorrection
- Timeout from Positive
  Reinforcement

Figure 5–2. Continuum of Educative Behavioral Interventions.

influence over, their own surroundings. Unlike many traditional behavioral approaches, a characteristic of these procedures is the weight given to the contextual variables that influence students. Another difference from the traditional approaches is that these procedures "package" several components into a single intervention (such as combining curricular enhancement with choice-making). These innovations include establishing and controlling a behavioral momentum, increasing the predictability of environmental expectations, and the ability to make choices.

Behavioral momentum. A recent procedure used to reduce resistance to change and transitions involves having adults establish a positive behavioral momentum prior to requesting that a student participate in a low preference task. When establishing a positive momentum, a teacher requests that a student engage in a series of easy, fast-paced, "high probability" activities (Davis, Brady, Hamilton, McEvoy, & Williams, 1992; Davis, Brady, Williams, & Hamilton, 1994). This is sometimes referred to as making pretask requests (Singer, Singer, & Horner, 1987). When the student performs these activities, the teacher provides rich praise. This first part of the momentum procedure results in substantial increases in the amount of reinforcement delivered to the student. It also "traps" the student into "playing the game" of responding positively to the teacher.

Once a student and a teacher demonstrate a reciprocal positive momentum of interaction, the teacher inserts a request for a student to display a "low probability" behavior (i.e., a low probability that the student will respond). The momentum of positive student responding "spills over" to the request that previously elicited noncompliance or other challenging behavior.

Establishing a positive behavioral momentum helps to create smoother transitions by reducing noncompliance. It also alters the relationships that have been established between tasks and teachers' efforts to engage students in these tasks. Often, as teachers try to direct students (and students fail to comply), a negative momentum or escalation emerges into a power struggle. Establishing a positive behavioral momentum, then controlling it, changes this interaction pattern. As the student is gradually eased into less preferred tasks, the teacher learns new ways of interacting with the student.

By preceding "problem" (or low probability) requests with positive and reinforcing interactions, the teacher increases the likelihood of student success and reinforcement. This new interaction pattern is an autism-sensitive, and even autism-polite, way of teaching students (Davis & Brady, 1993).

Increasing predictability. Resistance to change is often cited as a characteristic of autism. However, resistance to change may not be a characteristic of the disorder as much as a failure on the part of students to fully understand what will happen once a change is made. This inability to predict can be overcome by helping students understand what will happen in a subsequent activity or setting. The use of word or picture schedules is a simple way to increase predictability.

Another means of increasing predictability is to "preview" an activity prior to introducing it as a change in routine. For example, prior to introducing a new reading activity at school, parents might read the new story to the student at home as a bed-time activity. By familiarizing the student with the story sequence in advance, the parents help the student predict the story and content, thus helping assure a more enjoyable story session the next day in school. This procedure was described by Koegel, Koegel, Kellegrew, and Mullen (1996) as a means of substantially reducing disruption in preschool students. Such low intensity and creative procedures as developing individual schedules and providing activity previews help the student predict future activities. These procedures are especially well suited to students with autism.

Making choices. Traditional programming for students with more severe disabilities including autism often reduces choices by controlling the opportunities and routines for students. In many ways this disempowers students (Smith, 1997). The opportunity to make choices yields an array of positive outcomes. Students can learn to make choices involving self-selection of reinforcers, sequence of activities, use of materials, leisure and free time, and more. Choice-making provides a context for students to communicate; it gives students something to communicate about. For the educator it opens the door to more direct assessment of student preferences. Students with autism can make their choices known if teachers provide training in choice-making, make opportunities for choice-making obvious and routine, and expect students to make choices. Many students show little capacity to make choices, but this is not a fair basis for assuming that they cannot be taught to do so. Several recent studies demonstrated that most students, including those with extreme disabilities, are capable of making choices (Green et al., 1988; Parsons & Reid, 1990; Shevin & Klein, 1984). Providing opportunities for students to make choices should become part of the classroom routine. While it may take more time for the student, rather than the teacher, to make a choice about a student's lunch or recess activity, the genuine learning opportunity provided by student choice-making outweighs any short-term inconvenience.

LEVEL 2 (ANTECEDENT) PROCEDURES. Level 2 (antecedent) procedures prevent the need (or occasion) for challenging behavior by eliminating stimuli that are associated with and tend to trigger these behaviors. This includes a variety of cue and prompt systems.

Cue changes. Teachers can make alterations or modifications in the cues they use when teaching replacement skills. If verbal cues are being used, they might employ visual or gestural cues instead. This also includes giving a student a model or diagram of a task rather than a verbal explanation of the task. If the level of language is too complex for the student, the teacher might use simpler language.

Cue redundancy. Teachers can build redundancy into their cues by using multiple levels of cues. This will help to ensure a more complete understanding of the required task. In addition to a verbal direction, for example, teachers might combine a verbal cue with a picture, gesture, or physical prompt. Pointing to the group while asking a student to join the group is an example of cue redundancy. For many students with autism, the addition of a redundant visual cue is effective.

Distributed practice of new or replacement skills in natural settings. When teachers distribute the practice of a replacement skill, they provide opportunities for the student to rehearse the skill in different natural environments. Distributed practice allows a student to practice the skill in different places, with different people, and at different times, but this practice is not done in a repetitive "mass practice" fashion.

Mass practice of a new or replacement skill. Mass practice involves having the student practice the activity a number of times with supervision to ensure accuracy until the necessary level of mastery is reached. Mass practice can be helpful during initial acquisition or as a fluency building tactic; however, mass practice can lead to loss of motivation if not used sparingly and with reinforcement. Teachers who use discrete trial teaching formats are not limited to presenting trials in a mass format. Many students with challenging behavior display it when they are asked to perform a skill repeatedly. If this is the case, use of *distributed practice* is advisable.

Higher degree of assistance. Many teachers are familiar with teaching systems in which the teacher increases the level of prompt until the student is able to perform the replacement behavior (Alberto & Troutman, 1995). If, for example, the student is unable to perform the behavior with a gestural prompt, the teacher might increase to a physical prompt (or even hand-over-hand assistance) until the student is able to perform the behavior. Increased levels of assistance can be counterproductive for many students with autism, given their propensity toward prompt dependence. For others, touch may actually be aversive. Where increasing levels of assistance are required, introducing visual prompts often is successful and avoids student dependence on adults.

Graduated guidance. This procedure calls for the teacher to decrease the degree of physical assistance provided in direct response to the student's ability to complete the task. For example, a teacher might initially provide a verbal cue with as much physical assistance as necessary, then gradually reduce the physical contact until the task is performed without the teacher touching the student at all (Foxx & Azrin, 1972). Teaching a student to use a screwdriver, first by guiding one hand, then by touching the wrist or elbow, then by "shadowing" the hand movement, is an example of graduated guidance.

Permanent prompt systems. Students with autism often perform better when the cues to perform are stable and nontransient (in contrast to temporary cues). Permanent prompts also increase the likelihood that the student will perform the tasks without active intervention from adults. One example of a permanent prompt is the use of large color photographs in a binder to increase participation in a recreation sequence (MacDuff et al., 1993). The child is directed to engage in the activity depicted and to move through the sequence presented. Permanent prompt systems assist students by providing a permanent set of instructions or cues to which the student refers when she gets "stuck." Permanent prompt systems assist students who have problems moving through a multistep sequence (as might be found in hand washing) by prompting the student to perform each step. The most popular forms of permanent prompt systems include photographs, word lists, pictograms, and prompts saved on audio tapes. Although educators may be hesitant to spend the time and energy to create these materials, they provide long-term, permanent instructional benefits.

LEVEL 3 (REINFORCEMENT) PROCEDURES. Procedures on this continuum represent the simple alterations of the content, schedule, or delivery of consequences. Also included here are differential and noncontingent reinforcement. These interventions serve to replace the existing reinforcers for challenging behavior by making productive, replacement behavior more "profitable" (in terms of accessing reinforcers) to the student with autism.

Changing the content or nature of the reinforcer. If the student is not willing to perform a replacement skill for the available reinforcer, the item or activity may not be reinforcing for that student at that time. This logic is so fundamental that many teachers overlook the obvious conclusion that the consequence they intended to serve as a reinforcer *did not actually serve that purpose.* The solution: change the reinforcer.

Reinforcement schedule changes. If the student does not receive reinforcement often enough to maintain a new replacement behavior, among the major changes teachers can make are altering the *schedule* of reinforcement so that the student (a) obtains reinforcement more frequently or (b) accesses reinforcers for a longer period of time. Teachers who wait until the end of the school day to deliver free time as a reinforcer might use shorter free time periods throughout the day. A systematic "thinning" of the schedule of reinforcement in the classroom can help a student learn to generalize a new behavior to a new setting. Although a continuous schedule of reinforcement might be needed to teach a new behavior, a thinner schedule will maintain this skill and make it durable enough to use in places where frequent attention is not available. Once a student reaches whatever criterion has been set (such as 90% correct over 2 consecutive weeks), then the student might be reinforced every other time or every third time she uses the new skill in place of the problem behavior.

Differential reinforcement. In its most basic form, differential reinforcement means that teachers *actively* reinforce some target *other than* the problem behavior (Favell, 1993; Vollmer & Iwata, 1992). Although many forms of differential reinforcement have been used, two specific forms are found on this continuum because they include *instructional* rather than solely reductive procedures. differential reinforcement of alternative (DRA) behavior refers to the presentation of a reinforcer when a student produces a more socially acceptable alternative to the problem behavior. For example, a student may be reinforced for sharing materials rather than scratching a peer. The second form of differential reinforcement involves differential reinforcement of communication (DRC) responses. For example, touching a "help" card could be taught and reinforced in place of other inappropriate actions used to gain attention or assistance.

Noncontingent reinforcement. Teachers typically are urged to be highly contingent in their use of reinforcers and to reinforce only the behaviors they want to increase. Noncontingent reinforcement (NCR), on the other hand, runs counter to this logic. NCR is the delivery of reinforcers *in a systematic but noncontingent manner* (Vollmer, Iwata, Zarcona, Smith, & Mazaleski, 1993). The key to NCR is that a teacher must first identify the reinforcer that maintains a problem behavior. This reinforcer (or its equivalent) is then provided noncontingently (including at times when the problem behavior is *not* produced). The result is a reduction in the problem behavior.

NCR generally is used to interrupt escape behavior. NCR could be used for a student who tantrums for a preferred book. During the first phase of intervention, the student is allowed continuous and noncontingent access to the book. Tantrums, if they occur, are not consequated. Next, a short period of time without the book is followed by noncontingent access to the book. Whether the child tantrums or not during this interval, he still receives access to the book. The length of the interval is gradually increased and the duration of access to the book decreased. The problem behavior of tantrumming is weakened as it becomes ineffective in gaining access to the reinforcer.

NCR is a positive approach to problem behavior because it acknowledges the communicative purpose of a problem behavior with an active, reinforcement-based intervention. This intervention makes reinforcement available, but disrupts the relationship between problem behavior and a student's escape from demands. Teacher directives to stop working rather than student's problem behaviors result in escape from nonpreferred activities.

LEVEL 4 (CORRECTION AND OTHER CONSEQUENCE) PROCEDURES.
Level 4 procedures include strategies that interrupt and redirect challenging behavior. The two correction and consequence procedures on this continuum have an advantage for students who can accept correction without escalating their problem behavior and who can learn through modeling. Both procedures have explicit educative components that help teachers increase replacement behaviors as part of the effort to interrupt problem behavior. The two procedures included here are positive practice overcorrection and contingent observation time out from positive reinforcement (TOPR).

We recognize that many consequence procedures traditionally have been used with students with autism; these procedures are typically *reductive* in nature. For this reason, professionals with expertise in behavior analysis have often been viewed as "deceleration professionals" (Holburn, 1997). The disadvantage of this is obvious. Reductive consequences do not result in students learning new skills. Since students with autism already have skill deficits, the absence of instruction that increases functional replacement skills further robs students of the opportunity to learn. Also, reductive consequence procedures have numerous unintended negative effects, including student withdrawal from teachers and tasks. In addition, the problem behavior has *already* occurred when reductive strategies are implemented.

Positive Practice Overcorrection. Positive practice overcorrection is a procedure in which the student is required to engage in exaggerated practice of appropriate behaviors. Although much of the early research on overcorrection involved restitutional forms, positive practice is far more educative. A student who must hand an adult a word card requesting a brief break several times after screaming is engaging in positive practice overcorrection.

Caution must be exercised in the use of positive practice overcorrection. A student can become highly agitated and may actively resist efforts to practice the skill. In such cases other procedures will be more appropriate.

Contingent Observation Time Out from Positive Reinforcement (TOPR). Ample confusion exists regarding TOPR. TOPR involves restricting access to the consequence that reinforces a student's specific problem behavior (Mace, Page, Ivancic, & O'Brien, 1986; Ritschl, Mongrella, & Presbie, 1972; Roberts, 1988). Numerous forms of TOPR (e.g., exclusionary and nonexclusionary time out) have been shown to be effective reduction procedures, but seldom contain an educative component. Often teachers mistakenly use TOPR without establishing what reinforcer actually maintains the problem behavior. Others use isolation areas as punishment zones, again without attending to the specific reinforcer. Because many students with autism have problem behaviors that are motivated by escape, removal from a setting might inadvertently reinforce some students' problem behavior.

A form of TOPR consistent with the continuum presented in this text is the use of contingent observation. Contingent observation TOPR is used for students who learn by observing others, a skill found in some but not all students with autism. Contingent observation TOPR involves removing a student to a different part of the setting so that he may still observe the classroom activity but may not take part in the reinforcing activity for a short period of time (determined in advance). After the specified period has elapsed, the teacher asks the student if he is ready to rejoin the activity (or group). If the student indicates yes, he may return to the activity and participate in actions that would result in (increased amounts of) reinforcement. Designating a contingent observation chair where a student is positioned to see but not interact in a class activity is an example of contingent observation.

Aversive Interventions and the Continuum of Educative Behavioral Interventions

The procedures shown on this continuum reflect techniques that are used extensively in typical schools for students with and without disabilities. Properly applied, they represent an effective means of altering problem behavior. Other, more aversive procedures have received much attention in the field, particularly with more extreme forms of aggression and self-injury. Physical restraint, for example, involves the use of direct physical, bodily intervention to stop a behavior. Physical restraint has been used with stereotypic (Reid, Tombaugh, & Van den Heuvel, 1981) and self-injurious behaviors (Hamad, Isley, & Lowry, 1983; Luiselli, 1986; Matson & Keyes, 1988; Pace, Iwata, Edwards, & McCosh, 1986), including pica (Singh & Bakker, 1984; Winton & Singh, 1983) and aggression.

Indeed, where the use of restraint and other aversives is advocated, the problem behavior typically involves self- injury. Yet even with self-injurious behavior, educational programming has been effective and is advocated for long-term change (see Addressing Self-Injurious Behavior on the next page).

The use of aversives and similar restrictive treatments is fraught with problems (Johnston & Sherman, 1993). There are serious ethical concerns, and these procedures typically receive assessments of low acceptability in local communities. From a *teaching perspective*, a serious concern with these procedures is that adults who use them are not teaching students what they should do. Horner et al. (1990) asserted that positive interventions are now the *expected* technology and in no setting should this be more true than in public school programs for students with autism.

The authors of this text do not condone the use of aversive procedures, given the effectiveness of more educative and preventive procedures. This position is consistent with the Resolution on the Cessation of Intrusive Interventions presented by TASH (formerly The Association for

Addressing Self-Injurious Behavior

Lee Kern, Ph.D.

As many as 16% of individuals with developmental disabilities engage in self-injurious behavior. If left untreated, severe self-injury can result in permanent disfiguration and irreversible damage (e.g., blindness). Regardless of the severity, it is important to intervene immediately. Fortunately, recent advances have provided strategies to reduce its occurrence in classroom settings.

Recent research suggests that most self-injury occurs for environmental reasons. Although it occasionally occurs to satisfy a biologic or internal need (e.g., opiate release or sensory stimulation), more often self-injury is a learned behavior. Consequently, ecological or behavioral intervention is required.

To reduce self-injury effectively, it is critical to understand the environmental conditions that are associated with its occurrence. Three particular conditions have been shown to influence self-injury. The most frequent is when demands are placed on a child, particularly demands perceived to be unpleasant from the child's perspective. Self-injury also may occur when attention is not available. Finally self-injury may occur when preferred activities or items are removed or withheld.

There are several assessment strategies to assist teachers in identifying which of these conditions is associated with self-injury. The most common assessments are structured interviews and direct observation protocols (available commercially). These assessments are designed to identify events that precede self-injury (e.g., a request to perform a task) and events that follow it (e.g., removal of the task). By identifying the specific events surrounding self-injury, it is possible to determine the social purpose or function that it serves. With this information, interventions linked to the specific can be developed.

For an intervention to reduce self-injury effectively, several ingredients must be present. First, an alternative appropriate behavior to replace the self-injury must be specifically taught. Because most self-injury serves a communicative function (e.g., to gain attention), students must be given a different method for communicating their needs. Picture cards and microswitches are examples of alternative communication options.

A second strategy used to decrease the likelihood of self-injury involves modifying events that occur *prior* to the self-

(continued)

injury. For example, some students will persist with a task for only a certain amount of time before engaging in self-injury. For these students, shortening the task or providing frequent breaks may reduce its occurrence.

Finally, events occurring *after* the self-injury that contribute to its persistence should be discontinued. Specifically, children need to learn that self-injury will no longer get them attention, allow them to escape from a task, or help them gain access to desired materials or activities. Thus, teachers must avoid providing any of these possible reinforcers following self-injury.

Obviously, teachers who encounter self-injury in students must be aware of cautions. First, any self-injury causing damage to body tissues (e.g., bruising, swelling, open wounds) or to sensory organs (e.g., eyes) should be reported to a pediatrician immediately for medical care and/or protective equipment. Second, persistent self-injury that is not responsive to classroom interventions should be referred to individuals or programs that specialize in the assessment and treatment of self-injurious behavior. Professionals in programs like Children's Seashore House who have experience with this behavior can design prevention and rapid intervention programs to reduce or eliminate self-injury.

Lee Kern, Ph.D., works with children with autism and other disabilities with self-injury at Children's Seashore House at the Philadelphia Center for Health Care Sciences and at the University of Pennsylvania.

Persons with Severe Handicaps), the American Association on Mental Retardation (AAMR) Policy on Aversive Procedures, and the Council for Exceptional Children (CEC) Policy of Physical Intervention.

The position stated above should not be construed as condemning the use of physical restraint as an *emergency procedure.* At times, temporary emergency restraint may be necessary to avoid serious physical injury to a student or peers. Restraint should be considered an *emergency procedure.* It is not an educative behavioral intervention as no replacement behaviors are taught. Any restraint should be performed in accordance with the school's guidelines and only under supervision to avoid injury to either the student or teacher.

If self-injury or aggression occurs frequently, a formal program of behavioral support should be developed and implemented. Large school districts typically have one or more professionals with skill and training in applied behavior analysis; smaller districts often obtain such services on a contract basis. The latest reauthorization of IDEA (with requirements for functional assessment and active management of behavior) has brought considerable attention to the need for trained professionals with skill and experience in dealing with complex and dangerous behavior. Behavior that results in emergency procedures requires active interventions, not just the frequent implementation of emergency procedures.

Quality of Life Issues

Educational programming to address problem behavior of students with autism must be based on ongoing and sincere assessment of the quality of life for the student. This is among the prominent themes in the behavioral literature.

In the early life of a student this will involve actively teaching the child how to communicate in ways that are socially appropriate. At the same time, it is essential that all persons involved in a student's care (teachers, paraeducators, bus drivers, parents, grandparents, siblings, and others) be aware of and instructed in positive ways to foster empowering behavior and to avoid contributing to a student's problem behaviors. In many cases, parents seek to go beyond this and institute intensive early intervention efforts in the hope of dramatic improvement. The role that everyday life activities and experiences have on very young students' intellectual and social success is well established (Hart & Risley, 1995). Students with autism must be provided with everyday environments that offer rich opportunities for communication development, exploration, and structured learning. They must have environments equal to *or better* than those offered to the most fortunate children in our society if they are to have any chance of growth and development. These opportunities cannot be degraded by programming and interaction patterns that allow children to communicate by means of problem behaviors.

With children of school age, close attention must be paid to the development of social capacity. Students excluded from typically developing peers are placed at a distinct disadvantage and face inordinate challenges in regaining ground lost while in segregated environments. While relying on effective communication systems (whether speech, sign or picture exchange), the student must be taught with the most effective instructional techniques available. These students are difficult to teach. Without skilled teachers using the best instructional tools, these students will not learn easily, if at all. Fortunately, a wide array of instructional approaches is available to teachers. When these procedures are also consistent with students' preferences, student performance is enhanced (Dunlap & Kern, 1993; Dunlap et al., 1994). As Lindsley (1971), suggested, "the learner knows best" and good instruction, whether for students with autism or any other difficult-to-teach child, the teacher must become a student of the child's learning.

The same general orientation should be applied to older students. If teachers and others concerned with their education and development skillfully observe and then analyze their behavior, most problem patterns of behavior can be addressed with highly educative behavioral strategies. This is an important new feature of the 1997 reauthorization of IDEA. IEP development must consider the interaction of environment and behavior. Indeed, IDEA notes that the IEP team shall use positive behavior supports, approaches, and interventions for students' problem behavior.

This increased attention to the need for behavioral support (and not merely behavior management or discipline) is one of the most encouraging aspects of IDEA. What are these supports or strategies likely to be? Not surprisingly, the primary "intervention" within the PBS model relies on improving the overall quality of life for a person with disabilities. At one level, an improvement in one's life circumstances reduces or averts problem behavior; it is also an ethical response of educators. If severe challenging behavior could be effectively decreased over the long term using punishment alone, then teachers could operate happily as "deceleration professionals" (Holburn, 1997). However, a focus on quality of life, along with an understanding of problem behavior as communication, is a far more productive way of supporting growth and development. In the lives of students with autism, this requires attention to various aspects of their environment. To the degree that their environments can be changed, it becomes least intrusive and most effective to do so (and it is typically easier to change the environment than to change the student with autism).

A quality of life emphasis promotes a long-term and pro-social instructional focus. Oullette, Horner, and Newton (1994) write, "The quality of a person's life is tied directly to the nature of the social relationships he or she develops and maintain" (p. 55). The grim conditions in large public residential facilities for persons with disabilities as detailed by Blatt and Kaplan (1974) and analyzed by Wolfensberger (1975) served to degrade persons with disabilities and destroy any opportunity for meaningful life. This has been particularly true for students with autism. Now, the emphasis must be on upgrading the quality of life for these students and for others with serious disabilities.

SUMMARY

The new directions presented in this chapter will pose challenges to many educators, especially those who rely on traditional programming practices in special education. The challenging behavior of students with autism can no longer be assumed to be a fixed characteristic of autism. Rather it must be seen as an ongoing barometer of the quality of life and the degree to which the education and care they receive meets their needs. This orientation requires a major change in direction for many educators, school systems, and parents. It is possible, for example, to identify an accommodationist model for explaining the behavior of a student with autism. Using this model, any unusual behavior is explained by resorting to the "they do that because they are autistic" logic. If problem behaviors are *inherent* in the child's autism, no one is to blame for the behaviors and no professional is really responsible for changing them.

Behaviors that support independence can be directly arranged, taught, and supported. Challenging behaviors common to students with autism should become the focus of active and skilled teaching. Behavior is what we observe. Responsibility for children's behavior is shared by adults. Blame is not an issue, but challenging behaviors demand a skilled response from all involved in the education and treatment of students with autism.

REVIEW QUESTIONS

1. Why would a teacher attempt to determine the function of a student's challenging behavior?

2. How does the function of a problem behavior influence a teacher's choice of an intervention?

3. What role does a student's communication ability play in the display of problem behavior?

4. How do community standards affect the choice of an intervention for a challenging behavior?

5. How does the Continuum of Educative Behavioral Interventions differ from previous lists of effective interventions?

6. How does an adherence to an educative model of behavioral intervention relate to crisis intervention?

7. How does the behavior of a student with autism act as a "quality of life barometer"?

REFERENCES

Alberto, P. A., & Troutman, A. C. (1995). *Applied behavior analysis for teachers.* Columbus, OH: Merrill.

American Psychiatric Association. (1994). *Diagnostic and statistical manual of mental disorders* (4th ed.). Washington, DC: Author.

Anderson, J. L., Albin, R. W., Mesaros, R. A., Dunlap, G., & Morelli-Robbins, M. (1993). Issues in providing training to achieve comprehensive behavioral support. In J. Reichle & D. P. Wacker (Eds.), *Comunicative alternatives to challenging behaviors* (pp. 363–406). Baltimore, MD: Paul H. Brookes.

Ayllon, T., & Azrin, N. (1968). *The token economy: A motivational system for therapy and rehabilitation.* New York: Appleton-Century-Crofts.

Baer, D., Wolf, M., & Risley, T. (1968). Some current dimensions of applied behavior analysis. *Journal of Applied Behavior Analysis, 1,* 91–97.

Bambara, L., & Warren, S. (1993). Massed trials revisited: Appropriate applications in functional skill training. In R. A. Gable & S. F. Warren (Eds.), *Strategies for teaching students with mild to severe mental retardation* (pp. 165–190). Baltimore, MD: Paul H. Brookes.

Blatt, B., & Kaplan, F. (1974). *Christmas in Purgatory.* Syracuse, NY: Human Policy Press.

Brady, M. P. (1984). A curriculum and instruction synthesis model for teachers of the severely handicapped. *The Exceptional Child, 13*(1), 19–32.

Carr, E., & Durand, M. (1985). Reducing behavioral problems through functional communication training. *Journal of Applied Behavior Analysis, 18,* 111–126.

Carr, E., Levin, L., McConnachie, G., Carlson, J., Kemp, D., & Smith, C. (1994). *Communication-based intervention for problem behavior.* Baltimore, MD: Paul H. Brookes.

Carr, E. G., Newsom, C. D., & Binkoff, J. A. (1980). Escape as a factor in the aggressive behavior of two retarded children. *Journal of Applied Behavior Analysis, 13,* 101–117.

Cipani, E. (1990). Principles of behavior modification. In J. Matson (Ed.), *Handbook of behavior modification with the mentally retarded* (pp. 123–138). New York: Plenum.

Colvin, G., & Sugai, G. (1988). Proactive strategies for managing social behavior problems: An instructional approach. *Education and Treatment of Children, 11,* 341–348.

Davis, C., & Brady, M. P. (1993). Expanding the utility of behavioral momentum: Where we've been, where we need to go. *Journal of Early Intervention, 17,* 211–223.

Davis, C., Brady, M. P., Hamilton, R., McEvoy, M., & Williams, R. E. (1994). Effects of high-probability requests on the social interactions of young children with severe disabilities. *Journal of Applied Behavior Analysis, 27,* 619–637.

Davis, C., Brady, M. P., Williams, R. E., & Hamilton, R. (1992). Effects of high-probability requests on the acquisition and generalization of responding to requests in young children with behavior disorders. *Journal of Applied Behavior Analysis, 25,* 905–916.

Dunlap, G., dePerczel, M., Clarke, S., Wilson, D., Wright, S., White, R., & Gomez, A. (1994). Choice making to promote adaptive behavior for students with emotional and behavioral challenges. *Journal of Applied Behavior Analysis, 27,* 505–518.

Dunlap, G., & Kern, L. (1993). Assessment and intervention for children within the instructional curriculum. In J. Reichle & D. Wacker (Eds.), *Communicative alternatives to challenging behavior* (pp. 177–203). Baltimore, MD: Paul H. Brookes.

Durand, V. M. (1990). *Severe behavior problems: A functional communication training approach.* New York: Guilford Press.

Durand, V. M., & Carr, E. G. (1991). Functional communication training to reduce challenging behavior: Maintenance and application in new settings. *Journal of Applied Behavior Analysis, 24,* 251–256.

Favell, J. (1973). Reduction of stereotypies by reinforcement of toy play. *Mental Retardation, 11,* 21–23.

Foxx, R. M., & Azrin, N. H. (1972). Restitution: A method of eliminating aggressive-disruptive behavior of retarded and brain-damaged patients. *Behavior Research and Therapy, 10,* 15–27.

Gaylord-Ross, R. (1980). A decision model for the treatment of aberrant behavior in applied settings. In W. Sailor, B. Wilcox, & L. Brown (Eds.), *Methods of instruction for severely handicapped students* (pp. 135–158). Baltimore, MD: Paul H. Brookes.

Green, C. W., Reid, D. H., White, L. K., Halford, R. C., Brittain, D. P., & Gardner, S. M. (1988). Identifying reinforcers for persons with profound handicaps: Staff opinion versus systematic assessment of preferences. *Journal of Applied Behavior Analysis, 21,* 31–43.

Hamad, C., Isley, E., & Lowry, M. (1983). The use of mechanical restraint and response incompatibility to modify self-injurious behavior. A case study. *Mental Retardation, 32,* 213–217.

Hart, B., & Risley, T. (1995). *Meaningful differences in the everyday experience of young American children.* Baltimore, MD: Paul H. Brookes.

Heward, W. L., Dardig, J. C., & Rossett, A. (1979). *Working with parents of handicapped children.* Columbus, OH: Merrill.

Hobbs, T., Westling, D., & Hatoum, R. (1996). Treatment of positive behavioral support concepts in currently used textbooks. *Teacher Education and Special Education, 19*(1), 71–80.

Holburn, S. (1997). A renaissance in residential behavior analysis? A historical perspective and a better way to help people with challenging behavior. *The Behavior Analyst, 20,* 61–85.

Horner, R., Dunlap, G., Koegel, R., Carr, E., Sailor, W., Anderson, J., Albin, R., & O'Neill, R. (1990). Toward a technology of "nonaversive" behavioral support. *Journal of the Association for Persons with Severe Handicaps, 15,* 125–132.

Iwata, B. A., Dorsey, M. F., Slier, K. J., Bauman, K. E., & Richman, G. S. (1982). Toward a functional analysis of self-injury. *Analysis and Intervention in Developmental Disabilities, 2,* 3–20.

Johnston, J. M., & Sherman, R. A. (1993). Applying the least restrictive alternative principle to treatment decisions: A legal and behavioral analysis. *The Behavior Analyst, 16,* 103–115.

Koegel, L. K., Koegel, R. L., Hurley, C., & Frea, W. (1992). Improving social skills and disruptive behavior in children with autism through self-management. *Journal of Applied Behavior Analysis, 25,* 341–353

Koegel, L. K., Koegel, R. L., Kellegrew, D., & Mullen, K. (1996). Parent education for prevention and reduction of severe problem behaviors. In L. K. Koegel, R. L. Koegel & G. Dunlap (Eds.), *Positive behavioral support* (pp. 3–30). Baltimore, MD: Paul H. Brookes.

Lindsley, O. R. (1971). From Skinner to precision teaching: The child knows best. In J. V. Jordan & L. S. Robins (Eds.), *Let's try doing something else kind of thing: Behavior principles and the exceptional child.* Reston, VA: Council for Exceptional Children.

Lovaas, O. I. (1987). Behavioral treatment and normal educational and intellectual functioning in young autistic children. *Journal of Consulting and Clinical Psychology, 1,* 3–9.

Luiselli, J. (1986). Modification of self-injurious behavior. An analysis of the use of contingently applied protective equipment. *Behavior Modification, 10,* 191–203.

MacDuff, G., Krantz, P., & McClannahan, L. (1993). Teaching children with autism to use photographic activity schedules: Maintenance and generalization of complex response chains. *Journal of Applied Behavior Analysis, 26,* 89–97.

Mace, R., Page, T., Ivancic, M., & O'Brien, S. 1986. Effectiveness of brief time out with and without contingent delay: A comparative analysis. *Journal of Applied Behavior Analysis, 19,* 79–86.

Matson, J., & Keyes, J. (1988). Contingent reinforcement and contingent restraint to treat severe aggression and self-injury in mentally retarded and autistic adults. *Journal of the Multihandicapped Person, 1,* 141–148.

Maurice, C. (1996). *Behavioral interventions for children with autism.* Austin, TX: Pro-Ed.

Mullen, K., & Frea, W. (1994). A parent-professional consultation model for functional analysis. In R. Koegel & L. Koegel (Eds.), *Teaching children with autism* (pp. 175–188). Baltimore, MD: Paul H. Brookes.

O'Neill, R., Horner, R., Albin, R., Sprauge, J. Storey, K., & Newton, J. S. (1997). *Functional assessment and program development for problem behavior.* Pacific Grove: Brooks/Cole.

Oullette, L., Horner, R., & Newton, J. (1994). Changing activity patterns to improve social networks: A descriptive analysis. *Behavioral Interventions, 9,* 55–66.

Pace, G., Iwata, B., Edwards, G., & McCosh, K. (1986). Stimulus fading and transfer in the treatment of self-restraint and self-injurious behavior. *Journal of Applied Behavior Analysis, 19,* 381–389.

Parsons, M. B., & Reid, D. H. (1990). Assessing food preferences among persons with profound mental retardation: Providing opportunities to make choices. *Journal of Applied Behavior Analysis, 2,* 183–195.

Reid, J., Tombaugh, T., & Van den Heuvel, K. (1981). Application of contingent physical restraint to suppress stereotyped body rocking of profoundly retarded persons. *American Journal of Mental Deficiency, 86,* 78–85.

Repp, A. C., & Deitz, D. E. D. (1974). Reducing aggressive and self-injurious behavior of institutionalized retarded children through reinforcement of other behaviors. *Journal of Applied Behavior Analysis, 7,* 313–325.

Repp, A. C., & Deitz, D. E. D. (1979). Reinforcement-based reductive procedures: Training and monitoring performance of institutional staff. *Mental Retardation, 17,* 221–226.

Repp, A., & Singh, N. (1990). *Perspectives on the use of nonaversive interventions for persons with developmental disabilities.* Pacific Grove, CA: Brooks/Cole.

Ritschl, C., Mongrella, J., & Presbie, R. (1972). Group time out from rock and roll music and out-of-seat behavior of handicapped children while riding a school bus. *Psychological Reports, 31,* 967–973.

Roberts, M. (1988). Enforcing chair timeouts with room timeouts. *Behavior Modification, 12,* 353–370.

Rogers, S. (1996). Brief report: Early intervention in autism. *Journal of Autism and Developmental Disorders, 26,* 243–246.

Schloss, P. J., & Smith, M. S. (1998). *Applied behavior analysis in the classroom.* Boston: Allyn & Bacon.

Scott, J. (1996). Recruiting, selecting and training teaching assistants. In C. Maurice (Ed.), *Behavioral interventions for children with autism* (pp. 231–240). Austin, TX: Pro-Ed.

Shevin, M., & Klein, N. K. (1984). The importance of choice-making skills for students with severe disabilities. *Journal of the Association for Persons with Severe Handicaps, 9,* 159–166.

Singer, G., Singer, J., & Horner, R. H. (1987). Using pretask requests to increase the probability of compliance for students with severe disabilities. *Journal of the Association for Persons with Severe Handicaps, 12,* 287–291.

Singh, N., & Bakker, L. (1984). Suppression of pica by overcorrection and physical restraint: A comparative analysis. *Journal of Autism and Developmental Disorders, 14,* 331–340.

Skinner, B. F. (1968). *The technology of teaching.* New York: Appleton-Century-Crofts.

Smith, J. D. (1997). Mental retardation as an educational construct: Time for a new shared view. *Education and Training in Mental Retardation and Developmental Disabilities, 32,* 167–173.

Stokes, T. F., & Baer, D. M. (1977). An implicit technology of generalization. *Journal of Applied Behavior Analysis, 10,* 349–367.

Taylor, S. (1988). Caught on the continuum: A critical analysis of the principle of the least restrictive environment. *Journal of the Association for Persons with Severe Handicaps, 13,* 41–53.

Turnbull, H. R. (1997). *Keynote address.* Presented at the annual conference of the Association for Persons With Severe Handicaps, Boston.

Van Houten, R., Axelrod, S., Bailey, J., Favell, J., Foxx, R., Iwata, B., & Lovaas, O. I. (1988). The right to effective behavioral treatment. *The Behavior Analyst, 11,* 111–114.

Vollmer, R., & Iwata, B. (1992). Differential reinforcement as treatment for behavior disorder: Procedural and functional variations. *Research in Developmental Disabilities, 13,* 393–417.

Vollmer, R., Iwata, B., Zarcone, J., Smith, R., & Mazaleski, J. (1993). The role of attention in the treatment of attention-maintained self injurious behavior: Noncontingent reinforcement and differential reinforcement of other behavior. *Journal of Applied Behavior Analysis, 26,* 9–21.

White, O. R. (1986). Precision teaching—precision learning. *Exceptional Children, 6,* 522–534.

Winett, R. A., & Winkler, R. C. (1972). Current behavior modification in the classroom: Be still, be quiet, be docile. *Journal of Applied Behavior Analysis, 5,* 499–504.

Winton, A., & Singh, N. (1983). Suppression of pica using brief-duration physical restraint. *Journal of Mental Deficiency Research, 27,* 93–103.

Witt, J., & Elliot, S. (1985). Acceptability of classroom management strategies. In T. Kratochwill (Ed.), *Advances in school psychology* (Vol., 4, pp. 251–288). Hillsdale, NJ: Lawrence Erlbaum.

Wolfensberger, W. (1975). *The origin and nature of our institutional models.* Syracuse, NY: Human Policy Press.

Chapter 6

COMMUNICATION: MEANING AND COMPETENCE

Key Points

- Students with autism present significant communication skill deficits.

- Students with autism learn to communicate by learning communicative "function."

- Many students have developed communicative competence using different behavioral approaches.

- Increased language "encouragements" and opportunities may result in improved communication development.

INTRODUCTION

Students with autism have difficulties in both the expression and understanding of verbal and nonverbal language. For some students with autism, echolalia, maladaptive behaviors, and other less efficient actions serve a communicative function. For all people, functional communication skills are vital to independent functioning. In this chapter we present a variety of techniques used to teach students with autism to communicate.

Communication Problems

Students with autism exhibit difficulties in both expressive and receptive communication. Qualitative impairment in verbal and nonverbal communication is one of the core deficits of autism (APA, 1994). This impairment can be exhibited in a number of ways, from a student who is completely nonverbal to one who is highly verbal but is unable to utilize or interpret body language or fully appreciate the pragmatic aspects of another's communication.

The impairment in communication skills extends to *nonverbal* communication including joint attention, eye contact, body postures, and gestures. Many young children with autism do not seem to anticipate being held; others stiffen or look away from a person when making a social approach (APA, 1994). This lack of anticipatory posture has long been recognized as one of the early indicators of autism (Kanner, 1943).

Without intervention, it is estimated that from 28% to 61% of the individuals with autism develop no functional speech (Fish, Shapiro, & Campbell, 1966; Lotter, 1967; Schopler & Mesibov, 1988; Wolff & Chess, 1965). Unlike persons with hearing impairment, for example, these individuals generally display no understandable *compensatory* behavior (i.e., gesturing or using joint attention) to communicate. For students who develop speech, there are likely to be impairments in the production areas of volume, pitch, rate, rhythm, or intonation. Thus, even if speech is present, it often sounds odd or different from the speech of students without autism.

Deficits in receptive language can have a far-reaching impact. They can extend from students who have difficulty comprehending idiomatic speech to those who are completely unable to process spoken language. Auditory processing deficits affect the use of information and often cause confusion with the *sequence* of information. Interestingly, for most students with autism, information that is presented simultaneously and is spatial in nature (e.g., spoken words combined with pictures, pictograms, or written words) is often processed much more effectively than speech alone.

Some students with autism have an enhanced facility or savant skill for languages. There are individuals who are fluent in speech, reading, or both in multiple languages and are able to work effectively as translators.

Pragmatic Issues

Traditional speech-language pathology teaches that language is comprised of the interaction between form, content and use (Bloom & Lahey, 1978). Form refers to the conventional system of sounds and words that make up a language, as well as the grammatical rules for phrase and sentence construction. Content refers to the ideas about the environment that are coded by language. Use (or pragmatics) refers to the functions for which language is used and to the set of community standards that guide our understanding of language. Students with autism might have problems with any one or more of these areas of language.

Often language use, or pragmatics, is the most severely affected area in individuals who have adequate speech production and vocabulary (Baltaxe, 1977; Fay & Schuler, 1980; Paul, 1987). A common abnormality in pragmatics is pronoun reversal: the use of "you" or the student's name instead of "I" when referring to oneself. Echolalia, or the repetition of words, phrases, or whole paragraphs, is exhibited by some students. Echolalic speech provides a serious pragmatic challenge for the person listening to the student with autism.

Idiomatic phrases also present problems for many students with autism. Idiomatic phrases rely on shared understanding of a phrase and contrast with a literal interpretation of that phrase. The phrase, "What's up?" for example, might cause a student with autism to look up to see what is in the air. As anyone who has tried to learn a foreign language knows, idioms are most difficult to learn because, if translated literally, they make no sense. An idiom must be learned as an entire phrase with a meaning specific only to that phrase. Mesibov (1991) noted that individuals with autism use English as a second language; thus phrases taken for granted by English speakers must be directly learned by students with autism.

Idiosyncratic speech is seen in some students. Words or phrases are used in uncommon contexts as a communicative attempt. "Go blue wheel" could be used to request a ride in the family car. Television jingles or slogans can be used to request an item or a category of items. "It's the real thing" could be used to request a drink.

A complex problem involving pragmatics is the use of problem behavior to express oneself. The relationship between problem behavior and communication deficits is now widely recognized and is clearly evident in many students with autism (Carr et al., 1994). The student with autism who cannot make his or her wishes known is likely to resort to behaviors that have in the past influenced the behavior of others in his or her environment. These unconventional communications (Prizant & Weatherby, 1987) are not always be problematic, but they sometimes become the genesis of serious problem behaviors. For example, a behavior that initially is exhibited at a low level, such as crying, may escalate to severe tantrums over time when people in the student's environment begin to respond positively to student's crying. A child whose parents respond when he cries might discover that they come much more quickly if the crying also is paired with hitting. The child's hitting may cause parents to present desirable items at a higher rate, hoping to find out what the child wants. The crying has now escalated into a more problematic behavior (crying and hitting), and both serve a "wordless" communicative function. The development of a successful, interactive communication system reduces the need for this problem behavior

The DSM-IV describes these readily observable communication difficulties across a wide range of ability levels. These are described in Table 6–1. As noted by Kanner (1943), the ability to produce speech is less important as a characteristic of autism than the lack of ability to effectively communicate with people in the environment.

The Need for Communication

Individuals need to be able to communicate with others in their environment to express their wants and needs, to comment on their environment, and to engage in reciprocal social interactions. Of course, verbal speech is highly desired, but more important is the ability to communicate effectively and appropriately. Communication programming can be difficult for parents and teachers and it may require the adoption of obviously different educational goals, activities, and arrangements for the child. Careful consideration of the student's needs and skills should be

---

Table 6–1. Communication Deficit in Autism—DSM-IV Criteria

Qualitative impairments in communication manifested by at least one of the following:

(a) delay in, or total lack of, the development of spoken language (not accompanied by an attempt to compensate through alternative modes of communication such as gesture or mime);

(b) in individuals with adequate speech, marked impairment in the ability to initiate or sustain a conversation with others;

(c) stereotyped and repetitive use of language or idiosyncratic language; or

(d) lack of varied, spontaneous, make-believe play or social imitative play appropriate to developmental level.

Source: From *Diagnostic and Statistical Manual of Mental Disorders* (4th ed.), by American Psychiatric Association, 1994, p. 72. Washington, DC: Author. Reprinted with permission.

Picture Exchange Communication Systems

Andrew Bondy, Ph.D.

Children who are unable to communicate in traditional ways are likely to communicate in ways that set the stage for severe problem behavior. The child who uses the threat of a tantrum to obtain a choice on something small may resort to a full blown tantrum to escape from a nonpreferred activity. Accommodating a child, while seemingly polite and in many ways "the special education thing to do" often leads a child farther away from independence and drastically increases the risk of severe problem behavior. Providing a child with a means of efficiently communicating in an independence-enhancing manner, in many cases, is far better than instituting an elaborate behavioral intervention.

Preventing/Decreasing Problem Behaviors Through Communication Training

Do you recall, especially as a teenager, having a conversation with your parents during which you were convinced you were speaking English but that no communication was actually taking place? Do you remember the feelings of frustration and anger while trying to make yourself understood? Now, imagine yourself as someone who does not have an established language and yet you want others to understand what you do and don't want. This difficult, often frustrating, situation is exactly what many children and adults with various developmental disabilities face. Family members and professionals working with these individuals often have to deal with the expressions of that frustration and the limitations associated with the difficulty in making their own simple instructions understood.

It is important for everyone to learn how to make direct requests for the things they most want. Although speech is the preferred mode of communication, many people with disabilities do not speak and may never learn to use speech. For these individuals, alternative communication modalities may involve pictures and other symbols, written words, or sign language. Perhaps most important is to teach people to initiate requesting; this removes reliance on other people asking questions, such as "What do you want?" If they only respond when asked such questions, they may be termed "prompt dependent." The Picture Ex-

(continued)

change Communication System (PECS) (Bondy & Frost, 1994) is one system that rapidly teaches spontaneous requesting to children and adults with autism and related developmental disabilities.

I worked with a 2-year child with autism who came to our school as one of the most self-injurious children I had ever met. Within moments of arriving in our classroom, he appeared to notice something that he wanted. He immediately threw himself from his mother's lap, twice slammed his head on the floor, ran face first into a wooden door, and jumped up and down on his knees. When I was able to pick him up, he scratched my face, and punched and kicked as skillfully as any 2-year-old could! We quickly realized that he wanted pretzels but had no direct way to communicate this. During the first day, we taught him to use PECS and within a few minutes, he was calmly approaching people who had pretzels with them. During the next few weeks, by improving his communication skills and providing consistent reactions to his tantrums, his behavior problems were greatly diminished and he looked like a much happier child.

In addition to learning how to request important items and activities, it also is important to be able to calmly reject things. Learning to communicate "No" is crucial. When a person has not learned to communicate in a calm fashion, everyone else may have to cope with more dramatic forms of expression. For example, I once worked with a young woman, Minerva, who became very agitated if a teacher provided vocational materials and simply said, "Time to work." Most often, Minerva would look at the work, look at the teacher, and then scatter the materials all over the room! Then the teacher would engage Minerva in picking up the materials, during which Minerva would cry and scream. The entire process could take 30 minutes or more and left everyone exhausted.

We realized that Minerva did not see the "profit" in doing many of these jobs and simply concluded it was not worth her effort. She preferred the struggle with her teachers. Rather than designing some punitive consequence for throwing the materials, we decided to teach her to say "No thank you." If staff heard her say this, they would understand that they needed to make a better, or at least a clearer, deal with Minerva. That is, Minerva expected to get paid for working and saying "No thank you" was her way to begin negotiating. Soon, if someone simply gave er work to do, Minerva would say "No thank you" and the teacher would then come up with a better deal. For example, she might immediately determine that Minerva would like to take a walk. The teacher would then say, "Minerva, if you want to take a walk, you'll need to finish your work." Most often, Minerva would do work and *then* go for a walk. There was a dramatic reduction in her tantrums, without a significant change in the teacher's reaction to the tantrum. By learning a new communication skill, Minerva learned to replace the tantrum with an action that more calmly achieved her goals.

When people do not understand what is expected of them, they often act out or refuse to do anything. When provided with more information, especially through visual systems designed to augment spoken communication, many children and adults begin to be more successful in their assignments. We often start a lesson or job by allowing the person to select what she would like to work for prior to telling her what we expect. We may use a picture or other symbol of what she would like and put it on a card as a visual reminder of what she is working for. As time goes by, we may put pennies or similar tokens on a set of circles on the card, teaching the person that when all the circles are filled, then she can get what she was working for. In this manner, children better understand what they are going to earn and how much longer they must work before "cashing in." Teaching children how to wait for desired items, and to follow instructions and a schedule of activities, can all be made easier with visual cues.

In general, many behavior management problems are related to the difficulties that people have in expressing their desires and in understanding what is expected of them. By providing systematic training in functional communication, we may be able to replace problematic behaviors with actions that are calmer but yield the same outcome for the person. By providing systematic visual systems to indicate what tasks are expected, when they will occur, how long they will last, and what rewards can be earned often leads to greatly improved performance and equally improved general behaviors.

Andrew Bondy directs the Delaware statewide program in autism. He has developed, with Lori Frost, the Picture Exchange Communication System (PECS).

taken to avoid unduly stigmatizing the student, either by using an unnecessarily elaborate system or by using an ineffective communication system. The goal of any communication system should be to provide an interface between the student and individuals in the environment for reciprocal interaction. Communication, whether gestural, verbal, or pictorial, is necessary for independent functioning in a community. For lack of a communication system, many people with autism have a lifelong dependence on others to help them meet their daily needs.

In schools, most standardized tests are, to some extent, language based. Students who lack language are likely to test lower on standardized tests than students who have language. In addition, teachers rely heavily on verbal language to impart knowledge to their students, particularly in general education settings. Students who lack language will not fully benefit from education presented in these settings.

Teaching communication skills should be a prime component of any educational program for students with autism. Whatever the modality or combination of modalities (verbal, gestural, or pictorial), students need to be able to express themselves and to receive information from people in their environment and have access to the systems that allow them to do so most effectively.

PROVIDING A COMMUNICATION SYSTEM

Communication is a vital component of any program design for students with autism. Approximately 50% of students with autism historically do not develop language and many of the students with language exhibit abnormalities in usage. With these factors in mind, it is imperative that all communication systems provide the utmost in clarity and ease of use. Tone of voice, use of pictures to augment spoken words, sign language, and the use of precise spoken language are all ways to make communication more clearly understood. These communication techniques all facilitate learning for students with autism.

Communication is a reciprocal process. Students need to have a system in place to express their wants and needs and to initiate and maintain conversation with others. In addition, the communication system has to allow the individual to receive information from people in the environment. Imagine being in a country where you do not speak the language, cannot read the signs, or tell what is in the boxes in the stores; you cannot understand the gestures and signals that the people in the country use. In addition, the people all around you cannot understand what you are saying and do not understand the gestures that you use. The sense of isolation and frustration would be tremendous. Most adults can learn the language in that other country, thereby reducing their frustration. For the student with autism, alternative communication strategies may be called for.

Alternative communication strategies have been adapted for students who have little or no functional language; alternative systems give students a viable means of accessing desired activities, protesting, and making appropriate choices. These strategies include sign language, picture communication, and electronic communication devices.

Picture and electronic communication systems are considered prominent forms of *alternative and augmentative communication* (AAC). AAC systems have been shown to be useful in teaching students to communicate (Kiernan, 1983), but successful implementation requires moderate to high levels of skill by communication disorders specialists. Electronic devices that provide synthesized speech have been most often used with individuals with physical impairments, but these devices can be used effectively for nonverbal or minimally verbal students with autism.

Careful assessment, skilled training, and adults' (including teachers and family members) commitment to use the chosen system are necessary if the student is to learn to use it successfully. Family support is a vital component to the successful implementation of any communication system. If the family believes that a system is too elaborate or stigmatizing, they will not support its use. Students with autism must be able to communicate effectively with their families. Lack of enthusiastic commitment to the communication system, even if it is used as a temporary measure while the child is acquiring verbal speech, will reduce the efficiency of the system as well as the child's desire to communicate.

AAC devices allow the student with limited or absent speech to communicate effectively and efficiently. There are a number of factors to consider when deciding which type of AAC is most appropriate for a given child. Factors such as the student's current level of language, fine motor skills, sensory and physical tolerance, and cognitive abilities are all important. A communication device that requires a level of fine motor skill beyond the student's current capability is not likely to be used. Likewise, a communication device that is programmed with a number of sentences, none of which will access items or activities that the child enjoys will likely not be used. Careful assessment by persons skilled in AAC and knowledgeable about the student can provide an excellent "fit" between the student and his or her communication system.

A major disadvantage of many AAC systems is that they often require prerequisite skills (i.e., joint attention and imitation skills) that are not in the repertoire of some students with autism. In addition, communication relies on social reinforcers, such as the attention of the communication partner. Many students with autism do not respond to social reinforcement and tend not to spontaneously seek out others. For these students, initial communication programming with AAC will be a challenge.

The development of an appropriate, functional communication system is a vital component to the normalization of the individual. Whether the modality is verbal, pictorial, or gestural, every individual needs to communicate with others in the environment to provide fulfillment of wants and needs, to comment, and to seek and respond to social rein-

AAC Interventions for Children with Autism

Dale Williams, Ph.D., CCC

Because of the likelihood of communicative disorders, many of which are severe, children with autism often benefit from augmentative and alternative communication (AAC) systems. AAC enhances or, with severe disorders, replaces an individual's means of communication. The simplest AAC devices are picture, word, or letter boards. With these, the child simply points to the appropriate symbol to communicate. AAC systems can be complex as well, such as sign language, voice output systems, visual tracking devices, and communication equipment utilizing keyboards (Alvares & Williams, 1995).

Selecting an AAC system requires a team of professionals (Beukelman & Mirenda, 1992; Prizant & Wetherby, 1988) to assess language, motor, cognitive, visual, and hearing capabilities and to match a child to an appropriate AAC system. A professional certain to be on an AAC intervention team is the speech-language pathologist (SLP). Speech and language disorders are central to autism and SLPs are trained to assess and treat such disabilities. In addition, many SLPs receive specialized training in AAC through continuing education. Speech-language pathologists are thus uniquely qualified to offer AAC management with communicative disorders.

Although estimates vary, a significant portion of children with autism have no speech at all (Mirenda & Schuler, 1988). Other students may present information processing abilities that differ from the general population (Wing, 1995). That is, they have difficulty sequencing and organizing material and make better use of visual-spatial skills than auditory skills for processing. Given these differences, it is worth noting that AAC systems use of visual cues, which help these children to organize information (Blackstone, 1991). Also, pictures, words, and letters, prominent with AAC systems are not as transient as spoken language and are thus easier to process (Reichle, York, & Sigafoos, 1991).

Many children with autism have good reading and writing skills, and an interest in text and symbols (Blackstone, 1991; Lord, 1988; Mirenda & Schuler, 1988). AAC systems that require typing or tracking symbols take advantage of these students' strengths and interests and may thus facilitate language development.

These modes, used in conjunction with verbal modes, may help to bridge the gap between echolalia and meaningful communication (Blackstone, 1991). Difficulties with the social aspects of language (pragmatics) may be manifested in limited responsiveness to people. Refined communication through AAC may not only involve the child in social interactions, but also alter perceptions and raise expectations of the children's peers.

In addition to language skills, other traits associated with autism may be positively influenced by AAC interventions. For example, tantrums and self-stimulating behaviors may decrease with the emergence of improved language skills through AAC (Blackstone, 1991). Also, these children may show an interest in, or even a preference for, inanimate objects, including mechanical devices (Blackstone, 1991). Many AAC systems (i.e., keyboard or voice output equipment) are mechanical and thus might be preferred by some students.

Unfortunately, many children with autism do not have access to AAC. The delivery of AAC interventions, devices and services is hindered by a shortage of university programs in speech-language pathology, especially those with specific training in AAC and autism (Mirenda & Schuler, 1988; Williams, Taylor, & Scott, 1994, 1995). Hopefully, in time, such training will be more readily available.

Dale Williams is a speech-language pathologist and an Associate Professor in the Department of Communication Disorders at Florida Atlantic University.

forcers. Family members also want to communicate with the student with autism in a positive, meaningful way. Pictorial, gestural, and other AAC methods allow two-way communication contact for individuals who not only have limited or no expressive language, but also have limited receptive language skills.

Function as the Key to Communication Development

"Function" is the key to the modern understanding of communication development for students with autism. The goal of language intervention is to help the person, "develop a variety of needs and wants and to encourage them to express their needs and wants in flexible, conventional, and appropriate ways" (Duchan, 1987, p. 703). These needs and wants are observable to sensitive persons in the environment. The student who requests food with nonconventional hand signals or who protests an activity by tantrumming is attempting to communicate. The function of these communications is to have needs met. These needs usually consist of two categories: the student *wants something* or the student *wishes to have something stop* (or to escape from it).

Two different schools of thought on language development are essentially unified on the critical importance of function in communication development for students with autism. The term "functionalism" is the term most closely identified with cognitive-functionalists such as Prizant, Wetherby, or Duchan, but similar emphases are shared by behavior analysts. Duchan (1987) examined the similarities and differences between cognitive and behavioral approaches to the role of functionalism in language development. The key difference between the approaches is the degree to which intentionality is important. As a practical matter, whether a child has a tantrum to escape a demand or to express a dislike for a demand has little significance. If the communicative behavor (tantrum) is reinforced by allowing the child to escape demands, a dangerous pattern can be learned and over time, strengthened. Table 6–2 summarizes Duchan's analysis.

The functional aspect of language extends beyond mechanics into the area of total communication. One of the most difficult things for nonverbal students to learn is to communicate spontaneously under ordinary conditions. While typical children are eager to use new language skills in many new circumstances, children with autism tend not to generalize new skills to new circumstances. As language is arguably one of the most difficult skills to learn, it is least likely to be generalized by students with autism without specific training. Many of the language skills that students with autism learn might be used only in highly structured circumstances. Essentially, these students learn to communicate only when an adult gives a specific directive or request (a discriminative stimulus) to communicate. These students learn to communicate only when an adult structures the communicative situation in the way that the child learned it. This is communication only in the most limited sense.

The TEACCH program in North Carolina created a developmentally based communication curriculum designed for nonverbal students with autism (Schopler, Mesibov, & Baker, 1982). The TEACCH curriculum developers recognized the uneven pattern of developmental skills shown in these students. Their curriculum allows for multidimensional assessment and programming, and the objectives chosen are developmentally appropriate. Recognizing that students with autism tend not to follow a

Table 6-2. Functionalism in Behavioral and Cognitive-Linguistic Models in Relation to Autism

	Behavioral Approach	Cognitive Approach (Cognitive-functionalism)
Motivation for using language	Function or purpose	Ability to communicate intents to an interactant to achieve some function (replacing linguistic or cognitive knowledge as featured in older language models).
Key difference is a focus on . .	Associative links between and among observable behaviors	Variety of mental constructs which equate to intention generators
Unit of analysis	Contingency relationships (antecedents, behaviors, consequences)	Intents
Functional categories	Frequency of interactions, functional analysis of behaviors yielding function or purpose achieved.	Classification of language by forms and functions based on impact on or perception of interactant.
A functional communicative behavior is one that:	Achieves a desired function regardless of form or degree of social acceptability or the extent to which it is conventional. Communicative behaviors are functional whether or not they are intended to be so.	Carry out the intent of the communicator.

Source: Based on "Functionalism: A Perspective on Autistic Communication," by J. Duchan, 1987. In D. J. Cohen & A. M. Donnellan (Eds.), *Handbook of autism and pervasive developmental disorders* (pp. 703–709). Silver Spring, MD: V. H. Winston.

typical developmental sequence, they assess students' strengths and existing abilities for spontaneous communication.

An assessment tool with a very useful communicaton section is the Psychoeducational Profile (PEP) developed by Schopler and Reichler (1979). This system assesses the students under a variety of conditions including traditional clinical test conditions and in actual day placements or home environments. These items are scored at one of three levels: passing (if the student is capable of performing the skill without any special help); emerging (if the student has some of the skill necessary for the task and may be able to complete the task with extensive assistance); and failing (if the student is totally unable to complete the task even with extensive assistance).

The Adolescent and Adult Psychoeducational Profile (AAPEP) (Mesibov, Schopler, Schaffer, & Landrus, 1988) is the upper level of the PEP assessment system and is designed, obviously, for adolescents and young adults. Two sample items from the assessment of communication capacity are featured in Table 6–3. Note that the first item, Comprehends Verbal Instructions or Gestures, is somewhat contrived for the assessment purposes, while the second item, Responds to Questions about Present State, is placed within the natural flow of activity. Both items yield valuable information on the communicative competence of the student. The scoring format allows the teacher to quickly bracket current skills. This helps the teacher to avoid selecting skills that are either too easy (passing) or too hard (failing) and to concentrate on skills that are at emerging levels.

The TEACCH curriculum builds on existing skills rather than selecting skills that are not in the individual's repertoire. The communication curriculum is individually based and is adapted to the student's developmental pattern. The TEACCH curriculum examines five different programming dimensions to help teachers plan instruction and select a communication system. These dimensions are shown in Table 6–4.

BEHAVIORAL APPROACHES TO SPEECH AND LANGUAGE DEVELOPMENT

Many researchers who study language development in autism note that language is subject to the same type of reinforcement contingencies as any other behavior. Although this reflects the observations of Skinner (1957) over 40 years ago, current behavioral approaches offer a wide variety of language acquisition methods.

Whether traditional or modern, there are features that are consistent across the various behavioral approaches. First and foremost is a belief that language (verbal or nonverbal) is behavior that can be acquired and

Table 6–3. Functional Communication Assessment: Two Items Adapted From the AAPEP

Procedure	Scoring Protocol

Comprehends Verbal Instructions or Gestures

Spread the pencils, box, and paper on the table from child's left to right. Say the instructions listed below to the child. After each instruction, wait to see whether the child carries out the task. If the child makes no response or an incorrect response, repeat the verbal instructions, adding gestures and emphasizing the key underlined words. After each trial, return materials to their original positions.

Passing: Carries out at least 4 verbal instructions without additional gestures or repetitions.

Emerging: Carries out 2 or 3 verbal instructions without additional gestures or repetitions or carries out 2 or more with gestures or repetitions.

Failing: Carries out 1 or more of the instructions with or without gestures and repetitions.

1. Give me the box.
2. Put the pencils on the paper.
3. Put the box on the floor.
4. Knock on the door.
5. Shake my hand.

Responds to Questions About Present State

At appropriate times during the session ask the following questions:

1. "Do you want some water?" (during break)
2. "Are you finished?" (after a task has been completed)
3. "Do you need to use the bathroom?" (in the middle of the session)
4. "Do you like these activities?" (after a series of tasks)

Passing: Gives appropriate and apparently accurate response either verbally or nonverbally to all 4 questions.

Emerging: Answers 2 or 3 questions appropriately and accurately.

Failing: Answers 1 question or none appropriately and accurately.

Source: Adapted from the Adolescent and Adult Psychoeducational Profile (AAPEP), by G. Mesibov, E. Shopler, B. Schaffer, & R. Landrus, 1988. *Individualized assessment and treatment for autistic and developmentally disabled children.* Austin, TX: Pro-Ed.

taught. Although cognizant of the possible limitations of neurology, communication is an achievable goal that can be learned through some modality. A corollary is the recognition that various techniques and approaches will facilitate or not facilitate the acquisition of language. By

Table 6–4. Dimensions of Communication Programming

Communication Dimension	Example
Function	Requests, comments
Semantic categories	Things the child will talk about
Specific words	Preference words; survival words
Communicative form	Verbal, pictographic
Context	Place, people, activities

carefully selecting communicative targets to pursue, then using the best modality, tools, and techniques for the student, learning is highly likely. This approach to language acquisition is active rather than reactive.

In addition to philosophy, behavioral programs teach through reinforcement rather than punishment. Whatever the targeted communication behavior (closer approximations, verbal initiation, correct labeling, asking for an item, etc.), the student is taught, then reinforced for practicing that specific behavior. Utilization of a reinforcement model teaches the child that communication is a rewarding activity.

Generalization of the communicative skills is a targeted end result of behavioral interventions. To be considered a functional skill, communication needs to be spontaneously used across all relevant environments and people. A number of different approaches are used to ensure generalization (see Chapter 8), but behavioral approaches to communication all avoid the "train and hope" phenomenon (Stokes & Baer, 1977); behavioral approaches make active efforts to help students acquire durable, generalizable communication behavior.

Although there are numerous variations of behavioral approaches to communication skills, three programs are often cited for their effectiveness. These programs are well organized, packaged for teachers, and have been validated specifically on children with autism. They include (a) the Lovaas Discrete Trial approach; (b) Drash's TALK program; and (c) Koegel, O'Dell, and Koegel's Natural Language Paradigm.

Discrete Trial

Lovaas (1981) developed a specific behavioral language program for children with autism. Lovaas found that many children responded in an undifferentiated way to language. That is, they used adult speech as a signal to display behaviors that they had learned, without understanding the adult's specific request or statement. After being taught to line up on request, they were as likely to line up on hearing, "Go line up" as "Draw a line." Lovaas postulated that a failure to develop language was a function of certain sensory problems that distorted incoming stimuli. To remediate language deficits, Lovaas suggested that *discrimination training* should be the focus of training. To facilitate discrimination, he recommended that simplified language be used initially. This entailed giving the child only the most relevant words to ensure success.

Lovaas' initial program recommended interspersing 3 to 5 minutes of verbal imitation drills with already mastered drills from other areas. Since imitation training comprised a large part of the program, children who were not successful in learning verbal language were taught signs as part of their imitation drills.

There were five steps in the initial Lovaas communication program. The first step was simply to *increase the frequency* of a student's vocalizations. The student was reinforced initially for each vocal response. The turn-taking concept was established by repeating the instruction (or discriminative stimulus) every 5 to 10 seconds. The goal of this step was to teach the student to control the frequency of reinforcement through vocalization.

The second step was to teach the child to *vocalize within a few seconds* of an adult's instruction. Bringing the vocalizations under temporal control increased the turn-taking concept and taught the student that vocalizing after listening to another person vocalize would be rewarded.

The third step in the Lovaas program taught *sound imitation*. The targets chosen for imitation were either sounds that were emitted frequently during the first two phases, or "easy" sounds that typically developing children first acquire (i.e., "ah," "mm," and "buh"). These sounds were shaped through successive approximation until the imitation was accurate. This procedure continued until the child had a "sound vocabulary" of approximately 10 sounds.

The fourth step taught *word imitation*. Initially, the words chosen were composed of sounds that the student could imitate. That is, they were made up of sounds that the student already had in his or her repertoire (e.g., mama, baby, cookie). Words that have similar sounds (bye bye) are easier to imitate than words with very different sounds (table). Closer approximations of the target words were reinforced, as in the previous step.

The final step involved *imitation of volume, pitch, and speed*. Using the same shaping techniques as the previous steps, the student was reinforced for imitating the way in which the adult said the targeted word.

Once the child reliably imitated targeted words, more advanced skills such as object and action labeling were taught. The Lovaas program also addressed advanced language skills such as size, color, shape, prepositions, pronouns, and phrases and sentence use.

The TALK Program

The work of Drash and his colleagues (Drash & Tudor, 1989, 1990, 1991, 1993) exemplifies a current behavior analytic approach to speech and language development for young children with autism. Drash and his colleagues have achieved remarkable success in improving the language and cognitive functioning of children with autism and similar disabilities. His research has shown average gains of 26 IQ points and average gains in expressive language of 2.5 months for each month in treatment (Drash & Tudor, 1989). Drash's interventions are intended to yield maximum benefit, and neither he nor the parents who adopt his procedures are timid about the role of reinforcement in language development. Drash works closely with parents and home-based teaching assistants to extend the center-based therapeutic gains to children's homes.

The TALK Program (Training for Acquisition of Language in Kids) was originally developed for use with children with autism (Drash & Leibowitz, 1973). The program is highly structured and data based. The student's level of expressive language is assessed on entering the program. A step-by-step program is implemented which increases the frequency of vocalizations, then systematically shapes and reinforces desired speech sounds. The sounds are shaped into words, then naming objects and pictures. Gradually, the ability to form sentences is shaped and reinforced. The treatment program typically lasts from 6 months to 2 years.

TALK differs from most other language development programs in several important ways. One of the key features of TALK involves acquisition of normal or near normal language functioning as a long-term goal. Behavioral and cognitive skills are addressed as well. Because negative behaviors may severely impair the ability of the student to learn language, these behaviors are targeted as part of TALK. A second key feature is the use of a natural manding approach to imitation training. One of the most difficult tasks in teaching language to children with autism is teaching initial imitation skills. TALK requires that students imitate words. In return for correct imitation, reinforcers are given.

Drash states that the factors critical to the success of TALK are age of the child at initiation of the intervention and the number of hours of intervention that the child receives each week. Drash argues that children over 4 years old have developed their own ways of obtaining what they want in the environment. These idiosyncratic ways involve nonverbal behaviors that become entrenched in children's behavioral repertoires and make teaching verbal behavior more difficult. For TALK to be effective, as many people as possible in the child's environment must use the TALK techniques. Since parents are a child's primary "teachers" during the preschool years, he argues that it is vital for them to carry out the intervention at home.

Drash's work might have seemed extreme to some only a few years ago, but it reflects an important extension of the work of Bijou (Bijou, 1976; Bijou & Baer 1961, 1978) on behavioral contingencies that promote or impede the development of behavior. Drash, more than any other clinician-theorist, has boldly stated what many professionals in autism believe but are too cautious to admit; parent behaviors play a critical role in determining whether a child with autism achieves better or worse language and cognitive outcomes.

Natural Language Paradigm

A highly naturalistic behavioral approach for the acquisition of language has been developed by Koegel, O'Dell, and Koegel (1987). The Natural Language Paradigm (NLP) uses a combination of behavioral techniques with a child-centered approach to facilitate language acquisition. The NLP is a "mand model" approach in which teachers "follow a child's lead" by teaching object and activity words that are of highest interest to the child, rather than items chosen by an adult. These items vary as the child's interest shifts. Skills that the child has already mastered are interspersed with acquisition level skills to promote a high level of success.

Because the items and activities requested are things that the child shows an interest in, they tend to be reasonably age-appropriate. Once requested, the items are played with by the child and adult, which makes requesting the items a naturally reinforcing, functional skill. This helps link language to play skills, turn taking, and social interactions. The NLP is not an "anything goes" approach to language acquisition; there are parameters for what responses are reinforced. Students are explicitly prompted and reinforced for a variety of communicative attempts. This leads to generalization more easily than a stricter approach in which one specific adult request leads to one specific student response, which is then repeated to a prearranged criterion.

ESTABLISHING COMMUNICATION GOALS

Most people use more than one system of communication. We speak, write, gesture, and use eye gaze and body language to communicate with others. Many students with autism lack this communication repertoire. Prizant and Weatherby (1988) suggested that students with autism be taught more than one system of communication so that they have a wider variety of communication skills.

The emphasis in communication training should be based on developmental and functional criteria. Students need strategies that initially help them get what they want or need from the environment. These environmental objectives also need to be developmentally appropriate. For example, appropriate communication goals for a preschool child might be to indicate toileting needs or to request a particular social game (e.g., swinging on a swing). Appropriate goals for a middle school age student might be to indicate a need for assistance with an academic task or strategies for joining a game with peers. Goal selection criteria are as important in teaching communication skills as in teaching any other lesson to students. For more information on criteria for goal selection, please refer to Chapter 8.

Generally, simply having students memorize a set of words is not effective instruction; considerable thought must be given to where the student's language will be used. Other considerations include the student's age, needs, and living circumstances. Peer approach skills will vary considerably with the age and gender of the student. For example, teaching a student to use the phrase, "Will you play with me?" is effective for many elementary school-aged students, but it is more likely to get teenagers ostracized than included in many neighborhoods. A thoughtful teacher must look to the phrases that are used in the student's community and peers. Different phrases are typically used with peers than with parents. Although much communication is rote ("Hi. How are you?" "Have a nice day."), simple memorization is not the best approach to language acquisition.

Rather than developing language by learning vocabulary words, students with autism need to be taught verbal and nonverbal strategies that help them interact functionally with people in their environments. Students need to be given the motivation and the opportunity to communicate. Because many tantrum behaviors are used as a form of protest, one of the first communication goals should be the acquisition of a socially acceptable means to protest or reject (Prizant, 1988; Prizant & Weatherby, 1987). This means, of course, that a socially acceptable expression of protest needs to be successful in allowing the student to *at least temporarily* escape from the given task or demand. Demanding student compliance in this circumstance will guarantee that a newly learned *appropriate* social expression will be extinguished and tantrum behaviors (or whatever behaviors were previously successful in reducing task demand) will be exhibited.

The environment should be structured to foster communications that are balanced and reciprocal. Some communication systems have neglected to teach students with autism to *initiate* communication or *to repair communication breakdowns*. Often teachers inadvertently do not encourage the use of balanced and reciprocal interactions; this results in students becoming passive receptors of information. The use of a facilitative style can shift the control of communication to the child or at least allow a balance of power in communication (Prizant & Weatherby, 1988).

A summary of considerations for communication programming is provided in Table 6–5.

Styles of Interaction

Prizant and Rydell (1993) suggest that most communication programming involves either a facilitative or directive style of interaction. The facilitative style is a more naturalistic approach to language training in which the teacher arranges for the student to initiate communication, either verbally or nonverbally. The teacher then shifts attention to the student, asks for language elaboration, or models a verbal response for imitation. The teacher subsequently indicates the correctness (or understandability) of the student's language and responds to the student appropriately.

To generalize the new communication skills, the other individuals in the child's environment need to use a similar facilitative style in their communications with the student in different settings. Consistent facilitative interactions help ensure a student's motivation to communicate. There is little motivation to communicate when a student's communication needs are anticipated by adults, nor is there any motivation to communicate when the student's role in the classroom is passive.

The facilitative interaction style is contrasted with a more directive approach to language interaction. With directive language interactions, the student is primarily a receiver of language, rather than an initiator of language. There is a strong focus on receptive language skills and a lesser

Table 6–5. Considerations for Developing Communication Skills

1. Make the communication an integral part of the child's life in and out of school.
2. Communication, rather than rote responses, should be the goal.
3. Emphasize spontaneous speech, whether pictorial, gestural, or verbal.
4. Give the child many opportunities to communicate in all settings.
5. Any socially acceptable attempt to communicate should be reinforced in all settings.
6. Communication goals should be part of any plan to change maladaptive behavior.
7. Initial communication goals should target obtaining items and activities that the student finds reinforcing.
8. Communication goals should be developmentally and chronologically appropriate.
9. Work together with all significant people in the student's environment to make the communication training as consistent as possible.

focus on spontaneous expression. Directive interactions are more common in the upper grades or in the traditional classroom atmosphere where teachers lecture and the students take notes. These students passively receive (or sometimes fail to receive) the information that is being disseminated. Little opportunity for interaction is given, except for student requests for clarification or to answer questions. Comparisons between the two styles of communication are shown in Table 6–6.

There are difficulties with either style when used exclusively for students with autism. The teacher using a facilitative style who waits for a student with deficits in social relatedness and communication skills to initiate communication may have to wait quite a long time. Without a clear understanding of how to provide effective *communication temptations*, the facilitative approach will not provide enough opportunities to communicate to be a successful intervention. Communication temptations need to be provided under good stimulus control. If students with autism can get what they want without communicating with others, they will not communicate.

Table 6–6. Facilitative and Directive Communication Styles

Facilitative Interactions	*Directive Interactions*
Child controls focus and direction.	Adult controls the focus and direction.
Child assumes conversational lead, adult follows.	Adult assumes the conversational lead, child follows.
Adult encourages the child to contribute to conversation.	Adult structures the nature of the child's contribution.
Majority of adult utterances are low constraint (reflective, adds new information, comments, etc.).	Majority of adult interactions are high constraint (directives, yes/no questions, "wh" questions, etc.).
Adult responses are imitations or elaborations of child's utterances. They fulfill child's request.	Adult's prompts specify the specific form and content of the child's response.
A period of silence is given before responding.	
Adult's prompts are for further communication, without specifying form or content.	Adult identifies child's response options.

Source: Adapted from "Assessment and Intervention Considerations for Unconventional Verbal Behavior," by B. M. Prizant and P. J. Ridell, 1993. In J. Reichle and D. Wacker (Eds.), *Communicative Alternatives to Challenging Behavior* (pp. 263–297). Baltimore, MD: Paul H. Brookes.

The directive style also has problems when used exclusively. Directive interactions do not offer enough opportunities for students to express themselves. Receptive language is difficult for students with autism. Many students will not be successful in following adult verbal directives unless provided with visual cues. This will result in teacher and student frustrations, and only minimally involve communication *learning*.

A combination of directive and facilitative styles may provide students with both expressive and receptive language opportunities. Allowing students to express themselves, modeling expanded responses, reinforcing appropriate communicative attempts with attention, and providing access to activities and items requested, as well as requiring specific responses to questions and directives will allow students to increase both receptive and expressive language skills.

The Communicative Intent of the Student with Autism

The key to successful communication is an alertness to the intended message coming from the student with autism. Given the host of unusual behaviors common in these students, determining intent is not always easy; in fact, it is often a serious challenge. However, establishing intent remains the key to fostering communication and successful interaction. Not all behaviors that have *communicative form* are actually communicative. These behaviors may serve a "self-regulatory" function or indicate a state of anxiety. Although an ability to identify a student's anxiety may be important for the sensitive teacher, it is not generally thought of as communication.

All behaviors do not have a communicative function, but it makes sense to treat virtually all behaviors that could be communication *as* communication. The child who heard, "Dancing, Dancing" days or weeks ago and echoes it repeatedly today may be indicating a desire to dance or to engage in more active physical activity—or his vocalizations may have nothing to do with intention. The safe assumption, however, is that the echoed speech is communicative. If this is an inaccurate interpretation of meaning, we can probe in an effort to determine what the student did intend. Once we find out the student's true intention in the utterance, we can teach him a more precise way to request the item or activity. In all cases, we are fostering communication and providing consequences for the student's communicative overtures.

These assumptions are really very natural. If a fellow teacher in the parking lot were to spontaneously launch into singing a few verses of a song, co-workers would likely respond to any implied message. If a peer started singing a dance tune we might say, "I bet you're looking forward to the holiday break," or "Got a big weekend planned?" The same assumptions should be in place for the student with autism.

Echolalia and Communicative Intent

Echolalia is echoing or repeating what has been heard. This is common in children with autism. Originally seen as an odd, even bizarre manifestation of psychological disturbance, we now have a far more complete and accurate understanding of the role and various functions of echolalia. Researchers such as Fay (1967, 1969), Weatherby (1986), and Prizant (1988) have greatly increased our understanding of echolalia.

Echolalia can be frustrating for parents and for teachers not yet skilled in teaching students with autism. The student may repeat statements, especially questions in such a way that effective communication is impossible. The student may accurately say each word and mimic the inflection but totally miss the message. On one hand, extended utterances are emitted whole, without change; in doing this a student may be able to recite Hamlet's Soliloquy but have no understanding of its meaning. On the other hand, utterances may be used to convey a message; the recitation of a Barney song may be a request for that particular video.

Fortunately, echolalia offers numerous relative *advantages* in terms of both the child's potential for progress and the teacher's ability to teach successfully. First, if students have echolalia, then they have speech. Although many adults would consider echolalia nonfunctional or useless speech, it is nevertheless speech and as such can be developed into more useful communication. Many students with autism who do not speak in any situation and who are not echolalic do not develop useful speech. Instructionally, teachers equipped with the right approaches and understandings of echolalia can be highly effective in dealing with this common problem.

Most echolalia serves a communicative purpose or function. It should not be surprising that the student with autism should adopt and refine such a communication strategy. Echolalia can be efficient in achieving several purposes. As most students with autism have relatively good memories, it is easy for them to recall the exact words and style of a message. It is thought that much language may be learned as a "chunk" or whole, similar to the way in which adults learn phrases in a foreign language. Once a phrase is learned, it is repeated as a unit. Repeating the message takes essentially no comprehension ability. Echoing a message very likely impedes or stops communication overtures of other persons. If students with autism do not wish to interact but would rather be left alone, they have a handy tool for doing so with echolalia. A single phrase or the other individual's words echoed endlessly will tend to make the other person lose interest in interacting. Thus, echolalia reduces the chances that others will want to talk to the echolalic student. This may be especially powerful with other children who will immediately perceive the oddness of the communication. Children without disabilities, not otherwise coached to interact, generally give up. Among the purposes of echolalia, blocking communication may be the easiest to recognize.

Another function of echolalia involves conversational turn taking. If the student with autism understands that communication involves one person talking for a bit, and then the other person talking for a bit, and back and forth, echolalia helps the student with autism take a turn. The echolalia provides a method of attempting to communicate or repair a communication breakdown in the absence of spontaneous speech. Even if the message is not understood, teachers and adults responsible for interacting will persist, at least for a while, and repeated attempts will provide the child with autism with attention and possibly other benefits.

A number of researchers have examined the multiple functions of echolalia. They have, in general, considered both immediate and delayed echolalia. Immediate echolalia is the repetition of words or phrases during the same interaction with the child. Delayed echolalia involves echoes in later sessions (or even days or weeks) after the phrase was originally heard. For some, it may occur many years after hearing the source statement. It may occur only when some common element between the original learning situation and the current situation is present, as though the common element were a "trigger" to the entire original learning situation.

Prizant and colleagues (Prizant & Duchan, 1981; Prizant & Rydell, 1984; Weatherby & Prizant, 1989) have differentiated the functions of immediate and delayed echolalia. Table 6–7 features the key elements of these functions.

One technique that has proven effective in working with students with echolalia is volume cueing. Lovaas (1977) used discrimination training combined with the command "don't echo" to increase appropriate verbal responses in students with autism. The goal of volume cueing is to have the student echo the desired response and not the instruction or question that preceded it. For example, the teacher may say, "How old are you? . . . I'm four." and want the student to say only, "I'm four." in response to the question, "How old are you?" To assist the student to discriminate which part of the teacher's utterance he is supposed to echo and which part he is not, the teacher says the question softly and the response loudly. The student will usually echo the louder words. The teacher gradually increases the volume of the question ("How old are you?") until it is at the same level as the prompt ("I'm four"). The final step is to fade the prompt until the student is independent with his response.

Lovaas, restating his caution against using more words than necessary, provided another technique that can be used during later stages of teaching. The word "say" can be used as a verbal "marker," signaling a

Table 6–7. Functions of Immediate and Delayed Echolalia

Category	Type	Function
	Interactive	
Immediate	Turn taking	Keep conversational exchange going
	Declaration	Label objects, actions, places
	Affirmation	Agree to previous statement or question
	Request	Request item, object, or action
	Turn taking	Keep conversational exchange going; Verbal completion
Delayed	Labeling	Label objects, actions, places in the environment; Provide information; Offer new information
	Protest	Protest or inhibit others' actions
	Request	Request item, object, or action
	Attention/calling	Establish or maintain attention of others
	Directive	Influence or direct others' actions
	Noninteractive	
Immediate	Nonfocused	No apparent intent other than to indicate pain, fear, anxiety
	Rehearsal	Repetition used as processing or memory aid
	Self regulatory	Regulates own actions, accompanied by motor activity

(continued)

Table 6–7. *(continued)*

Category	Type	Function
Delayed	Nonfocused	No apparent communicative intent
	Situation association	Self-stimulatory No apparent communicative intent; Triggered by object, person, situation or activity
	Self-directive	Regulates own actions, accompanied by motor activity
	Rehearsal	Practice at lower volume, repeated at louder volume
	Label	Label objects, actions, places in the environment

Source: Adapted from "The Expression of Communicative Intent: Assessment Guidelines," by A. M. Weatherby and B. M. Prizant, 1989. *Seminars in Speech and Language, 10,* 77–91.

word or phrase that is to be repeated. In this case, the word "say" would be said at a lower volume than the rest of the sentence and serves as a cue that the rest of the sentence is to be imitated.

Although this initially seems highly artificial, it allows the teacher of students with autism to use existing echolalia to build appropriate language. Typically developing young children are often urged to "say bye-bye" or "say please" in early stages of language acquisition. Volume cueing and the use of the discriminant "say" should be considered as a prompt similar to those used with typical children during early language acquisition. Students with autism can be taught responses and conversational interchanges using this technique.

NONVOCAL COMMUNICATION SYSTEMS

The difficulty in teaching verbal communication has led many researchers and practitioners to explore nonvocal communication systems. Generally, this has involved the use of (a) sign language, (b) picture communication systems, and (c) The Picture Exchange Communication System.

Sign Language

Sign language usually is divided into two types: American Sign Language (ASL) and Signed Exact English (SEE). ASL is a complete language, with syntax and grammar different from spoken English. ASL commonly is used throughout the deaf community, but rarely by students with autism. Signed Exact English is a signed (instead of spoken) application of the grammar and syntax of standard English. Because it mirrors spoken language, SEE is the sign language system most often taught to students with autism.

Sign language was taught more extensively in the past. Many older individuals with autism were taught some signs and still use them to communicate their wants and needs. Sign has the advantages of being readily available and visually processed. Many basic signs are naturalistic movements that can be readily understood by people in the community. Two disadvantages of signing are that it requires some skill in fine motor manipulation and the ability to learn through imitation. Because some signs are not related to naturalistic movements, they can be somewhat difficult to interpret for naive observers.

Many individuals with developmental disabilities who fail to communicate vocally can be taught to communicate gesturally (Bonvillian & Nelson, 1976; Carr, 1979; Sundberg, 1980). Sundberg's research (1990) illustrates how individuals with developmental disabilities who do not have a vocal repertoire can emit motor responses under verbal control. Lovaas (1981) suggested that young children with autism could be taught signs. Such programming relies heavily on imitation training. Imitation of gross and fine motor movements are some of the early skills taught to children with autism; thus signing could be a natural and functional extension of imitation programming. It is important to note that, even when a student does not have a strong imitative repertoire, it is easier to imitate motor actions than vocal sounds.

Sundberg (1990) found that when sign language programs failed they tended to do so because of problems inherent in the teaching strategy, rather than problems related to student learning. Teachers who use signs should pay particular attention to their delivery strategies. For example, signing, or any other communication system, needs to be used in all environments in which the child is present. Students being taught a communication system need to use it expressively as well as receptively. Many students with autism and other developmental disabilities do not spontaneously generalize object labels to requests for those objects; they seldom are taught to request items not present. Active procedures for teaching spontaneous use should be built into teachers' instructional delivery. Because communication is a reciprocal process, teachers will need to present information, requests, and dialog to the student in the same (signed) modality. Finally, some teachers may inadvertently teach signs that allow students to access reinforcers that *teachers* prefer, rather than teaching *student* preferences. These examples support Sundberg's contention that much of the learning problem related to sign language is a function of the instructional delivery.

Picture Communication

Picture communication systems have the advantage of being clear, visual representations of objects, actions, and other potential communication messages. Pictures can be words, photographs, or line drawings. The Mayer-Johnson (1992) series of line drawings, an extensive vocabulary in picture form, is used by many teachers of students with autism. The Mayer-Johnson materials are available in print form and as a computer software program (Boardmaker). The basic concept behind picture communication systems is that many students with autism are able to use visual input more easily than auditory input. Presenting pictures for communication is easier for many students because the stimuli remain in the visual field as long as necessary.

The advantages of picture communication systems are that they are visually processed, require minimal fine motor skills, and are readily understood in the community (Bondy & Frost, 1993, 1994). There are disadvantages as well. If pictures are not available communication breaks down. Unfortunately, many teachers who develop picture communication systems use the systems for classroom instruction (e.g., vocabulary or concept development lessons) but fail to build in portability. Others do not allow the system to leave the classroom fearing that the pictures may be lost or damaged (Brady & Cunningham, 1985). Another disadvantage is that advance preparation is necessary. Pictures likely to be needed in a given situation must be collected and added to a student's message system. A limited array of pictures limits communicative spontaneity.

For basic communication needs, a standard group of pictures or symbols can be kept on a key chain or in small notebook carried by the student. Specialized communication symbols, such as those needed for going to the movies or to an arcade, can be created ahead of time and accessed as needed. Pictures can be made almost any size to fit a portable system (wallet, key chain set, notebook) that students can manipulate.

Teaching Picture Communication

Often a "touch board" is used for initial training. Necessary pictures or symbols are placed on a Velcro strip at the top of the board. Another Velcro strip is placed in the center of the board. The teacher shows the student a desired object and a picture of it, then places the picture on the center strip. The board is exchanged between student and teacher and the picture is shown as the representative of the object. When one-word (labeling) communications are understood by the student, more extensive vocabulary is added. For example, initially, the word or picture "ball" can be placed on the center strip to gain access to a ball. Later "I want" can be added with "ball" to make a more complete communication. Then adjectives such as "big" or "green" can be added to facilitate discrimination. This method can be used by teachers with nonverbal students by placing a multiple choice question on the touch board and asking the student to touch the correct answer. Figure 6–1 shows one example of a touch board.

An alternative method is to place a number of pictures on the touch board, essentially providing the student with as complete a picture vocabulary as the student can accommodate. With this arrangement, the student can point to a desired item or make sentences by pointing sequentially to different pictures. The teacher can point to pictures sequentially and provide a spoken label for each picture. Learning the meaning of the pictures on the touch board can be aided by matching the item, activity, or emotion to the picture.

One difficulty in teaching students to communicate with pictures is that one of the first skills taught is object labeling. The child is taught to point to a named object when given a verbal cue (e.g., "Point to the dish"). Some teachers or therapists provide reinforcement that bears no relationship to the object in the picture and often simply provide a social reinforcer (e.g., "Good pointing"). Although social reinforcers are effective for some children, a better strategy may be to have the student request highly preferred items first, to understand that communication itself is a highly reinforcing activity.

Picture Exchange Communication System

The Picture Exchange Communication System (PECS) is a specific application of the more general picture communication system. PECS was developed at the Delaware Autistic Program to teach very young children to communicate in a social context (Bondy & Frost, 1994).

The logic behind the PECS program is that children do communicate their wants and needs. Students using PECS are taught to do this by giv-

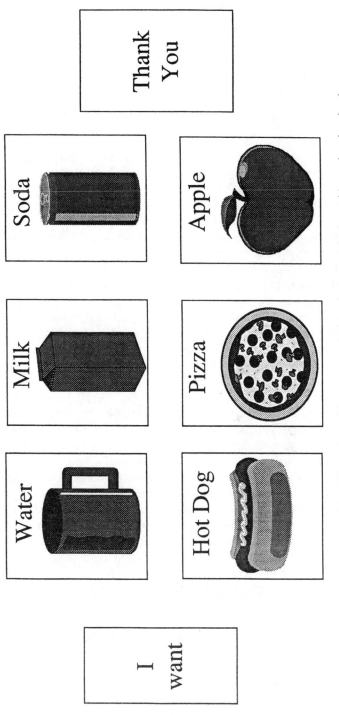

Figure 6–1. Sample communication board for a nonverbal student to assist in making a lunch selection.

ing a picture of a highly desired item to a communicative partner in return for the item. By having desired items *available but inaccessible without assistance*, communication becomes a necessary bridge between the child and the desired item. The value of communication is made clear to the child, as it is the only way to access these items. PECS is one of the few systems that teaches students to initiate social communication.

There are six phases in PECS' training process. The first phase involves *teaching the physically assisted exchange*. A group of items is placed on the table and the student is observed to determine which objects are picked up consistently. The teacher then assumes that these objects are *preferred* by the student. Once a preferred object is determined, the other items are removed. When the student reaches for the preferred item, a picture of the item is placed in the student's hand; the student is then guided by an adult from behind to place the picture in the teacher's hand. The teacher immediately gives the student the requested item. As the student learns to exchange pictures for objects, the physical guidance is faded. The teacher introduces, then fades an open-hand prompt by waiting longer to show his or her hand once the student has picked up the picture. No verbal prompting is used.

The second phase involves *expanding spontaneity*. The teacher gradually moves away from the student so that the student has to pick up the picture and take it to her to get the desired object. The student is taught to request a variety of different reinforcers, which are readily available, but, again, are not accessible without assistance (since the student does not need to communicate if she or he can get the item independently). During this phase, the pictures are placed on a touch board, which also is gradually placed at a distance. The teacher gradually moves away so that the child is required to go to the board, pull the picture off the board, and take it to an adult to obtain the desired item.

The third phase involves *simultaneous discrimination of pictures*. The student is taught to discriminate among two or more pictures on the communication board. Initially the student is presented with two pictures on the board, one of the preferred object and one of a neutral object. If the student gives the teacher the preferred object picture, he is given the object. If he chooses the nonpreferred item, he is told, "No, we don't have that," and guided to choose the preferred item picture. The location of the pictures must be changed randomly so that the student does not become location dependent (e.g., always choosing the picture on the left). More pictures of desired items are presented so that the student eventually has all the items learned in the first phase.

The fourth phase involves *building sentence structure*. When the student is able to request between 12 and 20 items, the teacher requires that items be requested using the phrase "I want _____." This method of "framing" a request assists in differentiation of sentences later. A single card with "I want" is placed on the sentence strip of the board. The student is assisted in placing the picture of the desired item next to the "I want" card. The sentence strip is removed from the board and given to the teacher in exchange for the item. Then the student is taught to put both cards on the sentence strip.

The fifth phase involves *responding to "What do you want?"* The question is asked and the child is prompted to take the "I want" card and the item card, place both on the sentence strip, and then give the strip to the teacher. Opportunities for spontaneous requests are presented as well. During the initial five phases of PECS, all of the communications involve objects or activities that the student prefers.

The sixth phase of PECS training is *commenting in response to a question.* To teach commenting, the teacher places a minimally preferred item on the table, and places a card with "I see" or "I have" on the sentence strip along with the referent picture. While holding up the object, the teacher asks, "What do you see?" The student is guided to pick up the "I see" card and place it on the sentence strip along with the referent card. The reinforcement offered is *different from the object* that was seen. This is done so that the student does not get confused and think that a request was made. When the student can answer differentially to the question, "What do you see?" then a second question, "What do you want?" is interspersed on a random basis. Over time concrete reinforcers for "What do you see?" are faded.

PECS training does not end after the sixth phase; additional language concepts are added. These can include attributes (big cookie/little cookie), verb concepts (throw/kick), and differentiated yes/no responses to such questions as "Is this a _____ " and "Do you want a _____?"

Similar to the logic of signed systems, students are expected to develop speech once some fluency in nonvocal communication is established. To date, that expectation has been realized for many youngsters. Bondy and Frost (1994) provided data for a group of seven children who used PECS. On average it took 3 days for each child to learn one picture exchange. By 5 months, these children each had one spoken word. A critical point in the intervention was the time at which each child used a larger number of spoken words than pictures. This was reached at 11.3 months when the students averaged over 70 words and pictures. These results provide evidence that PECS did not impede the development of speech, but appears to have enhanced it.

ADDITIONAL CLASSROOM CONSIDERATIONS

Although teachers have multiple options available when selecting the type of communication intervention they will use to promote communication for students with autism, there are several other factors to consider in making classrooms better communication environments. These factors include (a) using natural mands, (b) teaching imitation, (c) alternating the types of speech used in class, and (d) increasing language encouragements and opportunities.

Using Natural Mands

Mands are the requests, directions, and other verbalizations that a person gives in hopes of obtaining some action in return from another. Mands are a regular part of teaching, whether the teaching is structured or incidental. *Natural manding* involves teachers looking for and arranging opportunities throughout the day to "inject" mands into other routines, thereby providing students with natural, apparently spontaneous opportunities to use communication that the teacher is targeting for instruction.

Natural manding can begin by having the child ask for a particular preferred item. Initially, any sounds or vocalizations that the student makes (e.g., "buh" may be used to mean "ball" or "book") can be accepted as a student's request. Later, more accurate language forms are needed to obtain the same reinforcers. This use of mands as initial communication can help students make the association between "saying" and "receiving."

Natural manding requires that teachers determine reinforcers and preferences for their students in advance of a manding "opportunity." Next, the vocalizations that students use to ask for their preferences are written and made available to all adults in a classroom. Finally, teachers determine the times during a student's day when these "spontaneous" request opportunities will be provided. For example, if a student is known to enjoy a specific software program, a teacher might "just happen" to walk by a computer station with the student at the beginning of a scheduled work break. The presence of the computer, combined with the scheduled break, becomes a natural time for the teacher to ask, "Is there something you'd like to do during the break?"

To begin a mand sequence, the teacher must keep the preferred item visible but just out of reach while asking the student what she or he wants. The teacher has established what language form must be displayed by the student (e.g., a single word vs. a full sentence). When the student produces this communication request, the student has thus earned access to the preferred item. For the student above, using a full sentence request ("May I use the computer?") results in 10 minutes with the software program. Natural manding should also include the name of the item, as well as repetition of the vocalization the student made.

Teaching Imitation

Because many students with autism do not imitate, teachers should include imitation training as part of the educational program. Imitation training can be a structured lesson, presented incidentally, or both.

For many students, imitation training begins with imitation of sounds or actions already in the students' repertoire. For others, imitation of specific sounds (such as "ah" or "mm") may be an appropriate target. Students who do not produce a range of different sounds might be taught to imitate vowels and consonants in isolation, then sound combinations. Syllables and words are gradually shaped through the same process.

Many students will develop meaningful vocabulary by imitating words. Usually, these are words composed of the sounds that the student has already produced, either spontaneously or through imitation. However, many students will learn to imitate words quite rapidly when the words refer to high preference objects and activities. Even though all of the sounds in these words may not be well articulated, word imitation does not need to be delayed until a student can imitate all sounds. Sound approximations are acceptable and a regular part of learning.

Many students also learn to modulate volume, pitch, and speed through imitation. Volume is taught by saying the word to be imitated either very loudly or very softly, and then at different moderate volumes. The student is provided feedback for imitating the volume of speech correctly for each trial. Pitch and speed are taught using the same technique.

Finally, an imitation procedure overlooked by many involves teaching students to imitate people *other than* the teacher and adults in class. Students can learn to produce social initiations, protests and requests by imitating peers without disabilities, TV characters, personal heroes, and so on. Many students find it helpful to "try on" the communication abilities of others in an effort to develop their own personal communication skills.

Alternating the Types of Speech Used in Class

The type of speech and language used in the classroom should be understandable to the students. Students with autism often have difficulty with auditory processing, sometimes to the point of being unable to understand the function of spoken language. Even students who use language may use words in unusual ways or have a different understanding of some words than the speaker intends.

For students with minimal functional language, the overall number of words spoken in the classroom should be reduced. All staff should use the same phrases. Many teachers use conversational speech when making requests. Conversational speech is often wordy and includes terms with multiple meanings. For important classroom communications, a simpler (fewer words, more consistent meanings) type of speech is often necessary. When giving directions, for example, a teacher might provide only the most important words. "Sam, sit down" will be processed by some much more effectively than "Sam, I've told you many times that one of the most important classroom rules is to stay in your seat." Teachers can assess the effectiveness of their directions by observing how many steps the child follows without prompting. If a large number of directions are not followed, the teacher might reteach the directions using fewer words.

This should not be interpreted as saying that teachers of students with autism should only use "telegraphic" speech. Conversational speech is rich and a rewarding part of all classrooms but should not be used when delivering critical information or mands. If teachers have students with widely varied language abilities, it is important for teachers to learn to monitor *their own* use of language to ensure that each student can understand a teacher's attempt to communicate with the student.

Finally, just as students can learn to vary the tone, pitch, and volume of their voices, teachers should attend to the same vocal characteristics. A teacher's tone of voice is very important to some students. When language is not understood, the tone of voice often becomes a cue for the student. Also, a pleasant, soft tone is highly reinforcing to some students, whereas a flat tone is less reinforcing. Voice tone may be important to some students to help them determine the meaning of a teacher's feedback for a particular action. In addition, some students react differently to the pitch of a teacher's voice. Many parents report that their children with autism respond badly to teachers with higher pitched voices, particularly when the voice is also loud.

Increasing Language Encouragements and Opportunities

Does the failure of most children with autism to socially interact contribute to their poor language? It seems obvious that it would. A study conducted with young children offers some intriguing insights.

Hart and Risley (1995) recently reported the results of a large scale study of language development in very young children. Children were selected according to three socioeconomic and work characteristics of their parents: professional, working, and welfare. Extensive in-home observations were conducted. Hart and Risley found that the degree to which parents promoted language development correlated very highly with children's language performance as measured by formal instruments. The main pattern that emerged from their study was that the more language opportunities young children had, the better their language development. *Critical was the ratio of parental "encouragements" to "discouragements."* In both professional and working families, parental encouragements far exceeded discouragements. Very troubling was the finding that in families on welfare, the discouragements greatly exceeded encouragements. The cumulative weight of hundreds of thousands of these encouragements and discouragements is more than sufficient, in most cases, to account for children's language differences. Hart and Risley were extremely critical of attempts to attribute racial or cultural causes to language and intellectual development problems, instead showing that the *language environment* of the child accounted for most of the differences.

It is important to remember that this work was conducted with children without disabilities. In many ways, however, the results are potentially relevant to the development of children with autism. A factor as simple as the total number of verbal interactions could be a vital piece of the language acquisition puzzle. It is currently unclear whether the lack of some critical number of verbal interactions, due to poverty, disinterest, or lack of understanding of the communication, could influence the acquisition of language in students with autism.

If there is some critical number of successful language interactions, then certainly the stage is set for high intensity early intervention efforts to facilitate successful language interactions in children with autism. The challenge to low intensity or highly child-directed approaches would be to find a way to increase the total number of language interactions, or to make the child highly motivated to communicate, then provide for high levels of success.

One of the authors asked Dr. Risley about his work in light of Lovaas' interventions. Risley agreed that, if the total number of encouraging or positive language opportunities is critical, and if a student with autism fights off parent attempts to verbally interact, then the child is at high risk for poor language outcomes. He further suggested that, given the total number of language opportunities provided by an intensive, Lovaas-style intervention, children in this intervention had approximately the same cumulative number of opportunities as the high performing group of children found in his own study.

Hart and Risley have offered their data sets to other interested researchers. This allows the development of other hypotheses on children's language development. In the meantime, it is important to consider the total number of language opportunities and the number of completed verbal interactions of students with autism. Educators have enormous opportunity for increasing students' communication opportunities. In light of the tremendous potential for altering language and cognitive development, increasing communication opportunities is quite likely to be a highly successful, easily performed, and inexpensive intervention for students with autism and other disabilities.

SUMMARY

Communication is a vital part of every student's education. As communication deficits form one of the diagnostic areas of the autistic disorder, students with autism are likely to need strong communication interventions.

Gestural, verbal, and pictorial and technological systems exist and can be used by or adapted for students with autism. A multimodality approach, advocated by Prizant and Weatherby (1987) and others, gives students a variety of communication options that can be used to communicate wants and needs, initiate social interaction, and develop and maintain conversation ability. A key to the success of any communication program is a careful consideration of the student's cognitive and motor strengths, preferred modality of communication, ease and efficiency of communication, and the cost and time of acquisition. Communication programming is one area in which individual differences have a great impact. Consideration of individual determining factors makes the difference between success and failure in teaching students with autism to communicate.

REVIEW QUESTIONS

1. What communication problems are typically associated with autism?

2. What is a communication "system" and how might systems differ for students with and without autism?

3. How are problem behaviors and communicative competence related by "function"?

4. What different functions are served by echolalia?

5. How would a structured language program be similar to and different from a natural language program?

REFERENCES

Alvarez, R., & Williams, D. F. (1995). Students with speech and/or language impairments. In R. Taylor, L. Sternberg, & S. Richards (Eds.), *Exceptional children: Integrating research and teaching* (2nd ed.). San Diego: Singular Publishing Group.

American Psychiatric Association. (1994). Diagnostic and statistical manual of mental disorders (4th ed.) Washington, DC: Author.

Baltaxe, C. A. M. (1977). Pragmatic deficits in the language of autistic adolescents. *Journal of Pediatric Psychology, 2,* 176–180.

Beukelman, D. R., & Mirenda, P. (1992). *Augmentative and alternative communication: Management of severe communication disorders in children and adults.* Baltimore, MD: Paul H. Brookes.

Bijou, S. W. (1976). *Child development: The basic stage of early childhood.* Englewood Cliffs, NJ: Prentice-Hall.

Bijou, S. W., & Baer, D. M. (1961). *Child development: A systematic and empirical theory.* Englewood Cliffs, NJ: Prentice-Hall.

Bijou, S. W., & Baer, D. M. (1978). *Behavior analysis of child development.* Englewood Cliffs, NJ: Prentice-Hall.

Blackstone, S. W. (1991). For consumers: AAC and autism. *Augmentative Communication News, 4,* 1–3.

Bloom, L., & Lahey, M. (1978). *Language development and language disorders.* New York: John Wiley and Sons.

Bondy, A., & Frost, L. (1993). Mands across the water: A report on the application of the picture exchange communication system in Peru. *The Behavior Analyst, 16,* 123–128.

Bondy, A., & Frost, L. (1994). The picture exchange communication system. *Focus on Autistic Behavior, 9,* 1–19.

Bonvillian, J. D., & Nelson, K. E. (1976). Sign language acquisition in a mute autistic boy. *Journal of Speech and Hearing Disorders, 41,* 339–347.

Brady, M. P., & Cunningham, J. (1985). Living and learning in segregated environments: An ethnography of normalization outcomes. *Education and Training of the Mentally Retarded, 20,* 241–252.

Carr, E. (1979). Teaching autistic children to use sign language: Some research issues. *Journal of Autism and Developmental Disorders, 9,* 345–359.

Carr, E., Levin, L., McConnachie, G., Carlson, J. I., Kemp, D. C., & Smith, C. E. (1994). *Communication-based intervention for problem behavior.* Baltimore: Paul H. Brookes.

Drash, P. W., & Liebowitz, J. M. (1973). Operant conditioning of speech and language in the non-verbal retarded child: Recent advances. *Pediatric Clinics of North America, 20,* 233–243.

Drash, P. W., & Tudor, R. M. (1989). Cognitive development therapy: A new model for treatment of an overlooked population, developmentally delayed preschool children. *Psychotherapy in Private Practice, 7,* 19–41.

Drash, P. W., & Tudor, R. M. (1990). Language and cognitive development: A systematic behavioral program and technology for increasing the language and cognitive skills of developmentally disabled and at-risk preschool children. In M. Hersen, R. M. Eisler, & P. M. Miller (Eds.), *Progress in behavior modification* (Vol. 26, pp. 173–220). Newbury Park, CA: Sage.

Drash, P. W., & Tudor, R. M. (1991). A standard methodology for the analysis, recording, and control of verbal behavior. *The Analysis of Verbal Behavior, 9,* 49–60.

Drash, P. W., & Tudor, R. M. (1993). A functional analysis of verbal delay in preschool children: Implications for prevention and total recovery. *The Analysis of Verbal Behavior, 11,* 19–29.

Duchan, J. (1987). Functionalism: A perspective on autistic communication. In D. J. Cohen & A. M. Donnellan (Eds.), *Handbook of autism and pervasive developmental disorders.* (pp. 703–709). Silver Spring, MD: V. H. Winston.

Fay, W. (1967). Mitigated echolalia of children. *Journal of Speech and Hearing Research, 10,* 305–310.

Fay, W. (1969). On the basis of autistic echolalia. *Journal of Communication Disorders, 2,* 38–47.

Fay, W., & Schuler, A. L. (1980). *Emerging language in autistic children.* Baltimore, MD: University Park Press.

Fish, B., Shapiro, T., & Campbell, M. (1966). Long-term prognosis and the response of schizophrenic children to drug therapy: A controlled study of trifluoperazine. *American Journal of Psychiatry, 123,* 32–39.

Hart, B., & Risley, T. (1995). *Meaningful differences in the everyday experience of young American children.* Baltimore: Paul H. Brookes.

Kanner, L. (1943). Autistic disturbances of affective contact. *Nervous Child, 2,* 217–250.

Kiernan, C. (1983). The use of nonvocal communication techniques with autistic individuals. *Journal of Child Psychology and Child Psychiatry, 24,* 339–373.

Koegel, R. L., O'Dell, M. C., & Koegel, L. K. (1987). A natural language paradigm for teaching non-verbal autistic children. *Journal of Autism and Developmental Disabilities, 17,* 187–199.

Lord, C. (1988). Enhancing communication in adolescents with autism. *Topics in Language Disorders, 9,* 72–81.

Lotter, V. (1967). Epidemiology of autistic conditions in young children: II. Some characteristics of parents and children. *Social Psychiatry, 1,* 163–181.

Lovaas, O. I. (1981). *Teaching developmentally disabled children: The ME book.* Austin, TX: Pro-Ed.

Lovaas, O. I. (1987). Behavioral treatment and normal educational and intellectual functioning in young autistic children. *Journal of Consulting and Clinical Psychology, 55,* 3–9.

Mayer-Johnson, R. (1992). The picture communication symbols. Solana Beach, CA: Mayer-Johnson Co.

Mesibov, G. (1991) Lecture given at Division TEACCH, Chapel Hill, North Carolina.

Mesibov, G., Shopler, E., Schaffer, B., & Landrus, R. (1988). *Individualized assessment and treatment for autistic and developmentally disabled children.* Austin, TX: Pro-Ed.

Mirenda, P., & Schuler, A. L. (1988). Augmenting communication for persons with autism: Issues and strategies. *Topics in Language Disorders, 9,* 24–43.

Paul, R. (1987). Communication. In D. J. Cohen & A. M. Donnellan (Eds.), *Handbook of autism and pervasive developmental disorders* (pp. 61–84). New York: John Wiley.

Prizant, B. M. (1988). Communication problems in the autistic client. In N. Lass, J. Northern, L. McReynolds, & D. Yoder (Eds.), *Handbook of speech-language pathology and audiology* (pp. 1014–1039). Toronto: B. C. Decker.

Prizant, B. M., & Duchan, J. (1981). The functions of immediate echolalia in autistic children. *Journal of Speech and Hearing Disorders, 46,* 241–249.

Prizant, B. M., & Rydell, P. J. (1984). An analysis of the functions of delayed echolalia in autistic children. *Journal of Speech and Hearing Research, 27,* 183–192.

Prizant, B. M., & Rydell, P. J. (1993). Assessment and intervention considerations for unconventional verbal behavior. In J. Reichle & D. Wacker (Eds.), *Communicative alternatives to challenging behavior* (pp. 263–297). Baltimore, MD: Paul H. Brookes.

Prizant, B. M., & Weatherby, A. M. (1987). Communicative intent: A framework for understanding social-communicative behavior in autism. *Journal of the American Academy of Child Psychiatry, 26,* 472–479.

Prizant, B. M., & Weatherby, A. M. (1988). Providing services to children with autism (ages 0 to 2 years) and their families. *Topics in Language Disorders, 9,* 1–23.

Reichle, J., York, J., & Sigafoos, J. (1992). *Implementing augmentative and alternative communication: Strategies for learners with severe disabilities.* Baltimore, MD: Paul H. Brookes.

Schopler, E., & Mesibov, G. (1988). *Communication problems in autism.* New York: Plenum.

Schopler, E., Mesibov, G. B., & Baker, A. (1982). Evaluation of treatment for autistic children and their parents. *Journal of the American Academy of Child Psychiatry, 21,* 262–267.

Schopler, E., & Reichler, R. J. (1979). *Individualized assessment and treatment for autistic and developmentally disabled children. Vol. 1: Psychoeducational profile* (2nd ed.). Austin, TX: Pro-Ed.

Skinner, B. F. (1957). *Verbal behavior.* New York: Prentice-Hall.

Stokes, T., & Baer, D. M. (1977). An implicit technology of generalization. *Journal of Applied Behavior Analysis, 10,* 349–367.

Sundberg, M. L. (1980). *Developing a verbal repertoire using sign language and Skinner's analysis of verbal behavior.* Unpublished doctoral dissertation, Western Michigan University, Kalamazoo.

Sundberg, M. L. (1990). *Teaching verbal behavior to the developmentally disabled.* Danville, CA: Behavior Analysts.

Weatherby, A. M. (1986). Ontogeny of communicative functions in autism. *Journal of Autism and Developmental Disorders, 16,* 295–316.

Weatherby, A. M., & Prizant, B. M. (1989). The expression of communicative intent: Assessment guidelines. *Seminars in Speech and Language, 10,* 77–91.

Williams, D. F., Taylor, R., & Scott, J. (1994, November). *Collaborative training in autism and assistive augmentative communication at FAU.* Paper presented at the American Speech-Language-Hearing Convention, New Orleans.

Williams, D. F., Taylor, R., & Scott, J. (1995, November). *Multidisciplinary training in assistive augmentative communication and autism at FAU.* Paper presented at the American Speech-Language-Hearing Association Convention, Orlando, FL.

Wing, L. (1985). *Autistic children: A guide for parents and professionals.* New York: Brunner/Mazel.

Wolff, S., & Chess, S. (1965). An analysis of the language of 14 schizophrenic children. *Journal of Child Psychology and Psychiatry, 6,* 29–41.

Chapter 7

SOCIAL SKILLS AND SOCIAL COMPETENCE

Key Points

- Students with autism present significant social skill deficits.
- Direct, effective, skillful training in social skills is necessary.
- To effect lasting change, teachers must carefully analyze students' social capacity and social networks.
- Teachers must draw on an array of specific approaches to meet long-term goals.

INTRODUCTION

Students with autism typically have difficulties with social skills. Their problems include deficits in specific social skills, as well as problems with social relations. In this chapter we examine the problems with social relatedness experienced by students with autism and present various models for improving their skills and relationships.

THE IMPORTANCE OF SOCIAL SKILLS

Social contact is an important part of children's development and community living. People engage in reciprocal social interactions at home, at school, at work, and during leisure activities. Buying groceries, shopping at the mall, going to a movie, and playing with friends all involve social contact. For most people the acquisition of social skills begins at home, where language, turn taking, and play are taught incidentally by parents to young children. This process continues through visits from friends and family, venturing out into the community, and later by going to school.

The acquisition of good social skills helps students gain access to reinforcers. For example, when a child looks at an adult and says "please" and "thank you," that child is likely to be perceived as a "nice" child, predisposing the adult to offer praise, attention, and opportunities. The child who plays appropriately with peers, shares toys and treats, and does not steal toys is likely be sought as a playmate.

As children become adolescents and adults, interaction skills become even more important. Students must have the skills to approach peers in a socially recognized manner or they are not likely to be accepted into the social group. Further, skills must be differentiated so that they have a repertoire of social skills for peers and an overlapping but essentially separate repertoire of skills for approaching older or higher status individuals (such as teachers and employers).

Social skills play a major role in children's growth and development. These skills have an immediate role in a student's ability to interact with peers and adults, but they also play a primary role in establishing long-term relationships. Given the difficulty students with autism have in developing social skills, it is no wonder they also have problems establishing and maintaining social relationships.

Nature of the Social Deficit in Autism

Students with autism often fail to acquire reciprocal social interaction skills. Indeed, this deficit is an essential feature of the diagnosis of autism.

The social deficit in autism is sometimes manifested as rather mild impairments (i.e., difficulty establishing eye contact, making or interpreting facial expressions, or altering body postures). More serious manifestations include a failure to develop Students with autism often lack joint attention (Mundy & Sigman, 1989), and few seem able to share interests and experiences with others. Many students with autism appear oblivious to other individuals in the environment. Even among students with advanced language and cognitive skills, many fail to understand the perspective of others. These students are unable to infer knowledge, intentions, beliefs, or desires held by other people. (Baron-Cohen, Leslie, & Frith 1985; Ozonoff & Miller, 1995)

The social behaviors of students with autism vary over time and with the developmental level of the individual. In the earliest descriptions of autism, Kanner (1943) described young children who showed so little attention to social stimuli that they appeared to be deaf. Often these students do not respond to environmental sounds, to their names being called, or even to a very loud noise in close proximity (Lovaas & Newsome, 1976). Young children sometimes stiffen and move away from cuddling and parental contact; alternately, some show the opposite extreme and "cling" to a particular individual.

Home videos of children have shown that characteristics of autistic withdrawal are evident in some children at an early age (Osterling & Dawson, 1994). Videos also have documented that some toddlers begin to develop social interactions, but then lose these social skills over time (Eriksson & de Chateau, 1992). Typically, as students with autism grow older, they engage others in social contact, but this "engagement" often is so passive that peers do not recognize the behavior as an attempt to play or socialize. That is, these students often lack key "pivotal social skills" needed to initiate and maintain interactions (Koegel & Frea, 1993). Even in students who actively seek social contact, the nature of the social engagement tends to be somewhat unusual (Stone & Lemanek, 1990). Teenagers with autism may insist on specific responses to their questions or talk about a favorite topic endlessly, regardless of the interest of the listener. Adolescents and adults with autism tend not to pick up on the social cues presented by others.

Traditional Approaches to Teaching Social Skills

Most students without disabilities acquire social skills without formal training. When there is a deficit from either lack of exposure to particular environmental circumstances or disabilty, several approaches have been used to ameliorate the deficit. These approaches include counseling, modeling, and group social skills training.

Although these approaches appear to have helped some students acquire social skills, they have little value for youngsters with autism due to the idiosyncrasies of autism (perseveration, communication deficits, apparent lack of interest in social interaction, rigid adherence to routine). For example, a **counseling approach** to social skills development requires language and self-awareness skills beyond those held by many students, particularly students with communication deficits. Effective counseling also requires reciprocal social exchanges *with a counselor*. Since many students with autism do not have this basic reciprocity, the effectiveness of the counselor is limited.

Modeling or learning through observation also plays an important role in acquiring social behaviors, gender roles, and language (Bandura, 1971). Most students without disabilities learn social skills through models and reinforcement of the social behaviors by important people in their environments. Young children who walk and talk "just like daddy" or who who play house and have tea parties for their dolls have learned through modeling. Games like "cops and dealers" model behaviors seen (and reinforced) on television. In school, students wear the types of clothing and adopt the mannerisms of popular students in that school and popular adults in society. Successful modeling of the more popular students may increase the likelihood of being considered "popular" and increase their circles of friends. These behaviors are not taught. Rather, they occur as part of a process of acculturation and are highly reinforced by parents or peers. Most students with autism are not skillful imitators, and they tend not to engage in fantasy play or benefit from the modeled play of others. They seldom play house or have tea parties. Play tends to be a solitary activity using concrete objects, often in a manner not thought of as play at all by people without autism (i.e., flapping a puppet's arms or twirling a toy attached to a string). For these students, learning through modeling is ineffective; *learning to model* becomes a specific skill that must be taught.

Finally, various curricula that rely on **group social skills training** have become popular in many schools. These curricula treat social skills similar to any other subject area, specifying social outcomes that should result after students proceed through the curriculum. For example, the Walker Social Skills Curriculum (Walker et al., 1983) teaches social behavior including responding to criticism, responding to peer pressure, and so on. These curricula, which often are quite effective for students with learning and behavior disorders, use group instruction formats with modeling, role playing, and discussion as the primary methods of instruction. For most students with autism, however, instructional approaches relying on imitation, fantasy play, role reversal, and complex language have limited utility.

Current Approaches to Teaching Social Skills

Current approaches to social skills training for students with autism can be characterized as (a) direct instruction, (b) social communication training, (c) social story development, or (d) leisure related skill development (Shores, 1987, Simpson, Myles, Sasso, & Kamps, 1991). Prior to picking a method of promoting social skills, it is necessary to examine students' social relations and the strengths and challenges that these students face in their school, home, and other environments. One method of learning about students' social relations and skills in different environments is found in the TEAMS story on the next page.

Although the various approaches to teaching social skills differ in methods of delivering instruction, each approach reflects a conceptualization of social learning based on social reciprocity theory (Strain & Shores, 1977). Social reciprocity refers to the *exchange* of social behavior between two, or among several, people. To participate in a social exchange, people must produce social behaviors that have four distinct functions: social initiations, responses to these initiations, a continuation of the interaction, and an event that terminates the social exchange. **Initiations** serve to start an interaction. For example a social conversation might be initiated by a sentence such as "Do you want to play?" or "I need help." Other initiations might be physical or motoric in nature, such as handing a ball or a video game to a peer. **Responses** serve to connect a person to the initiator by responding to what is said or done when another individual initiates an exchange. This might include joining a peer in response to "Do you want to play?" or saying "Sure, I'd like to play Uno." **Continued interactions** refer to the total length of time that individuals interact with each other, either verbally or physically through play activities. Finally, **terminations** refer to the manner in which participants "call it quits." Like the other social functions, terminations can be verbal (e.g., "Got to go now.") or motoric (e.g., smile and wave).

Direct Instruction of Social Skills

Children and adults with autism can be taught directly to initiate social exchanges, respond to others' initiations, increase the durations of exchanges, and end exchanges appropriately (Myles, Simpson, Ormsbee, & Erickson, 1993; Simpson & Myles, 1993). Initial research demonstrating the effectiveness of direct instruction simply involved validation of teaching procedures including teacher prompts and reinforcement, and encouragement to interact by peers without disabilities (Strain & Fox, 1981; Strain, Kerr, & Ragland, 1979). Later research sought to extend students' learning by promoting generalization of the new social skills to different peers and in different places (Brady & McEvoy, 1989; Brady, Shores,

Using Team Environmental Assessment Mapping System (TEAMS) to Plan Educational Programs for Students With Autism

Patti C. Campbell, Ed.D.
Juliann Woods Cripe, Ph.D.

Jeremey, a 3-year-old with a history of significant developmental delays, is ready to transition from home-based early invention services to a school-based program. Jeremey's family and many of the professionals who work with him would like to see him go to his neighborhood elementary school. Because of his severe behavior outbursts, however, there is fear that a more restrictive placement (in a separate program for students with behavior disorders) will result.

Jeremey is a child who presents many challenging behaviors for both his family and the professionals who work with him and his family. His family describes him as, "being in a world of his own, a world that is difficult for others to enter." Jeremey spends much of his day engaged in stereotypic behaviors such as rocking and head banging. Jeremey appears to need intense sensory stimulation. He attempts to communicate with people around him using grunts, cries, and head banging. When people fail to respond to his signals, he will first butt them with his head; next he will begin slapping; and finally he will pull their hair until his needs are met. Jeremey also uses slapping or hair pulling when he wants to escape doing something.

Jeremey's family is worried that a separate program would further isolate him and permanently label him as a disrupter. To prepare for the planning meeting with school personnel, Jeremey's early intervention home-based team suggested that the group produce a written or pictorial display—in this case a TEAMS ecomap—to get a "picture" of the systems interacting in Jeremey's world.

Persons contributing to the TEAMS included Jeremey's mother, Teresa, his grandparents, the early interventionist, and his occupational and physical therapists. Jeremey is physically a healthy child who receives regular well child checkups. His vision and hearing appear within normal ranges. At first glance, the first thing the TEAMS map reveals is an extensive family support net-

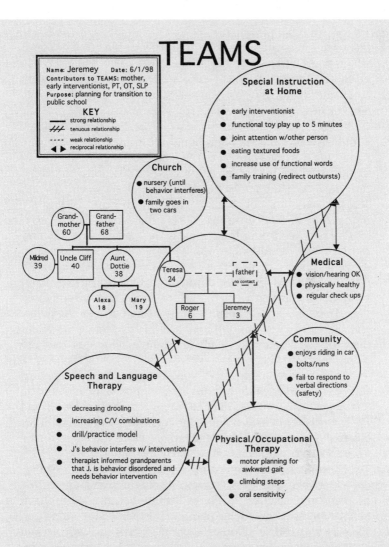

TEAMS

Name: Jeremy   Date: 6/1/98
Contributors to TEAMS: mother, early interventionist, PT, OT, SLP
Purpose: planning for transition to public school

KEY
——— strong relationship
⧸⧸⧸ tenuous relationship
- - - - weak relationship
◀ ▶ reciprocal relationship

Special Instruction at Home
- early interventionist
- functional toy play up to 5 minutes
- joint attention w/other person
- eating textured foods
- increase use of functional words
- family training (redirect outbursts)

Church
- nursery (until behavior interferes)
- family goes in two cars

Grand-mother 60
Grand-father 68

Mildred 39
Uncle Cliff 40
Aunt Dottie 38

Teresa 24

father
no contact

Alexa 18
Mary 19

Roger 6
Jeremy 3

Medical
- vision/hearing OK
- physically healthy
- regular check ups

Community
- enjoys riding in car
- bolts/runs
- fail to respond to verbal directions (safety)

Speech and Language Therapy
- decreasing drooling
- increasing C/V combinations
- drill/practice model
- J's behavior interfers w/ intervention
- therapist informed grandparents that J. is behavior disordered and needs behavior intervention

Physical/Occupational Therapy
- motor planning for awkward gait
- climbing steps
- oral sensitivity

work. This is a strong group because each of the four families live next door to each another on a family-owned plot of land. Teresa, her father, and her sister work at the prison across the highway from their land. Teresa is a guard and works during the day; her father works in the maintenance department at night. Their work schedules allow Jeremy to be cared for by family at all times. Uncle Cliff and his wife Mildred take care of Jeremy every Sunday afternoon. Teresa's sister's two teenage daughters

(continued)

fill in when needed. Jeremey also has a 6-year-old brother, Roger, who is doing well in first grade. Roger likes to play with his brother, especially when they play outside. Jeremey requires constant adult supervision and going outside sometimes presents a problem because there is no fence.

Because he does not respond to verbal directions Jeremey's world basically consists of his home, the homes of his extended family, the car, and church each Sunday morning. Jeremey loves to ride in the car, but for safety reasons he only gets out to attend the nursery at church. The family usually takes two cars in case Jeremey loses control of his behavior before the services are over. Jeremey's other environments are characterized by the services he receives from professionals. The services that Jeremey receives from the early intervention team include functional language and play activities that focus on engaging Jeremey with family members during their day-to-day activities. The early intervention team also provides training to Teresa and the grandparents. There is a strong positive relationship between the family and the early intervention team. The family feels good about the progress Jeremy has made and how much better they are interacting with him.

The physical therapist (PT) and the occupational therapist (OT) have worked with the early intervention team, resulting in a very positive, well-coordinated training program. The OT and PT have also provided training for Jeremy that help him in his day-to-day activities. The grandparents carry out most of the exercises with Jeremy as part of his daily routine.

Speech-language therapy for Jeremy has been a very different experience. The speech therapist told the grandparents that he really could not do much for Jeremy because his problem behavior interfered with the therapy. The therapist reported that since Jeremy had situation behavior disorders, he really needed programming for his inappropriate behavior before speech-language therapy could be beneficial. The therapy design for Jeremy is best described as a "drill/practice model." Most of the therapy sessions end early because of Jeremey's behavior. None of the activities have functional use in Jeremey's day to day routine. Jeremey does not like the speech therapist and spends most of the therapy sessions butting or banging his head. The family feels very uncomfortable around the therapist but will not say anything because he is a professional. The other service providers have not been able to work cooperatively with the therapist and some very negative relationships have resulted.

In summary, the family and others who participated in developing the TEAMS learned that while Jeremey presented some very challenging behaviors for a public-school-based program he also had some positives. He has a very strong family support network. Service providers have made gains using functional play and communication activities that impact directly on Jeremey's day-to-day functioning. The team felt that the information collected in the TEAMS process would have a powerful positive impact on the placement planning team's decisions.

Note: A complete description of TEAMS is available in Campbell, Campbell, and Brady (1998).

Patti C. Campbell is Associate Professor of Special Education and Director of several teacher education and technology projects at Valdosta State University. Juliann Woods Cripe is Associate Professor of Communication Disorders and Director of several intervention projects at Valdosta State University.

McEvoy, Ellis, & Fox, 1987; Gunter, Fox, Brady, Shores, & Cavanaugh, 1988; Odom & Strain, 1984).

The basic technique used in this line of research was to provide short periods of time each day for structured interactions between students with autism and nondisabled peers (or "student trainers"). Specific training sessions were provided for each child. The nondisabled peer was taught how to initiate or respond to the initiation provided by the student with autism. The students were placed in a setting with toys and games and the teacher prompted, modeled, or physically assisted the student with autism to initiate, respond, or continue the interactions. Gradually, the teacher faded the prompts and simply observed the interactions. These demonstrations were arranged between preschool and young elementary school-aged students (Davis, Hamilton, McEvoy, & Williams, 1994; McEvoy et al., 1988; McEvoy, Twardosz, & Bishop, 1990), older students (Brady et al., 1984, 1987; Simpson & Myles, 1993), and adolescents and young adults (Breen, Haring, Pitts-Conway, & Gaylord-Ross, 1985).

In the most poignant studies, the students with autism were included in group social activities but were directly taught to interact with only one peer at a time. As the student with autism learned to initiate and respond to a nondisabled peer, a second or third peer was included in the training. This allowed the gradual introduction of different peers into the sessions. Typically, after training was applied with two or three nondisabled peers, the child with autism began to interact spontaneously with "untrained" peers (see Brady & McEvoy, 1989, for a review). The lesson of this research is unambiguous. Students with and without autism, across different age levels, could be taught to interact with one another successfully; and, by including multiple peers in the teaching, *spontaneous* improvements in students' social skills would be directed to novel peers in different social environments.

It should be noted, though, that the peers must be taught directly to interact with students with autism. Schreibman, Stahmer, and Pierce (1996) suggested four behaviors that teachers should encourage in typical peers:

1. The peers without disabilities should encourage and seek to extend the social communication attempts of students with autism. Commenting about a preferred activity or toy of the student with autism is one way to do this.
2. The peers should exaggerate positive affective statements and behavior. Bold and obvious statements and behavior by the peer will affirm that the interactions are positive.
3. The peers should model socially appropriate statements and behavior. The peer should offer numerous "friendly" models and emphasize statements and behavior that can be easily imitated.
4. The peers should ignore and/or redirect behaviors or statements that are inappropriate. This includes looking for positive pathways for interaction.

Discrete trial training of social responses is a variation of direct instruction for social skills (Lovaas, 1981; Taylor & McDonough, 1996). The same discrete trial format used for academic and behavioral skills acquisition can be used to teach social skills such as turn taking or exchanging social information. The use of a discrete trial format generally involves substantial one-on-one teaching, although group formats can be used to increase practice opportunities. Turn taking, for instance, can be taught in a one-on-one format using puzzles combined with "My turn, your turn" verbal cues until the student anticipates the other person's turn. Then, a third person can be brought into the group and "My turn, your turn, his turn" cues can be used. Additional trials would involve asking, "Whose turn?" to elicit verbal or gestural responses.

When the students are able to indicate whose turn is next, a specific game (e.g., Bingo or Candyland) can be introduced. Initially, the game can be played with whatever level of prompt is necessary. As the students become more independent, the prompts and the teacher are gradually removed until the students are able to play the game unassisted. As turn-taking skills increase, more complex activities, sports, and playground games such as baseball and kickball can be introduced. When teaching playground games it is helpful to have a number of adults available initially to give cues to the individual players. This ensures that each student receives an adequate number of trials and that trials receive instructional consequences.

Social Communication Training

For students with more complete verbal language, a variation of the direct instruction strategies has involved social communication training. Students with autism tend not to interact in verbal conversations with others. This lack of conversational skill reflects a deficit in approach and initiation skills, responses, continuing interactions, and even social terminations. Social communication training allows adults to provide students with instruction involving "who to ask," "when to ask," "what words to use," and "what to do next." Two examples of social communication training stand out. Taylor and Harris (1995) used direct instruction and a time delay procedure to teach students with autism to ask questions and seek new information. Charlop and Milstein (1989) used videotapes of language models to teach conversation.

Classroom teachers can teach social communication content through direct instruction, social stories, role play with scripts, or video modeling (Breen et al., 1985; Reamer, Brady, & Hawkins, 1998). For example, teachers might need to teach nonverbal social cues such as moving away to indicate that a conversation is over and backing up to indicate that the social distance needs to increase. These social communication targets will increase the social acceptance of the student and allow him or her to be positively reinforced by successful social contact.

Since conversation topics and functions differ across situations and settings, conversation training must be quite flexible. For example, teaching peers to have an in-depth discussion with a friend at home requires different teaching methods than instruction designed to teach a student to answer a teacher's question in class. Language use, length of conversation, and nonverbal interactions such as social distance will vary with factors such as type of question, status and level of intimacy of the individual asking the question, and time before the next activity occurs. Turn taking during conversations is an equally important skill. Questions to ask to keep the conversation going, how long each person's "turn" should be, and how to know when the conversation is over are teachable skills even though they vary considerably across situations. Scripting is one social communication strategy that has received attention for students with autism. Krantz and McClannahan (1993) used a social script and a fading procedure to teach students to initiate interactions with peers. Hunt, Alwell, Goetz, and Sailor (1990) used similar procedures to teach conversation skills. The success of scripting as an intervention may relate to its use as a visual cueing system. Many students with autism learn most easily when instructional stimuli are presented visually. For students with verbal language and reading abilities, a script can be used to signal the conversational topic, use expressions and idioms, or as a guide to turn taking. Scripts also can be used to teach telephone use and job-related social skills (e.g., job interviewing). An object (such as a colored card for children or a coin for adolescents) can be passed from speaker to speaker and combined with a script to guide turn taking. As students develop proficiency through role playing and practice, portions of the scripts can be deleted. Directions or cues to the student with autism can be provided, prompting him or her to use different language and make choices regarding activities.

A variation on scripting that also incorporates students' visual strengths is the use of a flow chart or other visual diagram. A social conversational flow chart provides a visual sequence with all possible conversation topics written out. Lines connect each section, depending on the other person's response (If they say this, then you say that). The student following these visual patterns of a conversation thus has a visual prompt and may become more facile in a social situation. An example of a conversational flow chart used by one of the authors to help a student to ask another student for a date by telephone is provided in Figure 7–1.

Social Stories

A recent addition to the array of social skills strategies is the development of social stories (Gray, 1995; Gray & Garand, 1993). The stories are used to teach the concepts and strategies behind social skills before students enter a real social situation or to ameliorate problems when they arise. Social stories help students to identify positive social behaviors that will be needed in a social setting. Social stories are scripted scenarios of social situations. The scripts generally are discussed by teachers and students, then written by students, with or without teacher assistance depending on the writing fluency of the student. Social stories address problems with social reciprocity by describing social situations in terms of the relevant social cues and appropriate responses. Students problem solve the situations by writing behavioral descriptions of possible solutions and then rehearsing these responses. Social stories typically are used with students who have reasonable amounts of verbal language, although some teachers have adapted them for less verbal students much the same way preschool teachers use Language Experience stories for prereaders (i.e., the teacher writes a student's story from dictation).

A typical social story consists of two to five sentences that describe four components of the story. Students first write about the situation (a **descriptive** sentence) and then give an appropriate behavioral response (a **directive** sentence). Coaching is used to help generate the directive if the student does not offer an alternative behavior that is social in nature.

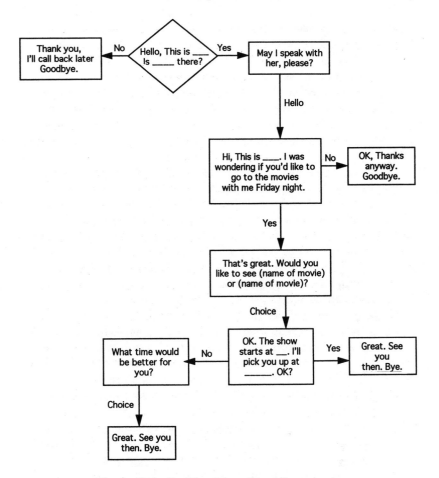

Figure 7–1. Social conversational flow chart.

Next, the student writes a sentence that describes the feelings and reactions of the other individuals involved (a **perspective** sentence), followed by analogies of similar actions and responses utilizing nonhumans such as pets (a **control** sentence) (Gray, 1995; Gray & Garand, 1993). The social story is placed in a book, typically with one to three sentences per page. Photographs, drawings, or icons can be used to illustrate the desired behavior. Advanced readers, of course, could have more elaborate stories.

Social stories can be written by the teacher or the student and are usually read in a repeated reading format over several days. They also can be given to the student for independent study and to use as a social behavior reference guide. Gray (1995) suggests that teachers should use social stories as a group-oriented language activity and provides general teaching suggestions. We recommend that a more systematic use would include:

1. **Identify a social problem behavior** that, if improved, will result in increased adaptive behavior, social acceptance, or safety.
2. **Define the social skill that would ameliorate the problem.** Since the purpose of the stories is to promote social competence, it is important that the student and teachers know exactly what behavior they are addressing.
3. **Collect baseline data on the desired social behavior** for at least 3 to 5 days. This information will provide a sensible basis for evaluating the effectiveness of the social story.
4. **Have the student write a short story.** Stories should be written either in present or future tense at the reading and writing comprehension level of the student. Stories should be written in the first person. A teacher can write a story from the student's dictation for students who do not write.
5. **Use photographs, line drawings, or pictorial icons.** Use of visual cues such as pictures can assist the student's understanding, especially where a student has minimal reading skills.
6. **Have the student read the social story and rehearse the desired social behavior.** This should become part of the student's daily schedule. The story can be read just prior to the situation in which the social skill should be used. Rehearsal should be linked to the student's story.
7. **Collect intervention data.** Evaluate whether reading the story results in improvement in the social skill by collecting data. Teachers also might collect data on improvements in students' reading or spelling of the stories.
8. **Change social-story procedures** if improvements in the social behavior do not occur within 2 weeks. If changes need to be made, keep the changes simple.
9. **Teach for maintenance and generalization.** Once improvements in the social skill are noticed, the utility of the stories can be expanded into other situations in which the social skill would be useful or necessary.

An alternative approach for young children includes the creation of social songs. Social songs are teacher-developed songs that are used to instruct and promote social/interactional skills such as greetings or turn taking. Social songs are similar to social stories in general format and concept. They differ in several important ways. First, they use a familiar song and offer the benefits of a rhythmic vocal activity. Second, they are intended to be learned by a group of students in a cooperative, high participation format. Finally they are designed to offer generic social problem assistance in contrast to the more problem specific format of social stories. Examples of social songs can be found in Table 7–1.

Finally, teachers can create a personal reference library with a student by saving the stories for a student's future reference. Over time, a "library" of appropriate responses to social situations can be assembled. This is similar to the phenomenon described by Grandin (1995) who wrote of viewing a "video in [her] imagination" or replaying a scene from a CD-ROM to gain an understanding of social situations. By describing the settings, appropriate responses, and the perspectives of other individuals involved, these stories can assist the student with autism to better understand their social behaviors and the feelings of others.

Although an empirical basis for social stories has yet to be developed, many teachers find this teaching approach useful because it attaches language to behavioral episodes and encourages rehearsal. Swaggart et al. (1995) and Gray (1995) summarized several advantages of social stories, including the development of language to describe situations, personalization of social skills instruction, and the rehearsal of routines. An example of a social story created by a student for one of the authors is provided on the next page.

Table 7–1. Social Songs

Turntaking

(To the tune of "Row, Row, Row Your Boat")

Wait, wait, wait your turn.

It is coming soon.

First his turn, then her turn,

Then we'll get to you.

Greetings

(To the tune of "Frere Jacques")

He's my friend, she's my friend.

I say hi, they say hi.

"Hi" says that I like you,

"Hi" says that you like me.

We are friends, we are friends.

Note: These Social Songs were contributed by Carolyn Nancy Frank.

Social Story

This is an example of a social story created by an 11-year-old boy and his teacher as a means of helping him control his voice volume and tone. Note the guides designed to help evaluate the student's reading skill development. Thus, this story is used to help the student control his voice as well as improve reading performance.

Teacher's Starter: "We will be reading a story to help you learn how to use your words in nice ways."

My Voice (89 words)

We use our voices to tell things to people.
The sounds we make tell people how we feel.
When a person laughs, it shows they are happy.
When a person cries, it shows they are sad.
Loud noises mean that a person is hurt or upset.
If my friends hear me making loud noises, they might think something is wrong and worry about me.
I should use my words to tell people how I feel and save loud noises for times when I am hurt and need help.

Time: _____

# of corrects _____

# of errors _____

Social Components of Leisure Skills

Another approach to social skill development that incorporates social reciprocity involves the development of leisure skills. Social-based leisure skills tend to be very difficult for many students with autism. This difficulty may stem from the lack of structure inherent in most leisure activities, from the social interaction demands on the student, or a combination of both. Teaching leisure skills assists students with autism in learning the social rules of play and interaction.

An important part of leisure programming involves teaching skills that are enjoyable and promote participation. Enjoyment increases the likelihood of natural reinforcers in students' environments contributing to the maintenance of the behavior. Targeting skills that involve the participation of family and friends also promotes maintenance. Communication with peers and families is necessary when targeting initial leisure skills. The skills required to play slow-pitch softball with peers are quite different from the skills required to attend a movie with the family. Initial leisure training should target skills appropriate to one setting. As the student learns the leisure skill and his or her social competence increases, a variety of skills can be taught to help the student learn to discriminate among settings.

When teaching leisure skills, teachers must build in *social exchanges as part of the leisure activity.* Many students with autism already are able to engage in solitary activities. For leisure activities to produce social competence, there must be regular opportunities to interact with others. For example, the social demands of a simple card game include teamwork, turn taking, sharing, and appropriate responses to winning and losing. Some playground games do not have obvious rules; instructional activities might involve teaching students in these activities to fit in (Breen et al., 1995; Haring & Breen, 1992). For some students, this will include self-management skills to help control stereotypic behaviors, although leisure and social engagement itself sometimes leads to a decrease in these patterns of behavior.

Finally, when teaching leisure skills it is important to remember that, for many students with autism, the demands of play exceed the demands of work. The rules of work are usually clear-cut and job tasks are usually structured. In contrast, social and leisure activities, playground games, or "coffee break" conversations generally lack structure and obvious rules, which makes them much more difficult for students with autism. This poses challenges to many teachers who assume that social and leisure skills will be learned without directly teaching them.

Strategies for Selecting Peers and Materials

Regardless of the teaching approach used to improve students' social skills, teachers should select peers and materials with care. We believe that the selection of peers and materials involved in teaching social skills requires even more careful consideration than when picking materials and activities for reading or math instruction. Since social skills instruction involves the time and energy of students *other* than the target students, the instruction must be time and energy efficient. During social skills instruction, the *stimulus materials* of the lesson are other students, while the *medium* of the lesson is the materials and activities. The peers, materials, and activities used in a social skill lesson must promote specific social outcomes. For example, students with autism are not likely to engage in reciprocal social interactions if teachers arrange social experiences only with *other students with autism or with activities that are better pursued alone* (Strain, 1983; Strain, Hoyson, & Jamieson, 1985). Fortunately, several sets of guidelines are available for selecting peers and materials during social skills instruction (Brady & McEvoy, 1989; Kamps, Locke, Delquadri, & Hall, 1989; Stremel-Campbell, Campbell, & Johnson-Dorn, 1985).

Selecting Peers for Social Skills Instruction

Strain and Fox (1981) examined the initial research on peer interactions. Based on the first generation of studies, they identified the need to prepare the nondisabled peers to recognize the interaction patterns of students with autism and teach them to persist in their interactions with students with autism. This included practice opportunities in which the peers without disabilities rehearsed initiating and responding to overt and subtle initations with adults and peers prior to interacting with target students (Brady et al., 1984, 1987; Strain, 1983). Peers also have been taught to understand the unusual communication patterns of each student with autism, to cope with any idiosyncratic or disturbing behavior, and to contrast those patterns with their own communication and behavioral idiosyncracies (Shores et al., 1985). This line of research produced four criteria for selecting peers involved in social interaction lessons and school integration activities:

1. willingness on the part of each student to participate;
2. a good school attendance record;
3. evidence that students involved in the lesson will generally follow teachers' requests; and
4. reasonable social interaction skills in most social situations.

For students with strong verbal skills or for students with disabilities other than autism, selecting peers for social skill lessons typically relies on existing social networks. For students with autism and others with a long history of extreme withdrawal, peer networks typically do not exist. Garrison-Harrell, Kamps, and Kravits (1997) described a method of evaluating potential peer networks that included teacher nomination, peer status evaluations, and direct observation. An alternative procedure was described by Forest and Lusthaus (1989) who used sociograms—maps of social preferences—to identify peers and potential "circles of friends." Campbell, Campbell, and Brady (1998) established a curriculum planning tool that delineated a student's social opportunities and needs in various current and future environments. Their planning tool links a student's social network to his or her instructional, recreational, and vocational settings. All of the approaches to identifying peer networks described here provide useful strategies that teachers can use to help identify nondisabled peers who would be central to the social skills development of students with autism.

Selecting Materials and Activities for Social Skills Instruction

Materials and activities should be selected for their congruence with the intended outcomes of the lesson. The degree of "reactivity" of a material is one characteristic that should be evaluated. Highly reactive materials (e.g., some video games) respond to a user's manipulation by producing sound, visual display, or movement. Reactive materials sometimes draw the attention of the students to the activity rather than to the peer interaction and thus might inhibit some social interactions. Materials with low reactivity, on the other hand, may be so subtle that they do not lead to interactions at all (Gaylord-Ross, Haring, Breen, & Pitts-Conway, 1984). Although it is difficult to predict all students' reactions to a particular game or activity, teachers can observe students' participation and ask themselves specifically if the materials *promote* social interactions or simply the use of the game or material.

Educators have long recommended that instructional materials be age-appropriate (Brown et al., 1979). Since a social exchange involves two or more students, materials and activities that do not match students' chronological ages may become stigmatizing for all participants. This may inhibit some youngsters' willingness to participate. Numerous peer interaction demonstrations have shown that students without disabilities will interact in meaningful ways with students who have autism when taught how to do so and when given regular opportunities to do so. Teachers can help to maintain these interactions and to promote social relations over time by facilitating common, nonstigmatizing activities around which the youngsters can interact. Indeed, it is our contention that meaningful long-term social relations are not likely unless teachers provide skillful instruction and numerous opportunities for students to engage in different types of social experiences.

SUMMARY

Social skills and social competence are important to the normalization of any individual. Because of the specific social skills deficits inherent in the disability, students with autism are likely to need direct training of social skills. Assessment of students' interests is important before beginning any social skills instruction. A student is more likely to interact to attain preferred peers and activities than nonpreferred peers and activities. However, if they have not had the opportunity to explore the materials and to learn to interact with peers, students with autism may need to *discover* what their activity preferences are.

A variety of techniques can be used effectively to teach social skills to students with autism. Adaptations and modifications to accommodate students of different ages, developmental levels, language facility, and interests can be used to help almost any student learn to engage in positive social interactions with peers.

We recognize that social skills are difficult to teach. Most educators are not taught to address these nonacademic skills. However, social skills are vital to the independent functioning of students with autism both in the classroom and in their nonschool lives. Lack of social skills, regardless of a student's cognitive strengths, isolates a student with autism from family and community resources.

Teachers may envision a life full of rich social opportunity for students with autism. Indeed, it is now popular to set such a vision for these students (Mount & Zwernik, 1994). But students will not learn social skills if they are not well taught. When a vision lacks a mechanism for articulation, the vision is likely to remain a dream.

REVIEW QUESTIONS

1. What social problems are typically associated with autism?

2. How can functional social skills be taught in a classroom, playground, or community setting?

3. What are four components of successful social interactions?

4. What methods increase the probability that newly acquired social skills will maintain over time and generalize to different people and places?

5. How can teachers of students without disabilities prepare their students to become socially competent with students who have autism?

REFERENCES

Bandura, A. (1971). *Social learning theory.* New York: General Learning Press.

Baron-Cohen, S., Leslie, A. M., & Frith, U. (1985). Does the autistic child have a "theory of mind?" *Cognition, 21,* 37–46.

Brady, M. P., & Mc Evoy, M. A. (1989). Social skills training as an integration strategy. In R. Gaylord-Ross (Ed.), *Integration strategies for students with handicaps* (pp. 213–231). Baltimore, MD: Paul H. Brookes.

Brady, M. P., Shores, R. E., Gunter, P., McEvoy, M. A., Fox, J. J., & White, C. (1984). Generalization of a severely handicapped adolescent's social interaction responses via multiple peers in a classroom setting. *Journal of the Association for Persons with Severe Handicaps, 9,* 278–286.

Brady, M. P., Shores, R. E., McEvoy, M. A., Ellis, D., & Fox, J. J. (1987). Increasing social interactions of severely handicapped autistic children. *Journal of Autism and Developmental Disorders, 3,* 375–390.

Breen, C., Haring, T., Pitts-Conway, V., & Gaylord-Ross, R. (1985). The training and generalization of social interaction during breaktime at two job sites in the natural environment. *Journal of the Association for Persons with Severe Handicaps, 10,* 41–50.

Brown, L., Branston, M. B., Hamre-Nietupski, S., Pumpian, I., Certo, N., & Gruenewald, L. (1979). A strategy for developing chronological, age appropriate and functional curricular content for severely handicapped adolescents and young adults. *Journal of Special Education, 13,* 81–90.

Campbell, P. C., Campbell, C. R., & Brady, M. P. (1998). Team environmental assessment mapping system (TEAMS): A method for selecting curriculum goals for students with disabilities. *Education and Training in Mental Retardation and Developmental Disabilities, 2,* 264–272.

Charlop, M. H., & Milstein, J. P. (1989). Teaching autistic children conversational speech using video modeling. *Journal of Applied Behavior Analysis, 22,* 275–285.

Davis, C., Brady, M. P., Hamilton, R., McEvoy, M. A., & Williams, R. E. (1994). Effects of high probability requests on the social interactions of young children with severe disabilities. *Journal of Applied Behavior Analysis, 27,* 619–637.

Eriksson, A. S., & de Chateau, P. (1992). Brief report: A girl aged two years and seven months with autistic disorder videotaped from birth. *Journal of Autism and Developmental Disorders, 22,* 127–129.

Forest, M., & Lusthaus, E. (1989). Promoting educational equality for all students: Circles and maps. In S. Stainback, W. Stainback, & M. Forest (Eds.), *Educating all students in the mainstream of regular education* (pp. 43–57). Baltimore, MD: Paul H. Brookes.

Garrison-Harrell, L., Kamps, D., & Kravits, T. (1997). The effects of peer networks on social-communicative behaviors for students with autism. *Focus on Autism and Other Developmental Disabilities, 12,* 241–254.

Gaylord-Ross, R. J., Haring, T. G., Breen, C., & Pitts-Conway, V. (1984). The training and generalization of social interaction skills with autistic youth. *Journal of Applied Behavior Analysis, 7,* 229–247.

Grandin, T. (1995). How people with autism think. In E. Schopler & G. Mesibov (Eds.), *Learning and cognition in autism* (pp. 137–156). New York: Plenum.

Gray, C. (1995). Social stories and comic strip conversations: Unique methods to improve social understanding. (Available from Jenison Public Schools, 8375 20th, Jenison, MI 49428.)

Gray, C., & Garand, J. (1993). Social stories: Improving responses of students with autism with accurate social information. *Focus on Autistic Behavior, 8,* 1–10.

Gunter, P., Fox, J. J., Brady, M. P., Shores, R. E., & Cavanaugh, K. (1988). Non-handicapped peers as multiple exemplars: A generalization tactic for prompting autistic students' social skills. *Behavioral Disorders, 13,* 116–126.

Haring, T. G., & Breen, C. B. (1992). A peer-mediated social network intervention to enhance the social integraton of persons with moderate and severe disabililities. *Journal of Applied Behavior Analysis, 25,* 319–333.

Hunt, P., Alwell, M., Goetz, L., & Sailor, W. (1990). Generalized effects of conversation skill training. *Journal of the Association for Persons with Severe Handicaps, 15,* 250–260.

Kamps, D., Locke, P., Delquadri, J., & Hall, R. V. (1989). Increasing academic skills of students with autism using fifth grade peers as tutors. *Education and Treatment of Children, 12,* 38–51.

Kanner, L. (1943). Autistic disturbances of affective contact. *Nervous Child, 2,* 217–250.

Koegel, R. L., & Frea, W. D. (1993). Treatment of social behavior in autism through the modification of pivotal social skills. *Journal of Applied Behavior Analysis, 26,* 369–377.

Krantz, P. J., & McClannahan, L. E. (1993). Teaching children with autism to initiate to peers: Effects of a script-fading procedure. *Journal of Applied Behavior Analysis, 26,* 121–132.

Lovaas, O. I. (1981). *Teaching developmentally disabled children: The ME book.* Austin, TX: Pro-Ed.

Lovaas, O. I., & Newsom, C. D. (1976). Behavior modification with psychotic children. In H. Leitenberg (Ed.), *Handbook of behavior modification and behavior therapy* (pp. 303–360). Englewood Cliffs, NJ: Prentice-Hall.

McEvoy, M., Nordquist, V., Twardosz, S., Heckaman, K., Wehby, J., & Denny, R. K. (1988). Promoting autistic children's peer interaction in integrated early childhood settings using affection activities. *Journal of Applied Behavior Analysis, 21,* 193–200.

McEvoy, M. A., Twardosz, S., & Bishop, N. (1990). Affection activities: Procedures for encouraging young children with handicaps to interact with their peers. *Education and Treatment of Children, 13,* 159–167.

Mount, B., & Zwernik, K. (1994). *Making futures happen.* Minneapolis: Minnesota Governor's Planning Council on Developmental Disabilities.

Mundy, P., & Sigman, M. (1989). Specifying the nature of the social impairment in autism. In G. Dawson (Ed.), *Autism: Nature, diagnosis and treatment* (pp. 3–21). New York: Guilford.

Myles, B. S., Simpson, R. L., Ormsbee, C. K., & Erickson, C. (1993). Integrating preschool children with autism with their normally developing peers: Research findings and best practices recommendations. *Focus on Autistic Behavior, 8*(5), 1–14.

Odom, S. L., & Strain, P. S. (1984). Peer-mediated approaches to promoting children's social interaction: A review. *American Journal of Orthopsychiatry, 54,* 544–557.

Osterling, J., & Dawson, G. (1994). Early recognition of children with autism: A study of first birthday home videotapes. *Journal of Autism and Developmental Disorders, 24,* 247–257.

Ozonoff, S., & Miller, J. N. (1995). Teaching theory of mind: A new approach to social skills training for individuals with autism. *Journal of Autism and Developmental Disorders, 25*, 415–433.

Reamer, R., Brady, M. P., & Hawkins, J. (1998). The effects of video self-modeling on parents' interactions with children with developmental disabilities. *Education and Training in Mental Retardation and Developmental Disabilities, 33*(2), 121–143.

Schreibman, L., Stahmer, A. C., Pierce, K. L. (1996). Alternative applications of pivotal response training. In L. K. Koegel, R. L. Koegel, & G. Dunlap (Eds.), *Positive behavioral support: Including people with difficult behavior in the community* (pp. 353–371). Baltimore, MD: Paul H. Brookes.

Shores, R. E. (1987). Overview of research on social interaction: A historical and personal perspective. *Behavioral Disorders, 12*, 233–241.

Shores, R. E., McEvoy, M. A., Fox, J. J., Brady, M. P., Denny, R. K., Heckaman, K., & Wehby, J. (1985). *Social integration of severely handicapped children* [Training manual]. Nashville, TN: George Peabody College of Vanderbilt University.

Simpson, R. L., & Myles, B. S. (1993). Successful integration of children and youth with autism in mainstreamed settings. *Focus on Autistic Behavior, 7*(6), 1–13.

Simpson, R., Myles, B. S., Sasso, G., & Camps, D. (1991). *Social skills for students with autism.* Reston, VA: Council for Exceptional Children.

Stone, W., & Lemanek, K. (1990). Parental report of social behaviors in autistic preschoolers. *Journal of Autism and Developmental Disorders, 20*, 513–522.

Strain, P. S. (1983). Generalization of autistic children's social behavior change: Effects of developmental integrated and segregated settings. *Analysis and Intervention in Developmental Disabilities, 3*, 23–34

Strain, P. S., & Fox, J. J. (1981). Peer social initiations and the modification of social withdrawal: A review and future perspective. *Journal of Pediatric Psychology, 6*, 417–433.

Strain, P. S., Hoyson, M., & Jamieson, B. (1985). Normally developing preschoolers as intervention agents for autistic-like children: Effects on class deportment and social interaction. *Journal of the Division for Early Childhood, 9*, 105–115.

Strain, P. S., Kerr, M. M., & Ragland, E. U. (1979). Effects of peer mediated social initiations and prompting/reinforcement procedures on the social behavior of autistic children. *Journal of Autism and Developmental Disorders, 9*, 41–54.

Strain. P. S., & Shores, R. E. (1977). Social reciprocity: A review of research and educational implications. *Exceptional Children, 43*, 526–530.

Stremel-Campbell, K., Campbell, R., & Johnson-Dorn, N. (1985). Utilization of integrated settings and activities to develop and expand communication skills. In M. P. Brady & P. L. Gunter (Eds.), *Integrating moderately and severely handicapped learners: Strategies that work* (pp. 185–213). Springfield, IL: Charles C Thomas.

Swaggart, B., Gagnon, E., Lock, S., Earles, T., Quinn, C., Myles, B., & Simpson, R. (1995). Using social stories to teach social and behavioral skills to children with autism. *Focus on Autistic Behavior, 10*, 1–15.

Taylor, B. A., & Harris, S. L. (1995). Teaching children with autism to seek information: Acquisition of novel information and generalization of responding. *Journal of Applied Behavior Analysis, 28*, 3–14.

Taylor, B. A., & McDonough, K. A. (1996). Selecting teaching programs. In C. Maurice, G. Green, & S. Luce (Eds.), *Behavioral intervention for young children with autism* (pp. 63–177). Austin, TX: Pro-Ed.

Walker, H. M., McConnell, S., Holmes, D., Todis, B., Walker, J., & Golden, N. (1983). *The Walker social skills curriculum: The ACCEPTS program.* Austin, TX: Pro-Ed.

Chapter 8

AN EDUCATIONAL MODEL FOR TEACHING STUDENTS WITH AUTISM

Key Points

- Effective instruction requires an understanding of the unique learning characteristics of students with autism
- Teachers have an active role in determining *what is worth teaching*
- Assessment instruments exist but have varying purposes and standards of adequacy
- Decisions involving how to teach include how to *organize* a lesson and how to *deliver* a lesson
- Evaluation of instructional progress is based on careful measurement and should indicate trends in student learning

INTRODUCTION

Many teachers believe that students with autism are among the most difficult students to teach. Because these students have learning characteristics that are unlike those of most other learners, teachers must have powerful tools in their teaching repertoires. These tools include planning strategies, techniques for selecting curriculum targets, procedures for organizing learning environments, and a mastery of instructional delivery and evaluation tactics. Within this context, actively avoiding bad tools is essential. In this chapter, the unique learning characteristics of students with autism are described. Next, a model is presented to help teachers identify important skills that should be taught and to demonstrate how this information leads to teachers' decisions involving how to teach and how to evaluate the effectiveness of their teaching. Finally, several examples of educational programs designed specifically for students with autism are presented.

LEARNING CHARACTERISTICS
OF STUDENTS WITH AUTISM

Students with autism often have learning characteristics that challenge their special education and regular education teachers. While educators with experience teaching these students are seldom surprised at these challenges, even experienced teachers encounter stumbling blocks with some students with autism (Grandin & Scariano, 1986). Teachers new to autism typically find that these youngsters challenge their former beliefs about learning; others may question their ability to be successful in teaching these students.

Although students with autism present challenges, understanding the nature of autism provides teachers with practical skills for becoming effective teachers. As noted in Chapter 1, students with autism often have serious difficulties communicating with other students and adults. For example, students who do not express their confusion or request assistance with a task give their teachers the impression that they understand the demands of an assignment and can perform needed tasks without difficulty. Other students have difficulty understanding teachers who make multistep requests or who imply but do not directly state their expectations.

Another characteristic of autism that challenges many teachers is the student's reliance on visual input rather than auditory input. Teachers skilled in presenting information via lecture, asking frequent questions, or leading discussion groups often find it difficult to accommodate students who acquire information in a predominately visual manner. This is even more challenging when students behave as though certain sounds (like a teacher's voice) are aversive and work to avoid them.

Several specific learning challenges are frequently associated with autism. The first involves difficulty in generalizing skills and knowledge from one set of conditions to another. Generalization problems in students with autism have been described in their social development (Sasso, Garrison-Harrell, McMahon, & Peck, 1998), spontaneous language production (Sundberg & Partington, 1998), self-care and community living skills (Belfiore & Mace, 1994).

A second learning problem involves students' tendency to become prompt dependent. Although many students with autism have the ability to perform useful and productive skills and routines, they often fail to initiate these actions until an adult requests that they do so. Students with autism are *taught* to become prompt dependent. When a student does not know the answer to a question or how to perform a skill, teachers often prompt the student. This allows the student to finish the skill and allows the teacher to provide reinforcement. With repeated practice, the student becomes dependent on the prompt and will not exhibit the desired response unless the prompt is delivered. Prompt dependency can be quite subtle. One of the authors worked with a student who was able to hand the teacher any requested number in a very large array, not by knowing his numbers, but by presenting the last card that the teacher looked at prior to the request. Other students will hover over a matching item or puzzle piece until they see the teacher begin to smile or otherwise prepare to deliver a reinforcer, then will place the item on the table in that location. This has also been seen when students fail to initiate to others (McEvoy et al., 1988) or dress or care for themselves (Lasater & Brady, 1995; Reamer, Brady, & Hawkins, 1998). Clever Hans, the horse reputed to have computational abilities (a standard historical lesson in introduction to psychology textbooks) actually performed his tricks in the same manner.

A third learning characteristic of many students with autism involves "stimulus overselectivity." This involves attending to a particular aspect of a task (e.g., shape or color) to the exclusion of more salient parts of the task. Students who experience overselectivity might follow directions only when given by one person or work only when sitting in a particular chair. This creates obvious difficulties for students who are expected to generalize a skill to novel materials, settings, or people. Students taught vocabulary using pictures, for example, may know all of the farm animals when presented in pictures, but may not be able to identify a real horse. Many teachers have discovered that a student's apparent "knowledge" of a concept was instead a student's selection of an irrelevant feature of the instruction—for example, the student selected a torn corner of the picture card showing a horse rather than the animal itself. A related learning characteristic involves difficulty *prioritizing* incoming stimuli or differentiating relevant from irrelevant information. Students with autism often have difficulty integrating ideas, sequencing, organizing, or generalizing information or tasks to other settings or people.

Many authors have written that students with autism do not respond well to changes in routine. Kanner (1943) saw this as one of the defining features of autism. Yet, structuring choices and teaching choice-making skills have been shown to be effective in promoting positive behavior and academic performance (Dunlap et al., 1994). Clearly, one skill needed by students in contemporary schools is the ability to adjust to frequent interruptions and changes in schedules and routines. Students and their teachers face a series of interruptions by telephone calls, visitors, and loudspeaker announcements. Schedule changes are equally frequent and often are the result of the large numbers of professionals who see students for brief interventions. As noted in Chapter 5, the assumption that students with autism are dependent on routines is better discussed in terms of students' need to *understand* what is asked of them, and *predict* the changes they face in their daily lives. It should come as no surprise that students react poorly when they do not understand why others are changing the people, places, and things around them. This is particularly true when students do not have the communication ability to question the people making these changes. Given this perspective, it is clear that students with autism present challenges to teachers in today's busy (and ever changing) schools.

Finally, perhaps the most paradoxical challenge involving students with autism is the impact they have on many teachers. Their lack of social reciprocity and the presence of problem behavior in many students with autism lessens the willingness of many teachers to persist in interacting with them (Carr, Taylor, & Robinson, 1991). Teachers need reinforcement from students as much as students need reinforcement from teachers if they are to maintain high levels of interaction. Interactions that are punishing for teachers tend to result in shorter and fewer teaching interactions directed toward the student. If a student screams, is aggressive, or ignores a teacher during instruction, that teacher will avoid placing demands on the student, if only to avoid disturbing the other students. At best, the likelihood of problem behavior challenges educators to remain motivated and persist with teaching. At worst, it leads educators to find instructional interactions so risky that they reduce them altogether. Obviously, it is much more reinforcing to teach a student who welcomes the interaction, companionship, and learning that the teacher offers.

Assessing the Learning Characteristics of Students With Autism

Any discussion of assessment should stimulate a guiding question: "What is the purpose of the assessment?" In special education, many professionals use a "shotgun" approach to assessment, expecting one assessment instrument (or procedure) to serve many functions. Assessment functions often have little overlap, however, and tools and procedures designed for one use seldom effectively serve other purposes. There are generally four purposes of assessment:

- establishing eligibility,
- determining instructional need,
- determining instructional progress, and
- determining the overall effectiveness of a program.

Assessment for the purpose of establishing whether any student is *eligible* for special education typically involves a mix of normative and criteria-based instruments. Students are evaluated first to determine whether a disability exists and second to establish whether the disability results in a need for specialized services. Assessment to determine instructional need often consists of learning profiles, family and community inventories, developmental checklists, and curriculum guidelines. To determine a student's instructional progress, educators need direct measures of how quickly and accurately a student learns an instructional objective. Finally, a host of measures are needed to establish the overall effectiveness of a program, including student progress and consumer (student and family) satisfaction. Taylor details the desirable characteristics of autism assessment instruments on the following page.

Assessment instruments designed for students with autism frequently meet the first purpose, establishing eligibility, although they often state their usefulness for instructional planning as well. To establish eligibility, instruments should be designed to provide an objective quantification of the extent to which a student matches eligibility criteria for autism in the DSM-IV. Additionally, some instruments differentiate autism from related disorders. Although each instrument has its strengths, none can be regarded as the *sine qua non* or essential autism assessment and each relies on the clinical judgment and skill of the diagnostician. Wasserman highlights these issues and emphasizes the need for high levels of expertise in the assessment of children with autism on page 279. To date, the instruments most common for establishing eligibility and program planning include the *Gilliam Autism Rating Scale* (GARS), *Childhood Autism Rating Scale* (CARS), *Autism Screening Instrument for Education Planning* (ASIEP), and the *Psychoeducational Profile—Revised* (PEP-R).

The Gilliam Autism Rating Scale (GARS) (Gilliam, 1995) is widely used by public school personnel for autism assessment. The purpose of the instrument is to identify and diagnose autism in children aged 3–22 years old. The GARS consists of 42 items clustered into Stereotyped Behaviors, Communication, Social Interaction, and Developmental Disturbances, based on the DSM-IV diagnostic indicators of autism. Behaviors indicative of autism are scored on a frequency based rating. Users are in-

Assessment of Children with Autism

Ronald Taylor, Ed.D.

Assessment of individuals with autism is a complex, multifaceted endeavor that should be both multidisciplinary and comprehensive. The many unique needs of individuals with autism require input from several different professions. Among the areas that should be addressed in a comprehensive evaluation are cognition, language and communication, social behavior, neurological status, educational needs, independent living skills, and vocational skills. Assessment should be conducted across the lifespan and should be modified as students' individual needs change. Professionals who are routinely involved in the assessment of individuals with autism include educators, psychologists, social workers, speech and language clinicians, audiologists, and medical personnel.

Because of the unique nature of autism, as well as the different levels of severity, assessment must also be individualized. This requires not only the identification of the areas to be assessed but also careful selection of the appropriate instrument or technique. For example, the amount of language is an important variable in determining which measure of cognition should be administered. Similarly, characteristics such as echolalia might interfere with traditional norm-referenced testing so that alternate methods must be used. Clearly, in addition to the standardized tests traditionally used in a psychoeducational evaluation, informal assessment through interviews and direct observation should be a principal component of any total assessment program.

In keeping with best practices, the specific purpose for the assessment must be identified and will help to determine the instruments or techniques used (Taylor, 1997). Among these purposes are diagnosis; development of educational, communication, behavioral, and/or vocational programs; and monitoring of progress. For example, several scales have been developed to aid in the identification of individuals with autism. These scales typically assess behaviors that are used as diagnostic criteria. They do not, however, provide specific information for the development of treatment programs. Two examples of these tests are *The Childhood Rating Scale* (CARS) (Schopler, Reichler, & Renner, 1992) and the *Gilliam Autism Rating Scale* (GARS) (Gilliam, 1995). A brief description of each scale follows.

CARS

The CARS was originally developed for use in the program called Treatment and Education of Autistic and Related Communication Handicapped Children (TEACCH). The CARS attempts to incorporate the components of various definitions and criteria used for the identification of autism, including Kanner's (1943) primary autism features. Individuals are rated on 15 items or areas: relating to people, imitation, emotional response, body use, object use, adaptation to change, visual response, listening response, taste, smell, and touch response and use, fear or nervousness, verbal communication, nonverbal communication, activity level, level and consistency of intellectual response, and general impressions. The scale can be used with children 2 years and up and has adequate technical characteristics.

GARS

The GARS is designed to use with individuals ages 3 through 22. Whereas the CARS does not provide standard scores in a traditional sense, the GARS does. Items for the GARS were based primarily on information from the *Diagnostic and Statistical Manual—4th Edition* (DSM-IV) and the Autism Society of America. The GARS is also easy and quick to administer, requiring only about 10 minutes. The items are grouped according to stereotyped behavior, communication, social interaction, and developmental disturbances.

The majority of instruments used with individuals with autism, however, are not specifically designed for this population. Instruments such as *The Test of Pragmatic Skills*, *The Vineland Adaptive Behavior Scales*, and the *Wechsler Pre-School and Primary Scales of Intelligence—3* are all used with children with autism. As noted previously, however, specific individual characteristics will dictate the most appropriate instrument to use. In many cases, nonverbal assessment is necessary. Newer tests such as *The Comprehensive Test of Non-verbal Intelligence* (Hammill & Wiederholt, 1995), might be appropriate for some children with autism. Also, as noted previously, the assessment should focus on skills that are age-appropriate and functional. As the child gets older independent living skills, social skills, and prevocational/vocational skills should be evaluated.

(continued)

In summary, assessing individuals with autism provides a challenge for the team of individuals involved in the process. Careful planning, communication, and collaboration among the team members is necessary. Decisions about the specific purpose for the assessment and the unique characteristics of the individual being assessed will, to a large extent, dictate the types of procedures and instruments that will be used.

Ronald Taylor, Ed.D., is a Professor in the Department of Exceptional Student Education at Florida Atlantic University in Boca Raton, Florida. He is also the editor of Diagnostique, *the journal of the Council for Educational Diagnostic Services of the Council for Exceptional Children.*

structed to apply ratings of Never, Seldom, Sometimes, and Frequently Observed to the behavioral indicators described in each item within a specific time interval. A sample item that represents the directness of the GARS is, "Repeats words or phrases over and over." Educators can administer the GARS in 5 to 10 minutes.

The technical adequacy of the GARS is based on norms from 1,092 children in 46 states. A full array of standard test statistics are reported and indicate that the GARS meets most of the criteria for technical adequacy for an instrument used for diagnostic purposes (internal consistency for subtests ranged between .88 and .93; test-retest measures were .88). The Likelihood Table restates the probability of a diagnosis of autism and is a very positive feature of the instrument.

The *Childhood Autism Rating Scale* (CARS) (Schopler, Reichler, & Renner, 1992) was developed first as a research instrument and then to evaluate children referred to the TEACCH statewide autism support system in North Carolina. It is now widely used for screening purposes and to establish eligibility. No age range is specified in the manual; however, the demographic information on the norming sample of typically developing children indicates that the majority of the sample was under 5 years old; only 11.4% were over the age of 11 years. The CARS consists of 15 items. Ratings from 1-4 (with intermediate ratings at 1.5, 2.5, and 3.5) are determined and brief notes or observations are provided to help the rater determine an item score. CARS scores can range from 15 to 60, with scores of 15–29.5 considered diagnostically as *nonautistic*, 30–36.5 as *autistic (mild to moderate)*, and 37–60 as *autistic (severe)*. Appropriate cautions are offered to prevent misuse of these single factor scores.

Clinical Skills in the Diagnosis of Autism

Theodore Wasserman, Ph.D.

Describing a uniquely psychological approach to the diagnosis of autism presents me with a significant challenge and quandary. Two descriptive data systems are utilized by psychologists. The first, group data, is most familiar. Psychologists frequently place their faith in the measurement of human behavior utilizing normed and standardized assessment procedures. These normed procedures gather specific individual data based on their relationship to the characteristics of the construct being measured. This method presents two problems when diagnosing autism. The first is that there is poor consensus as to how widely to cast the net when diagnosing autism (i.e., autistic spectrum disorder, regulatory disorder, Asperger's disorder, hyperlexia). The second problem is that the available instruments (i.e., CARS, GARS) often misidentify children as having autism based on the presence of autistic behaviors secondary to a different etiologic factor (i.e., mental retardation).

There is another method of behavioral analysis utilized by psychologists, which evolves analysis of data from a single subject. As a psychologist I have been trained to carefully observe and record data based on the systematic observation of an individual's behavior. I am aware that scientific knowledge involves essentially two paths of inference, inductive and deductive reasoning. "The latter involves drawing inferences from experiences and empirical data" (Franklin, 1999). I believe that, for the present, the diagnosis of autism involves the utilization of a single-subject design comparing observed data with the characteristics of a model of autism that describes the essence of the disorder.

At its core, autism is a social communication disorder. Children with autism avoid interpersonal interaction and display severe language phonemic processing and expressive language disorder. Young children with autism find comfort with the familiar and with routine. They are frequently overwhelmed by environmental stimuli and close down and actively resist its entry into their awareness. The children frequently display hyperactivity, obsessive-compulsive, and Tourette's-like characteristics.

(continued)

To diagnose autism then, I must create an environment that allows a child to demonstrate his or her interaction with the world and provide an environment that allows the child to demonstrate, or not demonstrate, the characteristics described above. The last thing I wish to do therefore is to control the environment in the way I have been taught to create an atmosphere wherein I can collect data consistent with the protocol of a particular testing instrument. On the contrary, what I wish to do is allow children to demonstrate how they organize their worlds and their places within it. My job is to systematically observe this attempt at organization and record data. To do this, I establish a number of sensors:

Free Play: When evaluating a young child (under age 5), I seldom attempt formal and intrusive testing procedures at the beginning of the session. I allow the child and the child's family to enter the testing environment and attempt to organize themselves within it. I frequently talk to the child's caretakers while observing the child's organizational attempts. I look for the following:

1. Does the child demonstrate awareness of the examiner (is he shy, avoidant, inquisitive)? Does the child recognize the examiner at all? Children with autism tend to avoid interpersonal contact, including interpersonal contact with the primary caretaker. Children at the mild end of the spectrum may relate to the primary caretaker but usually only as a "tool" utilized to get objects or to provide basic needs. Episodes of being comforted by the caretaker are infrequently observed and involve establishing physical contact rather than obtaining empathy.

2. Does the child rely on the caretaker to structure the environment or explore on his or her own? Children with autism usually haphazardly explore the environment on their own. If they allow the caretaker to structure an activity, it is usually an activity that is repetitively done, usually in a stereotypic manner. The caretaker has come to rely on this activity as a "babysitter" allowing the caretaker to get other necessary household chores done.

3. Does the child interact with the toys and other play objects in the room (my evaluations are usually done in a room where toys, dolls, and other objects are readily in view and available) or does the child wander about the room? Young children with autism frequently do not interact with toys in the prescribed manner.

4. Does the child share these new experiences with the caretaker? Children with autism do not allow others into their physical, cognitive, or emotional space. They are not good sharers in terms of reciprocity. These children will frequently walk away from a toy if another child starts to play with it.

5. Is the child overwhelmed by the new experience or completely oblivious to it? Overwhelmed children with autism frequently engage in stereotypies such as hand flapping, covering their ears with their hands, or pacing. All of these activities are designed to shut out external input.

6. Is the child interested in exploring at all or is the child so withdrawn from outside stimuli that this new environment is not perceived or interaction with it is not desired? More severely involved children with autism will withdraw from almost all environmental stimuli, limiting their interactions to a few well known objects.

7. If after a while, structuring attempts are provided, does the child accept them or resist them? Children with autism frequently will dramatically resist redirection or change in activities. At other times, they are completely indifferent. Their responses are extreme in either direction.

8. After selecting an object to interact with, does the child play with it or just manipulate it?

(continued)

9. Does the child line things up or attempt to impose compulsive order on things in the room? Obsessive-compulsive characteristics are always present in the behavioral pattern of autistic children. It is one of the main features that differentiates this disorder from the other classes of pervasive developmental disorder (i.e., retardation).

10. Does the child engage in autistic leading to get objects out of reach? This is a major discriminating feature of autism. Children with autism, and almost no one else, take their parents by the hand and lead them to things they want. The parent is treated like a tool rather than a person.

11. Does the child speak? Does the child respond to his or her name? Young children with autism usually do not.

After this phase of data gathering I usually move to establish whether the child can be structured or encouraged to interact with the evaluator. A new group of objects is introduced, frequently items from a standardized battery of developmental skill assessments (e.g., Mullin scales) and an offer of shared interaction is made. If the child is hesitant to interact with me, I will ask another team member (many of my evaluations occur in a transdisciplinary setting) or the caretaker to attempt the interaction. The important thing is to see if the child is willing or capable of demonstrating socially reciprocal interaction, not whether the child can interact with me.

After this phase, I attempt formal developmental assessment of the child to gain a measure of the repertoire of the child's skills. Two of the hallmarks of autism are the language and social deficiencies that pervade the behavior of these children. Frequently, children within the mild to moderate range will self-structure to visually directed tasks, and this performance discrepancy between visual- and auditory-based tasks is an important discriminator between autism and other pervasive developmental disorders. While attempting this assessment, I am also looking for a responsiveness to potential intervention methods (i.e., discrete trial or picture exchange). Frequently, getting the latter information is more important than the former.

After all of the above, I complete a standard checklist (CARS, GARS) hoping to quantify my observations and have the parent complete Form E2 from the Autism Research Society, which I utilize as sort of a second opinion.

I review my observations with the caretakers and complete taking a developmental history that assesses, among other things, the pattern of development that is consistent with autistic spectrum disorder. If I believe I am dealing with autism, I request the parent obtain an EEG and a metabolic workup to rule out competing etiologic possibilities. If all of the above sounds suspiciously like a fancy description of clinical judgment, so be it. Parents frequently ask me if I know after such a short time (no matter how long I actually took to do the assessment) that their child has autism. After observing and assessing thousands of children against the criteria described above, a predictable pattern emerges. You know it when you see it.

Theodore Wasserman, Ph.D., is a neuropsychologist and Director of the Child Development Center at the Richard and Pat Children's Hospital at St. Mary's Medical Center in West Palm Beach, Florida.

Educators can be trained in administration and scoring for the CARS quickly. Unfortunately, many of the technical features of the CARS are below the standards recommended for an instrument appropriate for eligibility decisions (Salvia & Ysseldyke, 1995). Measures for interrater reliability, for instance, are .71, although the test-retest reliability is much stronger at .88. An additional limitation is that item values are computed for the *undifferentiated* population of children (only children from North Carolina) on whom this instrument was standardized, thus limiting the representativeness of the instrument. And although the manual clearly indicates that the CARS is intended as a screening tool (and is adequate for this purpose), it is used extensively as a tool for establishing eligibility. Unfortunately, the widespread use of the CARS may limit access to a full evaluation if children do not meet the 30-point cutoff score for autism eligibility. Since no mention is made of Asperger's disorder, PDD/NOS, and other pervasive developmental disabilities, these children might not be assessed further (a false-negative error) and thus may be declared ineligible for special education even though they have a disability (albeit not autism). The CARS is not an appropriate screening instrument for students suspected of having these disorders.

The *Autism Screening Instrument for Education Planning* (ASIEP) (Krug, Arick, & Almond, 1993) was developed to identify children with autism for public school eligibility and to provide information on which to develop a school-based program. The most widely used element of the ASIEP is the Autism Behavior Checklist (ABC), which yields a general measure of autism. This is also the section of the ASIEP for which significant technical adequacy information is available. The instructional planning sections of this system lack full technical measurement information.

A strength of the ASIEP is the use of direct observation of student performance under standardized conditions. For example, raters are asked to evaluate body part recognition using a prescribed behavioral indicator, "Touch your head." The ASIEP in general, and the ABC in particular, are more appropriate for screening than for diagnostic purposes. It may help some educators supplement their instructional planning. A strength of the screening mode (ABC) is that, if students are not identified as having autism, information is provided that leads to other diagnoses.

The *Psychoeducational Profile—Revised* (PEP-R) (Schopler, Reichler, Bashford, Lansing, & Marcus, 1990) was designed by professionals at TEACCH to gather information for placement and programming for children with autism in preschool and elementary grades. The PEP-R testing protocol allows for a great deal of flexibility in administration to accommodate the heterogeneity of students with autism. The PEP-R is well supported by training tapes, workshops, and assessment kits and materials.

The test statistics necessary to evaluate the instrument's appropriateness for eligibility are not fully presented in the manual, which will concern many diagnosticians. In spite of this, the authors note that PEP-R conforms to the standards set for comprehensive evaluations. Recognizing the potential impact of the limited reliability and validity data, the test authors ask, "Can the PEP-R be used for effective educational and home programming?" (Schopler et al., 1990, p. 85). Their reply is to present the overall success of the TEACCH program (for which the instrument was developed) as an inference of the instrument's suitability.

Summary

Much is written about the *unique* characteristics of autism and the need to assess students and design instructional programs for them based on these assessed autism characteristics (Smith, Slattery, & Knopp, 1993). However, it is essential also to emphasize the need for unique skills, abilities, and attributes of *teachers* of these students. Some teachers, those who are inflexible, less resourceful, or are focused only on immediate demands and student compliance, will not be fully successful in their interactions with these students. These unique learners demand responsive and creative teaching and, in many ways, unique teachers.

DECIDING WHAT TO TEACH

Goal Selection Principles

Because students with autism can be difficult to teach and do not generalize their newly learned skills easily, care should be taken in selecting goals. Over two decades ago, Brown and his colleagues (Brown et al., 1979) delineated a set of principles or guidelines to consider when teachers try to decide the value of the lessons they teach to students with the most difficult learning problems. These principles are exemplified by six guiding questions about curriculum:

1. Will the skill help the student in the current or future environment?
2. Will the skill help the student access more reinforcement in natural settings?
3. Is the skill age-appropriate?
4. Is the skill socially valid?
5. Does the skill enhance special interests and talents of the student?
6. Will this skill assist the student in becoming a productive contributor to his community?

In a now classic paper on instructional programming for students with severe disabilities, Brown, Nietupski, and Hamre-Nietupski (1976) proposed that the curriculum principle central to these guiding questions involved the *criterion of ultimate functioning*. This criterion for selecting instructional goals posed a simple but central question:

If the student could not perform the proposed skill, would another person have to do it *for* the student, or could the task go undone?

The impact of this criterion for selecting curriculum was dramatic. Educators using the logic of the criterion of ultimate functioning refocused their instructional programs to target only the most important life skills for a student, de-emphasizing the selection of assumed developmental prerequisite skills (such as block stacking, puzzle use, and bead stringing) so often found in programs and considered appropriate for young children. Using this criterion and the resultant guiding questions, curricula for students with substantial learning problems have become more functional.

Applying these principles to students with autism, it is obvious that initial skills targeted for acquisition should be age-appropriate functional skills that (a) allow students to be as independent as possible and (b) lead to acceptance and reinforcement in typical settings. These skills are needed by all people, not just students with autism. Skills such as toileting, using utensils, and dressing are prerequisites for successful independent living. If a student cannot perform these skills, another person (usually a family member or paid service provider) will indeed have to perform the skills *for* the student. The ability to move from place to place independently also is consistent with these curriculum principles. Additionally, communication skills, both expressive and receptive, are necessary for social interaction, as well as to solve problems. In addition to these global skills, there are skills that many students need in particular school, home, and community environments. The ability to wait in line crosses community and school settings, but is seldom needed at home. Raising one's hand to ask permission to speak is required in school settings, but not in others. Reading, communicating, and matching to sample are skills that cross all settings. It is important to prioritize skills in terms of their utility to the student before teaching them. Skills that students enjoy, or have a personal interest in, are also relevant when deciding what to teach. High preference, personal interest skills can become leisure activities, an important part of the curriculum. These skills should be identified and supported so that the student has self-selected and sustaining activities. In many cases, such interests (e.g., baseball card collecting or geography information) are the basis for community involvement and friendship. Particularly when students are young, interests and skills that the family finds important or that help the student access leisure activities that the family shares help the student participate more in his family and can lead to increased reinforcement and acceptance in the student's community.

Critical Skills Needed by All Students

Part of a teacher's decision making about what to teach involves listing the skills that are needed by *all* students, regardless of whether they have autism. For students with severe disabilities, these skills are typically referred to as "critical skills" or "critical functions" (Gaylord-Ross & Holvoet, 1985). Critical skills for students with autism do not differ from the skills needed by all students and include:

1. Mobility
2. Self-care
3. Communication
4. Social interaction

Mobility

Mobility training, once the domain of educators of students with vision impairments, has been expanded to a host of community travel skills needed by sighted learners with severe disabilities (Westling & Fox, 1995). Although many students with other disabilities are assumed to need mobility assistance, this skill is often overlooked in students with autism because they typically do not require instruction to walk, run, climb stairs, and so on. Mobility training for these students might best be described as "destination training" or "route training."

If students are to participate in normalized community vocational, recreational, and domestic routines as adults, they must learn to become mobile within and between these environments as children. For young children, this might involve learning to find a classroom from the bus area, locating a chair or desk, or moving between learning centers within a classroom. As middle school-aged children, finding (and returning from) the library, gym, cafeteria, and other classrooms become mobility targets. Secondary-aged students might need to learn how to access a community work site, recreation center, convenience store, or public park using public transportation. Some students have no difficulty following a route per se, but have tremendous difficulty when a familiar route is noisy or crowded. For these students, the route is secondary to the more important mobility target of safe and controlled completion of the route. It is important for teachers to remember that these are teachable skills, and their mastery is critical to life improvement for students with autism.

Self-care

Nearly all students with autism need to learn or refine self-care skills. A major proportion of the instructional program for young children may be devoted to self-care; secondary students might need less emphasis on this. Self-care skills are often grouped into categories including:

1. Hygiene and toileting;
2. Dressing;
3. Home care (maintaining clothes, dishes, living environment); and
4. Food preparation.

Teachers should make an important distinction between self-care skills that need to be *taught* versus skills that need to be *strengthened*. Younger students often need direct instruction to help them learn the routines involved in putting on clothing, washing their bodies, and so on. Older students, on the other hand, may have these skills in their repertoires but not *use* the skills, and require supports other than reteaching to be able to use the skill reliably. This distinction has important implications for how teachers will teach. For example, Gast, Wellons, and Collins (1994) provided excellent descriptions of instructional programs designed to teach students home and community safety skills, and Reamer et al. (1998) designed a video-based teaching program to help parents teach toothbrushing, self-feeding, and dressing. On the other hand, Lasater and Brady (1995) used videos and self evaluation procedures to teach secondary-aged students with autism to become fluent in shaving, preparing lunch, doing laundry, and caring for their clothes, skills already in their repertoire that were never performed independently.

Communication

Communication deficits will be prominent in virtually all students with autism. Students with autism to some degree, unlike students with other significant limitations in communicative ability, often have the basic prerequisites for communication but are limited by social or cognitive disabilities in the use of or motivation to use their communicative abilities. Typical social and instructional interactions may not offer a sufficiently strong set of motivational factors to promote communication. Special techniques and teaching behaviors are required to optimize the communicative possibilities of the classroom. Functional demands on the child provide a host of naturally occurring communication opportunities that must be exploited. In addition, teachers must be comfortable with the unconventional communicative attempts of their students and be prepared to shape these attempts into more conventional and efficient forms. Increasingly, communication enhancement must be programmed across all environments. This requires educators to recruit parents as partners and to share essential skills with them. Finally, communication deficits are now recognized as the basis for most severe problem behavior. Teachers are forced to establish and to consistently implement a functional communication system for each learner. Obviously, this should be done before the student exhibits problem behaviors. If problem behaviors are already in place, teaching communication will be more difficult.

Social Interactions

As important as communication may be, it is now widely considered secondary to core deficits in social interaction and social perception. For most persons, social perceptions of others provide strong motivators to communicate or to display a good profile of self-care skills. Social benefits are a strong incentive to use mobility skills. In the absence of a social motivation, the desire to learn to use these and many other skills is reduced. Increasing social interactions becomes central to the use of all other skills. For social capabilities to be useful, they must be generalized to all relevant environments with other people and over time. Problems of misperception, nonrecognition, and faulty training and reinforcement all complicate the task for educators (Sasso et al., 1998). When educational programs are arranged so that students with autism have only other students with autism as their natural school social partners, the tasks are further complicated.

Getting Information Needed to Select Goals and Objectives

It can be difficult to determine appropriate instructional programs for students with autism, and educators should not try to do this alone. Information and the perspectives of the many persons significant to students should be gathered, and the IEP should be used as the planning mechanism for decision making.

The IEP is the document that acts as the decision-making framework for selecting the goals and skills that a student could reasonably learn within a year's time. The IEP is created with input from people who know the student best, including parents, teachers, and professionals who have worked with the student. The IEP, although not a contract, is a formal document that guides instruction.

More informally, talking with parents and former teachers can provide a wealth of information. Parents know, more than anyone else, how their child functions within the family structure. Skills that parents find important take a high priority when deciding what to teach. Parents are not the only family members, however, and input from siblings can help in identifying skills that should be taught. One of the authors, for example, discovered that a helpful family skill that was recommended by siblings involved asking an older brother to help start up a computer and software program. Once the student learned to ask her sibling for this help, daily afternoon disruptions were completely eliminated.

Talking with former teachers in an informal setting can provide information regarding the student's ability to function in the classroom. The information that an incoming student will transition easily if given a 5-minute warning but will tantrum if abruptly told to move to another activity can make the difference between a successful and unsuccessful school day for both student and teacher.

As often as possible, student preferences should be considered when selecting instructional targets. A student who dislikes reading fiction may be given more factual information, such as a textbook. Students who have difficulty with creative writing or in making inferences of character motivation based on reading a chapter may be allowed to complete an assignment by giving more factual information. If state or local curriculum standards call for mastery of a nonpreferred format, more individualized and supportive instruction can be provided. This could be as simple as allowing the student to work on preferred materials *after* completing nonpreferred work.

Although annual planning is required for the IEP, longer term planning (3–5 years) is very useful in selecting goals and objectives. Comprehensive long-term plans, such as MAPS (Vandercook, York, & Forest, 1989) or TEAMS (Campbell, Campbell, & Brady, 1998) hold promise for highlighting the skills that will be most important in future environments. Unfortunately, a relatively small percentage of students have these plans in the middle and high school grades, and an even smaller percentage have such plans in the elementary grades. Instructional programs for students with autism would be dramatically improved if all students with autism had carefully developed long-range plans.

Organizing Instruction: An Integrated Curriculum

One of the hallmarks of autism is a pattern of splinter skills—skills that are above the level of other skills, rather than a pattern of skills that fall on approximately the same developmental level. When deciding what to teach a student, it is important to decide how the lessons will be organized to avoid further splintering, and to promote the use of critical skills across a student's daily activities and routines. For example, some students learn language skills during one lesson, but are not required to *use* those skills during other lessons and routines. Rather than selecting single skills, educators should build skill practice into multiple routines, lessons, and settings.

Students with significant learning problems such as autism require a curriculum that actively integrates learning, where important instructional targets are built into the student's goals and routines throughout the day. Models for integrating curriculum are not unique to special education. In many general education classes, teachers use "thematic instruction" to accomplish this objective. Although instructional integration is a *preferred practice* in many areas of education (e.g., among reading teachers), it is a *critical practice* for students with autism. For example, a student learning to use a self-control procedure involving, "Wait for 5 seconds before asking" would have opportunities (and direct instruction) for that skill built into academics, transitions, and self-care routines. Figure 8–1 presents a curriculum planning matrix form; a sample for a secondary aged student is provided in Figure 8–2.

HOW TO TEACH STUDENTS WITH AUTISM

Making decisions about *how to teach* a skill to a student with autism requires educators to organize their instruction and deliver their lessons in

Curriculum Matrix

Name: _____

Objective 1							
Objective 2							
Objective 3							
Objective 4							
Objective 5							
Objective 6							
Objective 7							

Figure 8–1. Curriculum planning matrix.

an effective manner. If a student is to effectively use the new skill in school, family, and community settings, the way teachers organize and deliver instruction should match the learning characteristics of a student with autism. Organization for instruction refers to the process of getting ready to teach. Delivering instruction involves manipulations of the teacher's instructional interactions that are most likely to produce accurate student responses.

Curriculum Matrix

Name: _____

	Home Room	English	Social Studies	Lunch	Business Practices I
Objective 1 *Self Care (Checks ABCs of personal appearance)*	*Use common restroom.*	*Self-check before entering room.*	*Self-check before entering room.*	*Check clothing for food stains, use common restroom.*	*Self-check before entering room.*
Objective 2 *Initiates Social Interactions with Adults*	*Greet teacher upon entering classroom.*	*Greet teacher upon entering classroom.*	*Greet teacher upon entering classroom.*	*Smile at familiar teachers.*	*Greet teacher upon entering classroom.*
Objective 3 *Reads and Follows Written Directions; Identifies Problem Words*		*Use teacher provided advance organizer. Use highlighter in workbook for new vocabulary words.*	*Use teacher provided advance organizer. List any unknown words for tutor session.*		*Follow written instructions at computer work station. Keep dictionary program active. List unknown words for tutor session.*
Objective 4 *Organizes and Maintains Materials*	*Check and update personal schedule book.*	*Place homework in front of notebook. Bring English book and write homework assignment.*	*Place homework in front of notebook. Bring Social Studies book and write homework assignment.*	*Separate lunch money from other money.*	*Place homework in front of notebook. Bring business workbook and write homework assignment.*

Figure 8–2. Sample curriculum planning matrix for a secondary-aged student with autism.

Organizing for Instruction

Organizing lessons includes evaluating the strengths of the student and arranging and structuring the classroom environment (and the learning task itself) to facilitate learning. Organizing for instruction includes using visual structure, developing personal schedules for individual students, establishing work systems, creating work and nonwork areas in the classroom, assisting parents as tutors, and a host of other preparatory tasks. Organizing for instruction is perhaps the most challenging task a teacher faces. Although well-trained paraeducators can carry out many other teacher roles, organizing for instruction can only be done by a teacher. Students with autism challenge educators because they can be taught in the entire range of school and classroom settings. In autism-only classes, overt organizing and structuring modifications are common; in a general education class, the structure needed for the student to be successful will have to be tailored to that setting.

Using Visual Structure

Because most students with autism have relative strength in understanding visual instructions (rather than an auditory input), much of a lesson's organization should focus on providing visual structure and visual cues to the student. Structuring the environment effectively enables a student to move from place to place in the classroom with minimal disruption and to succeed in each area.

Visual structure involves providing cues in the environment by positioning and organizing furniture, materials, and information so that the method for successfully completing the task is obvious to the student *without the need for verbal information.* The use of visual structure extends from the overall classroom environment to individual tasks and lessons so that a student knows what is expected by going into an area or looking at a task. The visual structure of the classroom and the learning task should visually answer the following questions:

- Where do you want me to go?
- What do you want me to do?
- How will I know when I'm done?
- What do I do then?
- What happens if I do it?
- What happens if I don't do it?
- What happens if I don't know how to do it?

Visual structure helps students prioritize the most important stimuli in a classroom or a lesson. An effective visual structure highlights the most important information in an attractive format and in the area of the room in which the task should be conducted. Individual schedules, area labels, class rules, and overall classroom schedules can all be made interesting, informational, and appropriate. Noninstructional visuals (such as bulletin boards) can be placed toward the back of the room or near the break area for enjoyment during free time activities. Visual structure in an inclusive setting will be more subtle. A student's desk might be the obvious location for independent work. A daily schedule might be placed on one corner of the desk, or even in a student's notebook. Visual structuring of the tasks might include an outline, an advanced organizer, a transcript of the day's lecture, or a list of work to be accomplished that class period. Figure 8–3 shows one example of a room designed to highlight the visual arrangement for secondary students.

Developing Personal Schedules

A helpful application of visual structure for many students is the use of a personal schedule. Individual or personal daily schedules are used to help a student visually sequence activities (Schopler & Mesibov, 1995). Using objects, labels, or pictures, the personal schedule is a visual representation of the series of activities or events that make up a student's day. The schedule can cover part of the day or all of the day, depending on the student's needs. Personal schedules might be located in a common (transition) area (in a special education class) but do not necessarily require alterations to the classroom. In a more inclusive setting, schedules can be kept in a student's memo book, day planner, or pocket.

High School Vocational Classroom

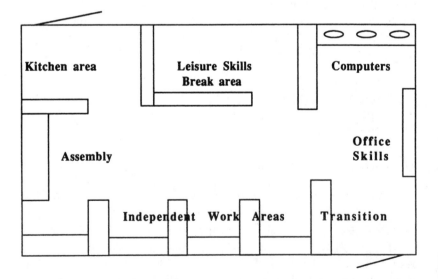

Figure 8–3. High school classroom arrangement that maximizes visual structure.

Most students must be directly taught how to use a schedule. When used regularly, visual schedules increase the level of student independence. Each component of the schedule is placed in a left-to-right or top-to-bottom order so that the student is able to use the same visual strategy for understanding the schedule sequence as a standard work sequence. The personal schedule visually answers "Where do you want me to go?" (to the designated area) and "What do I do then?" (do the work that is indicated on the work schedule). The use of personal schedules increases predictability of daily activities and reduces prompt dependence. Such predictability increases task accuracy and completion and lessens disruptive behavior associated with breaks in routine. Mac-Duff, Krantz, and McClannahan (1993) demonstrated that students with autism exhibit fewer maladaptive behaviors when a visual schedule is in place.

What do personal schedules look like? Most people without autism have "things to do" lists and personal notebooks. Personal schedules, conceptually, are the same. A personal schedule for home might include: make bed, take shower, wash hair, brush teeth, dress, eat breakfast, and go to bus stop. A schedule for classroom could include: Period 1: math, Period 2: English, Period 3: music, and so on. Figure 8–4 shows one example of a simple visual schedule designed for an elementary student.

Although many educators would intuitively plan to fade the use of schedules (and other forms of visual structure), it may not be necessary to do so. Many students become much more independent when their behavior is cued by some type of *permanent prompt*. Visual structure and personal schedules are examples of permanent prompts; if using a prosthetic device (such as a schedule) increases independent functioning, it need *not* be removed at a later point in time. This is similar to an educator's decision not to remove a wheelchair from a student who is unable to walk or to not remove a Braille writer from a student who is blind. If a student with autism needs a small stack of pictures of foods to support her ability to purchase these items from a store, it should be considered a necessary assistive device. Many students can learn to develop their own visual schedules, thus providing a lifelong skill.

Establishing Work Systems

All learners must be given a system for managing the tasks assigned to them. The hallmark of instruction that is well organized is set by Schopler and Mesibov (1995) who described "work systems" used at TEACCH, a state-wide autism learning and support project in North Carolina. Work systems establish visual clarity in tasks so that students can complete tasks accurately and with a minimum of verbal information or requests for assistance. Schopler and Mesibov (1995) advocated consistent stimulus formats (e.g., "left to right" and "top to bottom") so that

Visual Schedule for Justin

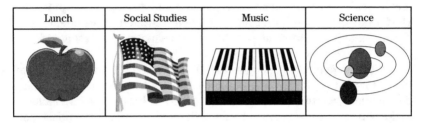

Independent Work	Computer	Playground	English

Lunch	Social Studies	Music	Science

Figure 8–4. Sample personal visual schedule for Justin, an elementary-aged student with autism.

students learn a strategy that can be used consistently to approach any new task. This procedure answers the questions, "What do you want me to do?" and "How do I know when I'm done?"

For academic work, a work system suitable for separate or inclusive settings might involve a list of written assignments and tasks placed in a labeled folder or a prepared assignment with the problems to be done highlighted with a yellow marker. A list of math problems and the pages on which they can be found is another method of providing visual structure for a student. In a vocational setting, a work system might involve a list of activities for the student to check off when completed. A vocational sequence might include activities such as: get your time card, put your time card in the machine, put your lunch in the refrigerator, go to your work area, and check your work schedule. These can be as simple as representational objects on a board or as subtle as a list of activities in order in a day planner.

Creating Work and Nonwork Areas in the Classroom

Given the difficulty many students have in identifying relevant cues, the physical environment of a classroom should be structured in ways that highlight the areas where work *should* and *should not* be done. One way is to have the room arranged into curriculum and leisure areas and teach students to rotate among these areas as their tasks are completed. In this arrangement, students work on math, science, or social studies (or self-care, community, and domestic skills) in specific areas of the classroom. Once the assigned work is completed, the student moves to another curriculum area or to a leisure area (e.g., a computer, art, or reading center) until the next subject lesson. Rotation between areas can be accomplished through verbal cues or through independent student scheduling.

Another way to structure the classroom is to have independent work areas where students work in their own designated areas on a specific sequence of tasks. These areas could be developed using individual desks or study carrels. Once tasks are completed, students check their personal schedules and move to a break or leisure area. The break area may or may not have other students in it, depending on whether other students have completed their assigned tasks. The break area should have both solitary and small group leisure activities so that students have a variety of choices. After the break, the student checks his or her schedule and returns to the work area (Schopler, Mesibov, & Hearsey, 1995). This could be adapted to general education classes by allowing students to work at their desks, then move to a computer or reading area until the next transition.

Helping students discriminate between work and nonwork areas helps distractible students to stay engaged in their work (or rest) tasks. Work and rest areas can be made as large or small as necessary, and visual access to the rest of the classroom can be controlled through the use of partitions and seating arrangements. If visual distractions are minimized, students will complete their work in a timely manner and proceed to a group area for break or leisure skills activities.

Classrooms for students with autism should also have a "transition area." A transition area is a central location to which students go after tasks are completed to check their personal schedules and see what activity is next. The purpose of teaching students to use a transition area is to reduce the ambiguity that often accompanies task completion. This ambiguity often produces preservative wandering or transition difficulties. By proceeding to a transition area after completing a task, a student learns to develop a routine of seeking out the next scheduled activity; all transitions are made from this area. In a more inclusive setting, a student who has difficulty with transitions can be asked to "check your schedule." If an actual place is still needed to ease transitions, that area might be in a space next to a teacher's desk or near another teacher work space.

Assisting Parents as Tutors

In Chapter 9 we noted that there are many models of family and professional interaction. One such model involves family members *co-teaching* particular lessons along with educators. For those who desire to play this role, parents and other family members can become very effective tutors. In the absence of special training and instructional methods, however, parents are likely to use a mixed bag of techniques, sometimes even resorting to coercive interactions. Some might even dwell on errors so often that the child becomes discouraged. Further, without a simple progress monitoring system, learner and parent frustration is almost inevitable.

If parents are interested in becoming home tutors, four guidelines should be followed by educators as they "translate" their instructional methods for use in students' homes. First, parents should be given the *opportunity to select* the instructional targets they believe they can realistically implement. Second, the student should *already be making progress* on this skill at school so that family tutoring involves building fluency or supporting generalization of a skill rather than initial acquisition. Third, home-based instruction should be *presented in brief segments* so that home does not take on the social characteristics of school. Finally, student *progress should be evaluated*, using a simple but direct data collection system.

One such model involves a parent tutoring program designed to strengthen students' reading skills. Although many home tutoring programs for students with autism target daily living activities, many of these students can become competent readers. Duvall, Delquadri, and Hall (1996) developed a program for nonautistic students, Parents as Reading Tutors (PART), to supplement the school's reading program. PART uses brief (11-15 minute) daily parent tutoring sessions, and involves simple instructional delivery and progress monitoring. PART consists of several easily understood practices:

1. Parents present a series of reading passages and record the number of words read correctly and the number of words read incorrectly per minute by the student.
2. Brief daily tutoring is initiated. The child reads a short passage aloud for 4 minutes. The parent records the end point and any errors made, then asks the child to read it again. On the second reading, the parent points to any error word and says it correctly. The child is asked to say the word and then to read the entire sentence. No other instruction is provided but praise is provided for success on error sentences. (Parents are asked to use a timer to provide just 7 minutes of tutoring for first and second graders and 10 minutes for children grades 3 and above.)
3. Comprehension is checked and enriched. Parents are directed to ask who, what, when, where, and why questions and to praise correct answers. For errors, parents provide a clear

correct answer, and ask the question again, praising correct second responses.

4. Reading rate is assessed after each reading session. Parents set a timer for 1 minute and ask the child to read aloud. The parent marks corrects and errors and notes them on a simple graph.

5. Last, a measure of weekly progress is determined by having the child read for a 1-minute period, similar to the daily rate assessment, on untutored materials. These data are similarly graphed and should show progress in generating new reading skills.

Home-based supports, including tutoring, must be simple to be effective. Family tutoring helps students extend their learning by increasing students' opportunities to respond (Hall, Delquadri, Greenwood, & Thurston, 1982) and by increasing the number of skilled people who intervene with the student (Duvall, Delquadri, Elliot, & Hall, 1992; Greenwood, Delquadri & Hall, 1989). This work is in its infancy with students with autism, but the simplicity and power of the intervention holds great promise for this field.

Although the *academic skill tutoring* described by Duval et al. (1996) has not been widely applied in autism, parents have been in the forefront as tutors for their preschool-aged children. The popularity and success of the home-based intensive early intervention programs typified by Lovaas (1981, 1987) have strengthened the concept of parent tutors. Lovaas' research indicated a need for training all of the people in the child's environment to provide a seamless intervention. Although many parents may not do "table time" teaching, they are the main generalization agents for the child, working with educators and other professionals to bring the skills from the one-on-one discrete trial sessions to the real world. In some areas, parents have formed support groups, providing information and training to educators, other parents, and paraprofessionals. Whatever the level of their involvement, parents are an integral part of the instructional process for students with autism.

Delivering Instruction

Once the classroom, tasks, and routines are organized and visually structured, decisions must be made regarding how the teacher will deliver the lesson to a student. Several methods of instructional delivery can be successful in teaching skills to students with autism. These methods include discrete trial teaching, using group formats, changing the levels of assistance, using incidental teaching, using time delay, task analyzing instruction, using precision teaching (PT), teaching students to generalize, using errorless and match-to-sample formats, and using permanent prompts.

Discrete Trial Teaching

Discrete trial teaching is a methodology of instruction that research consistently shows to be one of the most effective and efficient ways to teach new skills. Discrete trial instruction is part of the tradition of applied behavior analysis and is based on experimental research (Skinner, 1991). Lovaas (1981, 1987) successfully applied this methodology for young children with autism. Since then, it has been used in intensive behavioral home programs (Maurice, 1996) and in classrooms and research sites world-wide.

A "trial" or learning opportunity is "discrete" when it has a specific beginning and end. The process of giving a cue, observing the student's response, and presenting a correction or reinforcer comprises one discrete trial. Discrete trial teaching is most effectively performed in a one-on-one format, although it can be conducted successfully in group settings.

A discrete trial format is most appropriate for acquisition level skills. In the discrete trial procedure, a cue is given to the student to engage in the behavior to be taught (e.g., giving the student the verbal cue, "Draw a circle around the right answer."). Students who have severe deficits in receptive language may need a gestural cue, such as a sign or a picture, to accompany the verbal direction. Once the cue is provided, the student makes a response or is assisted in making a correct response. The student is also reinforced for responding correctly, although the criterion for reinforcement might require that the student respond correctly to several trials prior to obtaining reinforcement.

Discrete trials are usually taught in a series in the initial stages. Often, *massed trials* of 15–30 trials per lesson are used to teach a skill. Other times, two or three skills are taught in a *distributed format* where a few trials of each skill are interspersed throughout the lesson or the day. The success or failure at each trial is recorded, and ongoing assessment of the data determines whether any changes are needed. If a student does not learn a skill, changes need to be made in the assessment of prerequisite skills, the level of language used, or the amount or type of reinforcers. Data typically are collected after each trial.

Once the student has mastered the skill, the level of reinforcement is thinned until it approximates that found in the natural environment. There are many schedules of reinforcement that can be used in classrooms. An examination of a text devoted to behavioral techniques will give the teacher an extensive repertoire of schedules to use.

As the student gains mastery in the skill, the skills can be *embedded* into the daily functioning of the classroom. A student who has learned to respond to his name by making eye contact in a discrete trial teaching format can be expected to respond to his name in the classroom. Academic tasks can be placed in different areas of the classroom using different materials. One or two tasks using these materials would replace the massed-trial format.

Using Group Formats

Many teachers believe that the only direct instruction they can provide to students with autism is in a one-to-one format. Although one-to-one instruction is desirable on occasion, it is not necessary for many students' instructional programs and indeed has unintended side effects if used too frequently. For students with autism, these negative effects include prompt dependence, increased difficulty in generalizing skills learned in one-to-one instruction, and missed opportunities to learn to interact with peers (Kamps, Walker, Maher, & Rotholz, 1992; Munk, Van Laarhoven, Goodman, & Repp, 1998). Most students with autism must *learn how to* interact in a group before group formats can be used effectively (Alberto et al., 1980; Reid & Favell, 1984).

Gaylord-Ross and Holvoet (1985) summarized three group instruction formats appropriate for students with autism and other severe disabilities. The format most familiar to general educators involves *choral responding.* A teacher delivering a lesson in which the students respond to a teacher question (or cue) in unison is an example of choral responding. Because many general education students do not respond to this format, it is not surprising that many students with autism also do not participate in choral group lessons. For students in (or preparing for) general education classes, however, direct instruction in how to respond to this format, combined with opportunities to practice, are needed.

The second group instruction format described by Gaylord-Ross and Holvoet (1985) involves *interactive group instruction.* An interactive group format involves a teacher question (or cue) delivered to the group (or some members of the group), followed by peer-to-peer interaction. For example, a teacher might ask the group to, "Line up your rulers parallel to the Greenwich Mean line on the student's map on your left." Student participation in this group format involves (a) teacher-to-group mands, (b) peer-to-peer mands and responses, and (c) teacher feedback to the group *and* individual students.

Finally, Gaylord-Ross and Holvoet (1985) described their third group format as a *one-to-one in a group* (or concurrent individualized) format. This format provides features of both individualized and small group instruction. During a lesson involving an ant farm, for example, a teacher might form a group of eight students. Each student has specific objectives, some of which might *differ* substantially. Gary, a student with autism, might be learning to convert singular nouns to their plural forms, while Katie and two others are learning to describe extended family relationships. The teacher can teach and elicit information from each student individually while maintaining this group activity.

Finally, we note that effective teachers typically alter their instructional procedures, including their use of group instruction formats. As Munk et al. (1998) noted, the research on the efficacy of group instruction is unequivocal; only the willingness of teachers to experiment, modify, and adopt these procedures remains a question.

Changing the Levels of Assistance

Using different levels of assistance can help the student with autism to learn new skills. Levels of assistance can be physical, gestural, pictorial, or verbal and can be used in a most-to-least or least-to-most format.

The most-to-least format begins with whatever level of assistance is necessary to help the student respond correctly. For some students, this may involve hand-over-hand assistance for a student who is learning to write letters or an initial physical manipulation of the student's hand to position it correctly on the pencil. Other students may not need physical assistance, but may only require *gestural* assistance, which may include pointing at the top left hand corner of the paper to orient the student where to begin writing. *Pictorial* prompts, particularly helpful for students with autism, might include showing a picture of the student producing written letters. The least intensive prompt is verbal, where the teacher may remind the student to cross the "t" in a word.

The *most-to-least* format allows for few errors, since a level of assistance is provided to ensure correct responding. Many opportunities for reinforcement are available, because the student is reinforced for any responding above the designated level of assistance. In other words, if the student is expected to write his or her name with gestural assistance, the student will receive reinforcement if the name is written independently or with verbal, gestural, or pictorial assistance. The student would not receive reinforcement if physical assistance was required. Although this format maximally supports the student until the skill is well established, the student with autism is likely to become prompt dependent unless the level of assistance is faded as soon as possible. Some educators use a fifth level of assistance, *shadowing*, for students prone to prompt dependence. To shadow, a teacher might place his hand parallel to but several inches away from the student's hand, then move in synchrony with the student as she writes a letter. Shadowing has been a helpful step for students who are unsuccessful moving from physical to other prompts.

The *least-to-most* assistance format allows for more errors, but is less likely to facilitate prompt dependence. This format begins with verbal assistance (e.g., "Make sure that you put a capital letter at the beginning of your name"). The next level of assistance, *pictorial*, might involve giving the student a picture of the capital letter; a *gestural assist* might be to point to the capital letter in the alphabet above the board. The maximum level of assistance, *physical*, would be to assist the student in making the capital letter using hand-over-hand assistance. Because error responses are as likely to be learned as correct responses with repetition, care should be taken before using this format to ensure that errors are few and correct responses are highly reinforced.

Using Incidental Teaching

Incidental teaching is a valuable way of incorporating practice opportunities into a naturally occurring situation. First described by Hart and Risley (1968) with language instruction, incidental teaching has also been referred to as milieu, naturalistic, and mand-model teaching. The basic tactic of incidental teaching requires that a teacher "set up" a situation in which a student can see and request a desirable object or activity, then ask the student to use a form of language that the teacher has selected as an instructional target to gain access to the object or activity. Jones and Warren (1991) described three elements in an incidental teaching sequence: (a) the student initiates a communication, (b) the adult requests an elaboration of the request, and (c) the adult reinforces the elaboration, typically by providing access to the referent indicated by the student. If the student does not produce the instructional target, the adult then *models* the correct behavior.

Although this instructional format appears "incidental," the adult's teaching behavior is highly structured and planned. Incidental teaching can take place in virtually any setting but has been used most often at free play or activity times. For example, a student with verbal skills may need access to water to clean a paint brush. The student may stand near a sink and gesture for help. The teacher, having remained near the sink (and having set up the situation in advance), might say, "Tell me what you need." The child might then respond, "Help, please" and the teacher would then praise this speech and quickly provide access to the sink. The form of language needed to gain this access is the student's instructional target and is determined in advance by the teacher and IEP team.

Adult responsiveness to child initiations is critical to the success of incidental teaching. Sensitivity to the student's performance level and an ongoing effort to raise the level of language for each student is also essential. In any one instance, it may be easier for the adult to "read" the child's behavior or accept his or her minimal communication, and then provide what the child wants. However, such overaccommodation or detrimental teaching robs the child of a natural and perfectly contextualized learning opportunity. Professionals will need to train and monitor paraeducators and other adults in the routine use of incidental teaching.

Using Time Delay

Time delay is used to structure the amount of time between a teacher's cue for a student to engage in a target behavior and, when needed, the delivery of a prompt. When teaching for acquisition, prompts often are provided immediately after the teacher cue or request. This increases the chances that the student will correctly perform the skill. As the student learns the skill, the teacher systematically lengthens the time between the cue and the prompt. This increased time effectively reduces (or fades) prompts and is accomplished gradually with the student continuing to perform the task successfully. Several variations of this time delay tactic can be used including a *progressive delay* (small but steady lengthening of the delay) or a *constant delay*. In constant delay, the teacher prompts immediately only during the earliest phase of instruction, then shifts to one fixed delay interval. This may be useful for interactive activities or when the nature of the task logically demands a swift response for success.

Time delay might be used for a student with autism who has moderate to severe limitations in communicating a choice of lunch items. The teacher may present a variety of pictorial representations of the available choices and cue the student by saying, "Ted, what do you want for lunch?" After a number of days in which the teacher moved the child's hand between the array of choices without any delay (a delay of 0 s), the teacher now waits 3 seconds before providing the prompt (a constant delay of 3 s). Based on the student's success, the delay interval can be lengthened gradually. As with incidental teaching, time delay requires skill and effort on the part of the adult. Professionals may find it necessary to carefully describe the technique to paraprofessionals and others and to specify how time delay is to be used for an individual student.

Task Analyzing Instruction

Skill in task analysis is one of the hallmarks of a good teacher. Task analysis involves breaking a complex skill into its constituent parts for the purpose of maximizing learner acquisition of the skill. Bailey and Wolery (1989) noted that task analysis is both a *process* and a *product*. As a process, task analysis is a detailed analysis of a larger goal so that it can be broken down into manageable objectives that can be taught successfully. As a product, a task analysis yields a written plan or task sequence to guide teaching of the skill. Both process and product aspects of task analysis are essential when teaching students with autism. In most classrooms, the teacher will be assisted by other adults. These adults should follow the written task analysis developed by the teacher when working with a student.

In general, each step constitutes a discrete behavior and the completion of one step will usually provide a cue to initiate the next step. The actual number of steps and specification within each may differ based on the current and prerequisite skills of the learner and the time, resources, and skill of the educator. Cooper, Heron, and Heward (1987) offered five general methods for validating a task analysis. First, competent persons and their behavior when performing a target task can be analyzed, and the sequence of steps they follow becomes the basis for the task analysis. Second, persons with expertise in the task can be asked to specify the steps necessary for successful completion of the task. The third approach calls for the teacher to perform the task under conditions similar to those in which instruction will occur and to delineate each step in the process. A fourth method is to consider the temporal sequence of the tasks. Finally, a task can be conceptualized in terms of the degree of difficulty of each separate response. Easy tasks are taught first, and more difficult tasks taught later. (This strategy is not appropriate for skills that must be performed in a fixed sequence—like shaving.)

Many self-care and functional skills are fairly easy to task analyze. To teach students to wash and dry their hands, for example, a teacher might analyze this task by performing the skills and then writing down each step. This could be done with the help of a paraeducator. Some steps would have a clear termination (e.g., turning on the water results in water coming out of the faucet), whereas other steps may require the teacher to add a counting or other timing strategy (e.g., to determine how long students should rub their hands together with the soap). Successful acquisition of each step should be noted and recorded to show progress and guide future teaching.

Finally, note that task analysis is equally appropriate for teacher and student behavior. If a student would learn a skill best by practicing the entire skill each time (for example, flushing a toilet), it is best to task analyze the level of assistance provided by the teacher. The target objective might be, "The student will flush the toilet" and the task analysis might then appear as a most-to-least prompting hierarchy. This would involve an analysis of the *condition under which the lesson is presented* such as:

1. With finger-to-hand touch as assistance;
2. With pictorial cues as assistance;
3. With intermittent hand shadowing as assistance;
4. Without assistance.

For skills where the entire task might overwhelm a student, delivery of the lesson might work best if the student works on only a piece of the whole skill, adding mastered steps to the sequence (in either a forward or backward chaining format). For example, the target objective might be: "The student will shave his face with an electric razor" with the following task analysis (adapted from Lasater & Brady, 1995):

1. Shave right and left cheek;
2. Shave cheeks and chin;
3. Shave cheeks, chin, and neck;
4. Shave cheeks, chin, neck, and upper lip;
5. Shave cheeks, chin, neck, and upper lip, and trim sideburns.

Finally, some skills are most easily taught by teaching different actions as the different steps in a task analysis. For example, a task analysis for completing a meal for a young child might involve communicating food preference, communicating the order of food and drink presentation, eating different parts of the meal, requesting additional servings, and indicating that the child is finished (Reamer et al., 1998). Teaching each step separately allows for frequent trials distributed throughout the day, then a synthesis of those skills in context when needed as part of the meal activity.

Using Precision Teaching

Precision teaching (PT) is an instructional program originally developed for students who need academic supports. For example, Beck (1981) reported dramatic improvement of instruction for students at the Sacajewa Elementary School in all basic skills, the ability to use skills over time (maintenance), and students' ability to use a new skill in a variety of situations. A teacher who uses PT typically follows 10 steps when planning and delivering students' lessons. These steps include:

1. Carefully select a skill based on direct student skill assessment, usually with performance measured in 1-minute timings.
2. Select or develop a *probe* sheet to permit efficient assessment of progress. A sample probe for basic addition facts developed by a district is provided in Figure 8–5.
3. Establish an efficient *routine for timing* the student's performance. The routine should maximize student responding and minimize the punishing aspects of error correction.
4. Chart the student's performance data on a "standard behavior chart" using PT display conventions. An example of a standard chart is found in Figure 8–6.
5. The teacher uses *patterns* of performance data to make decisions. Changes to student lessons are guided by research-validated *decision rules*.

ORANGE COUNTY PUBLIC SCHOOLS
PRECISION TEACHING PROJECT
ORLANDO, FLORIDA

OCPS

see-write

(Sums 0-9)

```
 3   4   6   0   1   2   1   5   4   4   3   9   5   2   1   7   3   3
+1  +4  +0  +8  +1  +6  +6  +3  +1  +5  +3  +0  +2  +2  +7  +0  +6  +2    18

 3   3   0   2   6   4   8   2   6   8   4   1   5   7   3   6   5   1
+5  +3  +9  +1  +2  +2  +1  +0  +1  +0  +3  +8  +0  +2  +4  +3  +4  +5    36

 2   2   1   2   4   4   0   6   8   2   0   3   2   3   1   9   2   2
+7  +3  +8  +4  +5  +0  +9  +1  +1  +6  +3  +5  +5  +6  +2  +0  +7  +3    54

 0   4   4   0   5   5   3   0   2   3   3   0   0   1   3   6   1   1
+8  +2  +4  +1  +4  +1  +3  +2  +6  +4  +4  +5  +5  +7  +3  +3  +0  +5    72

 6   1   5   5   5   3   3   0   3   0   7   2   0   4   0   8   1   0
+2  +3  +3  +2  +4  +4  +6  +7  +5  +4  +2  +4  +1  +5  +6  +0  +4  +9    90
```

Figure 8–5. Sample precision teaching arithmetic probe sheet used by a public school district in Florida.

307

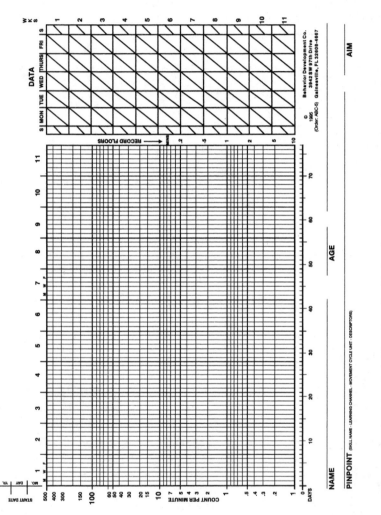

Figure 8–6. Precision Teaching Standard Behavior Chart used to evaluate student progress.

6. Select instructional techniques based on PT practice and research, with careful attention to a student's *stage of learning*. Acquisition learning strategies, for example, differ from those that work best for strengthening generalization.

7. Maximize the opportunities for *student responding* fostering self-correction, multiple practice, and focused drill on challenging skills.

8. Praise improvement and recognize that student performance can improve both for correct and error responding.

9. Work to achieve not just accuracy but, more importantly, *fluency* in each skill targeted for instruction. When students are fluent with their skills they can perform those skills easily and with accuracy. Fluent skills tend to generalize well.

10. Take responsibility for student achievement, recognizing that the *learner knows best*. To precision teachers, this means that an instructional program is "right" for a student when that student learns. Student learning is apparent from visual inspection of the charted data.

PT represents a technical, highly structured, and very powerful approach to teaching and learning. Surprisingly, PT has not be widely applied to instructional programs for students with autism. This is unfortunate as PT seems to have many autism-friendly attributes, including:

1. Instruction tends to be bare bones with material or presentation format distracters removed. Once a student begins a 1-minute probe, the student can fully concentrate on the task. This contrasts sharply with a discrete trial format, which may involve a number of redirections for each student response.

2. Time-keeping devices are used for all timed trials. Because many students with autism are very interested in timers, the instruction itself is linked with potentially powerful reinforcers.

3. Charting is a highly visual form of feedback. Sharing this information permits the child to participate in the instructional process. Because performance targets are indicated on student charts, a clear performance expectation is provided for each student's lesson. This allows students to work toward their goal and helps them predict what will happen on subsequent teaching days. Viewing good learning pictures tends to be a strong motivator for both learner and teacher.

4. The chief benefit of PT, the development of fluent responding, directly targets the primary instructional problems of

most students with autism: prompt dependency and a failure to generalize. PT has a fully developed technology for promoting generalization, which is highly applicable to students with autism.

Fluency is critical to successful teaching and learning. Binder (1996, p. 164) defined fluency as "that combination of accuracy plus speed of responding that enables competent individuals to function efficiently in their natural environments." He noted that our society has a fairly good understanding of fluency as tasks that are easy to do, are known well, or done very smoothly or automatically. Students with autism tend to do some self-selected things very fluently, but resist casual teaching efforts to help them achieve fluency on important academic tasks. Binder also analyzed the technical aspects of fluency. Here the relevance for teaching students with autism could not be greater:

> A more technical definition of fluency is related to its measured effects. When learners achieve certain frequencies of accurate performance they seem to retain and maintain what they have learned; remain on task or endure for sufficient periods of time to meet real world requirements, even in the face of distraction; and apply a skill, or combine what they learned in new situations, in some cases without explicit instruction. (Binder, 1996, pp. 164–165)

In one of the rare applications of this technology to students with autism, Clark and Scott (1999) illustrated the efficiency of raising some skills to fluent levels for preschoolers. They showed that establishing a fluent response set could promote higher rates of responding on a variety of readiness tasks. In an earlier study, Scott and Clark (1998) demonstrated that merely changing an instructional procedure from a discrete trial format to precision teaching could yield performance improvements of 200 to 300% for some students. Scott and Binder (1999) discussed the broader benefits of and impediments to rate-based fluency development techniques in autism and suggested that a revival of PT for students with autism may be at hand.

How would a teacher use PT for a student with autism? A simple application might target basic addition facts of two single-digit numbers in a vertical presentation for sums not greater than 18, with the student asked to "see problems-write answers." The teacher's decision to target this skill would be based on a direct assessment that determined that the student could answer some problems correctly and that the learner had the conceptual knowledge to engage in the skill. For example, the teacher might ask the child to show the problem "5+3" (using manipulatives or using dots to represent the number values). The teacher would select a probe sheet to assess performance on this skill (see Figure 8–5 for an example) and put the page in a plastic sheet protector to allow efficient multiple uses of the material with a water-based wipe-off pen. The teacher would then tell the student:

> I want you to answer each problem right on the page. Go from left to right. If you don't know an answer you should try your best or you can guess. I'll tell you when to start.

The teacher would then set a count-down timer for 1 minute and direct the student to begin while monitoring for adherence to the directions. At the end of 1 minute, the teacher tells the student to stop, corrects the work, records the number of correct and error digits for the 1-minute timing, and then plots these values on a standard chart. Based on the student's results, the teacher would design subsequent instruction tailored to the instructional "level" of the student on this task. For example, if the student obtained 13 corrects and made 6 errors (68% accuracy) during the timing, the teacher would use an array of acquisition strategies, emphasizing techniques such as modeling and error analysis and correction. Daily timings would confirm progress. With a few days of instruction on this specific task, the student might have *passed* a criteria of 83% accuracy (previously set by the teacher) with a performance level of 18 corrects and only 3 errors per minute (for an accuracy of 86%). At this point, the teacher would change from acquisition strategies to fluency instruction. To promote fluency, the teacher might tell the student to go faster, reinforce the student for a higher number of correct answers during a timing, and model how to move faster—perhaps incorporating "sprints" (a small set of problems done in a very short period of time). Simple drill and practice could be used, and the teacher would reduce the overall amount of direct teaching of this skill. The amount and frequency of reinforcement also should be thinned. Daily timings would again indicate if instruction was working. Finally, when the student produced approximately 70 correct math digits per minute, the focus of the instructional program would shift to generalization. Assuring fluency on a skill is an essential strategy for skill generalization.

Teaching Students to Generalize

Teachers of students with autism often teach a skill until it can be reliably demonstrated by the student when requested, then move on to teaching another skill. The downfall of this practice is that many students never learn skills well enough to make them functional; such skills essentially stay at the acquisition level and never progress to mastery. When teaching students with autism, problems with generalization are almost guaranteed. Thus, a student may have a series of skills that can be shown only under very specific circumstances, with certain people, using specific stimuli. One of the causes for the failure of these students to generalize is that they are seldom *taught* the skill past an acquisition level.

Generalization is the exhibition of a skill under novel (untrained) conditions. Both stimuli and responses can (and should be) generalized. Stimulus generalization is seen when a student, having learned to read the word "cat" from a flash card, spontaneously reads the word "cat" in a book. The student, having learned a skill (reading the word "cat") under one set of circumstances (flash cards), exhibits that skill under similar but not identical circumstances (a book). Response generalization can be seen when a student responds in any of several ways to the social initiations of peers. He may spontaneously respond, "hi," "hello," "hi there" or "what's up?" when a peer greets him. In this case, one of a series of behaviors is produced in response to a stimulus.

The use of simplified speech, often used when teaching acquisition skills through discrete trial formats, requires stimulus generalization from the student if the behavior to be used in other settings. The student who learns to give the instructor the ball when he or she is asked to "Give ball" may have great difficulty following that request when a more natural request, "Anthony, would you hand me the ball, please?" is used. Planning the expansion of language from simplified to more natural verbal stimuli can increase the likelihood of the student producing newly learned behavior in circumstances other than the training situation.

Students with autism, particularly those who have been intensively taught in one-to-one and discrete trial formats, often fail to generalize to novel stimuli in real world situations. A pink pig in a picture is correctly labeled "pig" but the animal at the farm saying "oink" may not be recognized as a pig. There are a number of ways of teaching students to generalize a skill (Stokes & Baer, 1977). The technique used will depend on the student, the skill, and the teaching environment. In the previous example, teaching the word "pig" with stuffed pigs, pictures of pigs, and a variety of real pigs at the local farm or petting zoo could give the student enough examples of "pig" to generalize the skill to novel stimuli. However, unless some stimulus discrimination is taught as well, it is quite likely that all four-footed animals will be labeled "pigs."

Teaching an older student to use office machines is an example of a skill that must generalize across materials and settings. The copy machine at school may be similar to the copy machine at a job site, but may be a different make, have function buttons in a different location, and have paper loading in the front instead of on the side. The copy machine at the office supply store may be different yet. A student should be able to generalize his copying skills to use all of these machines without direct instruction on each one.

Responses need to be generalized to real-world situations as well. We expect a preschool student to help put away plastic food and dishes in the housekeeping area as well as assist in tidying up the block area. We expect elementary school students to follow the written directions on their worksheets in all subject areas. In high school, we teach students to write an essay using a specific format. The use of that format to write on essay the effects of the Industrial Revolution or on the use of irony in Macbeth is an example of response generalization.

Skill selection is a teacher responsibility which relates to the likelihood of a skill being generalized. As early as 1968 Ayllon and Azrin suggested a *relevance of behavior rule* in which we would only teach skills that produce reinforcement for the person after formal intervention is completed (Ayllon & Azrin, 1968). The assumption is that these skills would be frequently used and reinforced in more typical settings. Consider alternatively that with poorly selected skills, a student might have few or no chances to use the new skill; mastery and generalization problems would be obvious.

As discussed previously, another critical barrier to generalization is the failure to develop fluency on a skill to be generalized. Binder (1996) noted that when students achieve a high level of accurate performance they "seem to retain and maintain what they have learned, remain on task or endure for sufficient periods of time to meet real-world requirements, even in the face of distraction" (pp. 164–165). Binder's analysis could not be more appropriate for students with autism. For any learner, if a skill is not yet mastered, it will tend not to generalize. Given the acknowledged generalization problems facing students with autism, developing fluent performance should be considered absolutely essential.

In addition to promoting fluency, another way to teach students to generalize is to teach with multiple examples. This strategy has been used successfully to produce generalized social, motor, self-care, and communication behavior, all important for students to be more fully integrated into the world outside the classroom. Teaching with multiple examples means that teachers implement their lessons using various materials, people, places, and language. For example, in teaching students with autism to interact with other people, teachers might apply direct instruction on initiating and responding with several "instructional" peers, then introduce others (noninstructional peers) until the student is able to approach a new peer and interact socially (Brady, Shores, McEvoy, Ellis, & Fox, 1987).

Teaching students to generalize takes teacher planning; more important skills should receive the greatest instructional planning. Before a skill is taught, the functional use of the skill should be determined and generalization of the skill from the classroom to the real world must be planned. Anything less can leave a student with a wide variety of splinter skills that are exhibited only under very defined and highly artificial circumstances.

Using Errorless Teaching and Match-to-Sample Formats

For students who do not respond to teacher requests, many educators advocate prompting and reinforcing *any* student response, including student errors just to "trap" the student into participating in instruction. Once students begin to participate actively in a lesson, teachers then differentially reinforce their responses until only correct answers are produced. Although this logic is clear to many teachers, a lesson format to teach this is lacking in many classrooms.

A simple errorless teaching procedure involves a *match-to-sample* format. For truly errorless responding, a teacher can present only one stimulus item and an identical example, then request the student to "Give me a _____" (name of item). In subsequent lessons, the teacher will add progressively more and different "distractors" until the student can make finer discriminations of the item. Thus the lessons move from an errorless procedure to a low error procedure and then finally to a more difficult one. An example of a task analysis of a teacher's materials used to teach a student to identify a picture of her mother is provided below.

Step 1: Student matches to the sample with no distracters. *(Matches picture of mother to identical picture.)*

Step 2: Student matches to the sample with two **very different** distracters. *(Matches picture of mother to identical picture. Also present are a toy truck and a telephone receiver.)*

Step 3: Student matches to the sample with three **moderately different** distracters. *(Matches picture of mother to identical picture. Also present are pictures of a group of children in class, teenagers in a car, and adults in a pool.)*

Step 4: Student matches to the sample with four **similar** distracters. *(Matches picture of mother to identical picture. Also present are pictures of other adult women including teachers and relatives.)*

This match-to-sample format can be modified as needed to ensure that the student continues to respond correctly. Modifications can include adding or deleting types and number of distracters, moving from photographs to line drawings, or pairing pictures with object miniatures. It is also important to note that a match-to-sample format can be used *without* errorless teaching.

Using Permanent Prompts

Prompts are not specific to individuals with disabilities, nor do they need to be removed over time. Signs reminding employees to wash their hands are posted in the washrooms of many companies. These signs are permanent fixtures, and are used to remind employees to perform a specific behavior. Students with disabilities also benefit from permanent prompts. Although educators often hope to remove artificial cues for students, such assistance need not be removed if:

1. removal would degrade a student's performance, and
2. the prompt can be made to blend into the normative social or cultural surroundings.

As noted earlier in this chapter, many students use visual personal schedules to help them organize their daily routines and remove the transition problems that accompany unpredictable changes in routines. These personal schedules are similar to the lists kept by many people without autism. Similar prompts include picture cards to prompt students to perform all tasks in a job sequence or a list of bus stops and bus transfers to get from home to work. Davis, Brady, Williams, and Burta (1992) and Alberto, Sharpton, Briggs, and Stright (1986) created audiotapes with personal messages to provide verbal prompts to assist students in performing work and school tasks. These prompt systems can be used to teach new skills or to maintain and generalize existing ones. If their removal results in skill deterioration, however, teachers can leave the prompts in place, thus making them permanent.

Summary

Students with autism are being educated in a wider range of school classrooms, including general education classes with peers who do not have disabilities. In these settings, especially in the elementary grades, the direct instruction and teacher-directed models emphasized in this chapter may not be prominent. Rather, teachers may rely on discovery learning approaches (Ausubel, Novak, & Hanesian, 1978; Barlow, 1985) and other methods that are not teacher-directed. These approaches are based on the assumption that students are active problem solvers, are curious and motivated to learn, and will work to make sense of a situation (Rosenberg, O'Shea, & O'Shea, 1998). In many general education classes, the emphasis of instruction is on generic problem-solving skills that rely on information processing strategies and other metacognitive approaches. It is precisely these metacognitive strategies that constitute the most obvious problems for most students with autism. Consequently, these discovery approaches build on students' weakest learning and cognitive capabilities. These approaches assume that motivation is largely internal, resulting from a student's desire to learn. Educators supervising students with autism in general education classrooms in which these methods are prominent should closely monitor students' progress and be prepared to offer support for more direct and effective instruction.

HOW TO TELL WHETHER YOUR TEACHING WAS EFFECTIVE

The learning difficulties that students with autism have are too serious to allow teachers to use guesswork when establishing the effectiveness of their instruction. Evaluation systems are needed to determine (a) whether the student is *learning* the lesson being taught and (b) whether the student is learning it *efficiently*. Fortunately several teacher-friendly instructional assessment systems are available to help teachers answer these questions.

Regardless of the type of assessment used, four principles drive its use. First, the assessment system must *directly evaluate* the actual skill being taught. An assessment system that relies on inference or indirect measures of skill progress typically is not sensitive enough to measure real but incremental progress. Second, the skill must be *measured frequently enough* to inform educators whether the instructor is having an impact on student learning. This typically involves assessment at least every 3–4 days. Third, if the lesson is important enough to spend considerable time and effort in teaching it, student progress should be *displayed graphically* to allow educators and family members to determine visually whether the student is actually learning the skill. Finally, the assessment system should help educators make instructional decisions involving (a) changes needed in the lesson, (b) moving to the next lesson, or (c) re-examining the utility and organization of the current lesson.

Using Rate Data to Measure Progress

Evaluating the rate of responding is one of the most sensitive measures of student progress. Rate is the number of responses over a fixed period of time—usually 1 minute for instructional purposes. Rate can be used to evaluate the progress of many skills, especially those that can be performed freely at a student's own pace (i.e., skills that do not require a teacher question or cue prior to a student response).

Calculating rate is simple. The number of student responses is divided by the time in which the behavior was to be performed. The product is then converted to the time unit (usually minutes); for example, 30 correct problems completed in 2 minutes is converted to 15 corrects per minute. The use of count per minute has become the convention and is featured on specialized standard behavior charts, which permit a wide range of response frequencies to be displayed on one chart format. Many data-based educators, however, also show rate on traditional, equal interval graphs as well.

Rate measurement and evaluation is based on the principle that the strength of a behavior (whether academic or nonacademic) can be sensitively measured by the number of responses over time. A skill that is well developed permits faster responding, whereas less well developed skills occur at far slower rates and are usually accompanied by more errors. Evaluation based on rate is not without criticism in autism. Many teachers believe that the unique characteristics of students with autism make it impossible for them to perform at high rates. Others who hold low expectations believe that these students should not be pushed and use only unstructured teaching interactions. These teachers believe that any expectation of high-rate performance is unwise. We believe that most students with autism can reach high rates when well taught. Given the strong correlation between fluent responding (high rate) and generalization, students should be taught to perform fluently.

Many educators are familiar with rate-based evaluation. Standard textbooks on applied behavior analysis (e.g., Cooper et al., 1987) provide details on the rationale and procedures for displaying rate data. The growing use of rate as a measurement system relies on graphic data display and allows easy communication between educators familiar with the conventions. A summary of the practices for using rate data includes:

1. Determine the baseline of the target behavior prior to implementing a lesson designed to teach the new skill. Measure the skill as many times as necessary to learn the natural range of the behavior prior to teaching. This will establish whether the behavior is consistently low, high, or fluctuating. During baseline, teachers can record both correct and error performances with a preference for 1-minute timing periods (for academic skills) or they can record a longer (naturally occurring) time period and convert the student's performance to rate per minute, as described before. The data should be graphed after each session. Student accuracy becomes obvious by examining the relative distance between the graphed patterns for correct and errored responding.

2. Continue recording and charting performance of the skill during instruction. The way the skill is observed and recorded should stay the same. When the lesson is provided, a brief notation on the graph should be made, with a fuller description provided in the teacher's lesson plan or comparable material. When instruction is effective, higher rates of performance will be seen on the graph.

3. The data patterns on each student's graphs (i.e., the trend lines for corrects and errors) show the impact of instruction. Day to day variation, or bounce, will be observed, but should not become the basis for changing teachers' lessons. Rather the *pattern* of a student's performance should notify a teacher whether any change is needed.

Teachers can summarize the rates of a student's performance in various ways. Some teachers simply present the graphs for visual inspection and describe the impact of their lessons on a student's overall learning. Others quantify the changes by presenting the differences in the means during baseline and during some aspects of their teaching. Widely used software (e.g., Microsoft Excel) simplifies this quantification. Finally, if fluency of responding is an objective, some teachers might wish to determine the percentage of mastery. For example, if a student averages 7 math problems correct per minute during baseline, the teacher's aim might be for the student to demonstrate fluency at 70 correct problems per minute. The *current mastery rate during baseline* would be 10% (7 divided by 70); the *mastery aim during the teaching* phase would be 100% (70 divided by 70). Performance gains of this magnitude are common in skillful, rate-based instructional programs of students with autism. Finally, an array of more elaborate techniques does exist, but generally these are used for research purposes.

Using Percentage Data to Measure Progress

Percentage is one of the simplest methods teachers use to evaluate progress. Scores on tests, classwork, and homework often are recorded as percentage data. There are times when percentage is appropriate, but for other lessons it is not a helpful assessment system. The calculation of percentage requires two numbers, the number of times the target skill was exhibited and the total number of opportunities that the skill *could have been exhibited.* When the total number of opportunities cannot be accurately determined, then percentage cannot be used. For example, to suggest that a student should "interact with peers 70% of the time" makes no sense, because "of the time" does not delineate the number of possible opportunities to interact. However, "responds to 70% of peers' social initiations" is an appropriate use of percentage as a measure of progress. There is a real number of social initiations, they can be counted, and the number of responses to those initiations also could be counted. Therefore, a student might respond to 13 of 17 initiations (or 76% of the initiations). Percentage data are an appropriate measure of progress for many academic (spelling words written correctly), self-help (wash hands after using washroom), and behavioral skills (transitions without protest) when assessing initial acquisition.

One teaching format that lends itself to measuring progress with percentage data is discrete trial teaching. When using this format, the number of trials is known and the number of correct trials is also known, since each student's response to a trial is usually counted as correct or error. Some teachers only take data on the last 10 consecutive trials of a particular skill, following a period of instruction. These last trials form the basis for calculating the percentage of accuracy for that session. When using percentage to assess progress, any number of trials can be used for the calculation; however, incorrect responses will significantly affect the percentage scores when they are derived from only a few trials. Figure 8–7 shows an example of a discrete trial data sheet. The data sheet can be transformed to a graph by converting each day's scores to percentage correct, then creating a line graph on the data sheet using the percentage values in the right-hand column.

Evaluation of progress using percentage data is identical to other direct measurement systems. A baseline measure of the target skill should be taken before beginning to teach. The baseline level gives the teacher the student's starting point before the skill is taught. The criterion for mastery of the skill should be established before teaching the skill. This criterion establishes the percentage of performance that the student has to exhibit to be considered competent. Different skills allow different criteria. A job skill such as making change at the cash register must be done at high levels (near 100%) of accuracy. Putting clothing in the correct drawer at home does not require as stringent a level of accuracy. Spelling words are usually considered mastered at an 80% level, whereas safety skills (such as street crossing) must have accuracy levels of 100%. Finally, assessment should continue during the instructional period, and the student's performance should show improvement until the preset criterion is reached. The performance shown as percentage data should be graphed to allow other teachers and family members to see clearly the impact of instruction on the student's learning.

Using Interval Data to Measure Progress

An especially teacher-friendly way to measure instructional effectiveness is to note the presence of the target skill during a particular (short) time interval. Interval systems are commonly used to record problem behaviors but they are also very useful when teaching a new skill. The new skill to be learned is identified and then the teacher simply observes to see whether that skill is shown during a predetermined interval of time.

Ten Trial Data Sheet

Name _____   Teacher _____

Objective _____   Sd _____

Date																					
Session	1	2	3	4	5	6	7	8	9	10	11	12	13	14	15	16	17	18	19	20	%
	10	10	10	10	10	10	10	10	10	10	10	10	10	10	10	10	10	10	10	10	**100%**
	9	9	9	9	9	9	9	9	9	9	9	9	9	9	9	9	9	9	9	9	**90%**
	8	8	8	8	8	8	8	8	8	8	8	8	8	8	8	8	8	8	8	8	**80%**
	7	7	7	7	7	7	7	7	7	7	7	7	7	7	7	7	7	7	7	7	**70%**
	6	6	6	6	6	6	6	6	6	6	6	6	6	6	6	6	6	6	6	6	**60%**
	5	5	5	5	5	5	5	5	5	5	5	5	5	5	5	5	5	5	5	5	**50%**
	4	4	4	4	4	4	4	4	4	4	4	4	4	4	4	4	4	4	4	4	**40%**
	3	3	3	3	3	3	3	3	3	3	3	3	3	3	3	3	3	3	3	3	**30%**
	2	2	2	2	2	2	2	2	2	2	2	2	2	2	2	2	2	2	2	2	**20%**
	1	1	1	1	1	1	1	1	1	1	1	1	1	1	1	1	1	1	1	1	**10%**
Initials																					
Changes																					

Change Notations:

1. _____   4. _____

2. _____   5. _____

3. _____   6. _____

Figure 8–7. Ten-trial data sheet.

The total number of intervals of observation is used as the denominator in the calculation, while the number of intervals in which the student engaged in the new behavior serves as the numerator. This value is then converted to a percentage and usually displayed on a graph.

Like any measurement system, the skill to be learned must be fully described in order to be easily counted and recorded. The definition of the skill must be a clear description of what the student actually does and must allow the teacher to know when the skill begins and when it ends. Merely not engaging in some behavior is not adequate.

Many teachers will find that a *partial interval* system works well to measure instructional outcomes. A partial interval system is one in which *any occurrence* of the behavior during an interval is recorded. A "Look-Record" recording convention also is helpful. Using this convention, a teacher observes the student for a brief period (e.g., 10 seconds); immediately after the end of each interval a short recording time (e.g., 5 seconds) is used by the teacher to mark whether the skill was observed. This "discontinuous" interval system (Bailey & Wolery, 1989) allows the teacher time to record the presence or absence of the new skill immediately after the end of each brief interval. Intervals of from 6–30 seconds permit many opportunities to observe use (or nonuse) of the skill. Teachers who use this measurement system find it convenient to create audiotapes with prerecorded observation intervals. For example one tape might give 20 minutes of a 20-second "look" and 10-second "record" schedule; a second tape might have another common schedule. These tapes can be used repeatedly and shared with others to increase the number of interval options available to teachers in a school. Finally, all observations are recorded on a coding sheet.

Interval recording requires care by educators. First, the observer must pay close attention to the student throughout the interval. Second, scoring must be done quickly and definitively in the brief recording time available. Finally, ongoing behaviors (such as a continuing social interaction) can be difficult to record accurately. However, this system is far simpler than many other approaches, and is truly a "teacher-friendly" measurement system. The results can yield a useful measure of how firmly a new skill is established and used.

The following example illustrates how an interval system works. A teacher has noted that DeBary, a student with autism, tends not to interact with other children when placed in an academic work group. The teacher defines Group Cooperation to include sharing, talking to the other children about the task, and behavior related writing and working. She then establishes a 10-second interval observation schedule. During each 10-second interval, she observes to see if the child cooperated at any time within the interval. If he did, DeBary is given credit for that interval. If not, the interval is marked with a "–." At the end of the observation period (a 15-minute portion of a science lesson), the teacher counts the number of intervals in which DeBary showed Group Cooperation and uses this number as the numerator of a fraction which has as its denominator the total number of intervals. This value is then converted to a percentage.

Percentage is a convenient way to use interval measures. Parents and other teachers can readily understand that DeBary engaged in Group Cooperation in only 30% of the intervals prior to instruction, but then improved to over 90% of the intervals observed after 3 weeks of instruction. It is important to note that the percentage value does not indicate the strength of the behavior, but rather is an indication of how likely it is to be used.

SUMMARY

An educational model for students with autism must be responsive to both the needs of the students and their unique learning characteristics. Because learning can be exceedingly hard work for these students, educational programs cannot be left to happenstance. Rather, education should be well planned, exquisitely designed, precisely delivered, and sensitively evaluated.

The model proposed in this chapter is a careful and logical model. We propose that educators and families work jointly to select target skills that would make a fundamental improvement in students' lives. This requires a rigorous effort in finding potential goals, followed by a serious effort in prioritizing them. Most students will require a combination of academic, social, communication, and community skills if schooling is to have an impact on their lives.

As important as it is to establish the specific content of a student's educational program, it is also necessary to carefully select or design an effective instructional delivery system. This requires attention to organizing the curriculum and the student's learning environment. It also requires teachers to gain fluency in the use of instructional delivery tactics with which they may have only cursory knowledge or familiarity.

Finally, educators should take seriously the calls for accountability being made by taxpayers and legislators throughout the nation. Stated simply, the citizenry wants to know that the time, energy, and money put into special education is making a difference to the students who need this assistance. So, too, responsible teachers want to know whether their instructional efforts are effective. If a direct assessment of student learning shows that they are not making progress, teachers (and our noneducator citizenry) want to know that we will not continue to do business as usual; rather educators will use student performance information to improve instructional programs.

The educational model presented in this chapter is an active one, but it is not beyond the means of educators who are both committed and prepared. Fortunately, it is also a model well grounded in the research on effective instruction. We consider the adoption of a proactive and accountable model of education as one of the fundamental challenges facing the field of autism.

REVIEW QUESTIONS

1. What are some of the key features of a student with autism that a teacher must take into account when planning an instructional program?

2. Describe at least four principles educators should use when selecting instructional targets.

3. What are the common assessment instruments in autism and what are their main functions?

4. What instructional arrangements are unique for teachers of students with autism? To what extent are these arrangements similar to or different from those common to general educators?

5. Describe at least four instructional delivery tactics that teachers will need to master to teach students with autism. How do these tactics differ from those common to general educators?

6. Describe two methods of directly assessing student outcomes.

REFERENCES

Alberto, P., Jobes, N., Sizemore, A., & Duran, D. (1980). A comparison of individual and group instruction across response tasks. *Journal of the Association for Persons with Severe Handicaps, 5,* 285–293.

Alberto, P., Sharpton, W., Briggs, A., & Stright, M. (1986). Facilitating task acquisition through the use of a self-operated auditory prompting system. *Journal of the Association for Persons with Severe Handicaps, 11,* 85–91.

Ausubel, D., Novak, J., & Hanesian, H. (1978). *Educational psychology: A cognitive view.* New York: Holt, Rinehart & Winston.

Ayllon, T., & Azrin, NH. (1968). *The token economy: A motivational system for therapy and rehabilitation.* New York: Appleton-Century-Crofts.

Bailey, D., & Wolery, M. (1989). *Assessing infants and preschoolers with handicaps.* Columbus, OH: Merrill.

Barlow, D. L. (1985). *Educational psychology: The teaching-learning process.* Chicago: Moody Press.

Beck, R. (1981). *Curriculum management through a data base.* Validation report for ESEA Title IV. Great Falls, MT: Great Falls Public Schools.

Belfiore, P., & Mace, C. (1994). Self-help and community skills. In J. Matson (Ed.), *Autism in children and adults* (pp. 193–211). Belmont, CA: Brooks/Cole.

Binder, C. (1996). Behavioral fluency: Evolution of a new paradigm. *The Behavior Analyst, 19,* 163–197.

Brady, M. P., Shores, R. E., McEvoy, M. A., Ellis, D., & Fox, J. J. (1987). Increasing social interactions of severely handicapped autistic children. *Journal of Autism and Developmental Disorders, 3,* 375–390.

Brown, L., Branston, M.B., Hamre-Nietupski, S., Pumpian, N., Certo, N., & Gruenewald, L. (1979). A strategy for developing chronological age-appropriate and functional curricular content for severely handicapped adolescents and young adults. *Journal of Special Education, 13*(1), 81–90.

Brown, L., Nietupski, J., & Hamre-Nietupski, S.(1976). The criterion of ultimate functioning and public school services for the severely handicapped student. In M. A. Thomas (Ed.), *Hey, don't forget about me! Education's investment in the severely, profoundly, multiply handicapped* (pp. 2–15). Reston, VA: Council for Exceptional Children.

Campbell, P., Campbell, C. R., &. Brady, M. P. (1998). Team Environmental Assessment Mapping System (TEAMS): A method for selecting curriculum goals for students with disabilities. *Education & Training in Mental Retardation and Developmental Disabilities, 33,* 264–272.

Carr, E., Taylor, J., & Robinson, S. (1991). The effects of severe behavior problems in children on the teaching behavior of adults. *Journal of Applied Behavior Analysis, 24,* 523–536.

Clark, C., & Scott, J. (1999, May). *Combining restricted operant and free operant responding to maximize instructional effectiveness for preschool children with autism.* Paper presented at the 25th Annual Convention of the Association for Behavior Analysis, Chicago.

Cooper, J., Heron, T., & Heward, W. (1987). *Applied behavior analysis.* Columbus, OH: Merrill.

Davis, C., Brady., M.P., Williams, R.E., & Burta, M. (1992). The effects of self-operated auditory prompting tapes on the performance fluency of persons with severe mental retardation. *Education and Training in Mental Retardation, 27,* 39–49.

Dunlap, G., dePerczel, M., Clarke, S., Wilson, D., Wright, S., White, R., & Gomex, A. (1994). Choice making to promote adaptive behaviors for students with emotional and behavioral challenges. *Journal of Applied Behavior Analysis, 27,* 505–518.

Duvall, S.F., Delquadri, J., Elliot, M., & Hall, R.V. (1992). Parent tutoring procedures: Experimental analysis and validation of generalization in oral reading across passages, settings and time. *Journal of Behavioral Education, 2,* 281–303.

Duvall, S. F., Delquadri, J. C., & Hall, R. V. (1996). *Parents as reading tutors.* Longmont, CO: Sopris West.

Franklin, R.D. (1999, February). *Science in pediatric neuropsychiatry.* Presentation at the World Conference on Pediatric Neuropsychology, West Palm Beach, FL.

Gast, D., Wellons, J., & Collins, B. (1994). Home and community safety skills. In M. Agran, N. Marchand-Martella, & R. Martella (Eds.), *Promoting health and safety: Skills for independent living* (pp. 11–32). Baltimore, MD: Paul H. Brookes.

Gaylord-Ross, R., & Holvoet, J. (1985). *Strategies for educating students with severe handicaps.* Boston: Little, Brown.

Gilliam, J. (1995). *Gilliam Autism Rating Scale: Examiner's manual.* Austin, TX: Pro-Ed.

Grandin, T., & Scariano, M. (1986). *Emergence: Labeled autistic.* Novato, CA: Arena.

Greenwood, C.R., Delquadri, J., & Hall, R.V. (1989). Longitudinal effects of classwide peer tutoring. *Journal of Educational Psychology, 81,* 371–383.

Hall, R. V., Delquadri, C., Greenwood, C. R., & Thurston, L. (1982). The importance of opportunity to respond in children's academic success. In E. D. Edgar, N. Haring, J.R. Jenkins, & C. Pious (Eds.), *Serving young handicapped children: Issues and research* (pp. 107–149). Austin, TX: Pro-Ed.

Hammill, D., & Wiederholt, J. L. (1995). *Comprehensive Test of Nonverbal Intellegence.* Austin, TX: Pro-Ed.

Hart, B. M., & Risley, T. R. (1968). Establishing the use of descriptive adjectives in the spontaneous speech of disadvantaged preschool children. *Journal of Applied Behavior Analysis, 1,* 109–120.

Kamps, D., Walker, D., Maher, J., & Rotholtz, D. (1992). Academic and environmental effects of small group arrangements in classrooms for students with autism and other developmental disabilities. *Journal of Autism and Developmental Disorders, 22,* 277–293.

Kanner, L. (1943). Inborn disturbances of affective contact. *Nervous Child, 2,* 217–250.

Krug, D., Arick, J., & Almond, P. (1993). *Examiner's manual: Autism Screening Instrument for Educational Planning.* Austin, TX: Pro-Ed.

Lasater, M., & Brady, M. P. (1995). Effects of video self-modeling and feedback on task fluency: A home based intervention. *Education and Treatment of Children, 18,* 389–407.

Lovaas, O. I. (1981). *Teaching developmentally disabled children: The ME Book.* Austin, TX: Pro-Ed.

Lovaas, O. I. (1987). Behavioral treatment and normal educational and intellectual functioning in young autistic children. *Journal of Consulting and Clinical Psychology, 55,* 3–9.

MacDuff, G., Krantz, P., & McClannahan, L. (1993). Teaching children with autism to use photographic activity schedules: Maintenance and generalization of complex response chains. *Journal of Applied Behavior Analysis, 26,* 89–97

Maurice, C. (1996). *Behavioral intervention for young children with autism.* Austin, TX: Pro-Ed.

McEvoy, M., Nordquist, V., Twardosz, S., Heckaman, K., Wehby, J., & Denny, R. K. (1988). Promoting autistic children's peer interaction in integrated early childhood settings using affection activities. *Journal of Applied Behavior Analysis, 21,* 193-200.

Munk, D., Van Laarhoven, T., Goodman, S., & Repp. A. (1998). Small group direct instruction for students with moderate to severe disabilities. In A. Hilton & R. Ringlaben (Eds.), *Best and promising practices in developmental disabilities* (pp. 127–138). Austin, TX: Pro-Ed.

Reamer, R., Brady, M. P., & Hawkins, J. (1998). The effects of video self-modeling on parents' interactions with children with developmental disabilities. *Education and Training in Mental Retardation and Developmental Disabilities, 33,* 131–143.

Reid, D., & Favell, J. (1984). Group instruction for persons who have severe disabilities: A critical review. *Journal of the Association for Persons with Severe Handicaps, 9,* 167–177.

Rosenberg, M. S., O'Shea, L., & O'Shea, D. J. (1998). *Student teacher to master teacher.* Columbus, OH: Merrill.

Salvia, J., & Ysseldyke, J. (1995). *Assessment.* Boston: Houghton Mifflin.

Sasso, G., Garrison-Harrell, L., McMahon, C., & Peck, J. (1998). Social competence of individuals with autism: An applied behavior analysis perspecitve. In R. Simpson & B. Myles (Eds.), *Educating children and youth with autism* (pp. 173–190). Austin, TX: Pro-Ed.

Schopler, E., & Mesibov, G. (Eds.). (1995). *Learning and cognition in autism.* New York: Plenum Press.

Schopler, E., Mesibov, G., & Hearsey, K. (1995). Structured teaching in the TEACCH system. In E. Schopler & G. Mesibov (Eds.), *Learning and cognition in autism* (pp. 47–78). New York: Plenum Press.

Schopler, E., Reichler, R., Bashford, A., Lansing, M., & Marcus, L. (1990). *Psychoeducational Profile Revised (PEP-R).* Austin, TX: Pro-Ed.

Schopler, E., Reichler, R., & Renner, B. (1992). *The Childhood Autism Rating Scale: CARS.* Los Angeles: Western Psychological Services.

Scott, J., & Binder, C. (1999, May). *Rate-based and free operant responding with individuals with autism.* Symposium presented at the 25th Annual Convention of the Association for Behavior Analysis, Chicago.

Scott, J., & Clark, C. (1998, October). *Fluent responding in young children with autism: A comparison of instructional formats and consideration of data challanges.* Paper presented at the 24th Annual Convention of the Association for Behavior Analysis, Orlando.

Skinner, B.F. (1991). *The behavior of organisms.* (Original work published in 1938). Acton, MA: Copley Publishing Group.

Smith, S. W., Slattery, W. J., & Knopp, T.Y. (1993). Beyond the mandate: Developing individualized education programs that work for student with autism. *Focus on Autistic Behavior, 8*(3), 1–15.

Stokes, T. F., & Baer, D. M. (1977). An implicit technology of generalization. *Journal of Applied Behavior Analysis, 10,* 349–367.

Sundberg, M., & Partington, J. (1998). *Teaching language to children with autism or other developmental disabilities.* Pleasant Hill, CA: Behavior Analysts, Inc.

Taylor, R. (1997). *Assessment of exceptional students: Educational and psychological procedures.* Englewood Cliffs, NJ: Prentice-Hall.

Vandercook, T., York, J., & Forest, M. (1989). The McGill Action Planning System (MAPS): A strategy for building the vision. *Journal of the Association for Persons with Severe Handicaps, 14,* 205–215.

Westling, D., & Fox, L. (1995). *Teaching students with severe disabilities.* Englewood Cliffs, NJ: Prentice-Hall.

Chapter 9

PARENTS AND FAMILIES

Key Points

- Educators should join with families as partners in the education of students with autism.

- Family decisions and choices reflect their resources and values; family-centered practices should reflect these family systems.

- The legacy of scapegoating of parents continues to influence attitudes and behaviors.

- Parental stress can be minimized when parents are well supported.

- Educators must strive to involve parents in class-room, school, and district level planning and decision making.

INTRODUCTION

The involvement of parents and families in educational programs has changed dramatically over the years. Although family involvement is needed for students with 24-hour-a-day disabilities, the model of involvement differs tremendously across families and within a family across time. This chapter examines family involvement, while describing the various family variables and stressors that teachers will encounter in working with families of students with autism.

FAMILIES AND PROFESSIONALS: CONTEXT FOR AN EVOLVING PARTNERSHIP

Much of the traditional thinking regarding parents of children with autism is counterproductive. We propose actively reconsidering the relationships between educators and parents. In most educational systems, a parent-professional partnership is the expected model. Educators can stand apart from this partnership or they can join in. No section of IDEA specifies that educators *must* join parents in partnership. Certainly no local educational agency or even specific school is likely to insist that educators join with parents to meet the many challenges of autism. Nevertheless, progressive educators will recognize the need for such partnerships and see the value of defining their roles within these relationships.

It is not possible to envision the full scope of services and supports for students with autism without educators playing a central role. This section presents the ways in which parents currently function as partners with educators. In some cases, parents are in a *leadership* role. In other areas a more equal partnership is apparent. In still other ways, educators assume a leadership role. For planning and implementation efforts to be truly successful, however, parents, families, and educators must interact as empowered partners.

Parent Strengths

Parents of children with autism face the same challenges as parents of any other child, plus many unique challenges. Historically, these parents were seen as actively contributing to, if not fully causing, their children's autism. The burden of guilt has been lifted, but many professionals still view parents in ways that are not conducive to good relationships. Educators should not prejudge parents; having a child with autism does not automatically mean that parents have needs that require elaborate supports. Typically, parents can and will do what is best for their children. Too often, professionals in general, and educators in particular, see parents as people to be helped. If parents and families need help, educators should be prepared to point the way while being careful not to impose prejudices or predetermined courses of action that may not be consistent with a family's wishes.

Marcus and Schopler (1987) offered six principles to guide professionals' behavior and attitudes toward parents.

1. Avoid judgmental attitudes. This calls for professionals to suspend judgment about family patterns of interaction and to respect the diversity of families.
2. Remember that raising children with autism is a complicated matter. Professionals should not assume that families have poor child management skills if their child demonstrates problem behavior. Few parents are naturally prepared to develop sophisticated behavior change procedures.
3. Professionals are guides, not experts, in family dynamics. Parent priorities are critical, and few parents want professionals to assume authoritarian roles.
4. Consideration of total family needs is necessary to keep the needs, or perception of needs, of one family member from overwhelming the entire family. Children with autism develop best in strong and unified families. The needs of siblings and others within a family also are important.
5. Fair and honest interactions between professionals and families are important. Collaborative relationships are not one-sided. They require openness and sharing, so that each party can participate in the joys and successes of the other.
6. Ultimately, families will maintain responsibility for their decisions involving their children with autism. Professionals must realize that their involvement typically constitutes only a small piece of the total picture for the child and family.

Summers, Behr, and Turnbull (1989) suggested entirely new ways of thinking about the families of children with disabilities. Instead of seeing families as troubled and under stress, Summers et al. advocated that the following positive elements be factored into any consideration of the family.

- Increased happiness
- Greater love
- Strengthened family ties
- Strengthened religious faith
- Expanded social network
- Learning to be patient

- Greater pride and accomplishment
- Greater knowledge about disabilities
- Learning not to take things for granted
- Learning tolerance and sensitivity

Athough some educators might think these recommendations are "soft," we propose that the Summers et al. recommendations form the heart of educational programs. Technical precision and clear goals are desperately needed when changing long-standing behavior patterns and when promoting continued growth and development. Yet the elements described by Summers et al. can help professionals and families remain focused on *why* students with autism and their families need support; these elements remind professionals of the ultimate outcomes they are working to promote. Scott's Advice to Parents on the next page provides an example of advice offered to families consistent with these emphases.

Although teachers play a critical role in the life of a child with autism, parents, obviously, play a far larger role. Teachers must be able to work together with families to optimize instruction. Although this is essential, it is not always easy. Numerous problems can interfere with good relationships, yet teachers must be prepared to be the consummate professionals to prevent, remedy, or manage problems. The demands of raising a child with autism can take a toll on families, but these factors also can foster extraordinarily close and fruitful partnerships. But just as autism in children often brings out the best in families, professionals who teach these children will discover and develop extraordinary skills to support families. On the page 336, the Levenes, the parents of a child with autism, write of the impact of autism on their family and the optimism which now propels their family's efforts.

Autism is not well understood by our society and even those familiar with special education may not understand autism. Parents, in general, prefer to hear an honest admission of an educator's lack of knowledge about autism rather than guesses or misinformation. This may be difficult for some educators who are comfortable in an authority role and have extensive knowledge on a broad range of other topics.

Two of the authors of this text have conducted surveys in graduate courses on autism offered under a federal teacher training project. Par-

Advice to Families—A Primer

Jack Scott, Ph.D.

I get many calls from parents who have just received a diagnosis of autism for their young child. In most cases, they are upset, lost, anxious, and sometimes angry, but they are also eager to learn all they can about autism. As a university professor I am not in a role to provide direct services. I can and do provide information and referrals and help them develop strategies for gaining supports and knowledge.

I tell them about other resources. In Florida we have regional Centers for Autism and Related Disabilities (CARD) funded by the state legislature to assist families and schools. I make sure that they have the name and phone number of a child neurologist with expertise in autism. I ask who provided the diagnosis and, if I do not recognize this person as someone with an extensive background in autism, I provide the name of a professional with diagnostic expertise. If they have not obtained a good diagnostic workup already, I strongly urge them to do so before I can sensibly give them additional information. Sometimes metabolic disorders, Rett syndrome, or even brain tumors can present a constellation of syndromes similar to autism, yet these disorders have very different courses of treatment. Families should not be playing a guessing game with autism.

I ask the parents if they have made contact with the parent groups and tell them about the local Autism Society of America (ASA) chapter, giving them the name and telephone number of the president or key contact person. I tell them about a regional parent skills training cooperative, Reaching Potentials, a group of parents sharing training expenses and organized to expand the array of intervention services in the area. I also tell them about the Family Network on Disabilities (FND), which offers information and training for parents to advocate more effectively for their children. I give them the name and number of a family of a child with autism (if the other family has given me permission to do so) so that they make parent-to-parent contact. I tell them that they can look for information on the Internet, but at this early stage, this level of information (and in many cases misinformation) is usually not what is needed.

(continued)

Depending on the age of the child, I give them contact information for the governmental or educational agency with responsibility for services. For parents of children under the age of 3 years, this will be an Early Intervention Program (EIP). For children over 3 years, two agencies are critical. For special education I provide the Child Find number for the school district in which they reside. Every local education agency must have an easy-to-access Child Find person. In addition, I give the contact person for our state developmental services program, which, in Florida, is within the Department of Children and Families. If the parents have a child with autism, which is a developmental disability, they must know about and be prepared to take advantage of these state-funded services. This agency can play a critical role in support and technical assistance, and, in the state of Florida, has moved progressively to improve the quality of life for persons with disabilities.

I ask the parents what they know about autism. Usually it is very little, so I share information on several books and articles including Catherine Maurice's, *Let Me Hear Your Voice* and Michael Powers' *Children With Autism: A Parents' Guide*. I also recommend Bryna Siegel's *The World of the Autistic Child: Understanding and Treating Autistic Spectrum Disorders*, and Sandra Harris and Jan Handleman's, *Preschool Education Programs for Children with Autism*. If they ask about outcomes, I tell them about the 1987 Lovaas article. I offer to send them a packet of information and invite them to visit our autism materials center at the university. I mention that our students are required to complete 30 hours of observation and participation with students with autism and ask if they would be interested in hosting one or more students (usually a teacher) for some of their experience hours.

I'll ask how they are doing. They will typically tell me all is well even if it isn't. I can't insert myself as an active helper, but I do urge them to call me if they need information or referral to other sources of support. I have the numbers and know the special strengths of several counselors and other human service providers who may be of assistance if the need arises. I do urge the family to rely on the strengths of their immediate and extended family to help meet any special challenges they may face. I encourage the family to seek support, respite care, or other help from their church or synagogue.

I do *not* tell the family that God probably had a special plan for them, or that they are blessed to have a child with autism. This is certainly not my place, even if I believed it to be true. Given the choice, most families would prefer that their child not have autism. I do tell them that my experience with parents of children with autism has been very positive. I tell them that when I compare different groups of parents, parents of children with autism are determined, persistent, energetic, and strong champions for their children. They may not believe me and I may not have data to back it up but I think, in time, they will find that they are the just the right kind of parents this child needed to have.

Jack Scott, Ph.D., is an Associate Professor of Special Education at Florida Atlantic University in Boca Raton, Florida.

ents of children with autism have been actively included in these courses. A test of general knowledge relating to autism was administered to parents, special education teachers, and speech-language pathologists. On pretests, parents consistently scored the highest of the three groups in their knowledge of this disorder. This is easily accounted for by several factors. First, parents with children who have autism have a sustained interest in the disorder. Second, information they receive is maintained by frequent use as they consider its application to their children and share information with other parents. Third, parents have a solid practical basis for understanding autism, as they have daily contact with their own children. The parents in this study knew a great deal about autism.

Teachers should be aware that parents may know more about autism than they do. Unless educators involved in IEP development and teaching have had *specialized training* in autism, the parents of their students are likely to have more knowledge on this topic than they do. Parent knowledge and insight are strengths that they bring to the effort to educate these students. This resource should be taken seriously.

Parents and Families: A Comment on Terminology

It has become standard practice to consider children within the context of their families. The term family is more inclusive than the term parent, including siblings and extended family members who may play an active,

The Power of a Word

Richard and Ann Levene

Autism. It is a frightening word. And to a parent it has many meanings, but no real explanation. The world is full of mysteries, but autism remains the most difficult for us to comprehend. This is how we felt when we first heard the pediatric neurologist diagnose Alex, our 19-month-old son, with mild to moderate autism. It was as if our dreams and hopes for our little boy disappeared with the utterance of one single word—autism.

After a period of grieving, we quickly realized that we were the only ones who were going to make a difference in our son's life. We were determined to beat this disorder. We wanted our son to become an active part of the family and the community around him. We wanted to go to sleep at night knowing that we were providing the best interventions available for our son. Intensive early intervention was the answer!

After several months of searching for the best program to help Alex, we discovered the Lovaas Program out of UCLA. This program and the work of many patient, loving therapists gave us the Alex we have today. In the beginning our son had no speech, no eye contact, no emotions or attachments, no appropriate play, and his behavior was very difficult. However, after intensive early intervention, Alex began to make progress.

Today we have a son. Alex enjoys playing CandyLand, he loves to play on the computer, enjoys dinners out, loves to go on vacations, sometimes talks too much. Most important, Alex has a wonderful relationship with his older brother. If we had given in to the autism, thinking there was no hope, we believe the Alex of today would not exist!

Dr. Richard Levene is a physician in West Palm Beach, Florida. Ann Levene is Parent Education Liaison with St. Mary's Preschool for Children with Autism in West Palm Beach, Florida.

and in some cases critical, role with the child. While sensitive to this tradition, it is also fair to recognize the special role played by the parents of a child with autism. They incur the greatest responsibility over the longest period of time and are the primary coordinating, planning, and support persons for their children. For these reasons, we refer to parents when the referent is most logically the parents of the child and use the term "family" when this term is most appropriate. Important decisions about the child's program are, in almost all cases, made by the parents with other family members possibly providing input.

Parents are likely to have opinions about how educational services should be provided. These opinions will emanate from their family values and philosophy and, to varying degrees, from information parents have received from the shared wisdom and collective experience of other parents of children with autism.

Best Practices in Parent-Professional Relations: Family Centered and Family Friendly

Public school programs for students with autism adhere to the requirements of IDEA. They focus on the needs of the student while assuring parent opportunities to participate in decision making. The focus of the school and the educational system is to help the student learn. Progressive practices for teaching students with disabilities, especially young children, are family centered (Turnbull & Turnbull, 1997).

There has been significant progress in providing family-centered services and supports in a relatively short time. Historically, scapegoating of parents of children with autism was a key element of professional practice. It is important to keep in mind that the scapegoating that occurred in the early years was not unique (Paul, Porter, & Falk, 1993), but rather reflected the broader scapegoating of parents of children with disabilities and even typically developing children. The efforts of parents (including parents of children with autism) to secure high-quality public education for their children became quite pronounced during the 1960s and 1970s, and has continued to the present.

Family-centered Services

A revolution has occurred in the way professional services are provided for very young children with disabilities. The foundation of this revolution is rooted in several different fields of study. Turnbull and Turnbull (1997) best illustrate the changes in professional services and care. Former practice called for parents to provide permission for professional services and they might be consulted on how these services could be delivered. The current view is that the young child is integral to and dependent on the family, so the family should be the center of the intervention effort. Professionals might arrange for supports that enable families to coordinate a variety of services for their children. Not only do parents "give permission" for an assessment, they *participate* in the process. Parents select treatment options and are supported while they gather information about the options and evaluate them. The parents benefit from training and education efforts. Therapists may assess the child, but increasingly direct services are provided to the parents, who are then able to *use* these new skills and ways of interacting with the child across all environments. This helps parents become skilled in helping to teach and advise others who care for the child about the most effective ways of interacting, thus maximizing therapeutic impact. Family-centered practice is fundamental to federally funded early intervention efforts and now constitutes best practice for those involved in early intervention (Bailey & Wolery, 1992), early language and communication intervention (Robinson, 1997), early autism intervention (Lovaas, 1987), and for prevention and reduction of serious problem behaviors (Koegel, Koegel, Kellegrew, & Mullen, 1996).

Brofenbrenner (1975) was among the first to suggest that family-centered intervention was essential to achieving enduring benefits for young children with disabilities. This is even more critical in families with multiple stress factors. Bailey and Wolery (1992) summarized family and early intervention best practices as:

1. Early intervention is increasingly family-, not child-, centered.
2. Early intervention should enable families to make decisions independently and to access services.
3. Services should be based on the needs of the family and child, not designed to meet the convenience of the providing agencies or systems.
4. Services should help a family achieve a normalized lifestyle.
5. Cultural sensitivity and respect for the values of each family are inherent in family-centered practice.
6. Services must be individualized to reflect the needs of the family and child.
7. Coordination of services across agencies is essential; families must be able to access services while professionals coordinate their efforts to avoid duplication.

These practices are central to early intervention services provided under Part C (formerly known as Part H) of IDEA. New community-wide forums for coordinating and developing services, such as the local interagency coordinating councils (LICCs) mandated under Public Law 99-457, are operating in all states that provide Part C services. The law called for the creation of a "comprehensive, coordinated, multidisciplinary, interagency program of early intervention services for infants and toddlers with disabilities and their families" (Swann & Morgan, 1993). These

LICCs include parents as key stakeholders; accountability to the parents is essential. These practices are cultivating higher levels of parent involvement.

Parents are not just the recipients of services but they, by means of active membership in forums such as the LICCs, have vastly increased *power* in the early intervention arena. These efforts to bring greater balance to the power equation help keep the system honest and promote the development of mutual trust and cooperation. Bailey and Wolery (1992, p. 28) suggested that, "Ultimately, the effectiveness of family support services will depend on the extent to which professionals can establish trusting and collaborative relationships with families and provide services in ways that enable families to make decisions for themselves."

Parents also make critical decisions on the overall plan for their children. A study by Buysse, Bailey, Smith, and Simeonsson (1994) examined the degree to which child characteristics influenced early placement decisions. Although a general pattern showed that children with moderate disabilities entered segregated settings more often than those with mild disabilities, large numbers of children did not fit the pattern. The largest influence on placement was preference, especially preference for more inclusive settings. Buysse et al. (1994) pointed out that the specific family factors accounting for these decisions are not yet well understood. One thing, however, is apparent: Parents are increasingly making their own decisions rather than just agreeing to the decisions made by educators and others.

In early intervention, the shift to family-centered practice is happening with remarkable speed (Agosta & Melda, 1996). However, the impact has not been as great in special education for students to grade 12. Obviously, the nature of these services is vastly different. Early interventionists typically are funded to meet with families in their homes. Public education for school-aged children has the school as its focus. Few teachers are expected to travel to students' homes to meet with families. Parents are expected to be active participants in the student's program, but school is the context for this participation. Working more closely with families does not require more resources, but rather more skillful allocation of resources already available.

Teacher trainers have been challenged to produce family friendly teachers. Pugach and Johnson, (1995, p. 242) suggested that teachers learn to actively collaborate and stated, "We believe it is essential that those who work in collaborative schools make family participation a central goal. However, merely setting this goal does not ensure that families will be treated as full members of the collaborative team. . . . Why is it that some teachers do not feel committed to making all families welcome in schools?" Pugach and Johnson went on to note some key differences in values, norms, or expectations that hinder families from feeling more welcome at school. They first recommended that the role of the family should be a regular topic for consideration among the staff. For teachers uncomfortable with family involvement, they suggested that these teachers invite parents or relatives to come into their classrooms. "Skeptical teachers need to come face-to-face with their beliefs and work with families directly as a means of overcoming possible stereotyping" (p. 243). Finally, they suggested that preservice students obtain far more experiences interacting with parents of students with disabilities. For professionals preparing to teach students with autism, this is easily accomplished through participation in home-based intervention programs (Scott, 1996). Many parents are eager to have adults volunteer or be paid to work with their children.

Concerns of Parents of Children with Autism

Parents of children with autism face many of the same challenges parents of other children with disabilities face. They also face some unique problems that stem from the combination of factors at the core of autism. For example, many children with disabilities have identifiable conditions that indicate disability. To most people, a child with autism appears to be developing normally. The child's lack of social awareness presents ongoing challenges as the child fails to respond to social expectations and cues from peers and adults.

In this following section, we explore several unique concerns in which families may need active support. Although educators may have a role in some of these areas, their responsibilities rarely include comprehensive support. Rather, educators who understand the issues can be sensitive to the support needs of the family.

The Parent Saga in Autism: From Scapegoat to Partner

Parents may have reasons to be skeptical of the professional community. It is hard to appreciate the impact of parent blaming on families already struggling under tremendous challenges with their children. Consider this passage from Bruno Bettelheim: "Throughout this book I state my belief that the precipitating factor in infantile autism is the parent's wish that his child should not exist" (1967, p. 125). Schopler and Rimland are credited with ending the unbridled and sanctioned blaming of parents. Schopler has characterized much of this as "professional scapegoating."

He suggested that scapegoating was the byproduct of a lack of knowledge of effective treatments. This scapegoating occurred within a broader context in which professionals were expected to be authorities and to have answers about human disorders. Professional ignorance gave way to blaming, with parents being the obvious targets.

Schopler (1971) analyzed this process in relation to parents of children with autism. He noted that scapegoating offered certain advantages to the person or group doing the scapegoating including guilt evasion and self-enhancement. For scapegoating to function, the victims had to share several characteristics. First, the victim had to be easy to identify. Second, the victim had to present little possibility of doing the scapegoater harm. This was because the scapegoater was stronger and/or had higher social status. Finally, the victim had to be readily accessible. Parents of children with autism met these conditions.

As parents removed the medical community as the source of authority in the field of autism, they took the mantle of authority upon themselves. This may be one of the earliest examples of constructivist empowerment in any area of disability advocacy. This "shared role as an authority" has had both positive and negative effects. For example, if a parent believed that a given treatment worked well for a child, regardless of the objective evidence, then this choice would be regarded as valid. The absence of an outside authority thus resulted in everyone playing a role as authority.

This ambiguity over who is capable of evaluating treatment effectiveness is inherent in the ASA Options Policy shown on the next page. Although respect for parents' treatment choices is not questioned, this tradition established an *implied endorsement* of virtually any treatment any parent may wish to pursue. When all options are made available and criteria for evaluating effectiveness are not articulated and rigorous, the stage is set for problems. Indeed, the debacle of facilitated communication provided one clear and tragic example of a lack of discernment that envelopes a field where anyone can be considered an "expert." Other treatments still compete for parent acceptance with little or no more evidence than that provided for FC.

The need for change has been recognized by ASA and is illustrated by their new treatment guidelines shown on page 343. These new guidelines represent a major departure from the reliance on parent *preference* as an indicator of treatment acceptability. While still respecting parent options, the importance of scientific, controlled studies and other evidence beyond a person's own experience, is emphasized in establishing whether an intervention is effective. Hopefully, with widespread use of these guidelines, the entire autism field will become more objective, more critical, and far slower to embrace dramatic claims made in the absence of evidence.

ASA Options Policy

The Autism Society of America promotes the active and informed involvement of family members and the individual with autism in the planning of individualized, appropriate services and supports. The Board of the Autism Society of America believes that each person with autism is a unique individual. Each family and individual with autism should have the right to learn about and then select the options that they feel are most appropriate for the individual with autism. To the maximum extent possible, we believe that the decisions should be made by both the parents and the individual with autism.

Services should enhance and strengthen natural family and community supports for the individual with autism and the family whenever possible. The service option designed for an individual with autism should result in improved quality of life. Abusive treatment of any kind is not an option.

We firmly believe that no single type of program or service will fill the needs of every individual with autism and that each person should have access to support services. Selection of a program, service, or method of treatment should be on the basis of a full assessment of each person's abilities, needs, and interests. We believe that services should be outcome based to insure that they meet the individualized needs of a person with autism. With appropriate education, vocational training and community living options and support systems, individuals with autism can lead dignified, productive lives in their communities and strive to reach their fullest potential. The ASA believes that all individuals with autism have the right to access appropriate services and supports based on their needs and desires.

Policy of Autism Society of America, Bethesda, Maryland. (Adopted by the ASA Board of Directors on April 1, 1995)

The Parent-Professional Alliance

Just as Rimland brought about a change in thinking about the cause of autism, Schopler operationalized a set of practices that revolutionized the relationship between professionals and parents. In the early 1970s Schopler began the TEACCH (Treatment and Education of Autistic and

ASA Guidelines for Theory and Practice

The following guidelines were developed to assist people with autism, parents/guardians, practitioners, and advocates in evaluating theories and practices related to autism. The guidelines will provide such consumers with a set of parameters under which they can better determine the threats and opportunities associated with theories and practices.

In assessing theories and practices, consumers need to ask professionals the following questions.

1. Do you adhere to the Priorities of Professional Conduct promulgated by ASA? (See Autism Society of America Priorities of Professional Conduct.)
2. What is the purpose of this theory/practice?
3. What do I have to do to benefit from the theory/practice, and what are its lasting effects?
4. What is the status of this theory/practice relative to controlled (scientific) investigation, and is there a reference list of publications?
5. How long must my child be involved in this theory/practice to gain benefit?
6. Are there any physical or psychological harms which might come to my child as a function of participating in this theory/practice?
7. What are the personal costs of time and money that I will have to endure, and will I be able to be reimbursed for these expenses?
8. How do I know that the costs for the implementation of this theory/practice are fair and reasonable?
9. Are the theoreticians or practitioners competently and appropriately trained and prepared to implement the provisions of the theory or practice, and how is this competence assured?
10. What steps will be taken to protect my privacy?
11. Are there any legal actions, current or past, against promoters, consumers, or practitioners of the theory/practice?
12. How will the effects of this theory/practice be evaluated for my child?

(continued)

13. By choosing this theory/practice, what alternatives (proven/unproven) are not being pursued?
14. Does this approach exclude other alternative approaches and does it mesh with my child's total program?
15. Which individuals with autism has this theory positively benefited, and under what conditions?

Policy of Autism Society of America, Bethesda, Maryland. Developed by the Panel of Professional Advisors and approved by the Autism Society of America Board on January 17, 1997. Reprinted with permission.

Related Communication Handicapped Children) program founded as a collaboration between parents and professionals. The nature of this collaboration is illustrated by four relationships:

1. The professional is sometimes in a trainer role and the parent is in a trainee role. The professional is expected to hold legitimate expertise.
2. The parent is sometimes in a trainer role and the professional is the trainee. Here, parents' knowledge of their children and their motivation to help is the key element.
3. A mutual support context is maintained. With a severe, chronic disorder, progress may be difficult to achieve. When there are disagreements, parents and professionals agree to be "gentle" with one another.
4. Parents and professionals sometimes collaborate to gain community support

These four relationships set the stage for the tremendous progress that has been achieved for persons with autism in the last 25 years. These relationships are now clearly recognizable to most special educators, but they represented a major breakthrough in the autism field. Although they appear quite logical and easy to implement, they are not always easily achieved in public education. Consider how each can be problematic from the perspective of a traditional educator.

1. *Professional as trainer of the parent.* This is perhaps the most easily accomplished, as educators can readily impart

information and dispense expertise. But, with a unique disorder such as autism, the temptation to dispense inaccurate information may occur. This could plant the seeds of parental distrust.

2. *Parent as trainer of the professional.* This may be difficult for educators, especially those who believe it is their role and responsibility to have all the "answers." In the often-sensitive team deliberations and IEP development process, parent knowledge may be viewed skeptically by educators, as it could lead to parents seeking unfair advantage in requesting services.

3. *Mutual support.* A strong and continuing tradition in American education is to blame the parents for a child's failure. This is endemic and not unique to autism. Educators should admit that neither they nor the parents can do the job alone.

4. *Collaboration for advocacy.* Schools seek parents as supporters and junior partners, but real advocacy may mean unsettling some well-established practices. Educators tend to be very conservative; often they are hesitant to speak boldly for fear of breaching unstated "compliance expectations" by recommending services that a school district might not wish to supply.

Certainly enlightened educators can see and move beyond these potential barriers. The collaborative partnership can be achieved and, in so doing, enhance the education and overall quality of life of students with autism.

Parent-Identified Issues

A number of parents of children with autism have identified key issues that interfere with their ability to interact effectively with educators. Maurice (1993) emphasized the need for easier access to advice and information on effective interventions that is unbiased and empirically valid. She described the challenges she and her family faced in obtaining accurate information on autism and treatment. Maurice was given abundant erroneous information about behavior analytic interventions, much of it from misinformed or biased clinicians. Moreno (1992) offered a highly useful synthesis of the problem issues faced by all parents of children with autism. Moreno had two focal points in her treatment, one involving parenting and the other involving issues for care providers. The parenting issues identified by Moreno included:

- Getting a diagnosis
- Coping with the medical and psychological bureaucracy
- Receiving and understanding the diagnosis
- Searching for good sources of help
- Learning to manage behavior
- Coping with fatigue and managing time
- Making medication decisions
- Selecting good schools and teachers
- Teaching social skills
- Deciding what to tell family, friends, and peers about autism
- Planning for better living environments
- Helping the person with autism cope with loneliness
- Learning to take reasonable and intelligent risks

Moreno also identified factors unique to the parents of more sophisticated youngsters, which included such diverse issues as whether an adolescent should be allowed to drive and how to pursue special abilities in college. Each of Moreno's issues should be recognized as a major source of concern for a large percentage of parents of children with autism. These issues are not just by-products of the parenting styles of less capable parents; they are the kinds of problems inherent in the parenting process for all diligent and concerned parents in our society today.

Moreno's advice for professionals is equally clear:

1. Do not say, "I know just how you feel."
2. Do try to include autistic loved ones in your social gatherings or outings whenever appropriate.
3. Do not say, "You must be a very wonderful person for God to have chosen you to have this child."
4. Do offer us a chance for respite whenever you can feel you can.
5. Do not offer unsolicited advice.
6. Do say that you care and ask how you may be of help.
7. Do not say, "But all teenagers/toddlers/young men/girls/etc. do that or have a problem with that."
8. If a parent seems unduly upset or discouraged over a particular problem, remember that the problem you see is not the only one the parent is dealing with.
9. When our autistic loved one is in an activity outside the home (e.g., scouting, church youth group, YMCA activity), do not assume we want to be there with them.

10. Do not try to cheer a parent by saying, "You don't know for sure that [the autistic loved one] won't ever be able to . . . "
11. It is all right say, "I wish I could say something to make it better, but I don't know what that might be. I hope that the future will be good to you and your child."
12. Regressed behavior in autistic loved ones often causes regressed behavior in parents.
13. Parenting any person with autism, regardless of functioning level, is a very challenging experience. (Moreno, 1992, pp. 100–101)

Educators share with other care providers a special contact with the family. It is essential that educators interact with parents in ways that strengthen family relationships. At times, this calls for simple but valuable listening skills and a willingness to see the world from the view of the family. At other times, it might involve instructional methodology that "fits" into the flow of family life. One method used to extend instructional support to students and their families involves video reviews and rehearsal. Reamer, Brady, and Hawkins (1998) demonstrated that watching a video of how parents interacted with their children with autism during daily self-care routines, combined with practice of less directive interactions, helped parents reduce interaction problems at home. For one family, the effects spread from the mother who used the videos to the father who simply shared conversation about the positive changes. An additional benefit of the video package was an increase in self-care skills in the children. Using similar methods, Lasater and Brady (1995) applied this technology to teenagers with autism by building videos and practice opportunities of home routines, then sharing these videos with the youngsters. In each case, the families viewed the interventions as "family-friendly." Each family used the videos to see the nature of their interactions and practice *within a family context* how problems might be solved.

Unfortunately educators are limited in the ways they can proceed. In many ways it would be better if teachers of students with autism could know and fully understand the nature of each family and be equipped with the tools (and time) to respond when needed. Obviously, this will not happen in most public schools. Rather, with an increased sensitivity to the issues of some parents, and a willingness to respond with family-friendly tools when able, teachers can anticipate and help to contain problems faced by the parents of their students.

Stress and Depression

Parents of children with autism face many challenges. These challenges are easily negotiated by some but most parents find them burdensome and unrelenting. For many, the strains imposed by care, advocacy, supervision, and loss of privacy compound to create stress. Some parents react to these stressors by becoming depressed. Teachers of students with autism interact with the parents of many children. Teachers will find that many parents cope with high levels of stress, while the ability to cope is impaired in others. The teacher of children with autism should understand the factors that increase the likelihood of stress in families and know productive ways to interact with and, if necessary, to help these families.

Clearly, not all families of children with autism experience heightened stress leading to depression, nor does autism *cause* parental psychological problems. DeMyer writing in 1975 commented in this regard. Her statement is as true today as it was 25 years ago:

> In well controlled studies, they [researchers] failed to detect any more mental illness or extreme personality types among autistic parents [parents of children with autism] as a group than among other groups of parents. (p. xi)

Parents do not cause autism any more than parents cause a child to be born with Down syndrome, and teachers should suspect any effort to find a cause in parent psychological attributes. But parents do respond to multiple and prolonged stressors. Knowing this will help a teacher be more effective.

Stress and Parental Coping

Stress may be a prominent feature of a number of families of children with autism. Early clinicians such as Kanner and Bettelheim saw these stressors. Consistent with their time, they theorized that the disorder evident in the child was caused by the parents' inability to cope with a high level of stress. Kanner noted that the children did place a large burden on the parents, yet the direction of transmission of disorder was hypothesized to be from the "disordered" parent to the child. Under this model, a parent, by virtue of his or her stress and other problems, gave rise to autism in the child. These unsupported theories did not survive long, but they did have a dramatic impact. Cantwell, Baker, and Rutter (1978) and others began serious studies into the nature and extent of parent stress and other psychosocial challenges in the mid- to late 1970s. These parents were seen as having a loss of self-confidence and loss of a fundamental joy in life. However, these studies made it clear that parent stress, when it was evident, was not the cause of autism in the child.

Stress in parents of children with autism has been shown to be higher than that of parents of children with other disabilities. Wolf, Noh, Fisman, and Speechly (1989) conducted a study of 57 parents of children with autism and compared their stress levels and degree of depressive symptoms to that of parents of children with Down syndrome and parents of typically developing children. The parents of the children with autism had the highest stress levels and also showed the largest number of depressive symptoms of the three groups. Social support was found to lessen the impact of stress. The authors pointed to the need for additional counseling and targeted support services to offset the negative impact of stress. A study conducted in Australia by Gray and Holden (1992) added to the parental stress picture. These researchers surveyed 172 parents of children with autism and found a lower level of depression, anxiety, and anger for those who received more social support. An interesting finding was that even parents otherwise skilled in coping with stress did not cope well with the special demands made by their child's autism. This may suggest that otherwise very capable and even self-reliant parents will confront new psychosocial challenges if their children have autism. Parents who never have sought help may be reluctant to do so. This adds to the challenges they face as they interact with professionals.

The pervasiveness of autism in the child contributes to the stress and associated psychosocial problems in many parents (DeMyer, 1979). One of the findings by Wolf et al. (1989) was that mothers of children with autism tended to have more depressive symptoms, whereas fathers tended to have reactions little different from fathers of typically developing children. The greater care role assumed by mothers was a factor. Mothers also showed higher ratings for dysphoria, a measure of depressive symptoms. Fathers of the children with autism had a slightly elevated measure of depression. Wolf et al. considered the factors that moderated stress for the families and determined that perceived social support offset the stress and dysphoria symptoms in both mothers and fathers. They further speculated that the needs of fathers are often neglected and that, if professional support is focused on fathers, then the perceived stress level of the mothers could be reduced. They concluded: "Parent counseling should focus on the needs of the entire family specifically at critical periods, increase parents' understanding of their child's development, and enhance their parenting confidence and self-esteem" (p. 164). The moderating effects of social supports have been found in other studies (Fong, 1991; Gill & Harris, 1991). The consistent message for educators is that parents who show very high levels of stress are communicating that their present levels of support are not adequate.

DeMyer's work continues to be a rich source of information and insight. More recent research on parents of children with autism appears overly cautious toward the sensitivities of parents and may, in many important ways, "miss the mark" in family dynamics. DeMyer's work was strengthened by the degree of understanding she achieved with families and the honest and often unflattering portrayals of efforts to meet the challenges of their child's autism. She did not focus solely on stress but her work highlighted its critical position in the lives of many families. The stress came from quite predictable sources in these parents:

> The inability of the autistic child to understand what is expected of him or to master the usual developmental tasks of childhood. Autistic parents, far from being aloof and akin to disinterested spectators, were intensely affected by the developmental failure of their autistic child. [DeMyer quoted one mother as saying] "I've tried and tried to do things right with him, but I must have failed. My oldest daughter seems to do things better than I do." (1979, p. 149)

DeMeyer provided a summary of the effects of the child's symptoms on the mothers, the primary caregivers in her study. All of the mothers studied reported feelings of physical and psychological tension in relation to their child's autism. Additionally, 66% reported a sense of guilt and 33% were "unsure of mothering ability." Considered together, a picture emerges of mothers who are stressed and who feel guilty about their failures with their children.

It may be helpful to consider the insightful summary DeMyer (1979) provided on what she believed the spouses wanted from each other. She wrote:

> When all the verbiage was cleared away, the mothers seemed to be asking of fathers:
> Please support me in trying to do the best I can with this different and trying child. Tell me I'm doing a good job. Let me cry on your shoulder, listen to my observations about our child, go with me to see the doctors, don't retreat from us. Take us out for some fun even though you are embarrassed . . . Don't criticize me, but help me.
> In turn fathers seemed to be asking of mothers:
> I'm trying to do the best I can to earn a living and to understand what's going on, but I understand our autistic child less than you do and I'm uncomfortable because of all your painful emotions. . . . You're not that way any more and you are immersed in the problems of one child. (p. 169)

For many families, DeMyer's observations are telling. Sensitive educators will understand that autism is a pervasive disorder. Autism transcends learning problems with the child who has it and has an impact on the entire family.

This impact also reaches to the adjustment of the siblings. In general, siblings are well-adjusted and resilient. Mates (1990) studied 33 siblings of children with autism. The siblings of children with autism all lived in families that had received services through the TEACCH statewide support network. He found no significant differences between the siblings of the children with autism and nonautistic children on any of the measures used in the study. His results come with a very optimistic caution. Even a small amount of support can be beneficial to siblings.

Supports Needed by Families

Parents of children with autism and other disabilities share many concerns, including long-term care, housing, and estate planning. Although many professionals translate these concerns into a need for counseling and psychological supports, many families report that their needs are more practical. Practical supports are those that involve managing everyday life routines, (Martin, Brady, & Kotarba, 1992). Martin et al. found that routines made complex by their children's disabilities involved such simple daily events as grocery shopping, meal preparation, and parental intimacy; longer term practical concerns involved home ownership, insurance coverage, and job mobility.

As students leave public school and reach an age at which other children would leave home, many parents seek residential options. Finding quality residential options is a major challenge for families, regardless of whether the residence is a group home, assisted living facility, or shared ownership in a house linked with specialized supports. Some residential options may not be of high quality; others accommodate only persons with very severe challenging behaviors.

A major source of family concern is the long-term financial status of their child with autism. The adult child may qualify for significant federal or state benefits that may be jeopardized if they inherit a large sum of money. Careful estate planning can help ensure that assets are passed along to ensure the child a high quality of life. Guardianship after the death of the parents can constitute a planning dilemma, especially if the child with autism does not have siblings. If a substantial sum of money is passed on, other factors must be considered. Some states require that a minimum of two guardians be involved, one to oversee financial issues and the other to oversee care. Parents will typically structure their estate to provide a high quality of life for their child while not inadvertently curtailing eligibility for state and federal benefits. Parents usually work with professional estate planners to make these arrangements. Although these areas are not the province of the school system, educators may provide information on these topics during parent training sessions or in state and local conferences.

Parents and Conflict With Educational System

As Will (1986) noted, the development of the IEP can become a battleground for services. Parents and school personnel sometimes engage in struggles over resources and services. While parents have always had due process under federal special education laws, this adversarial process polarizes issues in an effort to make the most effective presentation at a hearing. The win-lose nature of the process increases the likelihood of a nonproductive post-due process relationship. For these and other reasons, many parents have been hesitant to access this system. Schools have the option of offering mediation, but until recently this was seldom done.

Mediation

The 1997 reauthorization of IDEA *requires* LEAs to offer mediation services when a conflict arises. Parents are not obligated to accept mediation. If they do accept mediation, they retain the right to seek a due process hearing or other procedural remedies. This may permit a more reasonable consideration of the needs of the children when a conflict arises. Decisions about educational programming for children with disabilities are rarely black and white. The best solution is likely to be someplace between the two positions. With mediation, more reasonable outcomes are likely.

The mediation requirement represents an important change and one that should be well known to families of children with autism. Mediation is voluntary on the part of both the parties. It is not used to deny or delay a parent's right to a due process hearing. Under IDEA, mediation is conducted by a qualified and impartial mediator who is trained in effective mediation techniques. Mediation services are to be established by each state or local educational agency, which must provide a "disinterested party" with knowledge of special education laws and procedures. The following requirements must be met during the proceedings:

- The state, not the parent, assumes the cost of mediation.
- Mediation sessions must be held in a convenient place and in a timely manner.
- If an agreement is reached, it must be recorded in writing.
- All mediation discussions are confidential and may not be used as evidence in any future due process or civil proceedings. Both parties may be required to sign a confidentiality pledge.

The last stipulation serves at least two major purposes: First, it encourages each party to reveal their honest concerns without jeopardizing any future rights. Second, as the information is kept confidential, it keeps any one mediated settlement from becoming a precedent. School district personnel are often apprehensive about providing particular services for fear that an expensive or cumbersome precedent may be set.

This is understandable from a risk management perspective but contrary to the spirit of meeting the individual needs of the child who is the focus of a dispute. Using mediation, a more child-focused dialogue, one that extends the problem-solving process of IEP development and implementation, should be possible.

PARENT SKILL DEVELOPMENT

The old model of meeting family needs can be seen as one of providing counseling and psychological services. This model has given way to a dynamic set of approaches to meet the educational and skill needs of family members. Parents are now seeking to learn how they can most effectively respond to their child. Support groups continue to play a role, but these groups may only be important for some families and only for a limited time. No longer are support groups the primary service provided to families.

Many of the emotional support models had a basis in psychological counseling. The common assumption of the models was that families were dysfunctional due to the strains of coping with the child with autism. As Maurice (1996) noted, these models did not serve adequately as the springboard for relevant information or effective interventions. In many cases, the models based on counseling approaches became patronizing and another example of the unequal and disempowering relationship between parents and professionals. The movement toward parent-professional partnerships has not always been easy, as seen by Maurice's comments on the following page. Following Maurice, Kleinfield-Hayes offers suggestions for families seeking to become advocates and system change agents.

Behavioral Teaching Skills

Parents typically place a high priority on obtaining knowledge and skills that will promote positive behaviors in their children. Just as skills and program models based on behavior analysis are judged to be crucial by experts in the field of autism (see Pfeiffer & Nelson, 1992), parents have also recognized how critical it is to have these skills. Rapin (1995) makes a strong case for parent knowledge and use of basic behavioral skills. She is widely respected for her ability to bridge highly technical information with the very practical and immediate concerns of parents. In the excerpt that follows, she is responding to the question: "Do you think there is one particular thing that is essential to do when setting out to make a difference in the life of a child with autism?"

In Strength and Humility

Catherine Maurice

When Dr. Jack Scott invited me to submit to this book a short section on "empowerment strategies for parents," I called him and told him that while I would be happy to support his work, I was a little reluctant to undertake that particular subject.

There is, to my mind, only one consistently legitimate way in which a parent can address other parents: That is by candidly and honestly relating our experiences, and not by preaching to anyone. In this candor, we can freely admit our moments of blindness, our prejudices and false assumptions, as well as our acts of courage or strength. From this honesty, we can explore our pain, our joy, or our uncertainty, and other parents can find in our experiences some reflection of their own struggles. I made many mistakes in my family's journey through autism. I would hope that people could learn as much from my mistakes as they did from my moments of wisdom.

Other than displaying that tapestry of lived experience, from which other parents may draw images and echoes of their own, I am really not in a position to tell anyone else how to be strong or how to cope. As to treatment, my individual experience with my children has applicability to others *only* to the extent that I can point to the extensive objective research foundations of applied behavior analysis and the documented evidence of its effectiveness with other children.

Yes, I believe that autism demands extraordinary strength from parents, and that all of us must find some source of "empowerment." But I also believe that being strong means being wise. Being strong sometimes means being humble, asking ourselves, "Am I right in making this statement? Do I have all the facts? Have I considered the reliability of my impressions, my beliefs, my opinions?"

I think that in autism today we have the myth of the Lorenzo's Oil Mom or the Lorenzo's Oil Dad—a kind of superparent, who takes on the narrow-minded establishment, and triumphantly invents a cure through sheer gutsiness and determination. I believe that we are also living in an era of backlash. Parents, who for decades were victimized and blamed for their child's autism, are now tending to react strongly in the opposite direction: No longer victims, many parents are taking up a mantle of authority, expertise, and infallibility. Sometimes this "parents always know best" dictum is encouraged by professionals (perhaps trying to be popular?), and sometimes it definitely gets out of hand. You've probably noticed the same phenomena as I have: Parents getting onto the Internet, and lecturing each other on issues of treatment and causation. Other parents putting their kids into three or four different kinds of therapy at once, and then proceeding to make authoritative statements about the curative power of their "eclectic approach"—as though they could possibly know what is or is not working in their uncontrolled home experiments. Nevertheless, these authoritative statements are regularly disseminated widely on the Internet or in the *Advocate*, thereby perpetuating the cycle of fad treatments, untested miracle cures, and wholesale medical or dietetic experimentation on vulnerable children.

Where does true and effective parental empowerment come from? I think it comes from a combination of self-reliance and reliance on others, of heroism tempered by wisdom, of courage channeled by caution. I believe it springs from a growing awareness of what we do know, and what we do not know; of the place for instinct and common sense, and the place for humility before our ignorance.

How do we empower ourselves to create the best possible opportunities for our children's growth and development? I don't know how you empower yourself, but here are some of the sources from which I drew, and continue to draw, my strength:

- I pray, and ask God to guide me through my ignorance, and sustain me in my weakness and fear.
- I take a hard look at all the supposed experts out there, and I ask myself which of them, in making pronouncements about autism, are relying on their own opinions, instincts, clinical intuition, and which of them consistently refers to a body of published scientific evidence backing those opinions. Over the years, I have learned how to better discriminate between these two groups. The first has led to an endless parade of weak or harmful "treatments," endless hairsplitting over diagnostic terminology, and a never-ending supply of coping books. The latter has led to progressively more effective interventions for autism.

(continued)

- I shun anyone purporting to have solved the enigma of autism, or purporting to explain the "world view" of people with autism. No one speaks for all people with autism, and no one can climb inside the brain of a person with autism to translate how he or she experiences the world.
- I drew significant power from all that I learned about applied behavior analysis. ABA has provided me with a model for teaching my children, and a model of how they learn, that goes far beyond any hand-holding support group or trendy fad in education. ABA has given me the true power to make a real difference in my children's lives. ABA enabled me to understand that, whether they recovered or not, my children could learn, and I could communicate with them on some level. I drew strength from ABA when my children struggled with the severe deficits and excesses of autism, and I draw the same powerful insights from ABA as they progress through regular schools. Once I grasped the basic principles of task analysis, behavior shaping, prompting and fading prompts, systematic reinforcement, and so on, I found, and continue to find, multiple applications of these principles in my daily life with all three of my children. I do not believe that ABA is the only possible present or future treatment for autism. However, it is the most effective treatment we have right now, and it can give back to us parents some measure of the strength and peace that autism strips from us.
- I listen to and observe other parents. I ignore the things they do that seem misguided, and I pay attention to their interactions with their child that seem wiser than my interactions, more effective than my interactions, or kinder. I did this when I was running an intensive behavioral program for my children, and I do it today.
- I try to pick my battles and do not feel guilty about all the other things I could or should be doing. Your most crucial battle at this time may be funding. Mine was to resist the almost universal denigration of behavioral intervention, and not believe what all the "experts" told me about the hopelessness of autism. Your primary battle right now might be finding good thera-

pists. Mine, for a while, was just trying to hold my family together as we went through autism a second time. There are times that I have been very active in the wider community and times that I needed to concentrate exclusively on my own husband and children. There are times that I had to focus much more on one child, and tried not to suffer too much over not being a perfect mother to the other two. The point is that we cannot do it all, and I think that if we succeed in instilling in all our children, autistic or not, the knowledge that they are loved and treasured, we are already fulfilling our most important work.

- I drew great strength from the good behavioral therapists I found. Unfortunately, one would have to be naive not to know that there are some really bad therapists out there. Just as we parents have to learn how to judge and evaluate what researchers and psychologists are telling us, we also have to learn how to evaluate the therapists, the people who actually work with our children. A good therapist is confident about what she knows and humble about what she doesn't know. She seeks feedback from those who have more experience. A good therapist understands that there is *no formula, no universal curriculum* to suit every child. A good behavioral therapist knows that to be effective, she must be capable of performing a "functional analysis" of a child's behaviors before she prescribes programmatic intervention, and if she cannot perform such an analysis, she should find someone who can. A good therapist does not charge parents anything the market will allow her to earn, in spite of the fact that she can extort whatever amount of money she can from desperate people.

Where research and data were not available, I drew strength from my own reason and common sense. Nobody knows yet, with any degree of certainty, how many hours a child should be in discrete, one-on-one intervention. When my two children

(continued)

were in therapy, we had to constantly discuss the issue with our therapists. My children seemed to respond to a varying, flexible mixture of one-on-one discrete trial teaching sessions combined with a high degree of incidental teaching throughout the day. Until more research is generated, indicating with more certainty a reliable number of discrete trial hours as a necessary minimum, I think that parents have to exercise some common sense about how their child is responding to discrete trials, and not cling to any magic number as the absolute.

I drew strength from the people I love and who love me. And I drew strength from my conviction that, whether they recovered or not, nothing, including autism, could ever force me to stop loving my children. I don't know what autism is or why our children were afflicted by autism. I do not accept the politically correct ideology that autism is an alternative lifestyle that we should respect as a willful choice of our children. Autism to me is a devastating and catastrophic loss, and I have heard the weeping of too many other parents not to believe that it is a devastating and catastrophic loss for them as well. Those who wish to help parents deal with this trauma would do well to start by acknowledging the extent of this pain, and refrain from heaping us with platitudes about "the adjustment process" or the "specialness" of our children. I believe that only by acknowledging our pain in its fierceness and its scope can we ever hope to move beyond it, into peace and acceptance. In my hardest moments, moments beyond tears and beyond words, I needed to confront that loss and understand all that it meant to me. But it was in those moments, facing my worst fears about autism and facing the possibility of never having a meaningful conversation with my gentle dark-haired daughter or with my beloved little son, that I also found the seeds of a surer strength: the knowledge that I would always love them, no matter what. They were my children, and each was a child of God, enfolded in His heart and created by His will. I would love them forever, that I knew. I hope that other parents may find strength in that conviction: autism is strong, but love is stronger still.

Catherine Maurice is the mother of two children recovered from autism and the author of the best-selling Let Me Hear Your Voice.

Parents as Advocates and System Change Agents

Cyndy Kleinfield-Hayes

As parents consider a role as the lead advocate for their child, many ask themselves, "Can one parent or a handful of parents really make a difference?" It's certainly easy to get overwhelmed when you consider that being an advocate means that additional hard work and planning will be coupled with the already difficult family challenges within the home.

It's important, however, to consider the vast and diverse knowledge and experience you have within your local parent network. Often very small parent groups have many of the skills necessary to undertake a project of considerable magnitude. Making an inventory of your human and other resources can be very empowering. Additionally, the group's ability to collaborate with professionals enhances the resource base considerably.

Ironically, parents may actually have some advantage over large, complex organizations. The first step in pursuing any goal is to have a shared vision. Organizations typically struggle to organize their associates to develop common goals. Most parents, on the other hand, share the vision that their children will enjoy an environment that will allow them to *reach their potentials*. What that environment looks like and the best way of attaining that environment will vary across families. But the focus is, and must always be, the children.

Once the group is able to articulate their shared vision, they must go about the work of understanding and defining the process of attaining their vision. When discussing issues that will impact the quality of your child's life, using emotional energy productively is not an easy task, but it is a necessary one. Parents should make certain they know specifically what they are asking or working for, and why. They should be able to provide rational, objective information to support their efforts.

How requests or goals are positioned can have a significant impact on the level of results achieved. When solutions provide some mutuality, they are very likely to be supported. Outlining a win-win scenario essentially eliminates the adversarial position. Although the win-win solution may not be apparent at first, usually stepping back will provide a broader perspective and the benefits will become clear.

(continued)

Parents also walk a fine line. They must be very focused and committed to their goals; however, they must not become so enamored with their own perspective that they are not open to new information. Parents should constantly be on the lookout for information that may benefit their children. The challenge is to be a smart consumer.

Finally, it's important to set realistic goals. Just as we understand that we must celebrate our children's small victories, so must we celebrate our own successes. You can make a difference.

Cyndy Kleinfield-Hayes is a parent and founder of Reaching Potentials in Plantation, Florida.

One thing that I always talk about with parents is the need for control. Many parents of autistic children are being led by the nose by their child. The average child learns, between the ages of one and three, that the control the infant has of the parent is going to have to dwindle and disappear; that it is the parent who is now going to be in control of the child.

Autistic children because of their difficulty in reading facial expression, tone of voice, environmental cues, if you will, (what the people in England have pioneered in calling the "theory of mind") don't learn easily that the parent in now in control. . . . Once you start to make demands and impose activities which the child has not initiated, sooner or later you are going to precipitate screaming and temper tantrums. . . . You have to teach the parents how to deal with that. You cannot educate a child until the child has learned that doing what a grown up would like him to do and paying attention to what the grown up would like him to pay attention to is a benign thing—no big deal, might even be nice.

I consider this an absolutely critical skill that the parents of preschool autistic kids have to be taught. A child whose parents don't learn this by age ten or so, may be destroying the house, but being unable to physically control him anymore, they get on to this terrible slippery slope of medication and more medication and more medication—some of which may result in irreversible changes in the nervous system (Rapin, 1995, p. 21).

The implications of Rapin's comments are clear. Control, obviously, is not just a teacher convenience issue but is *developmentally essential*. The child with autism will have problems with behavior and communication. The parents may have trouble learning the skills necessary for successfully managing these and other problems.

Some of the intuitive approaches that parents prefer often backfire. Parents' attention to tantrums yields *more not fewer* tantrums. Allowing a very fussy child to escape demands increases the chances that the child will become more fussy in a wider array of circumstances. By the time parents catch on, control is held by the child. If the parents engage in a struggle for control, they encounter an escalation of problem behavior that can be, quite frankly, scary. Parents can hold out for the expected behavior for a period of time, but parents ultimately relent and the child prevails in the end. Behaviorally, the parents have increased rather than decreased the child's resistance to extinction. They have taught the child to resist parent behavior change efforts. Repeated trials further strengthen the child's problem behavior and they also strengthen the parents' conviction that the child is not amenable to change. Instead of viewing the problem as one of learning and behavior, problems that will respond to instruction, parents (and some educators) come to believe that the problems are fixed attributes of the child's autism. The parents have learned erroneously that the solution is to accommodate the child. They then seek to impart this ineffective strategy to all others who have responsibilities for helping their child. This very odd situation has the parents acting as the advocates for the *least* therapeutic course of action.

Just as Rapin implied, the age and size of the child become critical factors. As long as the child is small, the parents and other adults can physically manage a difficult situation. Difficult situations do not occur every day, and both child and parent learn the boundaries of this arrangement. But when the child grows to be physically as large as one or both parents, difficult situations take on an entirely new complexion. The child cannot be influenced by purely physical means. Stressful and possibly even dangerous struggles occur. As a result of such struggles, the child becomes aware of a new relationship. The parents may be less likely to resort to physical management and the child may be less likely to comply with attempts to be physically managed.

Our emphasis here is not that parents use physical management skillfully. Rather, we are in full agreement with Rapin that parents must gain the essential behavioral principles. Parents must then interact with their child in ways that are therapeutic as well as parental.

Parenting Style

Some parents have a style that is naturally very therapeutic for student with autism. These parents provide clear expectations, naturally reinforce cooperative behavior and work hard to not reinforce problem behavior. They tend to be directive and structuring. This makes it easy for the student with autism to be safe, learn the behaviors expected of him or her, and avoid behavioral complications. Although this direct style may be best, it is not popular in many parts of the country. Instead, a nondirective parenting style predominates. Here, the parents offer choices to children, suggest an array of alternatives, accommodate (or over-accommodate) children's preferences, and allow children to have their way whenever possible. Our goal is not to argue the relative merits of this parenting style for children without autism, but for those with autism and closely related disorders, it is not very effective. Regardless of their natural inclination for raising their typically developing children, adults should adopt a parenting style (a consistent and predictable set of interaction patterns) that will maximize the success of their child with autism. The more directive, structured, and behavioral styles hold the greatest chances for success. It is important to note that families will select from among the broadest array of options when considering how they respond to a child with autism. Their parenting choices, while worthy of respect, are not equally wise nor equally likely to yield positive growth.

Parent Education

A number of materials and training formats are available to assist parents in learning skills to help their children. Schools, agencies, and parent groups are in a position to assist. Parents of children with autism should be afforded easy access to specialized and parent-sensitive information about autism, child management, and skill development. Parents are considered the "first and best teachers of their children," but in the absence of specialized assistance and information, they may not be the first and best interventionists for their child with autism.

Maurice (Maurice, Green, & Luce, 1996) commented on the lack of information on sound treatment practices aimed at parents. She noted that an array of scientifically sound and parent-friendly books are available about many childhood medical disorders. Few such materials are available to guide parents as they seek to provide high quality education, treatment, and care for their children with autism. Certainly books for parents exist, but the content does not include best educational, psychological, or medical practices. Many of these works, for example, place cranial-sacral therapy or facilitated communication on the same level as functional analysis or positive behavioral support. Parents and families deserve to have ready access to valid information. They should be warned when the information they are given is "fluff."

Parents who either wish to supplement formal home-based programs or learn on their own can take advantage of parent-friendly behavioral training materials. Latham (1994), for example, has an easily read text with supplementary audiotapes. These materials emphasize prevention of problem behaviors using positive approaches and feature skill development within a natural, family context. Latham's materials are not autism-specific, a factor that may increase rather than decrease their acceptability. The general usefulness of behavioral interventions and analysis of problem behaviors allows families to use these same skills with all of their children and to anticipate problems and prevent them from escalating.

Behavioral Problem-solving Skills

Even when parents are very diligent and have good interaction patterns, problems can develop. Keeping small problem behaviors from becoming big ones is crucial.

For children who have problem behaviors, Mullen and Frea (1995) advocated a parent-professional consultation model in which the process of functional assessment serves as the cornerstone of the relationship. To understand the functions of problem behavior, professionals obviously must work closely with the parents. The value of descriptive assessment in natural settings is achieved when parents become co-assessors. Descriptive assessments of the child in everyday settings provide the basis for understanding the child's behavior. This more natural approach requires that interventions and data gathering be made more family-friendly and 'do-able' for the parents or other regular caregivers.

Mullen and Frea (1995, p. 184) suggested that "parents may be ideal candidates to take an active role in conducting their children's functional assessment." They noted four areas in which parents provide obvious advantages.

1. Parents are the logical experts on their children and their family.
2. Parents are uniquely positioned to provide round-the-clock assessment in natural settings for children.
3. These new skills acquired by parents can be used across the life-span of their children.
4. Functional assessment is a mechanism for effective collaboration between parents and professionals. (p. 184)

A person providing supports to a child and family must exercise several cautions. First, it is critical to assess the level of involvement parents wish to establish and maintain. Second, the relationship proposed here is one of partnership and not one in which the professional merely assigns the parent a role as therapist or data gatherer. Parents must continue to be the *parents* of the child. But, when the child is displaying problem behaviors and parent-friendly systems for intervention and assessment are readily available, most parents will warmly welcome the chance to be part of the intervention team.

Carr et al. (1994) provided a similar model for working with parents on functional assessment. In Carr's model, the professional and parent gather observational information on problem behaviors, then compare notes to form an hypothesis on the functions of the problem behavior. If the parents view a problem as an inherent characteristic of the child's autism, while the professional views it as serving an escape function, then additional observations and meetings are held to refine the hypothesis. Parents who have a very nonbehavioral inclination toward intervention learn to use behavioral approaches, while the professional appreciates the increasing complexity of an intervention in home and other natural environments.

Parents as Tutors

Parents who wish to take a direct role in the delivery of instruction can become very effective tutors. Educators can assist them by providing brief training and information about powerful instructional strategies. In the absence of training, parents are likely to use a "mixed bag" of tutoring techniques relying on coercive interactions or poor instructional techniques. Without a simple system for evaluating progress, learner and parent frustration are common.

Duvall, Delquadri, and Hall (1996) developed a family-friendly tutoring program. Although not specifically designed for students with autism, Parents as Reading Tutors (PART) offered a model that can be replicated by other parents and professionals. PART was designed for brief (11–15 minute) daily parent tutoring sessions. This program was designed to supplement, not replace, the school program. It relied on simple, proven strategies and careful monitoring of progress. The basic program consisted of five steps:

1. Parents determine their child's reading level. Parents present a series of passages and record the number of correct words read per minute and the number of errors.
2. Brief daily tutoring is initiated. The child reads a short passage aloud for 4 minutes. The parent records the end point and any errors made and then directs the child to begin again. Any error is corrected. The parent points to the error word and says it correctly. The child is asked to say the word and then to read the entire sentence. No other instruction is provided. Praise is provided for success on error sentences. Parents are asked to set a timer to provide just 7 minutes of tutor-

ing for first and second graders and 10 minutes for children in third grade and above.

3. Comprehension is checked and enriched. Parents are directed to ask who, what, when, where, why questions and to praise correct answers. For errors, parents provide a clear correct answer and ask the question again, praising correct second tries.

4. Reading rate is assessed after each reading session. Parents set a timer for 1 minute and ask the child to read aloud. They mark corrects and errors and note these on a simple graph.

5. Last, a measure of weekly progress is determined by having the child read for 1 minute similar to the daily rate assessment on untutored materials. These data are similarly graphed and should show progress in generalizing these new reading skills.

PART is based on research on learning involving opportunity-to-respond (Hall, Delquadri, Greenwood, & Thurston, 1982), peer tutoring (Greenwood, Delquadri, & Hall, 1989), and an experimental analysis of parent tutoring (Duvall, Delquadri, Elliot, & Hall, 1992). By combining these elements into a simple, highly structured program, parents can easily be effective tutors and their children can be eager learners.

Parent Involvement in School

Parents differ widely on the degree to which they wish to become directly involved in their child's education program. Some, hopefully few, parents will have essentially no involvement; if allowed to do so, others might easily become overinvolved. This section features formats for involvement including daily home notes, parent visits and observation, and parents serving as volunteers.

Daily Home Notes

Daily home notes let parents know how the child did in school. Teachers usually write a few minutes of notes in a spiral notebook that travels back and forth with the child. For younger children, the teacher simply puts the notebook in the child's backpack.With older children, the student can be made a partner in the communication process. Time constraints will dictate the length and complexity of the notes. The teacher and parent share important information, which might include sleeping pattern, meals, special events, and the student's daily performance. These might be as informal as simple exchanges regarding a student's demeanor or progress on a specific set of vocabulary items. The home note system can be used in a one-way (teacher to parent) mode for parents who seek a low level of involvement. It can become an interactive tool with a two-way dialogue for parents who wish to establish a higher level of involvement. Future applications of home notes will undoubtedly include the use of e-mail and other electronic systems.

Parents who transport their children to school may wish to brief the teacher on home activities and comment on school progress. Although each discussion may last only a few minutes, it is easy for teachers to have a backlog of parents, as most children come to school at the same time. To avoid this backlog, paraeducators or other adults should be positioned to assist and supervise the students while the teacher interacts with parents. The teacher can benefit from learning about any unusual occurrences and gaining information on the success of skill generalization efforts. The eagerness of some parents to engage in this format for information sharing seems to be most pronounced for younger children but the desire to share information and to have even brief contact with the child's teacher appears to serve many important functions for parents of students of any age.

Parent Visits and Observations

Some parents may wish to visit the class or program for their children on a regular basis. This can be a wonderful opportunity for parents to see how their children are learning. However, if not managed carefully, it can have a negative impact on students' learning. Frequent visits that involve in-class discussions between the teacher and parent take the teacher away from instruction. Having a parent in the classroom may distract some students and interfere with learning. This problem is reduced when the classroom has an observation capability. Parents and others may be able to directly observe students or may view them on a television monitor without interrupting the flow of instruction. Unfortunately, few schools offer this arrangement. A fair policy on visiting should be established and consistently implemented.

Parents as Volunteers

Parents of children with autism may be eager to serve as classroom volunteers. Motivated volunteers, especially those with an in-depth understanding of autism, are valuable. Volunteers typically must apply and meet some district or school criteria. They understand and agree to abide by a set of rules or expectations for their participation. A common set of expectations might include:

1. Participate on an announced and scheduled basis;
2. Sign-in at the office and display identification;
3. Maintain an environment of strict confidentiality about students and families; and
4. Assist the children as a group (unless otherwise specified). Do not dwell on your own or any other child;
5. Allow the teacher to set and maintain the instructional tempo in the classroom. Be responsive to the teacher's requests for instructional and behavioral assistance.

Such expectations help make explicit some aspects of parent participation. Unfortunately, parent involvement sometimes interrupts the instructional context. Teachers appreciate parents who are eager to donate their time and talent, but do not appreciate parents who enter the class and interfere with instruction. Parents should not ask teachers to justify programmatic decisions or practices affecting other students' programs, particularly during class. Obviously, a teacher cannot share the full range of child-specific information—almost all of it confidential—supporting these decisions.

A creative response to the wishes of some parents who sought high levels of productive involvement in their child's school was initiated in the Indian River County School District in Florida (Carbone, 1996). Several parents had an opportunity to receive training in observation and data recording. They assisted with behavior observations in selected classrooms on a voluntary basis. The parents gained further training and insight into child behavior and made an important contribution to the total school effort.

Many families, particularly of younger children, have intensive home-based behavioral programs. In addition to the instructional hours at school, these students may receive 20 or more hours of home instruction. Coordination between the home and school programs can be invaluable for efficient acquisition and generalization of skills. Although the teacher cannot be expected to implement all of the home goals, some goals can be coordinated across settings. Additionally, by informing the parents of the skills being taught in class, the parents can implement some of these goals at home.

The Teacher's Role Is Not Limitless

Parents find that their private life becomes more public as a result of having a child with autism. Similarly, a teacher of children with autism is exposed to greater attention and even scrutiny in contrast to other teachers. It is essential to keep the teacher's role and priorities in context. The teacher's role is to provide a safe environment in which students can learn and to provide documented and effective instruction consistent with the IEP. Some districts provide additional support for families through a social worker, guidance counselor, or ESE specialist. Other districts have established linkages with community support agencies. In the absence of such supports, these roles often fall on the shoulders of the teacher. Teachers traditionally assume many additional responsibilities, but when they are incorrectly expected to assume responsibility for the full range of supports for a student and family, they will surely be unsuccessful.

The Challenge for Educators

The minimum standard set by IDEA frequently becomes the de facto standard for special education. Educators know this. The process of informing parents that their requests, even when reasonable, are not mandated by IDEA can be problematic. How should educators deal with these dilemmas? We propose that they ask themselves, "If this were my child, what services would I want to see in place?" or in the case of a personnel situation, " Would I want this person teaching my child?" Educators can easily use this framework to get to the central issue on a number of important issues. The teacher of students with autism must do the same thing. Realizing that the system will not generally advocate for services much above a modest appropriate level, educators should exert pressure on these systems to obtain services that they would seek for their own children. Indeed, educators face multiple pressures to conserve resources, but they must act as empowered professionals who will press for the needs of a student with autism even when the system is not optimized to deliver a suitable level of service. This cannot be done alone. Educators must work creatively in direct partnership with families to build the attitudinal, programmatic, practical, and political resources essential in meeting these challenges. An example of how a parent cooperative can be used to provide resources is found on the next page.

District Forums for Planning and Program Development

The partnership between parents and educators is fostered by close cooperation and active sharing of information. As noted previously in this chapter, many circumstances will arise that could lead to conflict. One of the best ways to foster a positive context for sharing concerns and plans is a district-level advisory group. The Broward County School District in Florida, one of the largest districts in the nation, has a parent-professional autism forum. This group meets regularly to share informa-

Parent Cooperatives

Pamela Gorski and Ruth Singer-Strunck

Parents frequently receive conflicting opinions from professionals and well intending family members or friends. A necessary component to the emotional well being of a family is the ability to seek out the experiences of other families. Our parent support group was built because of the frustration we experienced as parents while trying to secure appropriate interventions and services for our children.

Our mission has been to provide a catalyst for parents and professionals to network. A meeting format that facilitates exchange of appropriate information on available interventions while addressing the emotional needs of parents and family members has proven to be very effective.

One of the most important things we discovered in building a successful parent cooperative is that it is imperative to develop close working relationships with the educational community. This includes individual teachers who influence the child with autism, the administrators within the school district, as well as the professors of special education at local universities.

Teachers frequently understand the educational and developmental needs of the child but may need help in fully understanding the emotional needs of the family. Educators often have a great impact on the student and their family but may find themselves torn between the needs of the family and the constraints of the school system. An effective parent cooperative can help to develop and enhance the relationship between parents and professionals, and provide essential collaboration with administrators within the school system. Professionals in the medical community can also play a positive role in building parent support systems. They are among the first professionals to consider the needs of the child and are in a position to refer parents to community services.

From our experience in building parent cooperatives, we've learned that there are a number of organizational steps that assure success. These steps include:

(continued)

- Develop a list of long- and short-term goals. Remember to include the needs of both the parent and professional community.
- Define a mission statement or statement of purpose.
- Identify a core group of members who can take an active role in developing the organization.
- Understand that the organization must be treated as a business and seek out appropriate guidance.
- File necessary documentation to establish yourselves as a non-profit organization.
- Secure the support of professionals in the autism community, such as speech-language pathologists, neurologists, psychologists, or other professionals.
- Find a meeting location that can accommodate your needs.
- Invite parents and professionals to attend the meetings; remember that collaboration is essential.
- Allow for networking time in your meeting format.
- Keep a personal tone to the meetings. Use name tags and include an opportunity for each person attending the meeting to introduce him- or herself to the group.
- Strive to keep abreast of current information in the community so that the organization will serve as an effective resource and referral network.
- Advocate for parent representative positions on the various community organizations that will have an impact on services to persons with autism.
- Choose a representative from your organization who can effectively convey the group's collaborative message to educators and the medical community.
- Establish a form of communication that will help to build awareness about your organization (such as newsletters, brochures, etc.).
- Educate the medical community about your efforts; become a referral source for families of newly diagnosed children.
- Try to become an effective information source by establishing a library of books, research articles, or other information related to developmental disabilities.

Parents of children with autism have suffered at the hands of the professional community in the past yet, as a whole, have managed to display a tremendous amount of courage and perseverance in sustaining their families. Always try to remember their determination to get help for their child and the hope that pushes them. We encourage you to get more involved, it is a rewarding "experience."

Pamela Gorski is the Director of Reaching Potentials, Inc. in Plantation, Florida. Ruth Singer-Strunck is the Director of SPEC Group, Inc. in Broward County, Florida. They also are parents of children with autism.

tion and to jointly explore needs of students with autism. Parents, agency representatives, teachers, principals, university faculty, and others meet to share perspectives. Sally Creswell, curriculum supervisor for this district, has outlined her vision on the next page.

When a district has a number of students with autism, it should have some forum to consider the nature and direction of the school district plan for these students. This may be conducted as a district-wide advisory forum. Unfortunately, the relatively low incidence of autism could result in parent underrepresentation in these advisory groups. The concerns of parents of students with autism could easily get lost. Regardless of the type or location of the advisory council, autism-specific issues must be addressed systematically and regularly.

Regional and State-Supported Efforts

School district initiatives and planning are essential but must be supported by regional and statewide efforts. The average school district in the United States enrolls fewer than 4,000 students; even with an estimated 1 student with autism per 1,000 students, this yields only 4 students with autism per district. It is rarely cost-effective to conduct specialized training for such a small number of persons, so multidistrict cooperation and collaboration is recommended.

State-supported regional efforts can further the partnerships of parents and educators. A system of regional autism centers in Florida, the Centers for Autism and Related Disabilities (CARD), currently operates six centers. Each center provides an array of services based on a common state mission, which is responsive to regional needs as expressed by

Autism Program Development: A District Supervisor's Perspective and Philosophy

Sally Creswell

One of our problems in school districts is the increasing number of students with the diagnosis of autistic spectrum disorder. This has created a need for experienced personnel in planning and delivering appropriate curriculum using sophisticated instructional techniques. This comes at a time when many educators lack specific training in this disorder. It also occurs as resources from the federal, state, and local governments are under scrutiny for downsizing and reducing the dollars available for all educational needs. This has become both a political problem and a leadership one. Leadership that will promote systemic and principled change in implementing family-professional partnerships is critical. Only through a true collaboration will there be changes in service delivery.

Currently, most state funding systems recognize the resource needs of the complex visually or hearing impaired student, but do not recognize the complex needs of the autistic learner. Carl Jung pointed out, "The artful denial of a problem will not produce conviction; on the contrary, a wider and higher consciousness is required to give us the certainty and clarity we need." Like Jung, we need to produce conviction about our problems by clearly defining the needs of students with autism and their families and clearly defining our process for obtaining services. In my role as curriculum supervisor for autism, I have found the following steps for change to be valuable:

A. Identify Key Staff and Their Roles in Autism
   *   *Bring teachers together* for workshops, support groups, or planning meetings. Objective is to find out their collective needs and concerns.
   *   *Visit classrooms* to further determine how the students are progressing and what conditions at the schools are conducive to their learning.
   *   *Attend the local Autism Society meetings* and become part of the group. Meet the parents. Volunteer to assist them with grant writing or other needs.
   *   *Provide a long- and short-term plan* and take it to district administration.

B. Create an Advisory Committee
    - *Create an advisory committee,* a small core of parents, teachers, and school administrators who are willing to meet three or four times a year, as a key element. Balance the membership equally. Keep it small. Broward began with six school staff, six parents, and six community personnel. Educators and parents represented the various grade levels. Parents also represented the Autism Society Parent Network. Six community agencies also were represented. The process was important. Ground rules were established honoring each member's views as essential. There are diverse opinions nationally and locally and there was agreement that all disagreements/debate remained within the group. Only proposed solutions went forward. All opinions were honored.

C. Create a 5-Year Plan
    - *Brainstorm an all-encompassing list.* Meet until you have a consensus for the 5-year, 3-year and 1-year priorities. Keep the 1-year goals limited (1–3 goals at most). All the rest of the meetings revolve around your annual list. The annual list ties into the 3- and 5-year plans.

D. Political Action Plan
    - *District Administrator prepares reports* to the supervisor for support and information for the executive/cabinet level.
    - *Advisory members contact* school board members as appropriate.
    - *Legislative platform* can be part of the school system's initiative.

E. Organizational Elements
    - *Use information from school-based staffings* for students with intense needs to document program requirements. Take this information back to departments to justify training and budgets requests.
    - *Obtain and analyze data on all the students.* How many students, grade levels, types of current placement, typical types of services offered (OT/speech/PT), number of aides, and how much actual time is spent with the student. How does the money go to the source: directly to the school or somewhere else? Does it come from a formula?

(continued)

- *Create a directory of names* (other than advisory council members) of all your local agency and professional resources within and outside the school system.
- *Create a directory of professionals in private and public institutions* who are doing current work in autism. Call them directly and get on the mailing lists. Find out their availability for consultation.
- *Form a regional network* among community agencies, professionals, parents, and universities. In our case it is the counties of Palm Beach, Broward, and Miami-Dade. Fifty percent of the state population with diagnosis of autism reside in these three counties. It is essential that we talk to each other about our efforts and our training.
- *Form a network of the public education administrators* responsible for autism programs from preschool to 12th grade. Discussion is limited to program issues and ways to have uniformity of program options and training.

Sally Creswell is a Curriculum Supervisor for programs for students with emotional handicaps and students with autism for the School Board of Broward County, Florida.

a parent constituency board. The CARD mission is highlighted in Table 9–1. The state of New Jersey also funds a parent-directed autism service and support group. The Center for Outreach and Services for the Autism Community (COASAC) has become the model for other groups that seek to be parent-directed, supportive of the most effective interventions, and highly responsive to family needs. State-wide agencies, whether organized like COASAC or CARD, serve an important role in promoting the interests of the entire autism community, a community in which educators play an important role.

Sullivan (1984) argued that parents are the key trainers of both professionals and legislators. In these roles they may speak in college classes, conferences, or with legislators. The education of legislators is critical for the enhancement of services. Educators are rarely empowered to meet directly with legislators to lobby for more funding for school pro-

Table 9–1. Center for Autism and Related Disabilities (CARD)

Mission	Philosophy and Values
The Center for Autism and Related Disabilities (CARD) provides support and assistance with the goal of optimizing the potential of people with autism and related disabilities.	CARD is founded on the belief that: All people, regardless of their abilities or disabilities, have the right to live as full participants in society. All people have the right to be treated with dignity and understanding. People with disabilities are members of families. All families have strengths and capacities. They have the right to be treated with sensitivity and respect and as integral members of a person's support system. People with autism and related disabilities have the right to be regarded as individuals who need services and supports that are based on their unique characteristics.

Source: From the Center for Autism and Related Disabilities at the University of South Florida, web site:http://card-usf.fmhi.usf.edu/CardRep97/CARD97TOC.html

grams, to make changes in insurance regulations, or to establish autism supports. But parents have no impediments to voicing their views, and astute elected officials are sensitive to citizens' opinions. This can work both for and against autism advocacy. A disjointed voice, with supporters "fussing" over seemingly minor issues, will not earn the support of legislators. But coordinated, strong, and well-documented advocacy and legislator education efforts, as Sullivan noted, have been highly successful.

SUMMARY

What We Hope Parents Will Do

The following list of eight items was developed by the authors in partnership with several parents of students with autism. It is a set of suggestions for parents on how to develop stronger partnerships with educators in their children's schools.

1. Participate actively in your child's school program.
2. Get and stay involved in the IEP process.

3. Volunteer, even if only for a few hours each month, at your child's school.
4. Understand the roles of other professionals in your child's education. Respect these professionals and expect that your role as parent will be respected.
5. Know what your child can do in school academically, socially, and communicatively.
6. Know what your child is learning at school and why it is important.
7. Know your rights but use them sparingly. Work on the assumption that teachers and administrators are trying to do the best they can for your child and the other children at his or her school.
8. Avoid insisting on services that will yield limited benefit. It is important to build and preserve positive relationships among students, teachers, and parents.

REVIEW QUESTIONS

1. What are the key benefits of parents and professionals forming partnerships?

2. What impact has the legacy of parental scapegoating had on the autism community?

3. What are the safe and faulty assumptions involving stress among families of students with autism?

4. What are some of the practices that can enhance communication between parents and educators?

5. What can educators do to support parent-directed efforts to enhance supports for students with autism?

REFERENCES

Agosta, J., & Melda, K. (1996). Supporting families who provide care at home for children with disabilities. *Exceptional Children, 62*, 271–282.

Bailey, D., & Wolery, M. (1992). *Teaching infants and preschoolers with disabilities.* New York: Merrill/Macmillan.

Bettelheim, B. (1967). *The empty fortress: Infantile autism and the birth of the self.* New York: The Free Press.

Brofenbrenner, U. (1975). Is early intervention effective? In B. Friedlander, G. Sterrit, & G. Kirk (Eds.), *Exceptional infant. Vol. 3: Assessment and intervention* (pp. 449–475). New York: Brunner/Mazel.

Buysse,V., Bailey, D. B., Smith, T. M., & Simeonsson, R. J. (1994). The relationship between child characteristics and placement in specialized versus inclusive early childhood programs. *Topics in Early Childhood Special Education, 14,* 419–435.

Cantwell, D., Baker, L., & Rutter, M. (1978). Family factors. In M. Rutter & E. Schopler (Eds.), *Autism: A reappraisal of concepts and treatment* (pp. 287–301). New York: Plenum.

Carbone, V. (1996, October). *Parents as observers and data gatherers.* Presentation at the Florida Association for Behavior Analysis, Daytona Beach, FL.

Carr, E., Levin, L., McConnachie, G., Carlson, G. I., Kemp, D. C., & Smith, C. E. (1994). *Communication-based intervention for problem behavior.* Baltimore, MD: Paul H. Brookes.

DeMyer, M. K. (1975). Research in infantile autism: A strategy and its results. *Biological Psychiatry, 10,* 433–452.

DeMyer, M. K. (1979). *Parents and children in autism.* Washington, DC: V. H. Winston & Sons.

Duvall, S. F., Delquadri, J., Elliot, M., & Hall, R. V. (1992). Parent tutoring procedures: Experimental analysis and validation of generalization in oral reading across passages, settings and time. *Journal of Behavioral Education, 2,* 281–303.

Duvall, S. F., Delquadri, J. C., & Hall, R. V. (1996). *Parents as reading tutors.* Longmont, CO: Sopris West.

Fong, P. (1991). Cognitive appraisals in high- and low-stress mothers of adolescents with autism. *Journal of Consulting and Clinical Psychology, 59,* 471–474.

Gill, M., & Harris, S. (1991). Hardiness and social support as predictors of psychological discomfort in mothers of children with autism. *Journal of Autism and Developmental Disorders, 21,* 407–413.

Gray, D., & Holden, W. (1992). Psycho-social well-being among the parents of children with autism. *Australia and New Zealand Journal of Developmental Disabilities, 18*(2), 88–93.

Greenwood, C. R., Delquadri, J., & Hall, R. V. (1989). Longitudinal effects of classwide peer tutoring. *Journal of Educational Psychology, 81,* 371–383.

Hall, R. V., Delquadri, C., Greenwood, C. R., & Thurston, L. (1982). The importance of opportunity to respond in children's academic success. In E. D. Edgar, N. Haring, J. R. Jenkins, & C. Pious (Eds.), *Serving young handicapped children: Issues and research* (pp. 107–149). Austin, TX: Pro-Ed.

Koegel, L., Koegel, R., Kellegrew, D., & Mullen, K. (1996). Parent education for prevention and reduction of severe problem behaviors. In L. Koegel, R.

Koegel, & G. Dunlap (Eds.), *Positive behavioral support* (pp. 3–30). Baltimore, MD: Paul H. Brookes.

Lasater, M., & Brady, M. P. (1995). Effects of video self-modeling and feedback on task fluency: A home based intervention. *Education and Treatment of Children, 18,* 389–407.

Latham, G. I. (1994). *The power of positive parenting.* North Logan, UT: P&T Ink.

Lovaas, O. I. (1987). Behavioral treatment and normal educational and intellectual functioning in young autistic children. *Journal of Consulting and Clinical Psychology, 55,* 3–9.

Marcus, L. M., & Schopler, E. (1987). Working with families: A developmental perspective. In D. J. Cohen & A. M. Donnellan (Eds.), *Handbook of autism and pervasive developmental disorders* (pp. 499–512). Silver Spring, MD: V. H. Winston.

Martin, S., & Brady, M. P., & Kotarba, J. (1992). Families with chronically ill young children: The unsinkable family. *Remedial and Special Education, 13*(2), 6–15.

Mates, T. (1990). Siblings of autistic children: Their adjustment and performance at home and in school. *Journal of Autism and Developmental Disorders, 20,* 545–553.

Maurice, C. (1993). *Let me hear your voice.* New York: Knopf.

Maurice, C., Green, G., & Luce, S. C. (1996). *Behavioral intervention for young children with autism.* Austin, TX: Pro-Ed.

Moreno, S. (1992). A parent's view of more able people with autism. In E. Schopler & G. Mesibov (Eds.), *Higher functioning individuals with autism* (pp. 91–103). New York: Plenum.

Mullen, K. B., & Frea, W. D. (1995). A parent professional consultation model for functional analysis. In R. L. Koegel & L. K. Koegel (Eds.) *Teaching children with autism* (pp. 175–188). Baltimore, MD: Paul H. Brookes.

Paul, J., Porter, P., & Falk, G. (1993). Families of children with disabling conditions. In J. Paul & R. Simeonsson (Eds.), *Children with special needs: Family, culture and society* (pp. 3–25). Fort Worth, TX: Harcourt Brace Jovanovich.

Pfeiffer, S. I., & Nelson, D. D. (1992). The cutting edge in services for people with autism. *Journal of Autism and Developmental Disorders, 22,* 95–105.

Pugach, M. C. & Johnson, L. J. (1995). *Collaborative practitioners: Collaborative schools.* Denver, CO: Love Publishing.

Rapin, I. (1995, July/August). Interview with Dr. Isabelle Rapin. *The Advocate,* pp. 20–23.

Reamer, R., Brady, M. P., & Hawkins, J. (1998). The effects of video self-modeling on parents' interactions with children with developmental disorders. *Education and Training in Mental Retardation and Developmental Disabilities, 33,* 131–143.

Robinson, N. (1997). Working with families. In L. McCormick, D. F. Loeb & R. L. Schiefelbusch (Eds.), *Supporting children with communication difficulties in inclusive settings* (pp. 109–148). Boston: Allyn & Bacon.

Schopler, E. (1971). Parents of psychotic children as scapegoats. *Journal of Contemporary Psychotherapy, 1,* 17–22.

Scott, J. (1996). Recruiting, selecting, and training teaching assistants. In C. Maurice, G. Green, & S. Luce (Eds.), *Behavioral intervention for young children with autism* (pp. 231–240). Austin, TX: Pro-Ed.

Sullivan, R. C. (1984). Parents as trainers of legislators, other parents, and researchers. In E. Schopler & G. Mesibov (Eds.), *The effects of autism on the family* (pp. 233–262). New York: Plenum.

Summers, J., Behr, S., & Turnbull, A. (1989). Positive adaptation and coping strength of families who have children with disabilities. In G. Singer & L. Irvin (Eds.), *Support for caring families: Enabling positive adaptation to disability* (pp. 27–40). Baltimore, MD: Paul H. Brookes.

Swann, W., & Morgan, J. (1993). *Collaborating for comprehensive services for young children and their families: The local interagency coordinating council.* Baltimore, MD: Paul H. Brookes.

Turnbull, A., & Turnbull, R. (1997). *Families, professionals, and exceptionality: A special partnership.* Upper Saddle River, NJ: Merrill/Prentice-Hall.

Will, M. (1986). *Educating students with learning problems: A shared responsibility.* Washington, DC: U.S. Department of Education.

Wolf, L., Noh, S., Fisman, S., & Speechley, M. (1989). Brief report: Psychological effects of parenting stress on parents of autistic children. *Journal of Autism and Developmental Disorders, 19,* 157–166.

Chapter 10

OFFERING A TRUE CONTINUUM OF SERVICES

Key Points

- A continuum must consider educational options beyond placement
- Schools are uniquely positioned to arrange a true continuum of supports and services
- A continuum of available services in a school district is not a continuum of student support
- A continuum for students with autism might differ from other common continua

INTRODUCTION

Often questions regarding a continuum of services are operationalized as decisions involving the degree of restrictiveness of a school placement. For students with autism, *a true continuum includes more than a focus on location* and includes educators' willingness to provide the types of structure and accommodations that will increase student learning. In this chapter we provide examples of an instructionally relevant continuum designed to support the learning characteristics of students with autism across different age groups.

WHAT IS A CONTINUUM?

The Individuals with Disabilities Act specifies that students with disabilities must have access to a continuum or array of educational placement alternatives. This is an effort to ensure that each student is provided with a quality educational program, regardless of how severe the disability or the degree to which the disability matches a district's existing resources and placement options. The congressional intent of IDEA's mandate should be clear. If not for this requirement, a local district could simply say that they do not offer a program appropriate for a child with autism and that parents should seek services elsewhere. Local educational agencies (LEAs) must be prepared to provide educational alternatives for students with autism, ranging from those with the mildest forms of the disorder to those with the most severe levels and with other handicapping conditions and complicating factors.

A dictionary definition of continuum states, "a continuous extent, succession, or whole, no part of which can be distinguished from neighboring parts except by arbitrary division" (Morris, 1978). Applied to education, this definition suggests *a seamless set of options* for students and educators. As the program for each student with a disability is individualized, a continuum of services is not a series of separate places or alternatives, but rather a locus on the continuum that can be tailored to meet the needs of that student. By providing more services, with a carefully crafted instructional program, only a few distinct "places" need be considered for meeting the needs of virtually any student. The degree to which a student is removed from close contact with typically developing peers is guided by the least restrictive environment requirements of IDEA, which mandates the use of the least restrictive settings in which an appropriate program can be delivered.

It is possible to consider a continuum of services for students with autism in at least three ways. At the most basic level is the view of many school administrators who focus on the letter of the law and seek to maintain close adherence to the minimum guarantees of the law. These decision makers view each placement decision not as an effort to develop a program that will have a lifelong impact on a child, but rather as a new challenge to the limited resources of the school system. Such challenges hold inherent opportunities for "bad" or expensive precedents to be set. In this mode of thinking, least restrictive environment might well be replaced with "least expensive environment."

The second way to consider the continuum is as the place or setting in which a student is best served to maximize his or her potential. This may require the creative and flexible use of several settings and different arrangements of services for different activities. A better placement decision could not be offered and any other setting or service arrangement would fail to offer the best package of supports. This best decision would maximize the student's progress and, in so doing, generally keep the overall costs of services lowest *over time*. This perspective of the continuum is somewhat idealistic as states are not required to provide the *best* programs that professionals can design, only ones that are "appropriate" for students with disabilities.

The third way to consider the continuum reflects the more community-based perspective of the developmental disabilities movement. This view defines a continuum by asking what supports or services are needed to help a person with disabilities become more successful in typical community environments. This view is best understood by considering the analysis of Taylor (1988), a critic of the traditional, placement-oriented conceptualization of the continuum. Taylor noted that the idea of a continuum falsely suggests a progression of skill development in which a student becomes progressively "more ready" for ever less restrictive services. Under the current continuum models, few students ever move from specialized placements and programs once located there. This is particularly true for students with more severe or obvious disabilities such as autism. In addition, students are most commonly placed in segregated settings and isolated from typically developing peers, which places additional hurdles to developing the very skills needed to "exit" from these environments. Taylor pointed out that this type of continuum unfairly validates the most restrictive and isolating placements. For these and other reasons, Taylor advocates discarding the notion of a continuum based on placement and replacing it with a more flexible model of providing supports in more typical environments. This position is fully explored at the end of this chapter in relation to the continuing preparation for autism-ready inclusive environments.

The wide variation in abilities and challenges of students with autism suggests that adopting a helpful view of a continuum will not be easy. A helpful continuum must be based on the characteristics of students representing the full spectrum of autism and must integrate what is known about effective programming for these students. Finally, a continuum should allow a differential emphasis on program elements for students at different ages or developmental periods, while maintaining an absolute commitment to education in less restrictive environments. Such a continuum is based on principles of learning and support and is not limited to what the schools must do simply for strict adherence to federal laws.

The needs of students with autism and their families are complex and multifaceted. The responses to these needs must be creative and break the limits that often constrain typical programming. These students often require after-care programs and supportive tutorial services. Many need home-based support for problem behaviors or to develop basic skills. Families commonly need respite care options. Many families also require access to support groups and counseling that is sensitive to their special circumstances. These services are not part of the continuum of *placements* provided in most school systems, yet they are critical parts of a full continuum of *services*. Here we are using continuum of services in a very different way to mean the full **scope** of services and supports necessary for the student with autism to be successful in his or her school, family, and community. Although schools are not obligated to fund or provide these additional services, they are uniquely positioned to play a central role to coordinate, plan, and, for some, even direct the delivery of these services. Of course, most LEAs are very, if not unduly, concerned with their core educational responsibilities. Consequently, many LEAs minimize or even reject the idea that they should be more fully involved in these services. This is understandable as school administrators fear that, once these subjects are broached, families may indeed request these supports. Some may even expect school districts to pay for them. Additionally, the families of students with *other* disabilities might demand the same level of "wrap-around" support. To develop a true continuum will require trusting partnerships of school leaders and parents of students with autism. Such partnerships are needed to cooperatively seek resources to provide nontraditional supports and services, and joint action is needed to develop shared support networks. Only in these ways will a full and true continuum of services be realized.

The Letter of the Law

IDEA mandates that a continuum of educational services be available to provide an education for individuals with disabilities in the least restrictive environment in which the individual can find success. Yell (1998) noted that the law provides options to meet the needs of students with disabilities to ensure their education in the least restrictive environment.

The IDEA requires that school districts have a range or continuum of alternative placement options to meet their needs. The continuum represents an entire spectrum of placements where a student's special education program can be implemented (p. 247).

This education is available without charge to all students who meet eligibility criteria. The law is specific as to the range of alternative (to the general education classroom) placements offered and for the provision of specialized education, related services, and supports necessary for students in regular and alternative placements. The law states that:

(a) Each [school district] shall ensure that a continuum of alternative placements is available to meet the needs of children with disabilities for special education and related services

(b) The continuum required . . . must:
  (1) Include alternative placements . . . (instruction in regular classes, special schools, home instruction and instruction in hospitals and institutions); and
  (2) Make provision for supplementary services (such as resource room or itinerant instruction) to be provided in conjunction with regular class placement. (IDEA regulations, 34 C.F.R. §300.551, 1997)

To qualify for special education a student must be evaluated by professionals and meet preset eligibility criteria. For eligible students, the resulting evaluations, combined with input from the parents, help the multidisciplinary team create the student's Individual Education Program (IEP). Based on the IEP, a determination is made for placement and related services for a maximum of 1 year. The placement reflects the multidisciplinary team's decision on where a student's IEP can best be carried out, that is, where the student is most likely to be able to achieve the targeted goals, given the supports and services for which he or she qualifies. These goals are expected to change as the student gets older, and the supports and services are likely to change as well.

The related supports and services are also mandated by law. They are intended to provide the assistance necessary to enable a student to benefit from education in the least restrictive environment. The implication of the law is that, without these related supports and services, the education of a student with a disability would have to be delivered in a more restricted setting. Note that the definitions are specific to allow the student to benefit from *educational opportunity* rather than a more global family-oriented support service or individual community living support. Depending on the IEP, however, these supports can move off the school campus and into the community as needed. Particularly as the student approaches the age for transition planning, more educational time is spent off campus in job-related activities. The supports and services would follow the student into the community as part of his or her transition plan (as stated in the student's IEP). The legal definitions of related services and supports are noted in Table 11–1.

Beyond the technical assessment of need documented by the professionals, an holistic assessment is necessary to create an educational plan that reflects the goals that the family finds important for the student, the family's resources and supports, and, to the degree that it is possible, to determine or infer the wishes, talents, interests, and hopes of the student with a disability. Goals that enable that student to function more effectively in the school, community, and family are vital skills that need to be addressed. These can include basic self-care skills such as toileting, household chores such as putting away dishes and clothing, or using manners in a cafeteria, movie, or mall. More advanced skills such as shopping from a list, making change, using public transportation, or simply waiting in line appropriately are all skills that could allow the student to function more effectively in the family and in the community.

Thus, the letter of the law regarding the continuum is narrow, even though the implications are far reaching. The continuum described in IDEA is placement-bound and, as such, requires a delineation of the *places* where a student's schooling will be carried out. However, in requiring a

Table 11–1. Definitions of "Related Services" and "Supplementary Aids and Services"

Related Services

Transportation, and such developmental, corrective, and other supportive services (including speech-language pathology and audiology services, psychological services, physical and occupational therapy, recreation, including therapeutic recreation, social work services, counseling services, including rehabilitation counseling, orientation and mobility services, and medical services, except that such medical services shall be for diagnostic and evaluation purposes only) as may be required to assist a child with a disability to benefit from special education and includes the early identification and assessment of disabling conditions in children. [Public Law No. 105-17. 111 Stat. 45 (20 USC 1401) §602 (22) 1997]

Supplementary Aids and Services

Aids, services and other supports that are provided in regular education classes and other education related settings to enable children with disabilities to be educated with nondisabled children to the maximum extent appropriate in accordance with section 612(a)(5). [Public Law No.105-17. 111 Stat. 45 (20 USC 1401) §602 (29) 1997] delineation of goals and objectives, IDEA also requires that educators examine a student's individual needs, and *make program decisions about placement, services, and supports based on those needs*. For many students with autism, this means that services and supports are needed that typically are not arranged for other students with modest learning differences. These supports become the basis for the active, *true continuum* of supports that will make an impact on students' education.

Flexibility of Services and "Point of View"

Within each school district, a wide range of services and delivery systems are necessary to accommodate the changing needs of students with disabilities from age 3 to 21. A continuum suggests an array of services with varying degrees of intensity or intrusiveness, depending on the needs of an individual student at a specific time. A highly flexible structure is required to provide needed supports and services across a student's school career.

The services that a student needs vary across time and circumstance. The focus of support is likely to change over time. During the preschool years a student may need intensive intervention in order to build a foundation for learning. The student may need specific instruction in self-help skills or in how to use an augmentative communication system. Elementary school may be a time to focus on building academic skills. During the middle school years, a student may need specialized vocational training to be ready to enter the job market after graduation. In high school, part of the day may be spent off campus at a job site with a job coach provided by the school. A student will have different needs at different ages and will require different supports and services.

The *level or intensity* of support is likely to change over time as well. A student with autism who is intellectually talented or who has Asperger syndrome may succeed academically, but need social support and instruction. Some students need less support during the preschool years, but need specialized social skills instruction in upper elementary or middle school grades. Other students with autism require intensive instruction during preschool and early elementary years, but are able to succeed in middle and high school with minimal support. Obviously, a continuum to support such a diverse population must be extremely flexible and sensitive to the changing needs of an individual as skills are acquired.

The "system," the family, and the student may view the concept of a continuum in very different ways. The system might view the continuum as a series of more or less restrictive placements or locations for cost-effective service delivery. This view might consider that groups of students with similar labels or disability categories will automatically have similar learning needs; these needs will be determined by disability label or level of severity.

An alternate point of view of a continuum represents the changing needs of students across the lifespan. This point of view considers the continuum as a flexible support system that provides individual supports based on the needs of a student at a given point in time. From this perspective, the types of supports available on the continuum will change as the students change. It also becomes clear that the continuum of service is relevant in its *availability to an individual student*. Because all students with autism do not share the same life and family experiences, each will have different needs for support. The continuum relevant to these students is one that represents the support each student needs, rather than one that represents all services provided by a district to any *hypothetical* student.

The "System" View: The Student Goes to the Service

The traditional system view of the continuum of services for students with disabilities is based on location and label. Students with mild disabilities traditionally have been taught in general education classrooms with pull-out or resource assistance. Students spend much of the day in a classroom with typical peers. An on-site or itinerant resource teacher provides specialized support services either in the classroom or on a "pull-out" basis for the amount of time designated on the student's IEP. Traditionally, students with moderate disabilities were often taught in settings where some integration with nondisabled students was possible.

Students with more severe disabilities were served in settings other than the general education classroom, either in separate classrooms on typical campuses or in separate "center" schools. Center schools typically are reserved only for students with disabilities, and some accept only students with a specific type of disability (such as students with autism). Hypothetically, these schools are staffed by specially trained teachers and may have a lower student-to-teacher ratio than special education classrooms in typical schools. Supporters of center schools believe that grouping students with disabilities together in one location is more cost-effective for a district than trying to provide services at different sites. For example, an on-site nurse might be responsible for 50 students with autism in a center program; this nurse would not be immediately available to the same students if they attended 10 or 15 different schools. Also, by grouping the students in one location, direct services could be provided to a large group of students by fewer personnel. For example, related services such as speech therapy, physical therapy, and occupational therapy could be provided for students with autism by fewer staff. Additionally, networking, problem solving, and teacher inservice was more easily delivered as a result of clustering teachers at the same school. Some students have also been served in residential placements or in hospital or homebound settings.

There are some inherent difficulties with the categorical programming viewpoint. While potentially cost effective, it tends to limit the programs available to individual students. That is, although the placements might represent a full continuum *from the district's perspective*, each student's access to supports is contingent on going to the separated location. A student with a label of autism, for example, would be placed in a specific school that had programs for students with autism. The curriculum is determined by the program that has been designed for that school, rather than the current student needs. And, since this location would accommodate a large number of students with similar characteristics, access to typically developing students and typical behavioral expectations is limited.

When students do not succeed in separate placements, different, more restrictive, placements are usually found. Moving from one placement into a less restrictive or more "normalized" placement is rare, because the supports and services a student needs often are available only in the more restrictive setting. In many ways, the logic of this continuum is that, if students need a particular service, they should be moved to where the services are currently located; the services do not exist as supports for students who need them to succeed in a more typical place. That is, the services should not be "exported" to the students.

A Continuum of Reasonable Accommodations

Reasonable accommodations, as mandated under IDEA, have a wide range. Accommodations refers to adjustments, changes, or adaptations to instructional format or curriculum. They may include individual (one-on-one) testing, changes to specific lesson formats (e.g., written rather than oral presentations), specific technology (e.g., large print books or AAC devices), or a unique aide (i.e., an individual hired to assist the student with disabilities in the classroom). Accommodations for students with autism might range from simple alterations in scheduling to the development of individual, personal schedules. Other accommodations might range from minor adjustments in the curriculum to the provision of various related services and specialized curriculum.

IDEA mandates that related services for which the student qualifies and which are deemed necessary for the student to benefit from instruction must be made available at no cost to the family. These services may include physical therapy, occupational therapy, speech therapy, and assistive technology. Eligibility for related services is based on an individual student's evaluations and is specifically noted on the student's IEP. A reasonable accommodation, related service, or support must be provided in whatever setting the child is placed at no cost to the family. IDEA specifically calls for the IEP to include:

(iii) a statement of the special education and related services and supplementary aids and services to be provided to the child, or on be-
half of the child, and a statement of the program modifications or
supports for school personnel that will be provided for the child

  (I) to advance appropriately toward attaining the annual goals;

  (II) to be involved and progress in the general curriculum in
accordance with clause (I) and to participate in extracurricu-
lar and other nonacademic activities; and

  (III) to be educated and participate with other children with disabilities and nondisabled children in the activities described
in this paragraph. [Public Law 105-17. 111 (STAT. 84 (d) (1)
(A) (iii) (1997)]

The accommodations and services listed here are typical of those provided to students with autism. They also are well within the tradition of
school-based services. What hinders fuller use of the supports available
to students is the continuum of convenience critiqued by Taylor (1988);
these services become **supports** for a student's growth and development
when they are used to help a student succeed in more typical community environments. A continuum should not be simply a collection of the
most services available, but should act *functionally* as supports for students and their families.

Unlike the hit-or-miss strategies of previous eras, educators today
have a wide variety of approaches that are effective for teaching students
with autism and other low-incidence disabilities. Educators are armed
with curriculum design strategies, group instruction methods, delivery
tactics, and data collection and analysis procedures that are known to be
effective in teaching new skills and promoting generalization of existing
skills. It is ironic that the success of the past two decades has resulted in
confusion about the continuum. Many of the legal challenges that schools
face involve questions of what services and supports are needed and
where they should be delivered (Brady et al. 1989). Often, these legal
challenges center on services provided in segregated schools, away from
typical peers. This was the basis for the legal challenge in *Orenich* (1988)
in which the court decided that public school officials must use the IEP
and placement processes to determine if a student with a disability could
be educated in a regular classroom with the use of supplementary aids
and services. School officials were required to take all steps needed to
implement the IEP in a regular setting with necessary aids and services
rather than requiring the student to move to the services. In a similar
challenge (*Briggs v. Connecticut Board of Education*, 1988), the court
determined that, if specialized services offered a student with a disablity
in a segregated setting could be offered in an integrated setting, they
should be, and the student should attend the integrated setting rather
than a segregated program. There was no set maximum cost to the school
board for provision of services. For students today, this would logically

include the most common related services such as speech therapy, language therapy, occupational therapy, and physical therapy.

Just as decisions about the continuum include, but are not limited to, placement, other issues involving placement become important. For example, not all integrated schools are *friendly* schools for students with autism. As Siegel (1996) noted:

> Despite parents' and teachers' hopes for an enlightened attitude on the part of the typical preteen, it is virtually never there when adults are not around. The teasing that a [student with autism] receives in this sort of setting is gross enough that despite his naive social skills, he can perceive that he is being humiliated and it hurts. (p. 222)

Perhaps Siegel is unduly pessimistic about teenagers' reactions to disability, but this observation might indeed reflect the culture of schools with no history of integration. Changing schools from segregated cultures (including schools with *no* students or those with *only* students with disabilities) to inclusive settings requires high level *adaptive behavior* on everyone's part. This includes students with *and* without autism, their teachers, and the other professionals in the schools.

A CONTINUUM FOR STUDENTS WITH AUTISM

The heterogeneity of students with autism makes the availability of a student-centered continuum vital for this population. Students with autism have such a wide variety of skills and abilities that any effort to "standardize" a continuum according to label alone is unhelpful. For example, students with autism who are also gifted have very different needs for support than those just recently assigned to general education classrooms. Similarly, many students with autism in special education classes participate in school activities with typical peers for varying amounts of time. Their needs for support and instructional programming will differ dramatically from one another and from students in different settings. Their autism is not the determining factor for a continuum of services; rather a continuum is established by identifying their needs for service and support that will help them be more successful in their current placement and in future less restictive, more typical places.

What Do Educators Consider in
Making a Personal Continuum?

How should families and educators decide what constitutes a continuum for a student with autism? First, a continuum should be based on a student's actual needs. Second, although placement decisions are part of the continuum, a list of places does not establish student's current or future *need* for these places.

Needs-based Continuum

A continuum of services or supports should be developed individually for students, based on their current and future needs, not merely on the availability of a service within a district. Said another way, the continuum should be student-centered rather than district-centered. Consider a student with severe autism who understands little speech and strongly resists changes in the daily sequence of activities. A continuum of service for this student might require an educational program that includes visual structure and minimizes speech in delivering instruction. Those factors alone might prompt some educators to seek placement in an autism-only class. However, if the student also has a strong need to learn how to interact with peers or co-workers, the *student-centered continuum* might include more integrated placements in activity and vocational classes. For another student with moderate levels of autism who is nearing graduation, more natural levels of language are needed. Consequently, that student's continuum might involve semi-structured, task-related conversation opportunities.

Planning a continuum requires attention to, *but is not limited to*, the types of supports known to be effective for students with autism. Siegel (1996), for example, noted that the specific deficits of students with autism require specific remedies. Most students with autism do not initially respond to social rewards and toys such as puppets and stuffed animals. Particularly at young ages or severe levels, food and sensory reinforcers are more powerful. Communication and imitation skills are often lacking. Proximal activities (e.g., table tasks) are likely to be learned before distal activities (e.g., circle time or physical education activities). A major learning problem is that, if left unstructured, many students with autism perseverate or regard things in an unfocused, undifferentiated way. Because many students with autism have difficulty with transitions, good educational programming teaches flexibility within routines.

When developing a continuum of service for students with autism, educators must consider these characteristics. However, this continuum could be delivered in many different places. An educational program that provides high levels of structure and individual or small group instruction may be immediately available in some special education classes, but these features could be delivered in general education classes as well. If a very low teacher-to-student ratio is absolutely necessary for most of the student's day, most general education classes will not be able to accommodate this.

Whatever the location of the continuum, the essential components of a good educational program remain the same. Egel (1989) identified eight components of an effective educational program for students with autism, regardless of age and current ability. These components include:

1. functional activities;
2. chronological age appropriateness;
3. procedures to replace high intensity or high frequency problem behaviors;
4. data-based instruction;
5. community-based instruction;
6. social integration;
7. extended year programming; and
8. parent and family involvement.

Functional activities are age-appropriate skills that are immediately used (and reinforced) in real-world environments. These skills need to be taught at appropriate times (e.g., table manners are taught at snack and lunch times), using materials found in the student's everyday environment. Teaching age-appropriate "chores" is likely to be reinforced by numerous adults.

Skills taught should be **appropriate to the chronological age** of the student. Giving infant puzzles and stuffed animals to adolescents is not supportive of a student's development and access to typical peer social environments. A continuum sensitive to age recognizes that useful skills (e.g., assembly tasks) can be developed using materials (e.g., film canisters instead of pop-it beads) that enhance the student's movement to a future, more typical work and social environment.

For many students, a continuum of services will include **positive programming to replace problem behavior**. In schools where mild punishers such as time out, verbal reprimands, and overcorrection are used, clear decisions need to be made as to whether those procedures will enhance or exacerbate students' problems. Typically, procedures will be based on a functional assessment of the problem behavior and lead to nonaversive interventions.

Data are needed to evaluate the effectiveness of instruction and to establish whether the services identified on a student's continuum are making any meaningful impact. Students with autism are highly variable in their day-to-day skill levels. Effective data collection over time with preset criteria for success will ensure that skills are mastered.

For most students, a continuum of support will include frequent and systematic **teaching in the community**. Community-based instruction increases the likelihood of skills generalizing across settings and trainers. For example, a first grader taught to walk the aisles of a supermarket holding onto the cart with the teacher increases the likelihood of walking the aisles with a family member. Skillful community-based instruction also increases the likelihood of learning correlated skills such as street-crossing or waiting in line.

Social integration is a critical part of the continuum for students. Students with autism do not exhibit social skills at high frequency and tend not to be reinforced for their social interactions by other students with autism. To develop a continuum sensitive to this need requires more than just social skill *instruction*; social experiences and social arrangements are necessary for most students.

Extended year programming allows the student with autism to continue increasing his skills or maintaining skills already learned. Often an extended "down time" will cause skills to be lost or at least forgotten.

Finally, **parent and family involvement** is a vital part of a student's continuum. This might include parent training (e.g., intensive or spot teaching), assistance with problem behavior, support for extending social networks to students' homes, or linkages with other parents and professionals. At a minimum, the contiuum should include an effective communication system between the teacher and parents.

Placement as Part of the Continuum

Some students with autism learn academic skills consistent with the general education curriculum; others participate in a more functional curriculum emphasizing self-care, daily living, and community skills. Given this heterogeneity, three principles apply to placement decisions. First, the place of schooling should match the content of a program for the student receiving that schooling. Second, placement determinations must be individualized rather than made based simply on the characteristics of autism. Finally, prior to considering placement decisions, IDEA requires that students' needs, goals, and objectives be decided. That is, an effective continuum of services should be established *prior to placement*. Although this is obvious in IDEA's regulations, it is commonly reversed in practice.

For many students with autism, the continuum of services is best delivered in the school the student would attend if not disabled. Unfortunately, for many students with autism, support in typical schools and classes is not a continuum option (Brady, Hunter, & Campbell, 1997). Any placement outside of typical schools should trigger two actions. First, the placement should be separated from the remainder of the continuum so that placement is clearly made *in support of the continuum* rather than placement being represented *as* the continuum. Second, placement outside of the school which the student would attend if not disabled should be considered an *atypical* placement. While atypical placements are accepted for *many* different students, for those with autism atypical placements should require (a) access to typical peers, (b) proximity to the family home, and (c) methods of transitioning back to more typical environments.

Inclusive Schools as Part of a Continuum

In recent years, increased attention has been given to including students with disabilities in general education environments. For many students with disabilities, particularly those with autism, this has been a very limited option (see discussion on next page). The reasons are as varied as the students within a district, but many educators believe that financial factors are a major influence. For example, Hasazi, Liggett, and Schattman (1994) compiled information on integrated schools in 6 states and 12 local school districts. Eight sites were considered "high users" of segregated facilities while 10 sites were "low users." Hasazi and her colleagues found that financial considerations were the cornerstone of influence for *all* of the sites.

Although finances do influence practice, the decision to include a particular student with a disability in a typical class or school relies on a number of factors; increasingly these factors are legal ones (Brady, McDougal & Dennis, 1989). For example, in *Sacramento City Unified School District v. Rachel H.*, the court established what came to be called the *"Rachel H. four factor test."* This test determined the suitability of a particular placement by balancing:

1. the educational benefits of a general education classroom (when paired with supplementary aids and services) compared with the educational benefits of a separate, special education classroom;
2. the nonacademic benefits of interacting with students without disabilities;
3. the effect of the student with disabilities on the teacher and other students in the classroom; and
4. the cost of the integrated programming.

Osborne and Dimattia (1994) presented a number of cases in which courts' interpretation of more inclusive arrangements differed. Early court interpretations often allowed placement in segregated settings if those settings could be justified as a way to deliver an "appropriate" education. In more recent court decisions, segregated settings have been approved only when students' goals could not be met in more inclusive settings. For districts with a philosophical preference toward placing students with similar disability categories in center schools, this trend presents a challenge. Courts increasingly uphold the IDEA requirement that **removal** of a student from typical settings requires substantial justifica-

Why So Much Confusion About Inclusive Schools?

Patti C. Campbell
Michael P. Brady

Few issues appear so consistent with mainstream thinking about American schools, yet so few issues have brought as emotional a response as the proposition that our schools should be more "inclusive." This proposition is debated in the professional literature, discussed in school lounges, requested by some and resisted by others—often with a level of invective seldom seen in educational debates. The finger pointing and mischaracterizations have not helped to lead educators to creative and careful implementation of school change, yet many schools in the past decade have become more inclusive. Why the confusion?

Who is Included in an Inclusive School?

To know how students with autism "fit" into inclusive education, it is important to understand what an inclusive school is and is not. Inclusive schools can be understood as a logical extension of the effort to move students with disabilities out of a separate *system* of education and into the mainstream of America's schools. Reynolds (1989) described the history of American education as one of "progressive inclusion," where schools increasingly take responsibility for educating youngsters who were previously *outside* society's mainstream. Reynolds observed that each generation of Americans has redefined schools to include children who were previously excluded due to social values about such demographics as race, ethnicity, language, or disability. Initial efforts to include these youngsters typically resulted in separate and parallel programs for them; as society becomes more inclusive, schools then establish the expectation that these children should be part of the typical school mainstream.

Inclusive schools differ from mainstreaming and LRE due, in part, to the magnitude of the changes needed to make school practices more effective for students with learning, language, and social differences. In many schools, the effort to become more inclusive is an issue of fundamental school reform (Smith, Hunter, & Schrag, 1991). This often requires a substantial restructuring of school operations (Goodlad & Lovitt, 1993; Sizer, 1992). Re-designing schools to support student diversity is no small feat; Skrtic (1991) pointed out that up to 40% of a school population may need support to function in a society that is growing increasingly more complex.

While mainstreaming typically has been advocated for *individual* students with disabilities, efforts to create inclusive schools involve support for all students who traditionally have been educated outside of (or are at-risk of removal from) the educational mainstream. This includes at-risk learners, students with disabilities, and students from families who do not speak English as their first language (Danielson & Bellamy, 1989; Hodgkinson, 1993; Reynolds & Wang; 1983; USED, 1993). The emphasis on school reform has been overlooked by many special educators who contend that "inclusion might work" for some children, but would certainly result in a loss of services for students with autism (Mesibov & Shea, 1996), emotional and behavior disorders (Braaten, Kauffman, Braaten, Polsgrove, & Nelson, 1988), and nearly every other category of disability (Fuchs & Fuchs, 1994). One implication is that inclusive schools are for *nobody*. An alternative implication is that the inclusion debates have left many confused about what an inclusive school really is.

Recently, Catlett (1998) surveyed educators and parents developing inclusive schools in several states. Parents, teachers, principals, professors, and others made clear that inclusion is *not* a project, an effort to mainstream a handful of students, or a placement for students with disabilities. Catlett's respondents emphasized that inclusive schools were an outcome of school reform. At a minimum:

- inclusive schools had written policies and practices where students attended their home schools (schools they would attend if they had no disability);
- classification and labeling existed *only* for child count and eligibility, not for program development or placement;
- any modifications to the typical school routine, activities, schedules, and curriculum were included on the IEP and delivered individually;
- students with disabilities were regular members of, and received special education in, general education

(*continued*)

classes with peers of similar ages. The number of students with disabilities in a class or school represented a natural proportion of similar students in the district; and

• inclusive educational experiences were on-going, not sporadic or episodic.

What these people described were schools involved in change. Inclusion was not a *program* limited only to students with certain disabilities, nor was it just a placement. Teachers were not "doing inclusion" by mixing students with and without disabilities for some activities during the day. Schools became inclusive when the children who went there *belonged* there.

Inclusion and the Stereotypic Behavior of Professional Educators

Often, the debate about inclusive schools resembles the stereotypic behavior common in students with autism and similar disabilities. Like other stereotypies, debating inclusion helps some educators (a) *escape from the difficult task* of working in schools to promote change, (b) *recruit powerful reinforcers* from others (social approval from readers and conference goers, speaker fees), and (c) *acquire certain physical sensations* during arguments. We believe a topography of Debating Inclusive Schools Stereotypy (DISS) exists, which includes:

• A delay in becoming involved in an issue in which the individual has not previously been engaged. This type of stereotypy is similar to Piaget's notion of egocentricity (Piaget, 1954) and often co-occurs with statements like, "I can't imagine how ... [therefore] it can't be done" and "We used to talk about mainstreaming but now we use 'inclusion.'"
• Repeatedly proclaiming that educators can make no changes in practice because, "the data aren't in yet." This typically coincides with a call for more research in one's own particular area of expertise. This stereotypy is most common among academics and employees of externally funded research centers.
• Using a worst case scenario to discount the concept for all students. For example educators with DISS

might argue that since "Mario," a 19-year-old with Lesch Nyan syndrome and a history of intense self-injury, could not participate in trigonometry, obviously inclusive schools are dangerous for other students with autism. This often co-occurs with statements about the naiveté of "inclusionists."

- Misrepresenting the interest in building inclusive schools as an effort to "destroy special education." Large bodies of literature distinguishing "supported education" from "separate education" typically are overlooked while engaging in this behavior.

It is our observation that, among educators of students with autism, DISS generally results in an emphasis on *autism* and a diminution of *childhood*. This is apparent when professionals use language like environments, facilities, units, centers, and clinics instead of "schools" to describe where students obtain their education.

Inclusive schools are not a unitary concept—they cannot be studied as we could examine a bacterium. Thus, it is true that, "all the data on inclusive schools are *not* in." Through interactions with the early developers of inclusive schools, however, educators with DISS would learn much about the practice of inclusive education. We know that many opponents of inclusive schools become strong supporters after they gain direct and positive experiences (Campbell, Campbell & Brady, 1998; Giangreco, Dennis, Cloninger, Edelman, & Schattman, 1993). We also know a lot about how to design curriculum and deliver instruction so that diverse students can learn and participate in typical instructional activities (Tralli, Colombo, Deshler, & Schumaker, 1996). And we know that most students with autism will not become socially competent adults unless they have regular and organized opportunities to learn to interact with nonhandicapped peers (Lord & Magill, 1989). Finally, we know that a range of behavior change methods exists that are effective and socially acceptable to society at large (Bishop & Jubala, 1995).

Inclusive Schools as Part of the Continuum

In many communities, students **without** autism have a vast array of school options—charter schools, magnet schools, flexible

(*continued*)

scheduling, and so on. Americans increasingly support the notion that children should have many educational options. Inclusive schools only recently have become an option, but they are not available in many communities. In special education terms, inclusive schools have not yet become part of the continuum. In districts across the nation, educators and parents must reinvent the argument in favor of inclusive schooling when they believe a child could be educated with support in a typical school setting. An inclusive school is not an option for many students with autism because it is not on the continuum, *not because of the student's disability*.

Educators historically have been reluctant to include students with disabilities in the absence of external pressures to do so. Most educators agree that students with autism would not receive special education today (whether in inclusive or separate settings) had the courts and Congress not required it. Further, where educators are reluctant or unable to establish a consensus on LRE (a developmental precursor to inclusion), the courts have been willing to define the parameters for us (Brady, McDougall, & Dennis, 1989). So too are the courts deciding issues about inclusive schools. In court decisions requiring inclusive education, Osborne and Dimattia (1994) described a preference for typical school settings unless strong, *actual* evidence exists that such placement is *not* appropriate. As in the LRE cases of a decade ago, the onus is on those who would exclude. Common to these decisions is the logic that educators must make good faith efforts *prior to* assuming students cannot benefit.

Conclusion

Years ago in speaking of ways to reduce self-injurious behavior, Lovaas (1982) reported his belief that we could reduce self-injury by at least half if we implemented what we already know. So it is today with inclusive schools. We already know how to include many, many more students than we choose to include. The restraint is not students' disabilities, but educators' ambivalence toward America's schools.

Educators will not abandon years of operations overnight because of a debate among academics. But society will continue its historical trend of bringing previously "out" groups in and reforming its schools so that these children belong and benefit.

Families will not accept education without input and choices. Parents of children with and without autism will pursue public schools for their children; others will seek private schools. In the public sector some parents will petition their districts for magnet schools or simply schools closer to the parents' place of employment. In the private sector, parents will search for schools operated by clergy, advocates of phonics instruction, or adherents to the methods of Lovaas. Within these different types of schools, educators will wrestle with the tensions created by new ideas. It should be no surprise that parents and educators of children with autism will seek a range of options, including inclusive schools. That is the nature of education, and it is what inclusive schools are all about. So why is there so much confusion?

Patti C. Campbell, Ed.D. is a Professor of Special Education at Valdosta state University in Valdosta, Georgia. Michael P. Brady, Ph.D. is a Professor of Educational Psychology and Special Education at Florida International University in Miami, Florida.

tion from a school district; more inclusive arrangements do not. Indeed, removal of a student from more typical and inclusive environments must not be based on the (a) category of handicapping condition, (b) configuration of the delivery system, (c) availability of educational or related services, (d) availability of space, or (e) method of service delivery (Boschwitz, 1988).

Students with autism present some specific difficulties with regard to inclusive schools. Many students with autism do not have spontaneous imitation skills, and often lack social mimicry. For these students, imitation must be taught directly; even then it may not be used spontaneously. Lacking direct instruction, these students often do not understand that, if everybody in class is doing a particular action (e.g., standing for the Pledge of Allegiance), then they should do it too. Finally, many students with autism are instrumentally motivated rather than socially motivated—they often do not engage in a behavior just because others are. In this way, students with autism are very different from typically developing students and therefore present their teachers with serious challenges.

Including a student with autism in a more typical setting is not appropriate if the student's achievement there is trivial. Education is far too serious to be trivialized! The challenge of every placement is that it supports student *learning.* As noted earlier, placement must specifically support students' learning objectives. Even with extensive support, not all students can be taught effectively in typical settings all of the time. This is the case for *any student who requires learning support, including those without disabilities.* Students with learning objectives that require extraordinary programming may also require extraordinary placements. Placements and programming are extraordinary when they promote substantial growth and development, meet the changing needs of a highly variable population of students, and include flexibility both in location and substance.

SUMMARY

A continuum of services and supports is not only a legal requirement, it is a necessity if educators are to provide a high quality education for a population as heterogeneous as students with autism. A continuum needs to provide not only a series of placement options, but also a series of services that function as supports for the student. These supports and services should address different levels of intensity as students' needs change and should be flexible enough to address different areas of need, including support, information, and services for families of the students. This logic is inherent in the philosophy and mandate of IDEA:

> Over 20 years of research and experience has demonstrated that the education of children with disabilities can be made more effective by
> (A) having high expectations for such children and ensuring their access to the general curriculum to the maximum extent possible;
> (B) strengthening the role of parents and ensuring that families of such children have meaningful opportunities to participate in the education of their children at school and at home;
> (C) coordinating this Act with other . . . efforts in order to ensure that such children benefit from such efforts and that **special education can become a service for such children rather than a place where they are sent**; [emphasis added]
> (D) providing appropriate special education and related services and aids and supports in the regular classroom to such children, whenever appropriate. [Public Law No. 105-17. 111 Stat. 39 601 (c)(5)1997]

A personal continuum of support facilitates smoother transitions as students move from early intervention services, prekindergarten education, school services, therapies, home programs, after school care, respite care, and transition to work, college, and adult living. This personal continuum requires, of course, multiagency cooperation and funding. Providing a flexible and personal continuum of services and supports requires that we break the bonds of a student's "label" and learn to see the student not as an individual with a disability, but as an individual who needs a certain pattern of support to be successful. That is the essence of special education for students with autism.

REVIEW QUESTIONS

1. What is Taylor's primary objection to the traditional notion of the continuum of services?

2. How does a common school district view of the continuum of services differ from the concept of a personal continuum of support?

3. How could the four elements of the "Rachel H. test" affect the placement of a student with autism?

4. How have placement decisions made by courts changed during the past 2 decades?

5. What is a true continuum of services and supports for students with autism?

REFERENCES

Bartlett, L. D. (1993). Mainstreaming: On the road to clarification. *Education Law Reporter, 76*, 17–25.

Bishop, K., & Jubala, K. (1995). Positive behavior support strategies. In M. Falvey (Ed.), *Inclusive and heterogeneous schooling* (pp. 159–186). Baltimore, MD: Paul H. Brookes.

Boschwitz. (1988). Education of the Handicapped Law Review ELHR 213:215.

Braaten, S., Kauffman, J., Braaten, B., Polsgrove, L., & Nelson, C. M. (1988). The regular education initiative: Patient medicine for behavioral disorders. *Exceptional Children, 55*, 21–27.

Brady, M., Hunter, D., & Campbell, P. (1997). Why so much confusion? Debating and creating inclusive schools. *Educational Forum, 61*(3), 240–246.

Brady, M. P., McDougall, D., & Dennis, H. F. (1989). The courts, schools and integration of students with severe handicaps. *Journal of Special Education, 23*, 43–58.

Briggs v. Connecticut Board of Education, et al. D. Conn (1988) EHLR 441:418.

Butler. (1988). EHLR 213:114

Campbell, C. R., Campbell, P., & Brady, M. P. (1998). Building-based decision-making: A shared planning model for inclusive schools. *Educational Considerations, 26*(2), 44–48.

Catlett, S. (1998). *Becoming an inclusive school: A predictable venture.* Unpublished doctoral dissertation, University of Houston, Houston, TX.

Danielson, L., & Bellamy, G. T. (1989). State variation in placement of children with handicaps in segregated environments. *Exceptional Children, 55,* 448–455.

Egel, A. L. (1989). Finding the right educational program. In M. Powers (Ed.), *Children with autism: A parents' guide* (pp. 169–202). Maryland: Woodbine House.

Fuchs, D., & Fuchs, L. (1994). Inclusive schools movement and the radicalization of special education reform. *Exceptional Children, 20,* 294–309.

Giangreco, M., Dennis, R., Cloninger, C., Edelman, S., & Schattman, R. (1993). "I've counted Jon": Transformational experiences of teachers educating students with disabilities. *Exceptional Children, 59,* 359–372.

Goodlad, J., & Lovitt, T. (1993). *Integrating general and special education.* New York: Macmillan.

Gorn, S. (1996). *What do I do when . . . The answer book on special education law.* Horsham, PA: LRP Publications.

Hasazi, S., Liggett, K., & Schattman, K. (1994). A qualitative policy study of the least restrictive environment provision of the Individuals with Disabilities Education Act. *Exceptional Children, 61,* 491–507.

Hodgkinson, H. (1993). American education: The good, the bad, and the task. *Phi Beta Kappan, 74,* 619–623.

Lord, C., & Magill, J. (1989). Methodological and theoretical issues in studying peer-directed behavior and autism. In G. Dawson (Ed.), *Autism: Nature, diagnosis and treatment* (pp. 326–345). New York: Guilford.

Lovaas, O. I. (1982). Comments on self destructive behaviors. *Analysis and Intervention in Developmental Disabilties, 2,* 115–124.

Mesibov, G., & Shea, V. (1996). Full inclusion and students with autism. *Journal of Autism and Developmental Disorders, 26,* 337–346.

Morris, W. (1978). *The American heritage dictionary of the English language.* Boston: Houghton Mifflin.

Orenich. (1988). EHLR 213:166

Osborne, A. & Dimattia, P. (1994). The IDEA's least restrictive environment mandate: Legal implications. *Exceptional Children, 61,* 6–14.

Piaget, J. (1954). *The construction of reality in the child.* New York: Basic Books.

Reynolds, M. (1989). An historical perspective: The delivery of special education to mildly disabled and at-risk students. *Remedial and Special Education, 10*(6), 7–11.

Reynolds, M., & Wang, M. (1983). Restructuring "special" school programs: A position paper. *Policy Studies Review, 2,* 189–212.

Sacramento City Unified School District Board of Education v. Rachel H., 14 F3rd 1398 (9th Cir. 1994).

Siegel, B. (1996). *The world of the autistic child.* New York: Oxford University Press.

Sizer, T. (1992). *Horace's school: Redesigning the American high school.* Dallas, TX: Houghton Mifflin.

Skrtic, T. M. (1991). *Behind special education: A critical analysis of professional culture and school organization.* Denver: Love.

Smith, A., Hunter, D., & Schrag, J. (1991). America 2000: An opportunity for school restructuring and inclusion. In T. Vandercook, J. York, C. MacDonald, & V. Gaylord (Eds.), Feature issue on inclusive education [Special issue]. *Impact, 4*(3), 4–5. (Available from University of Minnesota Institute on Community Integration, Minneapolis)

Taylor, S. (1988). Caught in the continuum: A critical analysis of the principle of the least restrictive environment. *Journal of the Association of Persons With Severe Handicaps, 13,* 41–53.

Tralli, R., Columbo, B., Deshler, D., & Schumaker, J. (1996). The Strategic Intervention Model: A model for supported inclusion at the secondary level. *Remedial and Special Education, 17,* 204–215.

U.S. Department of Education. (1993). *Reinventing Chapter 1: The current Chapter 1 program and new directions. Final report of the national assessment of the Chapter 1 program (EDD 355 330).* Washington, DC: U.S. Government Printing Office.

Yell, M. (1998). *The law and special education.* Englewood Cliffs, NJ: Prentice-Hall.

Chapter 11

PUTTING IT
ALL TOGETHER

This book summarizes the knowledge base in autism. As such, we have provided a broad and comprehensive review of issues; our approach, however, is to present this knowledge base within an educational context. For students with autism under 22 years of age, educational programs provide the best opportunity for minimizing the impact of the disorder while optimizing the unique characteristics of the syndrome. In this chapter, we revisit the educational implications of this knowledge base, and pose the following challenge for educators:

> Are you prepared to move from the stereotype of "autism as a puzzle" to the challenges and rewards of developing high quality, high impact, effective educational programs for these students?

THE DIAGNOSIS OF AUTISM

As we have pointed out in different ways throughout this book, a diagnosis of autism has substantial implications for the students who have it, their families, and the professionals who educate them. It is a spectrum disorder with three broad areas of deficit. These essential features are the presence of "marked and sustained" deficits in communication, behavior, and social relatedness. The pattern of these deficits is highly individualized, so that one student may be nonverbal, be quite interested in social contact, and have few problem behaviors; another student could be hyperlexic and verbal, but severely self-injurious. In addition, the onset of autism must be prior to the age of 3 years.

Autism is currently diagnosed through student observation and through reports from people who know the student well. Pediatricians, neurologists, and psychologists look for the pattern of deficits across the three areas. Students who have six or more "autism characteristics" across the three areas of deficit generally are diagnosed with autism. Fewer than six of these characteristics usually result in a diagnosis of pervasive developmental disorder. A diagnosis of Asperger's syndrome requires severe and sustained social and behavioral impairment, but no significant delays in either cognitive or language development.

Approximately 80% of students diagnosed with autism also can be diagnosed with mental retardation based on their standardized test scores. This figure undoubtedly overidentifies these students, given the extent to which test performance relies on social relatedness, receptive language skills, expressive communication ability, and a student's ability to transfer knowledge. Any strong "splinter skills," or skills that are significantly above the student's *general* level of ability, further complicate the diagnosis of other disabilities.

What does this knowledge of diagnosis mean for educators? Professionals who teach students with autism will necessarily spend energy and time on diagnostic issues, but an inordinate focus of re-sources on trying to identify autism is, we believe, counterproductive. Simply stated, quality education is *not* contingent on a diagnosis of autism versus another disorder. Students will benefit from many of the social, communication, behavioral, and other educational interventions outlined in this book regardless of how many total characteristics of autism diag-nosticians have found. Although diagnostic efforts are helpful, the results do not dictate the specific goals and methods used for an individual stu-dent's education. Rather, educators develop the most effective programs for students with autism by sustained analysis of an individual student's life progress.

USING THE STUDENT'S STRENGTHS AND WEAKNESSES

Each student's individual pattern of skills and deficits makes teaching these students a challenging and innovative experience. Teachers should know the interests and capabilities of each student and use these skills to find functional reinforcers to help establish new skills. A student who enjoys puzzles can be reinforced for learning a difficult task through access to a new puzzle, or for a few minutes of free time to work on a puzzle in progress. A student who enjoys facts about the solar system can be reinforced with books or cards giving information on the solar system. Alternatively, new skills in reading and math could be taught through the use of a solar system theme.

A student's fears and dislikes also need to be known as well. Some students may be afraid of toys and objects as innocuous as stuffed ani-mals. Others may dislike playing with sand or clay. A teacher who tries to use these items as reinforcers will not only fail to engage the student, but could end up in a lesson-disrupting struggle with an upset child. Items and objects used as reinforcers need to increase the likelihood that the student will perform the requested task to gain access to the item or object.

Many students with autism learn more efficiently through a visual modality than by listening to others. These students learn new skills through this relative strength. Written transcripts of lectures, pictures showing the steps in an activity, or a picture of a finished product can all be used to facilitate learning. Communication can be facilitated through the use of objects, pictures, or written words, as well as through gestures.

Because students with autism can become dependent on adults for prompts and other supports relatively quickly, independence can be fos-tered through the use of visual aids. Giving a student a list of classroom assignments to be completed (rather than hovering nearby and giving verbal directions as the student completes each assignment) is an example of fostering independence with visual aids. A picture of a completed table setting with dishes and silverware allows the student to set the table without the teacher prompting the student to place each item.

Generalization of learning is a common difficulty for students with autism. Teachers should include specific activities designed to promote generalized learning before beginning to teach any new skill. Using different materials, different locations, and different instructions are all ways that generalized learning can be produced. For example, a student who only learns to sort silverware will have much more difficulty generalizing that skill than the student who learns to sort silverware, socks, mail, and laundry. Likewise, a student who sorts objects sitting at a desk will have more difficulty generalizing that skill than a student who helps the teacher tidy up the classroom by putting the storybooks on one shelf, file folders on the desk, and the computer programs on another shelf.

Because autism commonly includes difficulty in learning, educators should look at the functionality of the skills they propose to teach. The educator needs to determine why a particular skill is being targeted for instruction. Some skills are prerequisites for other, more sophisticated skills (holding a pencil is a prerequisite to writing). Others are inherently important (hand washing, using a spoon). Skills that are not functional and are not prerequisite to other skills have a low priority. Teachers should always look to the manner in which the targeted skill will benefit the current or future life of the student. If the targeted skill is not likely to increase a student's independence, further access to a less restrictive environment, or facilitate participation in home and community activities, the teacher should examine the need for teaching that skill.

THE HISTORY OF AUTISM

From the time Itard decided to educate Victor to the present day, the history of autism has been one of controversy. Itard, arguably the founder of special education through his work with Victor, was probably considered quixotic by his colleagues. The difficulties inherent in "civilizing" a boy like Victor must have seemed the height of impracticality. Special educators owe a debt to Itard that the challenge did not deter him from the attempt.

Kanner (1943) wrote about a group of individuals whose disability shared specific features that were different from other disabilities. Asperger (1944) detailed his work with a similar group of students with better communication skills. Based on the individuals' lack of social interaction and preoccupation with self, Kanner called the syndrome "autism." His analysis of possible causes of autism set the stage for one of the most troubling controversies: parent blaming.

Bettelheim (1967) took Kanner's observation that the parents of children with autism seemed to be aloof and created an elaborate theory that, at its core, asserted that parents caused their children's autism. It took a parent who was also a psychologist, Bernard Rimland, to dispel the parent blame myth. Rimland inspired the search for physiological differences between individuals with and without autism that still continues today. Although no specific physiological or biochemical markers have been reliably found, neurological research has shown definite brain differences in some subjects and is moving closer to discovering multiple etiologies for autism.

Confusion over the classification of autism is central to the history of the disorder. Given its association with the European traditions of psychology during the middle 20th century, autism has long been considered an emotional disorder by many professionals. Indeed, in the growth of special education in the post-P.L. 94-142 years in the United States, students with autism often became eligible for services under a classification of *emotional* disorders. In 1990, autism became a stand-alone disability category, helping to disassociate students with autism from an intrapsychic orientation to services. However, even today, a psychogenic perspective of the needs of these students (and their families) can be found in some school districts.

The recent national interest in autism has largely been influenced by a grass-roots movement by families to provide research-based intervention for their children. Lovaas (1987) gave parents hope for dramatic improvement through intensive behavioral intervention. Many parents have tried to duplicate the intensity of Lovaas' interventions at home for their children. Families also have petitioned schools to provide some level of intensive behavioral intervention.

For educators, a knowledge of successful and unsuccessful previous interventions is necessary to deliver effective educational programs for students with autism. Understanding the research and being able to duplicate successful interventions in a data-based accountability model enables teachers to work toward specific student goals. An intervention that is not working should be changed before too much time is lost. Knowing what techniques, procedures, and methodologies have been found to work (and not work) with other students with disabilities enables educators to adopt the most practical and logical interventions.

MEDICAL ASPECTS AND CONCERNS

Some medical knowledge on autism is relevant to educators. We propose that knowledgeable professionals should be *aware of* developments outside their fields, even when these developments might not have direct implications for several years. We also believe, however, that educators of students with autism need not have mastery of the medical nuances of this condition. Recent neurological research suggests a number of differences in the structures and brain functioning of typically developing individuals and individuals with autism. To date, however, specific differences have not been correlated with specific levels or features of autism.

Other disabilities are sometimes found with autism. Students with Fragile X, a genetic disorder, have some of the symptomatology of autism. Individuals with other pervasive developmental disorders may also have some of the characteristics of autism. Approximately 25% of students with autism also have seizure disorders. Teachers should be aware of the possibility of seizure disorders and learn school policies regarding seizures. Teachers also should be prepared for students on pharmacological regimens, either to help control seizures or to help alleviate specific symptoms (such as self-injury or obsessive-compulsive behaviors). Some students may take multiple medications. Teachers should know the medications prescribed for a student and any likely side effects. School medication policies should be reviewed regularly with all classroom staff regarding safe storage, delivery, documentation, and monitoring of medications. Finally, staff should be aware that some medications will have strong effects on a student's (a) ability to learn, (b) need for fluids, and (c) need for rest or time away from demands.

An administratively approved policy is necessary for medications that are to be given at school. If there is no nurse on site to dispense medications, specific personnel should be designated in writing and approved by the parents to dispense medications. All medications should be kept in their original containers with a prescription on file from the student's physician. Dosages and distribution should be kept in a log and dated.

THEORIES AND CONTROVERSIES

There is no end to the controversy regarding theories of causation and corresponding theories of treatment. Treatments that have been disproven for students in other disability groups routinely make the rounds as the new treatment for autism. Treatments that have no basis in logic, fact, or research are promoted. From micronutrients to past life regression therapy to facilitated communication, unconventional and unproven treatments are rife in this field.

If they are to assist parents and provide them with information and recommendations, educators need to be aware of the current crop of unconventional treatments. Logical and careful evaluation of the research and other information is vital to avoid being misled. Consumers should note who is making the claims and whether there are any financial or emotional reasons for them to want the treatment to work. Teachers know that learning any skill requires effort and practice.

Interventions that minimize the need for effort and repetition should be carefully examined. *Extraordinary claims demand extraordinary evidence,* and educators and parents should insist on empirical appraisal before any claims are considered valid. If a treatment that sounds easy, fast, and wonderful worked, everyone would be using it.

Not everyone who promotes a novel intervention is a charlatan. The advocates of many controversial treatments do not intend to deceive families; many believe that their interventions truly make a difference. However, until their claims are replicated by researchers who do not have a financial or emotional investment in the treatment, such claims should be considered speculative, at best.

TEACHING COMMUNICATION

Communication is a major area of deficit in students with autism. Verbal and nonverbal communication is affected, as are both expressive and receptive language. The exact nature of the deficit varies. Some students do not understand simple directions; other students may be highly verbal but have difficulty interpreting body language. Still others have speech patterns that are stilted. Oddities of language, such as delayed or immediate echolalia and use of jargon, may have communicative intent.

For many students with autism, problem behavior is often used as communication. Carr and his colleagues (Carr et al., 1994; Taylor & Carr, 1992) clearly showed a correlation between students' problem behaviors and social contact with teachers. Tantrums and other problem behaviors often are effective in gaining attention and social contact. In effect, the tantrum may serve the communicative function of saying, "Please come here."

Tantrums can also be used as an effective communication to indicate protest. Upon presentation of a unwanted task, a tantrum can take the place of "No, thank you." The removal of the task or the demand condition sometimes reinforces (and strengthens) the efficiency of the tantrum. Similarly, tantrums can effectively prevent the removal of a desired item or activity. For example, students quickly learn that preferred toys will be returned if self-injury or aggression occurs when these toys are taken away. The establishment of a functional communication system allows students to get their wants and needs met without resorting to problem behavior.

Communication is a necessity and should be a top instructional priority for most students. All students need to have appropriate, effective, and efficient ways to communicate. To improve the quality of students' lives in more enriching environments, and to increase their participation in their families and communities, a method of communication must be established. Communication is vital to independence—individuals who need help communicating will require assistance all of their lives.

A number of communication avenues are available. Communication methods can include sign language, pictures, Picture Exchange (PECS), speech, or AAC devices. Picture Exchange was pioneered with students with autism and is currently being used successfully with students with other disabilities. A careful assessment of the prerequisite skills needed for each type of communication by a teacher and speech-language pathologist will establish the best fit between a student and a communication system. Families should be consulted to determine their preferences for a communication system, as well. If a communication system is to be meaningful for a student, the student needs the skill to use it— and it should be available in all environments.

SOCIAL SKILLS AND SOCIAL RELATEDNESS

The social deficit in autism varies from students who seem to be unaware of the existence of other people to students who want to make friends and have social relationships but are socially awkward. Lack of spontaneous sharing is seen in many young children with autism and is one of the early indicators of the disorder. Students with autism tend not to be reinforced by social praise. This can hinder learning in natural environments where frequently *only* social reinforcers are available.

Competence in social skills is important if students are to participate in their families and communities. Students who are not reinforced by social contact tend to isolate themselves, thereby limiting their participation in their families. An inability to interpret the social cues of others makes a student with autism different from his or her peers. This greatly hinders peer acceptance. Conversely, competent social skills permit a student to be more accepted in a peer group.

Social skills, like any other skill, can be taught. Teachers should understand the components of social interaction and be able to assess a student's interaction strengths and weaknesses. Teachers should assume that different students will have different instructional needs. Students' social targets will generally fall into one of four key components of social interaction: initiation (beginning the social exchange), response (answering the social initiation of another), continuation (the give and take of the exchange as well as repairing communication breakdowns), and ending the exchange.

Direct instruction of the four interaction target skills can result in vast improvement in students' social behavior. The use of nonsocial reinforcers can be paired with social praise and then be gradually removed. And, while many teachers will recognize that interacting is *inherently* reinforcing for most students, social exchanges usually are *not* reinforcing for students with autism until they gain the skills to become competent interactors with others. Students with autism who receive direct instruction in social skills and have frequent opportunities to *use* these skills in meaningful ways typically develop friendships and a range of other relationships common among typically developing children.

Students will be more likely to use the social behaviors that their family supports and values. A family in which going to pet shows or movies is a high priority will value (and support) social instruction that prepares a student to participate in these activities. It is also important to determine student interests and teach the social skills that relate to those interests. Behaviors appropriate for a chess match are very different from those at a rodeo.

TEACHING ADAPTIVE AND COOPERATIVE BEHAVIOR

Students with autism have "restricted, repetitive and stereotyped patterns of behavior, interests and activities" (APA, 1994, p. 67). They may line up or stack items, spin a toy repetitively, or engage in activities such as flapping, tapping, or rocking. They may read only books on chemical engineering or be interested only in airline schedules. They may become upset if the bus driver takes a different route to school.

Generally, behaviors can be evaluated as excesses, deficits, or inappropriate to the context. Excesses are "too much" of a behavior. It may be fine to line up crayons on one's desk, but may be inappropriate to line them up throughout the classroom. Most students tap their pencils or swing their feet, but tapping or swinging for hours is a behavioral excess. Deficits are too little of a behavior. Not knowing how to raise one's hand to ask for help or to ask to be excused from a task are examples of behavioral deficits. Taking off one's clothes in the classroom is an example of a behavior that is inappropriate to the context. It is acceptable (and even encouraged) to take one's clothes off when preparing for a bath but not acceptable to do so in a classroom. Using a toilet to urinate is an acceptable behavior, but not when the toilet is located in a display at the hardware store. The behavior itself is not problematic; the problem is that the behavior occurs out of context.

To target a behavior for change, it is necessary to determine the *function* of the behavior when the student produces it. Behaviors essentially serve three functions: they allow the student to obtain something; they allow the student to avoid, reduce, or escape something; or they are automatically reinforcing. Once the function of the behavior is known, an intervention can be developed and a new, more appropriate behavior that serves the same purpose (but in a more socially acceptable manner) can be taught. It is unethical to suppress a behavior without teaching the student a functional behavior in its place. Teaching should give students more skills, not fewer. The behavior targeted for acquisition should serve the same purpose or function as the problem behavior, be at least as easy to perform, and access reinforcers more readily than the problem behavior. Careful understanding of the function of an unacceptable behavior is necessary to a successful intervention. Placing a student in a time out from a reinforcement area for throwing a pencil may be highly reinforcing if the student threw the pencil to avoid doing a math worksheet.

Whenever possible, ask a student what skills she or he would like to learn. A student who tantrums when another student does not want to play on the playground may want to learn a better way to approach peers or a more appropriate way to handle a rebuff. The needs and desires of the student's family should also be considered when targeting problem behaviors. The family may find behaviors that the teacher considers minor to be very disruptive and ask that they be addressed first. It is important to target skills for acquisition that will be accepted in the student's community, allow the student greater access to less restrictive and more enriching environments, and increase independence.

Once the behavior program has been created, data must be collected and evaluated to ascertain whether the intervention is effective. Repeated measures should be taken and assessed in an ongoing manner so that the program can be changed as needed. Data collection is also essential for accountability and to show acquisition of a student's IEP goals.

WORKING WITH THE FAMILY

Parents tend to see educators as resources for information about disability in general and autism in particular. As parents talk to others and search the Internet, they hear about old and new treatments, swap information, and share opinions and anecdotes. Educators need to be aware of the current crop of unconventional treatments and share opinions and anecdotes. Knowledgeable educators can assist parents by providing information and resources to help them evaluate the new knowledge they receive.

Teachers are partners in the education of students, not the sole authority. Parents know their children and have valuable information relevant to a student's learning. Parents and educators can work cooperatively to help the student generalize skills learned in one environment to other environments. Educators should understand that the student is part of the family system and will participate as a member of that system.

There are inherent stressors when families and educators work to solve the problems of students with autism. In some families, these stressors make it difficult for family members to cope. Educators also face these challenges and may find it difficult to interact with some family members of their students. No single model of professional-family interaction is best; rather, these interactions should be driven by a shared focus on the needs of the student. Although the history of professional-family interaction involves parent-blaming, emerging practice centers on mutual support and partnership.

EDUCATIONAL STRATEGIES

The goals and objectives should be practical and useful, and any prerequisite skills should be identified. The frequency and type of data collection should be carefully considered. Logic and prioritization of objectives are necessary. Verbally requesting to use the bathroom may be a functional skill, but if the student has no communication system, then two *other* skills would logically precede this (using the bathroom and using a communication system). Once these skills are apparent, a request can be made. The criteria used to evaluate student progress also need to be taken more seriously. The criteria for mastery and data collection should reflect an accurate assessment of what the teacher can reasonably accomplish.

Once the IEP objectives have been set, the teacher should evaluate student strengths and interests that will help achieve these objectives. A student who is interested in cars and trucks might increase his or her reading skills through stories about cars and trucks. Access to cars and trucks (or books about them) could be used as a reinforcer for task accuracy or fluency.

Visual structure can be used to bridge gaps in receptive language. Providing a visual schedule of the day's activities can assist the student in transitions and facilitate independence in moving from one area to another. Visual work systems can assist the student to work more efficiently. Work systems show students how much work needs to be accomplished before reinforcement is given or before the student can take a break. The level of visual structure used should be tailored to the individual student.

Methodology used to teach skills needs to be individualized to the student's needs as well. Methods of teaching can be quite flexible. For some students, skills are learned most effectively using a discrete trial format. Others find the precision teaching approaches to be more efficient. Some students learn using a visual pattern or picture format. For others, the approach that works best depends on the type of skill being learned. Educators should be skilled in using a wide variety of methodologies to provide students with the opportunity to learn in the most effective, efficient manner.

Whatever the methodology or skill, many students have difficulty generalizing skills learned to new situations, new materials, or new instructors. Knowing this is a common problem, educators should program for generalization even before the skill is acquired. Many students become prompt dependent very quickly and find spontaneous exhibition of the skill difficult. An abrupt shift from high levels of reinforcement to more natural levels may also cause generalization difficulties. Teachers need to know what the skill will look like when the student has generalized it sufficiently. Will the student be able to use any soda machine after being taught how to use just one? Will the student be able to eat in any restaurant? Most importantly, will the student know what to do or whom to call if there is a problem? Independent problem-solving skills are important for a high quality of life.

Educators should know what level of performance is necessary to consider a skill mastered. An important point stressed in this book is that different skills have different criteria for mastery. Spelling accuracy of 80% correct may be acceptable. An employer may not be happy, however, with 80% of the customers being given incorrect change. Street crossing demands 100% accuracy. The performance expectation must be established before teaching a skill. Skills that are not learned well do not generalize well and are much less likely to be used independently.

MOVING THROUGH THE CONTINUUM

The requirements of IDEA mandate a full continuum of services for students with disabilities. In the past, that has often been interpreted as arranging for students with similar disabilities to go to the same locations. Programs in many areas were disability-specific; students with autism went to a program at school X and students with physical impairments went to school Y. Programs at these schools were staffed by teachers with training in a specific disability. There was a tendency to keep students in segregated settings rather than try to provide services in more typical classes and schools.

The mandate for education in the LRE is also a mandate for a more enabling environment. School settings should be ones in which students can find success while being prepared for active participation in their community. This mandate is often at odds with disability-specific school placements where services (e.g., PT, OT) were provided only if a student attended a school that already had these services in place.

Flexibility of service delivery has become an expectation for best practice and is consistent with the shift in thinking on the continuum. Students with autism may require different levels of support at different times of the day. A student may be quite capable of independently joining his age-peers for science and math, yet be quite unable to make it through a noisy cafeteria lunch line. Flexibility would allow this student to have more support during lunch than during math and science. The support would be available to the student when he is most likely to need it.

In the past decade, there has been a strong move toward providing supports to students in typical classrooms. An assumption is emerging that a student with a disability should be educated in the general classroom, with supports and services being provided on-site. If a student is to be removed to a more restrictive environment, the need for such a change must be clearly shown. Students should be given maximum support in the typical classroom before being placed elsewhere.

The expectation that many students with autism will be taught in general education classes does not mean that special education should or will be disbanded. However, the nature of some special educators' jobs may move from self-contained classrooms to general classrooms in a resource or collaborative arrangement with general education teachers. As this occurs, special educators will need a wider range of knowledge and skills and a genuine understanding of life and learning in regular classrooms.

LOOKING TO THE FUTURE

Educators of students with autism must be knowledgeable of current research and best practices. As the knowledge base in autism expands, the challenge to educators to use this knowledge in a progressive way will also expand. Educators will learn to work with different students and different professionals in many settings, including community settings. They will learn to work in roles that connect students with autism to their families and communities. Educators will learn to teach a specific student in the way that that student learns best. They will view students, not just their autism, and understand the specific patterns of strength and weakness that make each student unique. What an exciting time to be an educator of students with autism!

REVIEW QUESTIONS

1. How will changes in the knowledge base of autism affect the professional practices of educators in the next decade?

2. How will changes in the knowledge base of autism affect the interactions and relationships among students, their families, and professionals in the next decade?

3. What changes in your own professional practices, interactions, and relationships do you anticipate as a result of your

exposure to the information and perspectives presented in this book?

REFERENCES

American Psychiatric Association. (1994). *Diagnostic and statistical manual of mental disorders* (4th ed.). Washington, DC: Author.

Asperger, H. (1944). Die Autistischen Psychopathen; im Kindesalter. *Archiv für Psychiatrie und Nervenkrankheiten, 117,* 76–136.

Bettleheim, B. (1967). *The empty fortress: Infantile autism and the birth of the self.* New York: Free Press.

Carr, E. G., Levin, L., McConnachie, G., Carlson, J. I., Kemp, D. C., & Smith, C. E. (1994). *Communication-based intervention for problem behavior.* Baltimore, MD: Paul H. Brookes.

Itard, J. M. G.(1932). *The wild boy of Aveyron* (G. Humphrey, & M. Humphrey, Trans.). New York: Appleton-Century-Crofts.

Kanner, L. (1943). Autistic disturbances of affective contact. *Nervous Child, 2,* 217–250.

Lovaas, O. I. (1987). Behavioral treatment and normal educational and intellectual functioning in young autistic children. *Journal of Consulting and Clinical Psychology, 1,* 3–9.

Taylor, J. C., & Carr, E. G. (1992). Severe problem behaviors related to social interaction. I. Attention seeking and social avoidance. *Behavior Modification, 16,* 305–335.

INDEX